CAROLINA vs CLEMSON

CLEMSON vs CAROLINA

CAROLINA vs CLEMSON

CLEMSON vs CAROLINA

A CENTURY
OF UNPARALLELED RIVALRY
IN COLLEGE FOOTBALL

BY JOHN CHANDLER GRIFFIN

Published by Summerhouse Press
Columbia, South Carolina

to my wife and daughter, Betty and Alexis

Published in Columbia, South Carolina
by Summerhouse Press

Summerhouse Press
P.O. Box 1492
Columbia, SC 29205
(803) 779-0870
(803) 779-9336 fax

ISBN 1-887714-20-0

First Edition
10 9 8 7 6 5 4 3 2 1

Photographs courtesy of Clemson University and the University of South Carolina.
Materials presented on pages 282-299 courtesy of USC and Clemson Sports Information.

How You Play The Game

The gridirons are deserted now, and gone the season's strife,
But the game for us has just begun on the football field of life.

Never an intermission there the weary ones shall know,
Nor a time out call for the men that fall, nor the blessed whistle blow.

Never a sub can take your place, and never a man must yield,
For the Game is o'er for evermore for the men who leave the field.

Perhaps the world will see you win, and the pennants wave for you,
And your feet will tear the trampled turf, as you drive the touchdowns through.

Or perhaps upon your very goal the plunging bodies meet,
And the dusty lime of the last white line is crushed beneath your feet.

Perhaps the twilight wind is cold, and the goalpost shadows long,
And the victors swarm upon the field to chant their triumph song.

But if you play the losing game as but a hero can,
The men who buck your line will know they played against a MAN.

--W. W. Stephens, USC, Class of 1903

THE EARLY ERA
1896 - 1945

1896

OUR FIRST BIG THURSDAY EVER

It was Thursday, November 12, 1896, State Fair week, and for days enthusiastic throngs had been arriving at our capital city by wagon and by rail from all over the state. In fact, the State Fair was considered such a major attraction at that time that even the railroads, in a burst of of public spiritedness, were offering a special rate of a penny per mile to people traveling to Columbia, which meant that a family of three could make the long trip from Greenville, Augusta or Charleston to Columbia for the grand sum of only three dollars. Not a bad deal.

The Fair Grounds at that time were located on Elmwood Avenue (near the present site of the Logan Elementary School), approximately one mile northwest of the State House, on the opposite side of Columbia from its present location.

The main event planned for today, the event that always drew the biggest and most enthusiastic crowd, was the horse races, which were scheduled to begin at two o'clock sharp. As though the races were not enough to fill the stands, those in charge of events decided to introduce spectators to the latest in entertainment, a college football match.

Today's match would feature the Tigers from the Clemson Agricultural College versus the Jaguars from the South Carolina College. The game would be played on the race course infield and was scheduled to begin at eleven A. M. (to make sure that it did not interfere with the horse races). Admission was twenty-five cents.

To feature a contest between Carolina and Clemson was a stroke of genius on the part of our city fathers, for certainly no contest between any other two schools in the state could have generated more interest. It was simply a matter of the bad blood that already existed between these two institutions, hard feelings created when Governor "Pitchfork" Ben Tillman began lobbying for a state agricultural college.

Tillman, who had little love for the University of South Carolina (as it was known before Clemson became a reality), was quoted as making such inflammatory comments as "it's time the citizens of South Carolina had a state college they can be proud of." And he blamed what he called "the sorry plight of agriculture in this state" on the "pitiful and contemptible USC agriculture department." One state legislator, in response to Tillman, shouted: "The farmers of this state need a college education like they need a telegraph line to the moon."

As though all that were not enough to raise USC's hackles, once Clemson was charted in 1889, the University of South Carolina immediately lost its newly acquired status as a

Looking up Main St. from the State House in 1896. At that time the State Fair Grounds were located on Elmwood Avenue, just to the northwest of the church steeple in the upper left hand corner of the above photo.

university and again became simply the South Carolina College. A bitter pill for Carolina alumni everywhere.

Then, adding insult to injury, the far-sighted Tillman had a law passed imposing a special tax on fertilizer, the proceeds of which would go to support the Clemson Agricultural College.

Thus by 1896, while the SCC and Winthrop College were forced to go to the State Legislature, hat in hand to plead for operating capital, Clemson was granted over $200,000 in fertilizer tax proceeds, far more money than was granted to the SCC and Winthrop combined. It should also be noted that by 1896 Clemson could boast an enrollment of 446 students, while the SCC, founded in 1801, was struggling along with an enrollment that had dwindled to only 164 students.

So, yes, there did exist enmity between these two schools. And so a football contest between them became a grudge match even before the players ever laid eyes on one another.

This was the very first team ever fielded by Clemson, but already they had one game under their belt, having defeated a

The Clemson Tigers of 1896, Clemson's first football team ever.
Front row (L-R): Frank Tompkins, A. M. Chreitzburg, Captain R. G. Hamilton, J. D. Maxwell, C. W. Gentry.
Middle row (L-R): J. M. Blaine, J. T. Hanvey, W. K. Howze, G. H. Swygert, L. L. Hendricks, A. S. Shealy, George Hanvey.
Top row (L-R): C. K. Chreitzburg, Jim White, Jack Mathis, Coach W. M. Riggs, J. A. Stone, Theo Vogel, W. M. Brock.

strong Mountaineer team from Furman University less than two weeks before.

As for the Jaguars (they would become the Gamecocks in 1902), they had fielded their first team in 1892, losing to Furman 44-0. They had also fielded teams in 1894 and '95 and at this point had a cumulative record of one win and four losses. Today would be their first game of the '96 season.

It should also be noted that the Jaguars had never before employed a football coach, and perhaps they would not have done so in '96 were it not for the fact that the hated Clemson Tigers suddenly appeared on their schedule. But now, after all the other indignities the SCC had suffered at the hands of this upstate upstart, the SCC was determined to pull out all the stops. The Jaguars must beat the Tigers, even if it meant spending money to hire a coach. Thus came Coach Dixie Whaley.

By ten o'clock that fateful morning some 2,000 fans packed the grandstand and stood along the sidelines to greet the two teams when they arrived at the field. In addition to students from the two competing institutions, there were also in attendance gaily clad young women from both Winthrop College and Columbia's Methodist College (there were only four coeds enrolled at the SCC in 1896). Excitement was at a fever pitch, and the fans were in a very festive mood, with many sporting their school colors, waving banners, beating drums and blowing horns.

Indeed, *The State* newspaper reported: "The din from the students' yells and horns sounded as if the inmates from an insane asylum had broken loose."

Just after ten o'clock the two teams arrived by horse and wagon at the playing field and a cheer went up from their respective fans that could be heard all the way to the State House. The big Tiger team then trooped onto the field wearing orange sweaters, orange duck pants, and orange and blue striped stockings. The Jaguars wore their garnet sweaters, white duck pants, and garnet stockings.

As for padding, such was almost non-existent in 1896, except for leather shin guards (similar to those worn by baseball catchers), and an odd leather contraption known as a nose guard. Only sissies, it was said, wore helmets.

The Tiger team was somewhat bigger than the Jaguars, plus they had just enjoyed a whopping 14-6 win over mighty Furman, and thus the odds makers had the Tigers slightly favored in this contest. It would be several years before the "experts" learned that past records meant nothing when these two teams went at it on Big Thursday.

As for the game itself, Captains C. H. McLaurin and R. G. Hamilton met at midfield for the coin toss. The Jaguars won and elected to receive. (According to the rules of 1896, regardless of who scored, one team kicked off during the entire first half, the other team the second half.)

Clemson fullback A. M. Chreitzberg enjoys the distinction of being the first to kick off during the long series between these two schools, while Carolina quarterback L. C. Vass was

C. W. Gentry scored Clemson's first touchdown ever, versus Furman on October 31, 1896.

R. G. Hamilton, Clemson's first football captain and a member of the CU Athletic Hall of Fame.

Coach Walter Riggs, considered the father of Clemson football, was a professor of engineering who was asked to coach the team because he had himself played for Auburn and was one of only two people on campus who had ever seen a football game prior to 1896. He would later serve as president of Clemson College.

the first to return a kickoff, running the ball back to the Jaguars' 40-yard line.

The game seesawed back and forth for awhile, with the ball changing hands on several occasions. Then with twenty minutes elapsed, the Jaguars finally pushed the ball down to the Clemson three. On the next play N. W. Brooker crashed into the Clemson end zone and the SCC fans went wild. Captain McLaurin then kicked the extra point and the Jaguars went up 6-0 (touchdowns counted 5 points in 1896).

Indeed, it was reported that the "dopesters," who had their betting tables set up very openly behind the stands, were chagrined when the favored Tigers left the field trailing 6-0 at halftime.

But then in the second half, with only 85 seconds elapsed following the opening kickoff, Clemson's fleet J. A. Stone, subbing for the injured J. M. Blaine, took a handoff and raced around left end for 60 yards and the Tigers' first score against the Jaguars. Chreitzberg kicked the extra point and the score stood tied 6-6. *The State* newspaper reported: "At that point Clemson 's orange and blue goes mad by the wholesale, while the garnet and black wears a where-am-I smile."

But then Carolina's Brooker brothers went to work, hitting the big Clemson line repeatedly for nice gains. Then, on second down from the Clemson fifteen, Cantson Foster on what was described as a "cross-cross" ran the remaining distance for another Jaguar TD. Again McLaurin was true with the extra

point and the SCC took the lead 12-6. And that's the way this first game ever between these two blood rivals came to an end.

Oddly enough, this game was not marred by fist fights between the players (as was frequently the case back in those simpler times), nor were the two referees attacked by either the players or their fans. In fact, it was reported that both teams "conducted themselves as gentlemen throughout the contest, and that "the Clemson boys took their defeat gracefully with no show of ill feelings."

It might be commented, however, that just prior to the ending of the game the heavens finally opened and the rain began to fall, sending fans scurrying for shelter. It was one of the few times in history that rain has fallen on Big Thursday.

All in all, it was a grand beginning for what would become an integral part of our heritage in this great state, as well as one of the finest rivalries in the nation, one that continues to this day.

As for the Jaguars of 1896, they would go on then to lose to both Furman and Wofford while the Tigers would defeat both these institutions.

Coach W. H. "Dixie" Whaley in 1896 became the first coach ever employed by the SCC. A native of Charleston, he would later (running from his old halfback position) lead the Charleston YMCA to victories over the Jaguars. He was an attorney by profession and would go on to serve as Speaker of the House of Representives and later Chief Justice of the U. S. Court of Claims.

C. H. McLaurin, Captain of the '96 Jaguars. He played center and did the kicking for the SCC.

N. W. Brooker enjoys the distinction of having scored the first touchdown ever in this long series.

The South Carolina College Jaguars of 1896.
Standing (L-R): Coach Dixie Whaley, Mgr. D. D. McColl, L. M. Haseldon, Prof. LeConte Davis (for whom Davis Field was named), Frank Woodward (President of the college, 1897-02). Sitting (L-R): J. S. Verner, A. H. Brooker, Cantson Foster, B. A. Bolt, Christie Benet, Lee Hagood. On ground (L-R): J. G. Hughes, Mason Brunson, N. W. Brooker.

1897

TURNOVERS LEAD TO A BIG CLEMSON WIN

The first Big Thursday had proven such a roaring success, with over 2,000 fans in attendence, that it was decided in '97 to try such an extravaganza once again. This year Thursday fell on November 11, and both Carolina and Clemson enthusiastically accepted the State Fair's invitation to meet on that date.

In fact, it was announced a week prior to the game that Dr. Hartzog, president of Clemson College, had visited Columbia in order to secure living quarters for the 350 Clemson cadets who would arrive in Columbia by rail on November 10. Not only would these cadets attend the football game on Thursday morning, they would also march in the big military parade down Main Street on Thursday evening. (Among other "military companies" from around the state that would parade that evening were the Pomaria Rifles, the Tillman Volunteers, and the Gaffney Light Infantry.)

Hartzog announced his intentions of "keeping the cadets together during their stay in the city," and to that end he had rented the entire fourth floor of the Kendall Office Building on Main Street from a Mr. Swaffield, and had ordered 350 cots set up for his Clemson men. Mr. Swaffield had promised heat, and plenty of drinking and bath water. The cadets, it was noted, would bring their own blankets.

Both teams had employed new coaches for the '97 season. At Clemson it was Coach W. M. Williams, who had played under John Heisman at Auburn. Indeed, Williams was said to have been the finest blocking halfback in the South. During his single season at Clemson the Tigers would go 2-2 and win the state championship.

At Carolina it was Coach Frederick M. Murphy, a former star player at the University of Virginia, who would lead the Jaguars to a dismal 0-3 record during his year with the SCC.

For Carolina, Big Thursday would mark their first game of the '97 season. Following their loss to the Tigers on this day they would go on to lose twice to the Charleston YMCA by a score of 0-6 in both encounters. They would later blame these losses on their former coach, Dixie Whaley, who was now playing halfback for the Christians. The Carolinians complained that Whaley knew their signals and on every down would tip his teammates as to where the play would be run.

For Clemson, on the other hand, Big Thursday marked their final game of the '97 season. They had already lost to Georgia (0-24), beat the Charlotte YMCA (10-0), and lost to North Carolina (0-28). Since the SCC was the only state team on Clemson's schedule, a win today would mean that the

Coach Frederick M. Murphy, a star player from the University of Virginia and now a medical student who coached football in the fall. He led the Jaguars to an unenviable 0-3 record in 1897.

Lee Hagood, captain of the 1897 Jaguars.

The Jaguars of 1897. It should be noted that padding back in the early days generally consisted of quilted material that the boys' mothers had sewn onto their sweaters. (Their nose guards can be seen hanging from their necks in this photo.) As for the football itself, it resembles a watermelon far more than a modern day football.

The Clemson Tigers of 1897. Standing (L-R): Ansel (Sub.), Bowman (Referee), Coach W. M. Williams, Asst. Coach Walter Riggs, Mgr. A. M. Chritzberg, Garland (Sub.), LaBoon (Sub.), Joe Duckworth (Sub.). Middle Row (L-R): L. L. Hendrix, Norman Walker, George Swygert, George Hanvey, Jock Hanvey. Bottom ((L-R): Frank Sullivan, Jeff Maxwell, Captain W. T. Brock, R. T. Vogel, Charlie Gentry, Shack Shealy.

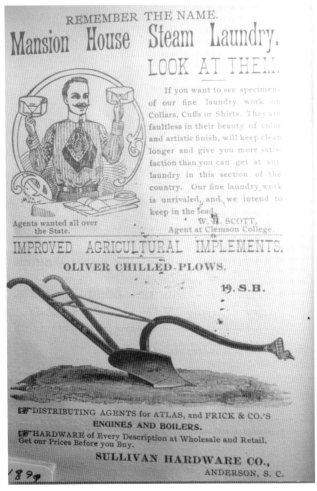

This ad appears in a Clemson publication for 1897.

Carolina's seven coeds of 1897 pose on campus with a trusted professor.

Tigers were undefeated in state competition and thus they would become undisputed champions of the great state of South Carolina.

And that is exactly what happened. Indeed, Big Thursday 1897 proved to be as colorful and grand as it had been the previous year, with over 2,000 exuberant fans jamming the grandstand. Just prior to eleven o'clock the SCC's Captain Lee Hagood met at midfield with Clemson's Captain W. T. Brock. This year Clemson won the toss and elected to receive.

Following the kickoff, Clemson ran three plays before Brock punted. Carolina ran one play, then was called offsides and the ball went over to the Tigers. After two nice runs by Maxwell and Vogel, the Tigers lost yardage on the next play and were again forced to punt. On first down Lee Hagood made a nice run but then fumbled on the SCC thirty. Brock scooped up the ball and ran it back for a Tiger touchdown.

Jeff Maxwell's kick failed and Clemson led 4-0. (Yes,

for reasons that remain obscure, touchdowns now counted 4 points, extra points, 2 points.)

The Jaguars again kicked off, and this time Charlie Gentry (he scored Clemson's first TD ever in 1896) returned it to the fifty. Then it was Maxwell, Gentry and R. T. Vogel running the ball and picking up good yardage. Finally Gentry dashed 35 yards for another Clemson score. Again the kick failed, and the score went to 8-0. And that's how the first half ended.

Later, only five minutes into the third period, Vogel again scored for the Tigers, Maxwell's kick was good, and the score became 14-0.

But moments later, just when things were looking bleak for the Jaguars, thanks to the fine running of Hagood, Foster, Herbert and Dial, the Carolinians found themselves on the Clemson one. But the Tigers held and the ball went over on downs.

Vogel attempted to punt out of his own end zone but the kick was blocked and Foster recovered in the end zone for a Jaguar score. Christie Benet was true with the extra point and the score became 14-6.

Later, following several drives on the part of both teams that were stymied by fumbles, Gentry again scored for Clemson, Maxwell kicked the extra point, and the score went to 20-6, Clemson's favor, and that's how the game ended.

Clemson, it was agreed, had a bigger, faster team in '97 and probably deserved the win, but the Jaguars did nothing to help their cause with their six fumbles, which might be an all-time Big Thursday record.

1898

THE TIGERS TRIUMPH 24-0

It was Thursday, November 17, a cool, brisk morning in Columbia, S. C., and already sports fans were beginning to make their way to the grandstand at the race track at the State Fair. This would mark the third annual meeting between Clemson and Carolina, and no one wanted to miss the eleven o'clock kickoff.

A month earlier Carolina had eeked out a 16-5 win over tiny Bingham College (a prep school in Asheville, N. C.), but they knew that today's game would prove far more difficult, one that would truly test their mettle.

As for the Tigers, they had already lost to Georgia 20-8, but had beaten Bingham 55-0. In fact, the Bingham game was Clemson's first home contest in history. The match was played on October 20, following the dedication of Bowman Field, Clemson's first football field. As for today's game, the Tigers were favored to win and they looked it.

Both teams had new coaches, W. M. Wertenbaker at Carolina and John Penton at Clemson. As for Penton, he would guide the Tigers to a 3-1 record and another state championship.

Both teams arrived on the field about 10:30 and began taking warm-up drills to the cheers and songs of their fans. As usual, the Jaguars were wearing their garnet sweaters and stockings, the Tigers wearing heavy yellow "work sweaters," orange pants and striped stockings.

The 2,500 fans that jammed the grandstand that morning also noticed that the players were wearing their hair long and shaggy. This was the latest thing in football strategy, for since the boys refused to wear helmets, it was reasoned that the long, shaggy hair would offer protection against head injuries. Indeed, it might be pointed out that according to the rules of 1898, players were penalized if they bowed to temptation and swung another player around by the hair. Besides, hair-pulling was not considered a manly thing to do.

As for the game itself, suffice it to say that the dopesters were quite correct in favoring Clemson by a margin of 5 to 3. In fact, the game was worse than that as the Tigers wound up taking it 24-0.

But, as the Jaguars happily pointed out, there is always next year.

Coach William Wertenbaker would lead the Jaguars to an 1-2 record in 1898.

J. Cantson Foster, captain of the '98 Jaguars, and a three-year starter at left end.

The 1898 Carolina Jaguars. Top Row (L-R): SCC president Franklin Woodward, C. J. McCallum, Harris, Othel Miller, G. T. Swearington, Minus, Hughes, Mgr. Witherspoon. Second Row (L-R): J. H. Haskell, Boyd Evans, Coach William Wertenbaker, Captain Cantson Foster, Lee Hagood, J. C. McIntosh. Seated (L-R): Beverly Herbert, W. E. Evans, Crawford, Monroe Shand, C. A.. Foster.

The Clemson Tigers of 1898. Coach John Penton is standing, third from left. Captain Shack Shealy, who would go to be a star with the Tigers, is holding the football.

The 1898 editorial staff of TAPS, the Clemson yearbook. This would mark their first year of publication.

Carolina's 1898 Blue Key Society.

Bowman Field was the home of Clemson football from 1898 until 1914. The Tigers defeated Bingham College in their first home game in history by a score of 55-0. (Clemson scored 11 touchdowns versus Bingham and W. C. Forsythe kicked 11 extra points, still an all-time Clemson record.)

1899

THE TIGERS WIN AGAIN

For the first time in their brief history the Jaguars played a five-game schedule in 1899. And, under new coach, I. O. Hunt, a former footballer from Brown University, the SCC jumped off to a winning start, beating the Columbia YMCA on their own Davis Field (located at the corner of Green and Sumter Streets).

As for Clemson, they had already lost close games to Southern powers Auburn and Georgia, but had beaten a good Davidson team by a score of 10-0. And with Coach Walter Riggs back at the helm, optimism for a good season was running high.

The entire Clemson student body arrived in Columbia by train on Wednesday afternoon. The train was bedecked with orange and purple bunting, and the 200 fans who greeted them at the depot were similarly dressed.

The Clemson football team was quartered at the Columbia Hotel. Some of these players, it was noted, were returnees from their great team of '98, and one member had been a starter since 1896. It was said to be the best Tiger team in history.

Immediately, several Clemson students began parading up and down Main Street carrying signs which read "Eat 'Em Up, Clemson!" The students had painted big tiger heads on these signs, and so for the first time Clemson displayed a mascot or logo in public.

Prior to the game on Thursday morning fans of both teams were given programs and urged to cheer for their particular college.

The Cheer for Clemson:

Clemson! Clemson! Rah! Rah!
Clemson! Clemson! Rah! Rah!
Hoo Rah! Hoo Rah!
Varsity! Varsity!
Rah! Rah! Rah!
Clemson! Clemson! Is our cry
V-I-C-T-O-R-Y!

And Carolina's big cheer was equally inspirational. (We only regret that no record exists today to indicate the identities of those creative students who wrote such stirring lyrics.) For Carolina:

Hien, Hien, Hica,
There's nothing like her, Carolina ever
Plays football.
She always beats 'em,
But never cheats 'em,
All teams both great and small.

Captains Monroe Shand of the SCC and Norman Walker of Clemson met at midfield for the coin toss. Carolina lost and was forced to kick off. This proved to be their first mistake. For Clemson's men were both bigger and faster, and the Jaguars thus spent most of the game struggling on defense, trying vainly to halt the big Clemson runners.

It was Shack Shealy, W. C. Forsythe and J. G. Kaigler ripping off nice gains for the Tigers as the game got under way. Then it was Monroe Shand, Harry Withers and W. A. "Coop" Cooper answering for the Jaguars.

After several exchanges, Shack Shealy broke through the line and dashed 25 yards for the Tigers' first score. Forsythe's kick was good and Clemson took the lead 6-0.

Following another exchange of punts, Captain Norman Walker carried around end for 25 yards and another Clemson score. This time the kick failed and the Tigers were up 11-0 with only two minutes left in the half.

Five minutes into the third period Shack Shealy ran for another Clemson score. This was Shealy's second TD of the day and his fourth against the Jaguars over the past two years. The point kick was good and Clemson went up 17-0.

By now the smaller Jaguar team was obviously exhausted and could do little to stop Clemson's big runners.

Coach Walter Riggs, in a show of sportsmanship, began to play his reserves at this point. But even that did little to lessen the effects of Clemson's superior speed and strength. Indeed, these reserves scored another 20 points before game's end, and the final score became Clemson 34, Carolina 0.

Coach Walter Rigggs after an absence of two years guided the Tigers to a 4-2 record in '99, with wins over Davidson, The SCC, NC State and Georgia Tech.

Coach I. O. Hunt, a former star for Brown University, compiled a 6-6 record during his two years with the Jaguars, including a win over Furman and two over NC State.

Monroe Shand, captain of the 1899 Jaguars.

The Tigers of '99 would enjoy a 4-2 season, including a 41-5 win over Georgia Tech.

The SCC Jaguars of '99 would go 2-3 on the season.

1900

CLEMSON ROUTS THE SCC

It was 1900, the final year of the nineteenth century, and hopes were running high at both Carolina and Clemson for a win on Big Thursday. Not only did the Jaguars have many players returning from the 1899 wars but Coach I. O. Hunt was also back for his second season. At Clemson, on the other hand, they now had the fabled Coach John Heisman at the helm and everyone knew what he could do.

The Jaguars had already lost a close one to a strong Georgia team 5-0 while beating Guilford 10-0. The Tigers, not surprisingly, had already demolished a good Davidson team 64-0 and Wofford 21-0. Thus the dopesters had Clemson heavily favored in today's contest. As it turned out, they knew what they were talking about.

The game was played on November 1 before a record crowd of some 5,000 fans at the State Fair. (It was reckoned that there were 1,000 fans seated in the grandstand, another 2,500 standing along the sidelines, and yet another 1,500 watching the game from the upstairs plazas of the main buildings at the fair.)

Captains Ted Bell of the Jaguars and J. N. Walker of the Tigers met at midfield, and the Jaguars won the toss, the only thing they won all day.

The SCC could not move the ball on the first series against the stronger Tigers, and already Jaguar fans could see the writing on the wall. Then, with less than two minutes elapsed in the game, Buster Lewis took the ball over from the five yard line for a TD. He then kicked the point, and Clemson went up 6-0. An audible groan went up from Jaguar fans, but the Tigers were just getting started.

Indeed, on the next series Claude Douthit again scored for Clemson. Lewis kicked the point and the score became 12-0. (And with less than five minutes gone in the contest!)

Two minutes later, believe it or not, Douthit again scored for Clemson, Lewis kicked the point, and the score became 18-0. At that point, with less than eight minutes elapsed in the game, the Jaguars' hopes had all but vanished.

For the Jaguars, Ted Bell, Dexter Otie, and Hogan Yancy made some nice runs on the next series, but finally they had to surrender the ball to the strong Tiger defense. The Jaguars thus punted.

Buster Hunter took the ball at the Clemson 45 and did not stop until he'd crossed the goal some 55 yards down field. The kick was no good, and the score became 23-0.

At that point the half mercifully came to an end.

For the Jaguars, the second half was even worse than the first, if such is possible. Indeed, only three minutes after the whistle blew, Claude Douthit again scored for Clemson, his third touchdown of the day, and the rout was truly on. From that point, the big Clemson runners moved at will through the exhausted Jaguar line.

Even Jake Woodward, a hulking Tiger lineman, scored on a fumble recovery (he remains one of the few linemen ever to score in this series).

At this point let us mercifully drop the curtain. The Jaguars were soundly thrashed by a superior team that day by a score of 51-0.

Following today's debacle the Jaguars would go on to defeat Furman, NC State (twice), while losing a close one to Davidson.

As for Clemson, they enjoyed a super season, defeating Georgia, VPI, and Alabama. Indeed, the Tigers of 1900 gave up only 10 points as they went 6-0 on the season, their first undefeated team ever.

The Clemson marching band of 1900.

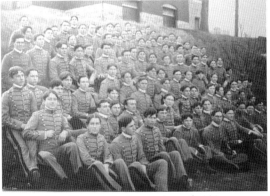

The Clemson freshman class of 1900.

The Clemson Tigers of 1900 would go 6-0 on the season, their first undefeated team in history, giving up a total of only 10 points, an all-time CU defensive record.

The Carolina Jaguars of 1900 would enjoy a 4-3 record, their first winning season in history.

The legandary Coach John Heisman (for whom the Heisman Trophy is named), would guide the Tigers from 1900-03, some of their best seasons ever. He is a member of the Clemson Athletic Hall of Fame.

Norman Walker (left), captain of the Clemson Tigers, 1899-1900, and Ted Bell (right), captain of the SCC Jaguars, 1900.

Fans pour out of the stands at the fair grounds following Clemson's drubbing of Carolina in 1900.

The SCC Glee Club of 1900.

Clemson's Regimental Staff of 1900.

1902

THE YEAR OF THE GREAT RIOT

The SCC and Clemson did not meet on the gridiron in 1901. Such a calamity occurred not as a result of carelessness or oversight but because the respective athletic committees from these two schools could not agree on terms. The SCC, therefore, met Davison on Big Thursday 1901, losing by a score of 12-5.

But now, in 1902, these two old adversaries were back again and everyone expected perhaps the best Big Thursday ever.

John Heisman was still head coach at Clemson, and would lead them to a 6-1 record in '02, including wins over such Southern giants as Georgia, Auburn and Tennessee. Indeed, their only loss would come this day, October 30, to the Jaguars of the SCC.

The new coach for the Jaguars was C. R. "Bob" Williams. During his two years with the SCC the Jaguars would win 14 games while losing only 3. Thus Bob Williams remains the winningest coach in the history of Carolina football.

As noon approached that day some 3,000 lustily cheering fans packed the grandstand and stood alongside the sidelines at the Fair Grounds as the Carolina squad lined up on the field and sang "We're Gonna Twist The Tiger's Tail." Indeed, there was nothing modest about this 1902 Gamecock squad. They had already demolished Guilford (10-0), NC State (60-0), and Bingham (28-0), and felt that they were the equal of anyone in the South.

While the two squads warmed up, two carriages drawn by white horses arrived on the field bearing the beautiful young coed sponsors for the opposing teams. Fans were in a festive mood and good-naturedly warred with cheers and songs.

Following the kickoff, only five minutes into the game, Guy Gunter scored for the Gamecocks on a five yard buck. Harry Withers kicked the point, and the SCC took the lead 6-0. Just eight minutes later Gunter raced around left end ten yards for another Gamecock score. Again the kick was good, and their lead became 12-0. And that's the way the half ended.

In the second half, neither team could make much headway against the other, but then Clemson's Vet Sitton burst through the Carolina line and out ran everyone 60 yards for a touchdown. John Maxwell kicked the point, and the score became 12-6.

But that was as close as the Tigers could get, and the game ended, a Carolina victory, 12-6.

For the SCC, it was their fourth consecutive win of the season, and one Carolina player, Bundy Davis, was quoted in *The State* as commenting: "Say, old pards, let's just lie down and die." And a bright eyed scrub, John Rhett, observed, "I only hope that Heaven will be like that game."

But the real action today didn't start until that evening once the big military parade down Main Street ended. And what antagonized the Clemson cadets was this: A Columbia merchant, in celebration of the game, hung a big transparency

Vet Sitton was named All-South as a Clemson end in 1903. He would later play pro baseball for the Pittsburgh Pirates.

John Maxwell, named to the All-SIAA team at quarterback in 1902-03, returned a kickoff 100 yards for a TD vs. Cumberland in 1903, still the longest kickoff return in the CU record book. He is a member of the Clemson Athletic Hall of Fame.

in his store window depicting a gamecock crowing over a poor, bedraggled tiger. It did not take the hooting young Carolinians long to borrow this transparency and begin parading it up and down Main Street.

Soon sharp words were being passed between the celebrating Carolinians and the Clemson cadets.

The Clemson men informed the Carolina men that it would be poor judgment to display that insulting transparency at the big parade that evening. Local police, alarmed at the Clemson threats and concerned for the peace and tranquility of the city, agreed. It should not be displayed that evening during the big military parade.

But of course, being human, that's just what the young Carolina men did.

At the conclusion of the parade that evening, some 400 Clemson cadets were dismissed at the foot of the State Capital on Main Street, just a short walk to the campus of the SCC. Armed with sabers and bayonets, the cadets quickly marched to the Sumter Street entrance to the Horse Shoe, where a band of some thirty irate Carolinians crouched behind quickly erected barricades to block the progress of the cadets.

And the Carolina boys were armed with pistols, rifles, and shotguns. And they were loaded. And the boys stated that they intended to use them. But fortunately, officials from both colleges arrived on the scene before blood could be shed. Still, as a result of this fiasco, the series would not be renewed until 1909, a hiatus of some seven years.

The Carolina Gamecocks of 1902 would go 6-1 on the season, still USC's most successful season ever. (Carolina defeated the Charleston Medical College 80-0 in 1902. Ten different USC players scored TDs in that contest, possibly an all-time USC record.) They gave up only 16 points to seven opponents, an average of 2.2 points per game, an all-time USC defensive record.

The remarkable Guy Gunter, Carolina's first great Super Star, who scored both Gamecock touchdowns in USC's 12-6 win over Clemson in '02. He later scored five TDs (including a 100-yard kickoff return) vs. NC State, all-time USC records.

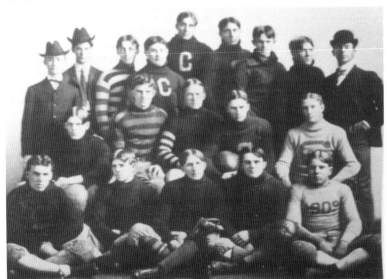

The Clemson Tigers of 1902 enjoyed a 6-1 record. and were named champions of the SIAA. Indeed, over the past three years under Coach John Heisman, the Tigers had a great 15-2-1 record.

Claude Douthit scored three touchdowns against the SCC in 1900. In '02 Heisman hired him to serve as manager of the Tiger team.

T. E. McCutchen, captain of the 1902 Gamecocks.

Bob Williams, coach of the Carolina Gamecocks. With a 14-3 record in '02 and '03, Williams remains the winningest coach in the history of USC football. In 1906, 1909, and 1913-15 he would serve as head coach of the Clemson Tigers. An attorney by profession, he would later be elected mayor of Roanoke, Va.

Clemson's beautiful young sponsors for the Carolina-Clemson game of 1902 arrived at the Fair Grounds in a horse drawn carriage.

Carolina's beautiful young sponsors for the Clemson game of 1902.

Hope Sadler, captain of the Tigers 1902-03, and one of the finest ends ever to play at Clemson.

During the Furman game of 1902, a Furman student fashioned a rooster from a pillow, then ran the length of the field at half time, plucking feathers from the pillow while the Furman students chanted, "Poor little gamecock!" The name stuck and thus the USC Jaguars suddenly became the Gamecocks. (This image appears in the 1903 Garnet and Black.)

1909

THE SERIES IS RESUMED

It was November 4, 1909, and today, after an interval of seven years, the Carolina Gamecocks and the Clemson Tigers would once again resume play on Big Thursday.

To date, the Gamecocks, under Coach Bob White, had suffered through a dismal season, losing badly to NC State, Wake Forest and Georgia Tech while beating only the College of Charleston. Thus the week prior to Big Thursday it was announced that former USC coach, Christie Benet, had been rehired to assist White in preparing the team to go up against Clemson. Unfortunately, no one thought to ask White's opinion about Benet's rehiring. White thus resigned in a snit, feeling that his talents had been insulted. (Under Benet the Gamecocks would go 1-3, beating The Citadel in the season's final game.)

Up at Clemson, almost their entire student body, including all but two members of the football team, had been expelled in 1908 for "lifting" the Civil War cannon that stood in front of the Pickens County Court House. Truly, this venture was nothing more than an April Fool's Day prank, but the president of Clemson College took a dim view of such ungentlemanly shenanigans and sent almost everyone home.

Thus in 1908 the Tigers, always one of the great powers of the South, managed to defeat only Gordon Military Academy in the first game of the season while losing to their other six opponents.

But by 1909 a sense of normalcy had returned to campus and the Tigers, again under Coach Bob Williams, formerly of USC, would go 6-3 on the year.

It might be pointed out that also in 1908 the State Fair Committee still wanted Carolina and Clemson to play a football game during State Fair Week even if they couldn't play each other. To that end, it was arranged for Clemson to meet Davidson on Wednesday afternoon, and for Carolina to meet Davidson on Thursday afternoon.

Well, you guessed it. On Wednesday the Wildcats beat Clemson 13-0, then on Thursday they beat Carolina 22-0. Not a bad day for Davidson.

Today's game was also historic in that it would mark the first time in history that a football game in South Carolina was broadcast on radio. The United Wireless Telegraph Company installed instruments at the Fair Grounds (now relocated to the corner of Assembly and Rosewood Streets) and broadcast the game back to the Barringer Building on Main Street.

A disappointing crowd of some 2,000 fans showed up for this encounter. But as the coaches pointed out, today was a beastly hot day, reminiscent more of August than of November.

Indeed, the heat was particularly hard on the smaller Gamecock squad. Try as they might, they were simply no match for the larger Tigers, and their exhaustion was apparent by half time.

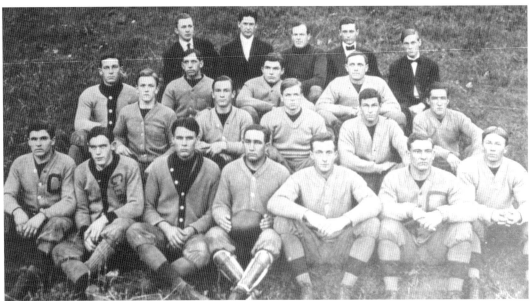

The Clemson Tigers of 1909. This team shut out five opponents while giving up only 43 points all year. Bob Williams was again their head coach.

Still, it was a hard fought contest and the soggy ground made it difficult for either team to mount much of an offense.

Captain James Hammond kicked off for USC, but Clemson could not move the ball and C. M. Robbs was thus forced to punt.

And so went the first quarter, ending in a 0-0 tie. In the second quarter Robbs attempted a field goal from the Carolina 18, but the ball barely cleared the line of scrimmage, and Francis Cain recovered at the 10. The ball then exchanged hands four more times without either side making a first down. Then, from the USC 20, Clemson quarterback E. H. Pinckney attempted to throw a forward pass, which was almost unheard of in those early days, but the pass fell incomplete and the Gamecocks took over.

Three series later, Clemson once more went to the air but this time Carolina intercepted, doubtlessly one of the first interceptions in the history of USC football. But it did the Gamecocks little good and four plays later Hammond again punted. Then, on second down, Witt Hankle dashed around right end for 40 yards, down to the Carolina 3. Robbs carried it in on the next play for a touchdown, W. P. White kicked the extra point and the score became 6-0, Clemson's favor.

By this time the wet field had become a quagmire and neither team could move the ball. Indeed, by now both elevens were punting on first and second downs, hoping for a break that would give them the ball in enemy territory.

But there were no more breaks, and the Gamecocks went down in defeat by a score of 6-0. Not a bad effort.

Coach Christie Benet of the USC Gamecocks. In 1902, the night of the big riot, it was Benet who climbed to the top of the barricade at the Horse Shoe and, hoping to diffuse the situation, offered to fight with any Clemson student who would step forward. There were no takers. Oddly enough, Benet would later serve as Chairman of Clemson's Board of Trustees.

James H. Hammond, captain of the 1909 Gamecocks. (In 1908, vs. the College of Charleston, Hammond completed two forward passes, a first for USC football. He also returned a pass interception 90 yards for a TD vs. Davidson in '09, a record that would stand at USC until 1973.)

The Carolina Gamecocks of 1909. This particular formation, with the quarterback close up under center, resembles a combination of the T-formation and the single-wing of a later era. It is also interesting to note that the players are now wearing shoulder pads beneath their sweaters.

Linemen (L-R): U. G. DesPortes, Berte Carter, B. T. Sharpton, Marion Mobley, A. F. Rawls, Robert Brown, Randolph Murdaugh. Back (L-R): Ben Beverly, Irvine Belser, Francis Cain, James Hammond. (Note: Ben Beverly was killed in France during World War I.)

Clemson cadets roll into Columbia on the Monday before Big Wednesday 1909.

C M. Robbs, captain of the 1909 Clemson Tigers. His TD today beat USC 6-0.

Big Thursday 1909. These are the earliest photos known to exist of a Carolina-Clemson football game. The Tigers are wearing striped jerseys and stockings.

1910

TIGERS LOSE 7 FUMBLES BUT WIN GAME

The day following Big Thursday 1909 Clemson's athletic director, the celebrated Walter Riggs, complained long and loud that the State Fair committee had thrown both teams a curve ball by increasing the rent on the football field at the Fair Grounds from fifty dollars to two hundred dollars. This was a sizeable amount of money, said Riggs, and perhaps the two teams would retaliate by playing their annual game at Carolina's Davis Field rather than at the Fair Grounds.

Nevertheless, as Big Thursday 1910 rolled around both teams were on hand for the kickoff.

Clemson at this point had another new head coach, Frank Dobson, who was given a three-year contract to coach all three major sports for the Tigers. A former professional baseball player, he received the first multi-year contract in the history of Clemson athletics.

To date, the Tigers had wins over Gordon Military, Howard, and The Citadel, while losing to both Mercer and Auburn.

Back in Columbia, meanwhile, John H. Neff was the new Gamecock coach. He had formerly played for Virginia and brought with him to USC the strange idea that the forward pass could be a devastating offensive weapon if used correctly. Indeed, the Gamecocks at this point, with Crip Whitner tossing the ball and Burnette Stoney doing the catching, had already defeated their first four opponents of the season (the College of Charleston, Lenoir, the Georgia Medical College, and Wake Forest) while not giving up a single point on defense.

Still, no one was fooled. Despite Carolina's superior record, Clemson had played a much tougher schedule, and their bigger team was clearly favored to win today.

November 3, 1910 was described as a cool, windy day, with a stiff breeze blowing diagonally across the field of play. Still, promoters of Big Thursday were gratified to see some 3,500 paying customers on hand for the game, a new Big Thursday record.

President Teddy Roosevelt attended the big military parade down Main Street following the 1910 meeting between Carolina and Clemson. Here he is seen on the front lawn of the State House.

Captains U. G. DesPortes of USC and W. H. Hankel of Clemson met at midfield. Clemson won the toss and elected to receive.

Carolina fans then went wild when Clemson fumbled P. R. McNair's kick and the Gamecocks recovered deep in Tiger territory. Whitner threw a pass to Stoney on first down, but Stoney fumbled the ball and Clemson got it back.

Joe Bates then picked up twenty yards on the next two plays for the Tigers. Three plays later they were on the USC 25, but the Gamecocks held at that point and took over on downs. After three plays USC punted once again. After three more exchanges Clemson fumbled for the third time and again Carolina recovered. Again USC punted.

But now the stronger Tigers began to go to work, showing that they themselves were no strangers to the passing game. Fullback Joe Bates hit W. H. "Cap" Hankel for ten yards, then completed another toss to Ben Britt for 15. Still the drive was stymied and Clemson was forced to punt. Carolina then ran three plays, was forced to punt, and again Clemson bobbled the ball. The Gamecocks thus recovered their fourth fumble of the game. Carolina then punted down to the Clemson 30-yard line.

Ah, but this time Paul Bissell, Clemson's fleet halfback, took the ball on the fly and electrified the crowd by dashing 65 yards down the sideline, all the way to the USC 5. At that point they fumbled once again. The Gamecocks now had five fumble recoveries under their belt.

But after three plays USC attempted to punt. The ball sailed far over the kicker's head and Frank Gilmer, Clemson's big center, recovered in the end zone for a Tiger score. Bill Connelly kicked the point and Clemson went up 6-0.

The Gamecocks fumbled the ensuing kickoff and Clemson recovered deep in Carolina territory. From there the Tigers smashed in for another TD, Bissell kicked the point, and the score became 12-0. And the half came to a close.

The second half began with Carolina kicking off and Clemson again fumbling the ball and Carolina recovering their sixth fumble of the afternoon. After three plays and no gains A. W. Metts punted for USC.

Clemson fumbled the kick and Carolina fell on the ball, their seventh fumble recovery of the game.

Again, unable to move the ball, USC punted. This time the Tigers held on, and behind the blocking of their big linemen their runners began to make headway. Three minutes later Bill Connelly went in for Clemson's third TD of the day, Bissell's kick was good, and the score went to 18-0.

In the fourth quarter, holding a comfortable lead, Clemson truly began to experiment with the forward pass, with B. E. "Boo" Lachicotte completing pass after pass to their big ends, Harry Woodward and Hankel. Connelly scored their final TD of the day on a short burst up the middle of Carolina's exhausted line, Bissell again kicked the point, and the final score became Clemson 24, Carolina 0.

The Carolina Gamecocks of 1910. They would blank their first four opponents of the season, then lose to the next four. USC's four consecutive shutout wins in 1910 remains an all-time Gamecock defensive record. (USC would record four consecutive shutouts, but they were not all wins.)

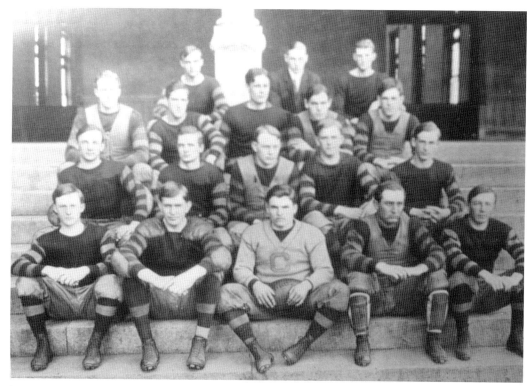

The Clemson Tigers of 1910. They would go 4-3-1 on the season, their best performance a 0-0 tie with Georgia.

Pitchfork Ben Tillman presents a state flag to the Clemson cadets in a special ceremony in 1910.

John F. Neff, coach of the Carolina Gamecocks, 1910-11. They would go 5-8-2 under his direction.

Frank Dobson, coach of the Clemson Tigers, 1910-12. The Tigers would go 11-12-1 during his tenure.

U. G. DesPortes, captain of the 1910 Gamecocks.

This "memorial" sketch appeared in Clemson's 1910 yearbook, a spoof of the "Pendleton Guards," all those young men who were expelled in 1908 for lifting the Civil War cannon from in front of the Pendleton Court House.

On the Wednesday prior to Big Thursday some 300 Clemson cadets pitched their tents at the State Fair Grounds where they would remain until Sunday.

Clemson cadets of 1910 make dorm life as comfortable as possible.

1911

BLOCKED KICKS FOIL THE GAMECOCKS

After a disappointing 4-4 record in 1910 Coach John Neff was back for his second season at Carolina.

By the time Big Thursday rolled around on November 7, 1911, the Gamecocks had lost to Georgia, beaten the College of Charleston, and tied Florida. They didn't know it at the time, of course, but the College of Charleston would be their only victim of the season as they rolled to a dismal 1-4-2 record.

The situation at Clemson was fairly similar. Coach Frank Dobson was back for his second season, and to date they had beaten only Samford while losing to both Auburn and Florida. Following today's game they would have only a win over The Citadel to show for their efforts as they struggled to a 3-5 season, their second losing season in history.

It was written at the time that a "record crowd" of some 3,500 fans filled the stands just before the eleven o'clock kickoff.

Meeting at midfield were captains C. W. "Crip" Whitner for Carolina and Paul Bissell for the Tigers. As usual, the Tigers won the toss and elected to receive.

Carolina kicked off, Clemson fumbled, Carolina recovered deep in Tiger territory and it seemed that luck was on the side of USC this day. But no. There was a penalty on the kickoff and the play was called back.

This time Clemson returned the kick, but was then unable to move the ball and punted to the Gamecocks' 25-yard line. Two plays later Whitner attempted to punt, but the kick was blocked. Alex Lewis, a big Tiger end, picked up the loose ball and ran it in for the TD. Alex Lewis' kick made it 6-0.

The ball changed hands several more times, then Clemson's Tom Perry punted to Whitner, who bobbled the ball. There was a scramble, but the Tigers recovered on the USC 10. On the next play Johnnie Kangeter went in for the TD, Alex Lewis kicked the point, and the score became 12-0.

As play progressed, Clemson's big runners began to assert themselves. Midway the second quarter Kangeter ran for 11 yards, then Clare Webb passed to Lewis for nine. Then Webb had runs of 7 and 5 yards, and a pass to Lewis for 10. Then came the inevitable Clemson fumble. USC recovered.

After three plays, Whitner again tried to punt, and again Clemson broke through to block the kick. This time it was Tom Perry. He scooped up the ball and made it all the way to the USC 15 before being dropped. From here Captain Paul Bissell drop-kicked a field goal and Clemson went up 15-0.

And so ended the half.

Neither team could do much against the other in the third quarter. In the fourth, Kangeter, Bissell, and Webb seemed to run at will against the Gamecocks, and after an extended drive Webb set up the Tigers' next score with a short pass to Lewis down to the USC 3. Webb then took it in for a touchdown, Lewis kicked the point, and Clemson was leading 21-0.

Later, with only moments left in the game, Whitner again had his punt blocked and Clemson recovered on the USC 10. Webb threw a short pass to Lewis right at the goal line, and two plays later Webb went in for the score, Lewis was again true with the point, ending the game, 27-0.

The Carolina Gamecocks of 1911 would experience a dismal 1-4-2 record. As for Big Thursday, they had now lost to Clemson for three consecutive years, and had not scored on Clemson since 1902.

Paul Bissell, Captain of the 1911
Clemson Tigers.

The 1911 Clemson Tigers would suffer through a 3-5 season.

A Clemson dorm of 1911. These young cadets, all outfitted in their colorful robes, seem to have
furnished themselves with all the comforts of home.

W. C. "Crip" Whitner, captain of the 1911
Carolina Gamecocks. Versus the Georgia
Medical College in 1911 Whitner threw
two TD passes to Burnette Stoney, the first
TD passes in the history of USC football.

Clemson's Ben Brittt takes a short pass for 10 yards.

Clemson's John Kangeter through the center of the Carolina line for six yards.

Tanny Webb circles USC's right end for 25 yards.

The Gamecocks pound the center of that big Tiger line.

1912

FRITZIE AND DUTCH SPARK USC WIN

It was October 31, 1912, and Gamecock fans could only hope that today would be different, that today would see them go home the victors over Clemson College, a team they had not even scored on since 1902. And this was the time to do it if they ever were. For Carolina now had in their backfield two of the finest runners in the South, Alfred Holmes "Fritz" Von Kolnitz and Ed "Dutch" Passailaigue. Both were transfer students, Von Kolnitz from the College of Charleston and Passailaigue from The Citadel.

To date, thanks largely to Dutch and Fritzie, the Gamecocks had beaten both Wake Forest and the College of Charleston, while losing close ones to mighty Virginia and Florida.

Plus Carolina had a new coach on hand, Dr. Red Edgerton, a star player from the University of Virginia, and a man of vision and ideas. Indeed, USC had given him a multi-year contract, their first such contract in history.

At Clemson, meanwhile, Frank Dobson was back for his third year as head coach. To date the Tigers had beaten Samford, Riverside, and The Citadel, while losing a close game to Auburn. They would finish the season with a disappointing 5-5 record.

In later years a big Clemson lineman, W. A. "Tubby" Schilletter, would recall his playing days in general and his Big Thursdays in particular.

Athletes received no special privileges, he recalled, and were required to meet all class and drills just like everyone else. Football practice began at five o'clock every afternoon and lasted until seven. He remembered the coaches having lights strung around the field so that the team could practice after dark, if necessary.

A typical practice session would begin with calisthenics, after which backs and ends would go through running and passing drills. The linemen would spend their time with the tackling dummies.

Then would come a live head-on tackling session, with the fullbacks and linemen going all out to level one another. Then would come 20 minutes of running plays.

"We dressed in our dorm rooms and hung our uniforms out the window to dry," Schilletter recalled. "I bought my own shoes, and my mother made my shoulder pads."

The school furnished padded pants, a leather nose guard, and a helmet made of cotton and leather. Each player was also issued an extra jersey for game use only. There were

This picture has significance for two reasons. One, it shows the happy 1912 Carolina squad, and some admirers, just after the Gamecocks had licked Clemson for the first time in 10 years. The other reason is that so far as known, this picture (along with some others) printed in The State the following morning was the first instance where a South Carolina newspaper printed pictures of a game the next day. The State had just put in the first photo engraving plant in South Carolina

This photo of happy Gamecocks was taken immediately following USC's big 22-7 win over Clemson in 1912. Prior to kickoff that day the Tigers paused in their workouts to watch in awed silence as the Gamecocks arrived at the field aboard the latest in transportaion, a 1912 Ford flatbed truck. With wins over the College of Charleston, Clemson, and The Citadel, the 1912 Gameocks were declared State Champions.

no numbers on the jerseys, so sports writers needed the help of spotters in order to identify the players.

Schilletter recalled Clemson's trips to Columbia for Big Thursday. The cadets would depart Clemson on Wednesday morning, traveling by train, then pitch their tents at the Fair Grounds and spend an exhilarating four days in the Capital City.

As for the football team, they would depart Clemson at noon and arrive in Spartanburg about three. They would hold light workouts at Wofford College, eat a light supper, then board an eight o'clock train for Columbia.

By midnight they would be comfortably in bed in a Columbia hotel.

Thursday morning the team ate a breakfast of poached eggs and toast. Then at 10:30 they were given a small portion of turkey.

As for Big Thursday 1912, Clemson took the opening kickoff but could not move the ball. But then neither could the Gamecocks. And the opening quarter ended in a 0-0 deadlock. But to begin the second quarter big John Kangeter ran 15

yards for a TD, kicked the point, and the Tigers went up 7-0 (touchdowns now counted 6 points).

Now, just when it appeared that the game would become another Clemson rout, USC's Bill Harth picked up a Tiger fumble and ran 35 yards for a Gamecock touchdown. Von Kolnitz kicked the point, and the score was tied 7-7.

Later in the quarter Fritzie Von Kolnitz gave USC the lead, 10-7, when he booted a 10-yard field goal.

Clemson kicked off to open the second half. On first down Von Kolnitz ripped off 35 yards on an end sweep. On the next play Passailaigue circled end for 20 yards and another Gamecock touchdown. The kick was blocked, and USC was now up 16-7.

Clemson again fumbled during the next series. Dan Harth picked up the ball and ran it back 20 yards, down to the Clemson 10. On the next play Dan Heyward ran it over. Again the kick was no good, and Carolina took the lead 22-7. And thus ended Big Thursday 1912.

To say that the Carolina fans were delirious with joy is an understatement.

Alfred Holmes "Fritz" Von Kolnitz, captain of the 1912 Gamecocks. He scored five TDs against Porter Military and kicked three extra points, giving him a total of 33 points scored on the day, an all-time USC scoring record. He is a member of the USC Athletic Hall of Fame. (Later, to save his family embarrassment, he would play baseball for the Chicago White Sox under the alias Alfred Holmes.)

Ed "Dutch" Passailaigue, another early Gamecock Super Star at fullback. Like Von Kolnitz, Dutch was a native of Charleston and had been a star for The Citadel before transferring to USC. Note: He tied Von Kolnitz's TD record when he scored five touchdowns versus the College of Charleston in 1912.

Dr. Red Edgerton, coach of the Gamecocks 1912-15. The team would go 19-13-3 under his leadership.

Ben Britt, captain of the '12 Tigers.

The 1912 Clemson Tigers would have a disappointing 4-4 record, losing to all the biggies on their schedule.

An Action shot from Big Thursday 1912. Clemson is wearing their striped jerseys and stockings.

1913

BIG TUBBY SCORES TWICE FOR CLEMSON

It was October 30, 1913 and fully 5,000 fans turned out to watch the latest match between Carolina and Clemson on Big Thursday, by far the biggest gathering ever to watch an athletic event in South Carolina.

And as usual the Tigers were favored to win by a rather handsome margin. Bob Williams was back as head coach of the Tigers (he had a three-year contract), and to date they had beaten Davidson while losing to both Alabama and Auburn. By year's end, in addition to their win over USC this day, they would also beat The Citadel and Mercer, while losing to Georgia and Georgia Tech.

As for Carolina, Red Edgerton was now in his second year as head coach and the Gamecocks were not really doing badly. Already they had beaten Wake Forest, while losing to both Virginia and UNC. And they would go on, following today's loss, to beat Florida, Davison and The Citadel. All in all, not a bad year for the Gamecocks.

There had been a few significant rule changes in 1912, by the way, that truly effected the game: the field must now be 100 yards in length; there would be a ten-yard area to the rear of the goal posts where forward passes could be legally caught; and the ball would now be kicked off from the 45-yard line instead of the 50; touchdowns now counted 6 points, the extra point 1 point. It was truly the beginning of modern day football.

On a negative note, certain irregularities were discovered in the way Fritz Von Kolnitz and Ed Passailaigue had transferred to Carolina, and thus in 1913 they were banned from play against SIAA member institutions, which included Clemson. And this hurt the Gamecocks tremendously.

At any rate, captains John "Big" Mills of USC and A. P. Gandy of Clemson met at midfield for the coin toss. Clemson won and elected to receive.

Dan Heyward then kicked to Clemson's Jimmy James who returned the ball to the 40. Johnny Logan picked up 25 yards on the first play and then 20 on the next and the Tigers were moving. But then came a fumble and the Gamecocks recovered.

Then came a stalemate of sorts, with both teams punting on second and third down. Finally, USC fumbled a return, Johnny Logan picked it up and ran it in for a Clemson score. James' kick failed, and the first quarter ended, Clemson leading 6-0.

In the second quarter the defensive struggle continued, with the teams exchanging punts on six occasions before Carolina fumbled and Jimmy James picked it up and rambled 20 yards for Clemson's next touchdown. Again James' extra point try failed, and Clemson led 12-0.

And thus ended the first half.

To open the second half, Dan Heyward again kicked to Tanny Webb who returned the ball to the Clemson 30. Several plays later the Tigers had advanced to the Carolina 25. From there John Logan made a "spectacular" run for

Clemson's Senior Privates Club of 1913 for those unconcerned, careless cadets who found themselves still wearing the single stripe of a buck private after four years of military training.

A Carolina yearbook cartoon cele-brating USC's win over Clemson in 1912.

Clemson's third TD of the day. James' kick was good and the Tigers went up 19-0.

Then, about two minutes later, Clemson's Kenny Caughman picked up a loose ball and ran it back to "within 6 inches" of the USC goal where he was tackled.

The Tigers then took three cracks at the goal, but lost a foot. At that point they tried some secret strategy. They moved big W. A. "Tubby" Schilletter from his tackle sport to fullback, handed him the ball, and sure enough Schilletter took it in for the score. James' kick missed, and the score became 25-0.

As though that were not enough, in the fourth quarter Tubby Schilletter scored again, this time with a fumble recovery, which must be some sort of record for Clemson tackles, and the Tigers finally took the game by a big margin, 32-0.

The Clemson Tigers of 1913. They would go 4-4 on the season under Coach Bob Williams. (Williams remains the winningest coach in the history of USC football.)

A. P. "Hop" Gandy, captain of the '13 Clemson Tigers.

The 1913 Carolina Gamecocks, under Coach Dr. N. B. "Red" Edgerton, would go 4-3 on the season. The two gentlemen pictured in the insets are Fritz Von Kolnitz and Luke Hill, both members of the USC Athletic Hall of Fame.

John "Big" Mills, captain of the 1913 Carolina Gamecocks.

1914

MAJOR AND WEBB LEAD TIGERS' WIN

October 29, 1914 was a beautiful day for a football game, with the temperature in the sixties and only a few small clouds scattered about to mar an otherwise deep blue sky. The sounds and smells of the State Fair just added to the festive mood of those who arrived early for the game.

Only about 4,500 fans turned out this year and for understandable reasons. Just two months prior to today's contest, Europe had erupted into what is now remembered as one of the most horrible wars in history, while here at home cotton prices had dropped to its lowest level in years.

Times were so hard, in fact, that Clemson, in an effort to conserve resources, had left their student body at home this year.

At Carolina, Dr. Red Edgerton was back for his third season as head coach, and was now suffering through a long losing season, having defeated only the Charleston Machinists Mates while losing to Georgia Tech, North Carolina, Virginia, and tying Newberry. The Gamecocks were playing their first 11-game schedule in history and would finally finish the season with a 5-5-1 record.

Coach Bob Williams was back for his second season at Clemson, and to date the Tigers had lost to both Auburn and Tennessee while beating Furman and tying Davidson. They would finish the season with a winning 5-3-1 record.

Captains Luke Hill of USC and Tubby Scilletter of Clemson met at midfield for the coin toss. Schilletter, with his two late TDs, had been the hero of the Tigers' win on Big Thursday 1913, but today he lost the toss and the Gamecocks elected to receive.

The first quarter was scoreless, but those in the know agreed that Carolina seemed to be getting the better of Clemson.

Nor did the second quarter see any touchdowns. But C.S.

"Dopey" Major put the Tigers up 6-0 with two long drop-kicked field goals, one from the 20-yard line, the other from the 15. And thus ended the first half.

USC kicked to Clemson to open the second half and Tanny Webb returned the ball to the Tiger 35. Two plays later, Webb faked a punt and made a "brilliant broken-field run" 65 yards for a Clemson touchdown. The kick failed and the Tigers were in the lead 12-0.

Then, following an exchange of punts, Clemson again found themselves on the USC 15-yard line. Two runs netted them nothing, so Dopey Major was again called on for a field goal. And again he calmly drop-kicked a 3-pointer for the Tigers, putting them up 15-0.

Then, only minutes later, following a pass interception, Tanny Webb again scored for the Tigers, running the ball into the end zone from 10 yards out. Webb then kicked the extra point and Clemson took the lead 22-0.

As the fourth quarter began Carolina desperately began firing passes all over the field, Burnette Stoney doing most of the throwing. Indeed, on USC's first possession of the fourth quarter, Stoney completed a 40-yarder to Brooker down to the Clemson 10. Two plays later Felix Langston took it in for a TD. The kick failed and Carolina now trailed 22-6.

On the next series Carolina again went to the air, but Clemson intercepted a pass and returned it to the USC 30. Two plays later Tanny Webb again scored for the Tigers, his third TD of the day. Then he kicked the point and Clemson went up by a score of 29-6, which would be the final score.

In addition to Dopey Major's three field goals on the afternoon, Tanny Webb scored three TDs and kicked two extra points, a total of 20 points scored on the day. Not a bad effort from either player.

The Gameocks of 1914. Linemen (L-R): William Fant, Otis Goins, Burnet Stoney, Ted Girardeau, Harry Hampton, Mack McMillan, Luther Hill. Backs (L-R): Runt Coggeshall, Jerry Porter, Felix Langston, Dan Heyward.

The Clemson Tigers would enjoy a winning 5-3-1 record under Coach Bob Williams in 1914.

Jerry Porter, a fine halfback for USC in 1914.

Dan "The Viking" Heyward, fullback for the Gamecocks of 1914.

W. A. "Tubby" Schilletter, tackle and captain of the 1914 Clemson Tigers who scored two TDs against Carolina in 1913. He is a member of the Clemson Athletic hall of Fame.

Luke Hill, captain of the 1914 Gamecocks. He was named to the All-State Team for three years and served as captain of that team in 1914. He also served as president of the student body in 1914. He is a member of the USC Athletic Hall of Fame and the All-Time USC Football Team.

1915

THE INFAMOUS RINGER INCIDENT

The year 1915 saw Coach Bob Williams back for his third year as head coach at Clemson. Plus they had a number of players back from their powerful team of 1914, and thus enthusiasm was running high for another winning season. As it turned out, the Tigers would indeed get off to a rousing start as they pummeled Furman 94-0 in their opening game. Then came a 6-6 tie with Davidson and a great 3-0 win over mighty Tennessee. The only blemish on Clemson's record as they prepared for Big Thursday was a 14-0 loss to powerful Auburn.

Following today's game with USC, unfortunately, Clemson would go on to lose to UNC, VMI, and Georgia, and wind up with a disappointing 2-4-2 record.

At Carolina, on the other hand, Coach Red Edgerton was beginning his fourth year as head coach. He had never experienced a losing season since signing on with the Gamecocks, but his overall 14-10-2 record (plus the fact that USC had lost to Clemson in both 1913 and '14) was a disappointment to many fans and some were surprised that his contract was extended by a year. But what happened was this:

Back in the spring of the year Coach Edgerton had stood up at an assembly of USC students and school officials and made an impassioned plea that his contract be extended for one more season. Should that happen, promised Edgerton, Carolina would beat Clemson and at least tie Virginia. He then received a standing ovation from all assembled. And he got his extension.

It was this promise that led to severe problems for Edgerton, the football team, and USC in the fall.

For almost immediately several influential USC alumni, hoping to be of assistance to Edgerton and the Gamecocks, put certain wheels in motion. They would comb the nation and secretly recruit the best football players that money could buy.

And they did.

Improvements in Carolina's football fortunes were obvious as the 1915 season got underway. In quick order they smashed Newberry 29-0, Presbyterian College 41-0, and N C State 19-10. Thus they were 3-0 going into Big Thursday.

Unfortunately for Carolina, however, Clemson students were curious as to the Gamecocks' early successes and thus launched an informal investigation which did reveal some amazing irregularities in USC's football program. These the Clemson cadets quickly "leaked" to the press.

Among other things, Clemson claimed that two of Carolina's players had previously played for Muhlenburg (Pa.) College, while another (enrolled at USC under an alias) had once played for both NC State and Brown University. And there were others.

Some, in an effort to receive free tuition, had listed their hometown as New Brooklyn, S. C., a nonexistent community.

At this point, in hopes of substantiating their charges, Clemson brought forward a telephone operator (called a "ringer") who testified that she had overheard a telephone conversation between a USC alumnus and an athletic broker

Riggs Field, Clemson's football home, 1915-41, was dedicated on October 2, 1915. The Tigers and Davidson then battled to a 6-6 tie.

in Pennsylvania who sold football players to the highest bidder.

USC initially denied that any such plot had taken place. But it is a fact that coincident with Clemson's probe, four prominent USC freshmen suddenly vanished from both the USC lineup and the USC campus and were never heard of again.

Just prior to kickoff on game day, as though in retaliation for Clemson's investigation, USC insisted that Clemson's players all be lined up and forced to take an oath that they were eligible to play.

Still, despite everyone's best efforts, following the contest a Clemson lineman, C.E. "Mule" Littlejohn, swore to the press that the USC lineman playing across from him had stated that he had once played pro ball in Bethlahem, Pa. before enrolling at USC.

Two weeks following the game, the president of USC wired the president of Clemson and admitted that his investigation had revealed some irregularities in the football program and offered to forfeit the game by any score Clemson might suggest.

Clemson's president very graciously refused to accept the forfeit. But Carolina was forced to forfeit their first three wins of the season.

Big Thursday 1915, by the way, was a viciously fought defensive struggle that ended in a 0-0 tie.

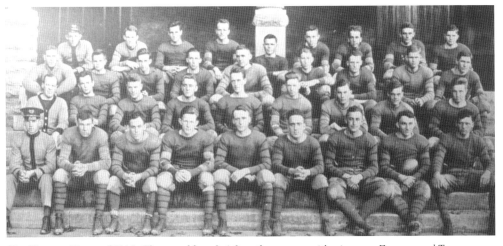

The Clemson Tigers of 1915. They would go 2-4-2 on the season, with wins over Furman and Tennessee, losses to Auburn, UNC, VMI, and Georgia, and ties with USC and Davidson.

W. K. McGill, Clemson captain in 1915.

The Gamecocks take on Newberry College in their 1915 opener at Davis Field, a game USC won 29-0. (Note the USC band standing in the background beneath the trees.)

Otis E. Going, USC captain in 1915.

Carolina's coed sponsors for 1915 arrived at the Fair Grounds in horse drawn carriages.

For the first time ever, Clemson in 1915 presented the latest in football pagentry, CHEERLEADERS!

And Carolina's CHEERLEADERS.

Two action shots from Big Thursday 1915, a viciously fought defensive struggle that would end in a 0-0 tie. A week following this game USC would offer a forfeit by any score Clemson would suggest. But the president of Clemson refused the offer, saying that the Tigers would win on the field or no where.

1916

BIG TIGERS SMOTHER GAMECOCKS

Gone now from the Carolina scene was Coach Red Edgerton and in his place came Dr. Rice Warren, USC's twelfth head coach since 1896. But already things were not going well for the Gamecocks. They had only two starters back from the 1915 squad, and going into Big Thursday they had merely a win over Wofford to show for their efforts, while losing to Newberry and Tennessee. By season's end the Gamecocks would experience only two more wins (over Mercer and Furman) while losing to Wake Forest, Virginia and The Citadel.

Clemson was facing a similar situation. Gone now was Coach Bob Williams and in his place came Wayne Hart. The Tigers had only four starters back from 1915 and had only one victory, a 7-6 win over Furman, to show for their efforts as Big Thursday rolled around. But their losses (to Georgia, Tennessee and Auburn) were to some of the most powerful teams in the South. Still, by season's end the Tigers would enjoy only one more win (over PC), while losing to VMI, Davidson and The Citadel.

The fact that both Carolina and Clemson suffered losses to the Citadel in 1916 says much, for the Bulldogs were considered the weakest team in the state at that time.

On Wednesday evening Carolina took 18 of their varsity players to a private home outside the city, away from all the excitement surrounding Big Thursday, where they would spend the night. The Tigers, on the other hand, were all quartered in private homes in a residential area of Columbia.

It should also be noted that for the first time in history Carolina players would be wearing numbers on their jerseys for today's game.

Also, as a result of the "ringer" incident of 1915, the outraged president of USC had passed a rule that freshmen could no longer play varsity ball at the University. Thus before kickoff at noon today USC announced that if they could not play their freshmen then neither could Clemson. The Tigers were initially dismayed by this announcement, but they finally agreed and the game proceeded.

Captains M. K. McMillan from USC and Dopey Major met at midfield and Carolina won the toss. The Gamecocks, said McMillan, would kick the ball, and thus Captain Major chose the east goal.

Harry Hampton kicked for USC and E. M. Wiehl made a beautiful run back, down to the Carolina 40. Indeed it was only a last-second tackle that stopped him from going all the way.

But led by Major, Wiehl, J. G. "Mutt" Gee, and F. L. "Fish" Witsell, the Tigers were simply too much for the outmanned Gamecocks. And though Babe Clarke, Mack McMillan, and the Hampton brothers, Frank and Harry, turned in excellent performances for Carolina, the Tigers finally triumphed once again, this time by a score of 27-0. Indeed, USC had not won on Big Thursday since 1912.

An action shot from Big Thursday 1916, a game won by Clemson 27-0. Carolina had not won now since 1912.

The Carolina Gamecocks of 1916. They would suffer through a 3-6 losing season under Coach Rice Warren.

Mack McMillan, captain of the 1916 Gamecocks and a unanimous selection to the All State team.

The Clemson Tigers of 1916. Under Coach Wayne Hart, they would go 3-6 on the season, one of their few losing seasons in history.

Dr. Rice Warren, a Columbia physician, would remain as coach at Carolina for only one year.

The Gamecocks defeated Wofford College 23-3 in 1916, one of only three games they would win all season, in a game played at Davis Field (at the corner of Green and Sumter Streets). Note the USC dorms in the background.

C. S. "Dopey" Major, captain of the 1916 Tigers. He is still remembered as one of Clemson's finest football players of the Early Era.

Coach Wayne Hart would lead Clemson to a 3-7 season in 1916. This would be his only year with the Tigers.

Clemson cadets watch excitedly as the Tigers defeat Furman University 7-6 at Riggs Field to kick off the 1916 football season.

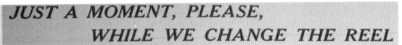

Clemson's "Senior Privates" again spoof their military training program in this 1916 TAPS photo.

1917
AMERICA GOES TO WAR

America entered the war against Germany in the spring of 1917, and young men from across the nation were being herded into service by the thousands. The effects of the war were being felt everywhere, and especially hard hit were our college athletic teams. Some, of course, were hurt worse than others.

At Clemson, for example, their students were largely left unscathed by the war, thanks to their fine ROTC program. Such was not true at USC.

Thus as 1917 rolled around at Clemson, Edward A. Donahue, a former star player for Washington and Lee, was named head coach and hopes were running high that the Tigers would better their 3-6 record of 1916. And those hopes were not in vain, for prior to Big Thursday the Tigers had already mauled both PC and Furman, while losing by a score of 7-0 to their old nemesis Auburn. Following today's game they would go on to beat Wofford, The Citadel and Florida while losing only to Davidson.

At Carolina, on the other hand, things were not going so well. In the spring of 1917 USC had an enrollment of 480 students. Of those 55 were female. Then, once America declared war on Germany, 125 students volunteered for service, leaving only 300 male students on campus. As for the football team, there were only four lettermen back from the team of 1916--the others were now training to go to France.

Regardless, USC had a new coach on campus, Dixon Foster, a star player from Hampton-Sydney University, and it was hoped that he could work miracles with the material on hand. But such was not to be. To date the Gamecocks had beaten Newberry and lost to Florida. Following today's match they would lose to Erskine, Wofford and PC while beating Furman and The Citadel.

But for years to come fans would remember Big Thursday 1917 as one of the most exciting games on record.

Carolina kicked off, but initially neither team could move the ball against the other and there ensued an exchange of punts. At that point, led by the smashing runs of Stumpy Banks, J. H. Bartlet, E. L. Witsell, and Boo Armstrong, the Tigers moved to the USC 15-yard line. Then Witsell threw a short TD pass to L. R. Kay in the end zone, then he kicked the point, and Clemson took the lead 7-0.

And that's how the first half ended, with Carolina doing surprisingly well against the favored Tigers.

In the third period Clemson's Stumpy Banks fumbled Rut Osborne's 50-yard punt, the ball rolled into the end zone, and USC's tiny 100-pound end, Bully Weston, recovered for a Gamecock score. The point try failed and Clemson kept the lead 7-6.

But it was in the fourth quarter that the fireworks really began. On the first play of that quarter, with the Tigers deep in Gamecock territory, Witsell tossed a short pass which was

Dixon Foster, coach of the 1917 Gamecocks. He would go in service following this single season at Carolina.

Rut "Dago" Osborne, an outstanding quarterback for the Gamecocks. He would serve as Chairman of the USC Board of Trustees, and is a member of the USC Athletic Hall of Fame.

Sumter "Babe" Clark, captain of the 1917 Gamecocks.

picked off by USC's Colie Seaborn at the twenty-five. Seaborn then raced 75 yards for another Carolina score, George Brown kicked the point, and the Gamecocks went up 13-7.

But then, following the kickoff, Clemson mounted a sustained drive that ended with Witsell taking the ball in for another Tiger score. His kick was good, and again Clemson led 14-13.

In the game's final moments Carolina went to the air. But this ploy failed as Clemson's L. P. Thackston intercepted an Osborne pass and ran it back 25 yards for the Tigers' final TD of the day. Final score: Clemson 21, Carolina 13.

The Clemson Tigers of 1917 would enjoy a good 6-2 season.

J. G. "Mutt" Gee, and F. L. Witsell. Gee was an All-Southern center for the Tigers. Witsell played quarterback and served as 1917 team captain.

Clemson's Anderson County Club of 1917.

Ed Donahue, coach of the Clemson Tigers 1917-20.

The Carolina Gamecocks of 1917. Linemen (L-R): Sumter Clark, Harry Hampton, James McGowen, William Brown, J. H. Moore, Heyward Brockington, Bully Weston.
Back (L-R): Lindsay Turner, Rut Osborne, Colie Seaborn, Clark Waring.

1918

THE FLU EPIDEMIC HITS USC HARD

Big Thursday 1918 was played on November 2, a day when thousands of men would die in the trenches of France, and just nine days prior to November 11, the day when all the killing would end.

Back home, the entire city of Columbia, including the University, was firmly in the grip of the great flu epidemic that swept the nation in 1918. By October 1 there were 84 cases on campus, and by November 1 the total had swelled to include almost the entire student body. The most serious cases were sent to the army hospital at Camp Jackson, others were treated at Woodrow College which had been converted into a hospital. Eventually four USC students would die of this terrible malady. Indeed, classes in all schools and colleges in the Columbia area, including the University, were cancelled on October 15 and did not begin again until November 6.

As a result of these negative conditions USC played an abbreviated schedule of only four games in 1918, and were probably lucky to play those.

Clemson seems to have been immune to the flu, but the war had hit them hard. Indeed, only one member of their great team of 1917 (Boo Armstrong) was on hand as the 1918 season opened, the others now being in service.

Coach Ed Donahue was in his second year as head coach,

and the Tigers had played two games prior to their date with Carolina, beating Camp Sevier 65-0 while losing to Georgia Tech 28-0.

Gone now from the Carolina scene was Coach Dixon Foster and in his place was Lt. Frank Dobson, on special assignment from the US Army. He had five lettermen back from 1917 and was determined to do the best he could under the circumstances. The Clemson game was USC's first encounter of 1918. They would then go on to beat Furman 20-12 and Wofford 13-0 while tying The Citadel 0-0.

(The State Fair did not open in 1918, thanks to the flu epidemic, and thus for the only time in history Carolina and Clemson would play at Davis Field on the campus of the University.)

But luck seemed to be running in favor of Clemson this afternoon as Carolina's most outstanding player, Ted Beall, had to be carried from the field following the very first play from scrimmage. USC had to punt, and the bigger Tiger team began a long march highlighted by a pass from W. L. Frew to R. E. Thornton down to the Carolina 30 yard line. Two plays later Boo Armstrong took it in for the score. Frew's kick missed, and Clemson was up 6-0.

In the second quarter it was all Clemson again as they immediately began alternating Boo Armstrong, Switzer

Carolina's 1918 State Champions basketball team.

J. H. Moore, captain of the 1918 Carolina Gamecocks.

Lt. Frank Dobson, coach of the 1918 Gamecocks. He was athletic director at Camp Jackson and on loan to USC.

Allison, and T. J. Reames for short gains until they'd reached the Carolina 3-yard line. Again it was Armstrong taking it in for the score. Frew's kick was good, and Clemson led 13-0.

It was said that the smaller Carolina team put up a vicious fight in the third period, but Clemson was irresistible, and "Carolina's well organized retreat became a rout." As the period came to a close, Reames turned Carolina's end and scampered 67 yards, down to the 3 yard line. Armstrong took it in on the next play, his third TD of the afternoon, the kick missed, and Clemson led 19-0.

On the next series Carolina tried a pass, but it was picked off by Allison and returned 68 yards for a TD. Yen Lightsey's kick was good, and Clemson's lead now went to 26-0.

Minutes later Clemson drove for another score, Boo

Armstrong going in for his fourth TD of the day. Lightsey's kick was again good, and the score became 33-0. Following the kickoff, USC then tried another pass. This time it was intercepted by D. A. Crawford who ran 38 yards for another score. The kick failed, and Clemson was up 39-0. And that was it for both teams.

Boo Armstrong's four touchdowns in this game set a record that has never been equalled by any other player from either team.

(In 1918 military authorities at neither Clemson nor The Citadel would allow their athletes to miss ROTC drill because of athletic events. Thus, because Clemson could not travel to Charleston and back in one day, USC loaned their Davis Field to these two schools so that their annual game could go off as scheduled.)

The 1918 Carolina Gamecocks. Linemen (L-R): Heyward Brockington, J. H. Moore, Marshall Durham, Ed Smith, LeRoy Mims, Ted Beall, Clark Weston. Backs: Spratt Moore (QB), L. S. Barringer (RH), George Brown (FB), H. S. Jones (LH).

F. E. "Boo" Armstrong scored four TDs versus Carolina in 1918, an all-time record for this series. He is a member of the Clemson Athletic Hall of Fame.

B. C. "Stumpy" Banks, Captain of the 1918 Tigers. In 1917 he scored five TDs against Furman, an all-time Clemson scoring record. He is a member of the Clemson Athletic Hall of Fame.

The Tigers defeat Camp Sevier 65-0 in a game played at Riggs Field in September of 1918.

Clemson's Sumter County Club of 1918.

The Gamecocks return a kickoff on Big Thursday 1918 in a game played at Davis Field. (The State Fair was cancelled because of the flue epidemic.) The Tigers would win it by a score of 39-0.

1919

ARMSTRONG, BANKS, KEY TIGER WIN

It was October 30, 1919, the war had been over for almost a year, and a sense of normalcy was returning to the nation.

Indeed, it was estimated that some 6,500 fans were on hand for the game, far too many to be accommodated by the limited seating space. According to *The State* newspaper, which took the fair committee to task for not having made better preparations for the large crowd, fans jammed every inch of space in the stands, stood five deep around the playing field, and indeed spilled out by the hundreds onto the playing field. Six policemen, it was said, spent the afternoon trying to persuade fans to move to the sidelines but without much success. These, it was said, were mostly USC fans, and on several occasions they actually impeded the progress of the Clemson football team.

One amused Carolina player was quoted after the game as saying, "Several times I couldn't return Clemson's punts until the police cleared the crowd back. If we hadn't waited, I'd of gotten lost in the crowd."

But Clemson's big Tiger team came into today's contest, as usual, the heavy favorites. Coach Jiggs Donahue was back for his third year at the helm and he had five of his mainstays from 1918 back for the 1919 wars. Already they had beaten Erskine, Davidson, and mighty Tennessee while losing only to Auburn and Georgia Tech.

At Carolina, meanwhile, Dixon Foster had bid farewell to the military and was back as head coach. Only two starters from 1918 were on hand to greet him, but as usual the Gamecocks resolved to do the best they could. Already they had lost to PC, Georgia, and Davidson, though they'd beaten Erskine. Not a glowing beginning by any means.

Carolina won the toss and elected to receive. Rube Skinner

returned the ball to the USC 30-yard line. But the Gamecocks couldn't move the ball and Martin Goodman then got off a long punt which rolled dead at the Clemson thirty.

The Gamecocks held the Tigers, but were offsides on several key plays which kept the Clemson drive alive. Finally, Switzer Allison took the ball in for a touchdown. L. D. Harris' kick missed, and the Tigers were up 6-0.

The rest of the first quarter saw the two teams deadlocked with neither able to move against the other.

The second period was pretty much a replay of the first with neither team able to make much progress against the other. Carolina's Burnette Stoney tried a field goal at one point but the ball sailed wide. But then, following another exchange of punts, USC's Martin Goodman attempted a punt from his own twenty. The kick was blocked and run back to the two. From there L. D. Harris ran it in for the score. His kick was no good, and Clemson led 12 to 0.

Again Armstrong kicked off. And then an odd thing happened. Harry Lightsey took the kick and was sprinting upfield when he was tackled by his brother L. M. Lightsey, an outstanding Clemson guard.

Carolina was down by 12, but five minutes later the Gamecocks intercepted a pass at the Clemson 12. From there Carolina finally managed to wedge the ball over for a TD, Herbert Timmons getting the honor. Ed Smith's kick missed, and the score became 12-6.

The third period was a scoreless defensive duel, but in the fourth Clemson gained a first down on the USC two-yard line. It took them four plays to smash the ball over, but they finally succeeded, Stumpy Banks taking it in, and the score became 19-6. And that is how the game ended.

J. C. "Suzie" Owens, a mainstay at tackle for the Tigers and a member of the Clemson Athletic Hall of Fame.

The Gamecocks of 1919 would suffer through a 1-7-1 season. They would not have a worse record until 1966, when they went 1-9 under Coach Paul Dietzel.
Linemen (L-R): Heyward Brockington, Mack McMillan, Harry Lightsey, Ed Smith, Alex Waite, Martin Goodman, Burney Smith. Backs (L-R): Herbert Timmons, Mike Blount, Gus Allen, Rube Skinner.

Clemson's offense on the move in this action shot from Big Thursday 1919.

In 1919 Mike Blount ran back a Washington and Lee fumble 85 yards before being tackled on the Generals' 10-yard line. This remains the longest non-scoring fumble return in USC history.

The Clemson Tigers of 1919. They would go 6-2-2 on the season.

Clemson beat Davidson 7-0 at Riggs Field in 1919. Note that many of the players are not wearing helmets in this shot.

Heyward Brockington, Captain of the 1919 Gamecocks and a four-year letterman. He was named to the All-State team in 1919.

1920

GRESSETTES' TOE UPENDS THE TIGERS 3-0

It was October 28, 1920, an unseasonably warm day in Columbia, and the players were perspiring heavily as they went through their pregame warmups prior to their annual Big Thursday shootout.

Jiggs Donahue was in his fourth year as head coach at Clemson, and had five starters, including Boo Armstrong and Switzer Allison, back from Clemson's great team of 1919, and hopes were running high for another successful season. Such, unfortunately for the Tigers, was not to be. Prior to today's game the Tigers had beaten Newberry and Wofford, while losing to Auburn and Tennessee. Following Big Thursday they would defeat only The Citadel while losing to Georgia Tech, Furman, and Georgia.

The picture at Carolina was somewhat brighter. Sol Metzger, a true professional, was the new head coach, and hopes were running high that he would bring with him the lessons he'd learned as coach at the University of Pennsylvania, where he'd won the national championship in 1908. He had four starters on hand from 1919, plus a new secret weapon by the name of Tatum Wannamaker Gressette, a punishing tailback and one of the finest field goal kickers in the South.

Prior to today's game the Gamecocks had beaten both Wofford and PC, while losing to Georgia and UNC.

Clemson kicked off to Carolina and the ball was returned to the USC 22-yard line. W. C. Sizemore skirted left end for 15 yards on first down. Then Gressette brought the crowd to their feet when he completed a 40-yard pass to David Robinson, down to the Clemson 23. But Clemson stiffened at that point, and the Gamecocks gained but 5 yards on the next three plays.

It was at that point that Tatum Gressette huddled with his teammates. Sizemore called for a field goal. Gressette nodded his head. "Just give me three seconds, " he said. "Hold 'em out for just three seconds and I'll get us three points."

And that's exactly what happened. Gressette took the snap from center, dropped back three paces, then drop-kicked the ball squarely through the uprights.

Only two minutes and 24 seconds were elapsed off the clock and Carolina had taken the lead 3-0.

From that point on the game became a terrific struggle, with Clemson determined to score and Carolina determined that Clemson would not score.

Indeed, the Tigers had a golden opportunity early in the second period when they carried for a first down on the USC seven-yard line. But three running plays gained them nothing, and a pass completion gained them only five yards, and USC took over on downs.

The following day newspapers across the state were lavish in their praise of both teams, but felt that Carolina's team, being much smaller than Clemson's, deserved much credit for holding the Tigers scoreless for 60 minutes this day.

Final score: Carolina 3, Clemson 0. For the first time since 1912 the Gamecocks had upended the Tigers.

The 1920 Lady Gamecocks basketball team.

Ed Smith, captain of the 1920 Carolina Gamecocks.

Sol Metzger, coach of the Carolina Gamecocks.

The Carolina Gamecocks of 1920. They would enjoy a 5-4 winning season under new head coach Sol Metzger, and were the first USC team to beat Clemson since 1912. They set a less enviable record when they lost to Navy 63-0, USC's worst loss ever. (Tatum Gressette is lined up at tailback, directly behind the center.)

Tatum Gressette. His 25-yard field goal beat Clemson 3-0 in 1920. Prior to his death in 1997, Gressette, at the age of 98, was the oldest living former captain of a Carolina football team.

The 1920 Clemson Tigers. Under Coach Jiggs Donahue they would suffer through a 3-6 season. Note: Yen Lightsey, R. C. Potts and Stumpy Banks were all named to the All-Southern Football Team.

James T. Crouch, a great Gamecock receiver, would become a member of the USC Board of Trustees in 1952.

L. M. "Yen" Lightsey, an outstanding Tiger lineman 1917-20, was named All-Southern. His brother Harry starred for Carolina.

Boo Armstrong, captain of the 1920 Tigers and a member of the CU Athletic Hall of Fame.

1921

GAMECOCKS PUNISH TIGERS

Never before had the Gamecocks beaten Clemson College two years in a row. But today, October 27, 1921, presented USC a golden opportunity to do the improbable. For prior to Big Thursday this unusually strong Gamecock eleven had romped over Erskine, Newberry, and PC, while tying a good UNC team, and had given up only two touchdowns in doing so. Thus the Gamecocks were undefeated going into Big Thursday, and optimism was running high that they would break their old Clemson jinx.

At Clemson, on the other hand, under new head coach Doc Stewart, the outlook was somewhat dismal. They had beaten only PC at this point while losing to both Centre and Auburn and tying Furman.

Fans who follow their heads instead of their hearts in such matters were right when they concluded that Clemson was no match for Carolina on this day. And sure enough, by day's end the Tigers would take home another loss to go with the five they'd suffer before the 1921 season ended.

Fully 8,000 fans were on hand to watch as Clemson kicked to Carolina. Al Ambs returned the ball to the USC 20-yard line, but three plays netted USC nothing, so Rock Snipes went back to punt. He fumbled the snap and the Tigers recovered on the Carolina five. For the next four plays then Clemson bucked the Gamecock line. But they failed to score and Carolina took over on downs.

Three plays later Carolina again fumbled on their own twenty, and again Clemson recovered. Four plays later the Tigers attempted a field goal, but the ball sailed wide.

For the rest of the quarter the two teams exchanged punts. Then, five minutes into the second quarter, the Gamecocks took over at the Carolina 30-yard line on a blocked punt. Al Ambs then electrified the crowd with a 35-yard run down to the Clemson 35. Then came Rock Snipes with a 20-yard burst down to the Clemson 12. Ambs went for four, then it was Alex Waite going in for the score. George Belk kicked the point, and the Gamecocks led 7-0.

And thus ended the first half.

Just three minutes into the second half George Belk intercepted an M. G. Stockum pass and returned it 60 yards for Carolina's second TD of the day. Belk again was true with his kick and USC went up 14-0.

As though things were not bad enough for the Tigers already, their Pinky Colbert attempted to punt but fumbled the ball at his own 15-yard line. Carolina recovered, and two plays later Alex Waite took it in for Carolina's third TD of the day. The score now became Carolina 21, Clemson 0. And that is how the game finally ended.

For Carolina, it was the first time in history they had beaten Clemson for two successive years, and it was written that celebrations lasted far into the night all over Columbia.

In particular, Joe Wheeler was singled out for his spectacular play on defense for the Gamecocks, some experts saying that they'd never seen anyone better.

Clemson, by the way, went 1-6-2 on the season, one of their worst records ever.

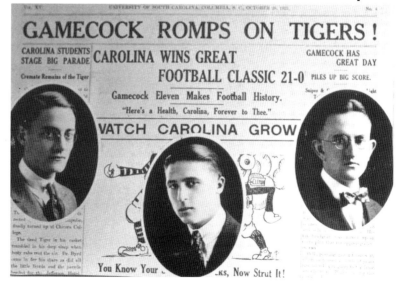

USC's student newspaper, "The Gamecock," trumpets carolina's big win over Clemson in 1921 (along with photos of the editorial staff.

The Clemson Tigers of 1921 would go 1-6-2 on the season, still their worst record in history.

E. J. Stewart, coach of the Tigers, 1921-22.

J. H. Spearman, captain of the 1921 Tigers.

Carolina's football managers of 1921 would take a back seat to no one when it came to dressing in the latest fashions.

Clemson's Oconee County Club, 1921.

The Clemson cadets on parade near Tillman Hall, 1921.

Tatum Gressette, captain of the 1921 Gameocks whose field goal upset the Tigers 3-0 in 1920, is a member of the All-Time USC Football team. He would later serve as head coach at The Citadel. (Oddly enough, his son would one day serve as Head Cheerleader at Clemson College.)

1922

LUCK AND CHARLIE ROBINSON DOWN USC

Some 8,500 excited fans swarmed through the gates at the Fair Grounds on October 26, 1922 to see if Sol Metzger and his Gamecocks could make it three in a row over Coach Doc Stewart and his Clemson Tigers. At this point Carolina had beaten Erskine, PC and Wofford while losing only to UNC by a close 10-7 margin. Clemson, on the other hand, had beaten PC and Newberry while losing to Centre by a 21-0 score. The game was therefore considered a toss-up.

By noon there was not a cloud in the sky and the temperature stood at a very agreeable 75-degrees as Carolina's Joree Wheeler kicked off to the Tigers' Pat Harmon. From that point on the first two quarters became a punting duel between Carolina's Rock Snipes and Clemson's Rhett Turnipseed, with neither team able to take advantage of the many breaks that came their way. And the first half ended a 0-0 tie.

The third quarter was incredible in that the Gamecocks kept possession of the ball the entire period except for one play when the Tigers punted. Yet USC could not take the ball in for a score. They had one first down on the Clemson six, and another on the Clemson ten. But no scores for Carolina.

But then came the fireworks. Rock Snipes broke loose on a 40-yard dash to the midfield stripe. But the Gamecocks were called offsides and ball was brought back to their 4-yard line. From there Rock Snipes made his only poor kick of the day, a 30-yarder that gave Clemson the ball at the Carolina 34.

The Tigers connected on two passes, then came a nice run by Pat Harmon and they had a first down on the USC 20. On the next play Charlie Robinson threw for ten yards to F. M. Zeigler and the Tigers were on the move.

But the Gamecocks held and on fourth down Robinson tried a field goal. The kick was blocked, but Robinson recovered for Clemson. Two runs failed to gain yardage, so again Robinson tried a field goal, this time from the USC 20. The kick was good and the Tigers finally took the lead 3-0. Which is how the game ended.

This game, by the way, was being broadcast by wireless to the chapel at Clemson College. It was said that their 700 students assembled to hear the game went wild when the final whistle blew. They had ended Carolina's big win streak at two games.

(USC intercepted ten passes vs. Furman in '22, an all-time Gamecock record.)

J. Strom Thurmond (back row, 3rd from left), a longtime senator from South Carolina, was a member of Clemson's state champion cross country team in 1922.

F. B. "Bull" Lightsey, an All-Southern tackle for the Tigers, 1922, 24-25, and a member of the Clemson Athletic Hall of Fame.

E. H. Emanuel, captain of the 1922 Clemson Tigers.

The 1922 Clemson Tigers.

Alex Waite, captain of the 1922 Gamecocks and an All-State performer. He was captain of the football, track and swim teams.

USC quarterback A. G. Ambs (#20) sweeps Clemson's end in this 1922 Big Thursday game won by the Tigers 3-0. Note that the players are now wearing numbers on their jerseys.

1923

GAMECOCKS FALL BY AN EXTRA POINT

Clemson's new head coach, Bud Saunders, had been an outstanding athlete at the University of Missouri and held a degree in law from that institution. He came to Clemson full of hopes and expectations but would enjoy only one winning season with the Tigers, and that in 1923 when his team would go 5-2-1 on the season. Worse, his Tigers would win only one game with Carolina over the next three years.

Back at Carolina, Coach Metzger was back for another year as head coach, though his Gamecocks were not setting the woods on fire in 1923. They'd beaten Erskine and Newberry while losing to NC State and PC prior to Big Thursday.

As for today's game, the experts considered it a toss up. The real difference, as it turned out, would be the toe of the Tigers' Charles Robinson, a Winnsboro boy, who once kicked four field goals in one game while playing for Mt. Zion High School. He'd kicked the field goal that beat Carolina in 1922, and his extra point this afternoon would turn the same trick.

Over 9,000 fans jammed the old grandstands today, by far the most people ever to witness an athletic event in South Carolina.

Captains Butch Holohan of Clemson and Joe Wheeler of USC met for the coin toss. Wheeler won and elected to receive.

The first half was a viciously fought defensive struggle with neither team able to move consistently against the other, and they went to the locker rooms tied at 0-0.

In the third quarter, following an exchange of punts, Clemson kicked out of bounds at the Carolina 15-yard line. Tom

Brice fumbled on the first play and Sam Jackson recovered for Clemson. On third down for the Tigers E. G. Dotterer passed to Charlie Garrison who took it in for a TD. Charlie Robinson then kicked the extra point and the Tigers led 7-0.

Then following several more punt exchanges, Charlie Robinson again went back to punt for Clemson, but Carolina's J. C. Long blocked it and Frankie Meyer picked it up and ran 15 yards for a Gamecock touchdown. W. C. Sizemore then attempted the extra point, but Clemson blocked it and thus kept the lead, 7-6. And that, finally, is how the game ended.

Clemson would finish the season with a good 5-2-1 record, while the Gamecocks would struggle through to a 4-6 record, their only losing season under Coach Metzger.

Following the game, reported *The State*, students from both Carolina and Clemson marched around the field cheering their institutions, their teams, themselves, and their opponents. As for the game itself, *The State* concluded (in a bit of florid prose):

That the Tigers scored but one touchdown is a tribute to the back-to-the-wall spirit of the Birds who fell before the rushing Tiger until the goal post hour glass flashed its warning danger signal and then emphasized with an inspiring resistance the dictum, "They shall not pass."

But despite these stirring last words, the Tigers did "pass" and in fact won the game with a pass. That plus the toe of Charlie Robinson.

The Clemson Tigers of 1923. Linemen (L-R): C. C. Garrison, Butch Holohan, Stonewall Jackson, J. B. Wertz, Dutch Tennant, Frank Strother, Gary Finklea.
Backs (L-R): Charles Robinson, E. G. Dotterer, Bratton Williams, Pat Harmon.

The Gamecocks' starting eleven of 1923.
Linemen (L-R): Marion Swink, T. B. Simmons, Henry Bartell, Joe Wheeler, Bob Gunter, J. C. Long, Frankie Meyer.
Backs: A. G. Ambs (QB), W. R. Jeffords (RH), Alex Jascewicz (FB), W. C. Sizemore (LH).

The Lady Gamecock basketball team of 1923.

Frankie Meyer who picked up a Clemson fumble and ran it in for a touchcown on Big Thursday. He would serve as captain of the Gamecocks in 1924.

W. C. "Sic" Sizemore. The Tigers blocked his extra point try, winning the game for Clemson.

Joe "Joree" Wheeler, captain of the 1923 Gamecocks and hero of USC's 1921 win over the Tigers. Wheeler is a member of the USC All-Time Football Team.

Bud Saunders, coach of the Clemson Tigers, 1923-25.

R. F. "Butch" Holohan, captain of the 1923 Tigers.

The Clemson baseball team of 1923.

It was the 1920s, the Jazz Age, and Clemson's Pep Band was in the forefront of all that was swingingly chic.

1924

BOATWRIGHT'S TOE WINS GAME FOR USC

It was 1924 and over the next three years the Clemson Tigers would suffer through some of their most dismal seasons in history, losing a total of 20 games while winning only five. Even worse, perhaps, they would bow to the Gamecocks in each of those three seasons. This particular year, 1924, still under Coach Bud Saunders, the Tigers would beat only Elon and PC while losing to their other six opponents.

The Gamecocks, on the other hand, still playing under Coach Sol Metzger, would enjoy one of their best seasons ever in 1924, winning seven games while losing only three.

Back for his senior year at Clemson was Charlie Robinson whose toe had beaten Carolina in both 1922 and '23, and Tiger fans hoped he might work just such a miracle again. But time would tell.

Only minutes following the opening kickoff, Clemson was forced to punt. Jack Wright returned the kick to the Tiger 30. Power Rogers then skirted left end for ten, then came Bill Jeffords for fifteen, and the Gamecocks had a first down at the Clemson five. But the Tigers held at that point and took over on downs.

Several minutes later the situation was reversed. USC was forced to punt from their own end zone and Charlie Robinson ran it back to the Carolina 25. Then runs by Bratton Williams and John Walker gave the Tigers a first down at the USC 12. But a 15-yard holding penalty against the Tigers drove them back and their drive bogged down.

And so went the first half, with neither team able to score against the other.

Then, five minutes into the third quarter, with Clemson in possession at the Carolina ten, the Gamecocks got the break they'd been waiting for.

Robinson attempted a short pass to a receiver in the flat, but the pass was picked off by Blake Edmonds. He dashed down the sideline with not an orange jersey in sight. But at the last moment, as he reached the Clemson ten, he glanced back over his shoulder to see if he would make good his escape. It was a fatal mistake. For he lost his balance, stumbled and fell at the Clemson five. The Gamecocks then tried three running plays and gained nothing. But then on fourth down the Gamecocks called on their ace kicker, P. J. Boatwright, for a field goal. He drop-kicked the ball squarely between the uprights and Carolina took a 3-0 lead.

And that, finally, is how the game ended. So for the past three years now Big Thursday had been decided by three points or less.

Frankie Meyer and Bill Jeffords, USC co-captains for the Clemson game, meet with officials just prior to kickoff on Big Thursday 1924.

Those rugged Gamecocks of 1924 went 7-3 on the season, including a 3-0 win over Clemson. Linemen (L-R): S. S. Seideman, Blake Edmunds, Bill Boyd, Robert Gunter, Alex Murdaugh. Backs: P. J. Boatwright (QB), Bill Jeffords (RH), Jazz Jascewicz (FB), Bill Rogers (LH).

The Morning After the Day Before

This somewhat partisan cartoon appeared in The State newspaper the day following Carolina's 3-0 win over Clemson in 1924.

In 1924 Bill Jeffords was credited with a 90-yard punt vs. UNC. This remains the longest punt in the USC record book. Jeffords caught three TD passes vs. PC in '25, again getting his name in the USC record book.

Captain Frankie Meyer, called one of the finest ends ever to play for Carolina.

P. J. Boatwright whose field goal gave USC a 3-0 win over Clemson in 1924.

The Clemson Tigers of 1924 would go 2-6 on the season. Note their natty new uniforms, the latest in football attire in 1924.

Captain Charlie Robinson whose magic toe beat USC in both 1922 and '23.

Wallace R. Roy, an outstanding end for the Tigers, was named to the All-American Track Team in 1925, and was voted the Most Outstanding Athlete in South Carolina in 1926. He is a member of the Clemson Athletic Hall of Fame.

The Iron Men of 1924 were expected to play 60 minutes of every game. Here Bratton Williams attempts to gain yardage through the middle of the Carolina line.
(Blake Edmunds' 85-yard non-scoring run with a pass interception against Clemson in 1924 remains the longest such run in the USC record book.)

1925

FOUR FIELD GOALS WIN FOR USC

It was 1925 and Carolina's new head football coach, Branch Bocock, a native of Virginia, enjoyed the distinction to being the only Protestant ever to serve as captain of the Georgetown football team. During his two-year tenure with USC he would compile a good 13-7 record, including two wins over Clemson.

Prior to Big Thursday this year, the Gamecocks had beaten Erskine, NC State and Wofford while losing a close one to UNC.

As for the Tigers, Bud Saunders was back for his third year as head coach, and fans were hoping he could better his terrible 2-6 record of 1924. To date, however, Clemson was 0-3 on the season, with losses to PC, Auburn and Kentucky. And thus Tiger fans were not optimistic about their chances against Carolina.

Some 13,000 gridiron enthusiasts turned out on October 22 to witness this contest, a new record for Big Thursday.

They had hardly gotten settled in their seats when they were again brought to their feet when Carolina's big fullback, Alex "Jazz" Jascewicz, booted a 20-yard field goal to put the Gamecocks up 3-0.

Then in the second quarter fans saw one of the most unusual plays they'd ever seen in this or any other game. Bill Rogers punted for Carolina, a long, high kick that Clemson's safety slightly misjudged. The ball came spiraling down, hit the safety's shoulder pads and bounced 10 yards across field into the arms of punter Bill Rogers who was flying down field to help make the tackle. Rogers neither broke stride nor was touched as he dashed the remaining 17 yards for a touchdown. Jascewicz's kick was good, and Carolina took the lead 10-0.

Later, just before half time, Clemson fumbled at their own 12, and Red Swink recovered for the Gamecocks. Rogers then ran to the seven, and on the next play, with the clock ticking down, Jascewicz kicked his second field goal of the day and Carolina went up 13-0.

Early in the third quarter Clemson took over on their own 12-yard line but couldn't move the ball, and on fourth down A. C. Link got off a short kick which only reached the 27-yard line. Two run netted the Gamecocks seven yards, and at that point they then called on Jascewicz for another field goal. It was good, his third of the afternoon. Carolina led 16-0.

Only minutes later Link again got off a poor punt for the Tigers from their own 32-yard line. The ball barely made it back to the line of scrimmage, and the Gamecocks took over there. Bill Roger then completed Carolina's only pass of the day, a 27-yarder to Red Swink, down to the Clemson five. Rogers then took it in for the TD, the kick was good, and Carolina led 23-0.

In the fourth quarter, following a long drive, Bill Jeffords scored for Carolina on a short burst up the middle. Again the kick was good, and the score became Carolina 30, Clemson 0.

Later, with only minutes left to play, the Tigers again got off a poor punt and the Gamecocks took over at the Clemson 25. Three plays later they again went for the field goal. This time, in a show of good sportsmanship, they called on Red Swink to show what he could do. He had never before kicked a field goal in his life, but this one was good and Carolina went up 33-0. Which was the final score.

As for Carolina they would finish the season with a good 7-3 record, scoring 150 points while giving up only 27.

Clemson, would have their worst season in history, with only a 6-0 win over The Citadel to show for their efforts while losing to their other seven opponents.

Bud Saunders and his coaching staff led Clemson to their worst season in history in 1925, with only a win over The Citadel to show for their efforts.

The Tigers of 1925 would suffer through their worst season in history, winning only one game while losing seven.

The Tiger basketball team of 1925.

G. I. Finklea, captain of the 1925 Clemson Tigers.

Clemson's Orangeburg County Club of 1925.

USC's Alex "Jazz" Jascewicz set a new Big Thursday record when he booted three field goals against the Tigers in 1925.

Captains G. I. Finklea and J. C. Long meet with officials just prior to kickoff in 1925.

Branch Bocock, Carolina's coach would go 7-3 in 1925, his three losses by a total of only 15 points. He would beat Clemson in both 1925 and 1926.

J. C. Long, captain of the '25 Gamecocks and a three-year starter at tackle.

Bill Rogers and Marion "Red" Swink would both be named All-State in 1925. It was Rogers who caught his own punt and ran it in for a TD against the Tigers in '25. He is a member of the USC Athletic Hall of Fame.

USC's Bob Wimberly (#7), behind terrific blocking, sweeps end for a first down in this Big Thursday match won by Carolina 33-0.
(Carolina's total of four field goals in this game remains an all-time record for this series.)

1926

BILL BOYD KICKS A RECORD FIELD GOAL

Big Thursday 1926 arrived on October 21, a beautiful but windy day in Columbia, with some 12,400 fans on hand to see if Carolina could extend their win streak to three games, something they'd never done before.

Clemson arrived on the field at 11:30 to begin their warmups. Ten minutes later the Gamecock team arrived, their appearance heralded by the blaring sirens on the big Columbia fire truck which cleared the way through the swelling crowd. Bands from both colleges entertained the fans with the latest in so-called jazz music.

In fact, according to *The State* newspaper, the Clemson band was in the process of delighting their faithful when, unaware that the USC band had just struck up their Alma Mater, they began playing their rousing rendition of *Charleston*, the song that was sweeping the nation, featuring a "negro dancer" who leaped upon the Clemson bandstand and began doing a frenzied dance. Carolina fans, standing at rigid attention across the way, did not find this exhibition amusing and a riot almost erupted. (Clemson later offered a sincere apology to USC.)

Following the kickoff, but still early in the first quarter, Carolina faced a fourth down at the Clemson thirty. At that point the Gamecocks called on Bill Boyd for a 47-yard field goal, an unheard of distance in those days. But amazingly enough, the ball sailed through the air, hit the cross bar, then bounced over, a record kick that would stand for many years.

The half ended with Carolina up, 3-0. Then, towards the end of the third quarter, Clemson punted from their own ten. The ball traveled only six yards, going out of bounds at the Clemson 16. Bill Rogers and Power Rogers then combined for a first down at the Tiger five, and Bob Wimberly took it in for the TD on the next play. Marion Swink's kick was good, and now the Gamecocks were up 10-0.

The Tigers seemed to fold at this point, and only minutes later Bill Rogers again carried the ball in for a score, the kick was good, and USC went up 17-0. Just before game's end Red Swink scored again for Carolina and the Gamecocks took their third consecutive game from Clemson, this time by a score of 24-0.

B.C.Harvey, captain of the 1926 Clemson Tigers.

The Clemson Tigers of 1926 would suffer through another losing season. They went through three head coaches that year, Cul Richards, Bud Saunders, and Bob Williams.

The Carolina Gamecocks of 1926 would go 6-4 on the season, including a 24-0 win over Clemson. The Tigers had not scored on USC now for the past three years.

Bob Wimberly, an ace halfback for the Gamecocks.

Captain W. R. Boyd, an All-State selection at center for USC. His 47-yard field goal on Big Thursday 1927 set an all-time USC record.

Bill Rogers and Bill Price were also All-State players for USC in 1926. (Bill Rogers passed for 282 yards in USC's 19-0 win over VPI in '26, a performance the press described as a "world's record passing performance." This record would stand until broken by Tommy Suggs in 1968.)

Incredulous players from both teams mill around following Rogers' kick, but the referees' decision was final: the kick was good.

This incredible shot captures Bill Rogers' 47-yard field goal just as it hit the cross bar, then bounced over to give USC a 3-0 lead.

1927

BUD ESKEW LEADS TIGERS TO WIN

It was 1927 and after suffering through their worst three-year record in history, the Clemson Tigers hired the fabled Josh "Big Man" Cody to guide their football fortunes. During his tenure at Clemson, 1927-30, his Tigers would defeat Carolina for four consecutive seasons, not losing to them again until 1931.

At Carolina, meanwhile, they had hired a former star Gamecock lineman, Harry Lightsey, to guide their fortunes. Lightsey, by now a Columbia attorney, accepted the USC coaching position on a temporary basis. Still, he enjoys the distinction of being the first USC coach in history ever to defeat the University of Virginia. In fact, in 1927 he defeated both Virginia and UNC. (USC would not duplicate this feat again until 1953.)

Big Thursday was described as a perfect day for football as 13,000 fans packed the grandstands at the Fair Grounds.

After five minutes of play it became obvious to everyone that the teams were very evenly matched, and that fans were in for a grim defensive struggle. And such was the case.

The first quarter consisted of a series of punts from both teams. And the same for the second quarter. In the third quarter Red Swink did try a field goal from the Clemson 31, but the kick was short and wide.

But then in the fourth quarter, the Tigers mounted a drive. Quarterback Bud Eskew ran for 14 yards, then threw to F. M. Zeigler for another 14 for a first down at the USC 36-yard line. Then came a triple-pass play, Eskew to Bob McCarley to Zag Mouledous, good for a first down at the 22. Three plays later Eskew again threw to McCarley who took the ball into the end zone for Clemson's first score against Carolina since 1923. W. P. Timmerman's kick was good, and the Tigers went up 7-0.

And the rout was on. On the next series, Rogers punted for Carolina, only to see his kick taken by Eskew who then snaked his way through the entire Carolina team 36 yards for another Clemson TD. McCarley's kick was good, and Clemson led 14-0.

Then, with time running down, Clemson started a drive from their own 37-yard line. But then Eskew threw a 50-yard bomb to H. B. "Hop" Cuttino who was finally cut down at the USC 17. Following runs by Eskew and McCarley, Eskew finally went in for the TD and the Tigers walked away with a 20-0 win.

Also today for the first time ever, the Clemson cadets rushed onto the field following the final whistle and tore down the goal posts. Their celebration later carried over to Main Street, where the cadets ran up and down the aisles of theaters, danced and laughed through crowded restaurants, and tore down decorations around the business district. Their celebration continued until the wee hours, and was taken good naturely by all concerned.

The Gamecocks of 1927. For the first time in history they defeated both UNC and Virginia during the same season, a feat they would not repeat until 1953.

Bob McCarley, Clemson's ace fullback for three years, 1927-29. He led the Tigers in scoring in '27 with 31 points.

Josh "Big Man" Cody, coach of the Clemson Tigers, 1927-30, would go 4-0 against Carolina.

Bud Eskew, captain of the '27 Clemson Tigers and hero of Big Thursday 1927.

Emmett Wingfield, captain of the 1927 Gamecocks and a quarterback who ran the team to perfection.

Captains Emmett Wingfield and Bud Eskew meet at midfield for the toss of the coin on Big Thursday 1927.

Harry Lightsey, a Columbia attorney and coach of the Gamecocks for only one year. (He was the brother of Clemson's Yen Lightsey.)

The latest in football fads arrived at Carolina in 1927. It was "the cheerio section," where students wore colored sweaters to spell out various messages.

The Tigers and Gamecocks embroiled in gridiron action on Big Thursday 1927, a game won by Clemson 20-0. Note USC's cheerio section in the background.

Carolina's cheerleaders of 1927 would take a backseat to no one when it came to school spirit.

The Jungleers of Clemson College, the latest thing in jazz band music of the 1920s.

1928

POOR KICKING GAME SINKS USC

Gone now from the Carolina scene was Harry Lightsey and in his place came the celebrated Billy Laval, a man of vision and creativity, who had built Furman University into a Southern football power. In fact, Furman had defeated Carolina for five successive seasons prior to 1928, and thus Laval stood high on the list when USC decided to hire a coach who knew how to win.

Indeed, USC was 5-0 going into Big Thursday in '28, including one of their greatest wins ever, a 6-0 triumph over Amos Alonzo Stagg's University of Chicago, one of the strongest teams in the nation.

As for Clemson, Josh Cody was back for his second season along with such tested veterans as Dick Magill, Ike Davis, O. K. Pressley, Ed Hall, Johnnie Justus, Bob McCarley, Dopey Major, Bob Jones and O. D. Padgett. A true all-star lineup. The Tigers too were 5-0 going into this contest, with an impressive 6-0 win over powerful Auburn to their credit. Indeed, the Tigers had not even been scored on when they arrived in Columbia to take on the Gamecocks.

(1928 remains the only season in history when both Carolina and Clemson were undefeated going into their annual battle.)

And the 14,000 fans who crowded into the stadium that afternoon were expecting a real shootout. As it turned out, unfortunately for Gamecock fans, Clemson did most of the shooting while the Gamecocks spent most of their time dodging bullets.

On the opening kickoff three of Clemson's star players, Bob Jones, O. D. Padgett, and Fatty Hall, were injured and had to be carried from the field, leading O. K. Pressley to yell to Coach Cody: "My God, they have killed us all on the kickoff!"

The first quarter consisted of missed chances by both squads and ended in a 0-0 tie.

Early in the second, after Padgett intercepted a J. F. Cooper pass, the Tigers took over on USC's 41-yard line. Then, behind the running of John Justus, Lewis Pitts, and Bob McCarley, the Tigers moved to the USC nine. From there Justus ran it in. The kick failed and the Tigers were up 6-0. And thus ended the half.

Midway the third quarter Clemson recovered a fumble at the USC 47. Again, behind the running of Justus and McCarley, the Tigers quickly moved to the Carolina five. McCarley ran it

in on the next play. H. W. Asbil kicked the point, making the score 13-0.

As the fourth quarter got under way, a close game suddenly became a rout. USC punted out of bounds at their own 33, and from there Ray McMillan carried the ball on five successive plays until he finally scored. The kick was good, and the score became 20-0.

Carolina then fumbled the ensuing kickoff, and Clemson recovered at the 24. Kitt Hane gained nine yards on first down, then Goat McMillan scored from 15 yards out to make the score 26-0.

Five minutes later Carolina again got off a poor punt, one that went out of bounds at their own 32. On first down Kitt Hane wove his way through the exhausted Gamecocks all the way for Clemson's last TD of the afternoon and a final score of 32-0.

So now Clemson was 6-0 on the season and still had not been scored on. As for Coach Laval, this was his first loss to any team in the state since 1924.

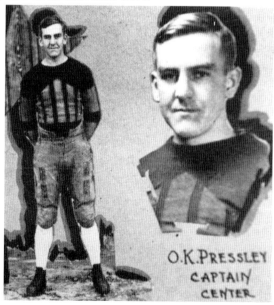

O. K. Pressley, captain and center for the 1928 Tigers. O. K. Pressley was Clemson's first All-American football player. He is also a member of the Clemson Athletic Hall of Fame.

Covington "Goat" McMillan, a star halfback for Clemson , 1928-29, and a coaching legend with the Tigers, 1937-64.

Bill Cooper, captain of the 1928 Carolina Gamecocks.

Billy Laval, former head coach at Furman, became head coach at Carolina in 1928. Only Rex Enright and Paul Dietzel had longer coaching tenures at Carolina than Billy Laval.

The Carolina Gamecocks of 1928. Noted for his creative genius, Coach Laval installed what he called "the Crazy Quilt" formation. The Gamecocks went 5-0 before opponents finally learned how to defend against it. Still, their 6-2-2 record that year was one of their best in history.

Captains Bill Cooper and O. K. Pressley meet for the coin toss just prior to the Big Thursday kickoff in 1928.

On a grim day in late November the Tigers beat a good Furman team 27-12, their eighth win of the season.

In 1928 Carolina upset Amos Alonzo Stagg's University of Chicago team 6-0, one of USC's greatest wins ever. Here Carolina's peerless Ed Zobel goes in for the score.

1929

GOAT MCMILLAN LEADS TIGER VICTORY

After going 8-2 under Coach Josh Cody in 1928, the Tigers were again on a roll with a 5-0 record as they prepared to meet the Gamecocks in 1929.

As for the Gamecocks, their 6-2-2 record in 1928 under Coach Billy Laval was better than anyone had dared dream they'd do, and hopes were running high that 1929 would bring even better things. In fact, they were 3-1 going into Big Thursday, with only a close 6-0 loss to mighty Virginia to mar their record.

The experts considered Clemson a slight favorite as the teams lined up for the kickoff.

Still, the Gamecocks were pulling out all the stops this afternoon, and on the first play from scrimmage Bru Boineau threw a long pass intended for Bob Gressette, but it fell incomplete. The Gamecocks came back with the same play on second down, but this time the ball was intercepted by O. D. Padgett at the Tiger 47.

Following two running plays, Goat McMillan threw to Bob McCarley down to the USC 14. Then came John Justus around end and into the end zone for Clemson's first score of the afternoon. McCarley's kick was good, and Clemson led 7-0.

And so ended the first quarter. The second quarter became a tragedy of missed opportunities for both squads. But late in the second, with time running out, a fourth down 9-yard pass from Goat McMillan to Bob Jones resulted in another Clemson score. The kick was good. The Tigers went up 14-0.

But then, with only moments left in the half, the Tigers went to the well once too often. McMillan tried another long pass, but it was picked off by Crip Rhame who ran it back 80 yards for a Carolina TD. Bru Boineau kicked the point, and the score was narrowed to 14-7.

The third quarter was scoreless, but only two minutes into the fourth, McMillan tried another long pass. This time it was picked off by Bru Boineau who raced 75 yards for another Carolina touchdown. Boineau then kicked the point, and suddenly the score was tied 14-14.

But the Tigers were undaunted. After a series of punts, Carolina had the ball deep in their own territory. Boineau attempted to run around end, but fumbled the ball. Clemson covered it at the 18. On the next play McMillan shot through the Carolina line and made it all the way into the end zone. McCarley's kick was good, and the game ended 21-14, another Clemson win.

Josh Cody's 1929 Clemson team shut out four opponents and became the second Tiger eleven to win eight games in a season.

Captain Julian Beall was the first Gamecock ever named All-Southern. He is a member of the USC All-Time Football Team.

Goat McMillan was named All-Southern in '29, and is a member of the CU Athletic Hall of Fame. He is also remembered as one of Frank Howard's finest assistant coaches.

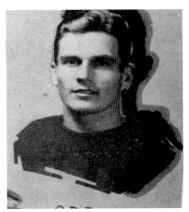

O. D. Padgett, captain of the 1929 Clemson Tigers and a devastating fullback. In 1928 Padgett won the first Jacobs Blocking Trophy ever presented.

The 1929 Carolina Gamecocks would go 6-5 on the season. Note their new starburst jerseys, another innovation of Billy Laval who thought these jerseys would make it easier to hide the ball.

A devoted fan struts her little rooster on Big Thursday 1929.

Ed Zobel (hero of the Chicago game in '28) and Bru Boineau were both named to the All-State Team in 1929 (along with Monk Shand). Boineau is a member of the USC Athletic Hall of Fame and the All-Time USC Football Team.

In 1929 Hugh Stoddard became the first Gamecock to be awarded the Jacobs Blocking Trophy.

Action shots from Big Thursday 1929. In this '29 game the Gamecocks intercepted four passes which they returned for 191 yards. This remains an all-time USC record.

The action was fast and furious on Big Thursday 1929. Here Goat McMillan carries for the Tigers.

Clemson "Rats" of 1929 lived a hard life. Still, as seen in the above photos, Clemson's upperclassmen were always available to teach them the joys of recreational activities.

1930

MAXCY WELCH SPARKS A TIGER WIN

In 1930 the Gamecocks played probably their toughest schedule in history, one which included such Southern powers as Duke, Georgia Tech, LSU, Clemson, and Auburn. It was a season wracked with inconsistencies, as the Gamecocks fought like gamecocks one week, like chickens the next, beating both Duke and LSU, then losing to Furman. Yet they still finished the season with a winning 6-4 record.

As for Josh Cody and his Clemson Tigers, they beat everybody on their schedule that they were supposed to beat while losing only to Tennessee and Florida. Indeed, Clemson would again win eight games in 1930, giving them a great 24-8 record over the past three years. (Only the Clemson teams of 1948-50 would enjoy a better three-year performance with a 24-4-3 record.)

The Great Depression was in full swing as the two teams squared off on October 23, 1930, but still a record crowd of 15,000 fans showed up for the game. Clemson, who had spent the past two days practicing at Camp Jackson, were the clear favorites to take another one, their fourth in a row.

But on this day Carolina drew first blood. With the ball on their own 34, they tried two smashes at Clemson's big defensive line, and got nothing. Then the ball was pitched out to Bru Boineau who turned Clemson's end and raced 66 yards for a USC touchdown. Boineau kicked the point, and USC took a surprising 7-0 lead.

In the second quarter the teams exchanged several punts, then Clemson punted out of bounds at the USC one-yard line. Boineau was forced to kick from his own end zone and Clemson returned it to the Carolina 34.

Maxcy Welch came out throwing for the Tigers. On second down he tossed to Bob Jones who ran it in for the TD. Lionel Harvin's kick tied the score.

Just before half time Welch passed to Lionel Harvin who broke into the clear and appeared headed for a Tiger score. But Harvin tripped at the Carolina three. Two plays later he redeemed himself by taking it in for the score. He then kicked the point, and Clemson was up 14-7 as the half ended.

In the third period, led by the brilliant running of John Justus and Maxcy Welch, the Tigers had a first down at the Carolina four. Welch took it in on the next play and Clemson went up 20-7. And thus ended the game.

Receiver Bob Jones, a longtime coach at Clemson and a member of the Clemson Athletic Hall of Fame.

In 1930 Grady Salley was awarded the Jacobs Blocking Trophy.

Maxcy Welch, hero of Big Thursday 1930, scored five TDs in Clemson's 75-0 win over Newberry, an all-time Tiger record. (His total of 33 points scored on the day remains another all-time CU record.)

JOHNIE JUSTUS

John Justus, captain of the 1930 Clemson Tigers.

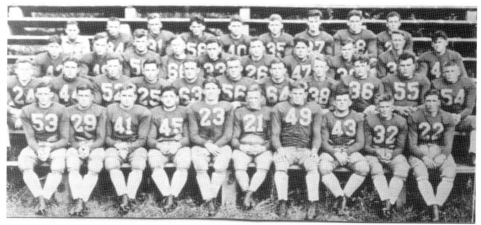

The Clemson Tigers of 1930 would enjoy a fine 8-2 season, including a 20-7 win over Carolina. (This was their third consecutive eight-win season.)

Clemson seems to have this NC State runner pretty well surrounded as the Tigers went on to win 27-0.

Clemson cadets suffered through two weeks of military training in Alabama during the summer of 1930.

"Swifty" is right, "The army ain't no place for a lady". Ferg looks "hot".

Pat Leardo, a native of New Jersey and an outstanding center for the Gamecocks.

Harry Freeman, an All-State guard for USC.

Captain Bob Gressette, an All-State end for USC.

Grady Salley coming off tackle against the Gamecocks.

USC's Bru Boineau throws a short one to Bob Gressette on Big Thursday.

Something new for the Gamecocks in 1930: coed cheerleaders!

1931

THE APPEARANCE OF THE GAFFNEY GHOST

1930 would mark the end of the Southern Conference as it had always been known. For this was the year that the ten teams of the lower Southern states broke away to form the Southeastern Conference.

Gone now from the Clemson scene was Josh Cody and in his place came Jess Neely, a man of vision who would guide Clemson to their first bowl game (1939) and to a level of national fame they had never experienced before. One of his first moves upon arriving at Clemson was to hire a young man named Frank Howard to serve as his line coach. Clemson fans would hear more from Mr. Howard in the years to come.

But for the moment things were not going well for Neely and his Tigers. They opened the season with an 0-0 tie with PC, then were drubbed 44-0 by Tennessee, then managed a close 6-0 win over NC State, then lost 6-0 to The Citadel. Hardly an encouraging beginning. The '31 Tigers lost 74-7 to Alabama, their worst loss in history.

The big news at Carolina was the appearance of a young man from Gaffney, S. C. named Barney Earl Clary, who was already setting records for the Gamecocks and standing opponents on their ear.

They had opened the season with a startling 7-0 upset win over Wallace Wade's Duke Blue Devils, a game in which Earl Clary was dubbed The Gaffney Ghost. Then came losses to both Georgia Tech and LSU, but they were close losses and thus Gamecock fans were optimistic that Carolina would snap their four-game losing streak as they awaited the kickoff on Big Thursday.

It was October 22, 1931, and the weather could not have been more perfect for a football game. As had so often been the case in the past, the first half of today's game became a punting duel between the two teams, with neither able to move against the other, and they went to their locker rooms tied 0-0 at half time.

At half time, by the way, Billy Laval had his team shed their black jerseys and don bright, shiny red ones. What affect this had on the team is unknown, but it is a fact that the Gamecocks came out and totally dominated play for the next two quarters, thanks to the running of Clary, Dick Shinn, and Miles Blount.

Early in the third, with the ball at their own 40-yard line, Clary turned end for 34 yards and a first down at the Clemson 26. Then came Shinn for another ten. Then it was Fred Hambright for another ten. Then Earl Clary took it in for a TD.

Chuck Hajec's kick was good, and USC tok a 7-0 lead. And thus ended the third quarter.

Early in the fourth period the Tigers punted out of bounds at their own 38. Then, following a 15-yard penalty against Clemson, Dick Shinn faked a pass and ran 23 yards for USC's next TD. The kick was good, and the score went to 14-0.

Five minutes later Carolina recovered a fumble at the Clemson 28. On first down Shinn ran it down to the two. Then Miles Blount hit that big Tiger line and struggled on in for the final score of the day. Hajek's kick was again good, and USC walked away with a 21-0 win. (Earl Clary, by the way, had 147 yards rushing on the day.)

Earl Clary, called The Gaffney Ghost, would become one of the most celebrated runners in the history of Carolina football. He would be chosen for the All South Atlantic Team in 1931. He would also spark Carolina to shutout wins over Clemson for three years, 1931-33.

Clemson coaching legend Frank James Howard, an Alabama All American, became Jess Neely's assistant in 1931.

Jess Neely, coach of the Clemson Tigers 1931-39, would lead them to their first bowl game and to national prominance.

Buck Priester, one of Clemson's greatest running backs ever.

A. D. Fordham, captain of the Clemson Tigers and an All-South Atlantic center in 1931.

Clemson and those pesky Furman Hurricanes, the bane of both Carolina and Clemson during the Early Era, played to a 0-0 tie in 1931.

Clemson's corps of cadets was in good hands in 1931.

The Carolina Gamecocks of 1931 would go 5-4-1 on the season under Coach Billy Laval.

To open the '31 season the Gamecocks upset Wallace Wade's Duke Blue Devils 7-0. Here Earl Clary goes in for the TD that gave USC a great win. Frustrated Duke players later said that trying to tackle Clary was like trying to tackle a ghost, and thus came his nickname.

USC quarterback Dick Shinn (holding ball) hands off to Miles Blount to score from three yards out to give Carolina their final TD and a 21-0 win over Clemson.

Miles Blount, captain of the 1931 Gamecocks, who scored Carolina's final TD on Big Thursday 1931.

USC quarterback Dick Shinn, hero of Big Thursday 1931.

Bryant Adair was named to the All-South Atlantic team at Guard for the Gamecocks in 1931.

1932

WILLARD, CLARY, LEAD USC WIN

It was October 20, 1932, and a hot day at the State Fair as fans began to pack into the grandstand area for today's matchup between the 2-2 Clemson Tigers and the 3-1 Carolina Gamecocks. Despite their similar won-loss records, one of Carolina's wins had been over mighty Sewanee and the other a tremendous upset over national power Villanova in a game played in Philadelphia. Thus Carolina was considered a slight favorite to take today's game.

As had happened so often in the past, the first half consisted of a punting match between Carolina's Grayson Wolf and Clemson's Bob Miller, with neither team able to take advantage of the opportunities that came their way.

Then came the second half, and the Gamecocks began to assert themselves. Following an exchange of punts, the Tigers kicked to the Carolina 35. Two running plays gained six yards, and again Wolfe punted, a high, floating spiral. Henry Willard raced down field in hopes of downing the ball inside the Clemson ten. Coming up to block him was Gene Willimon. The

two players tangled, and in the ensuing melee Willimon's foot hit the ball, sending it bounding behind the goal line. Willard then covered the ball, and after a prolonged discussion by the referees, it was declared a Carolina touchdown. Grayson Wolf kicked the point, and USC led 7-0.

Clemson was then unable to move the ball, and punted out on the Carolina 43. Earl Clary then thrilled USC fans with runs of 19 and ten yards, then fired an 18-yard pass to end Tom Craig, and USC had a first down at the Clemson nine-yard line. Three cracks at Clemson's line gained little, but on fourth down Clary fired a six-yard pass to Allie McDougal for a TD. The kick was good, and USC led 14-0. Which is how the game finally ended, and for the second year in a row Carolina had shut out the Clemson Tigers.

Following Big Thursday neither team would enjoy much success. Clemson would go 1-2-1 on the rest of the season, while Carolina suffered through a 1-3-2 post-Big Thursday season. (In Carolina's last game of the season they tied Auburn 20-20, depriving the Plainsmen of a trip to the Rose Bowl.)

Bob Miller, captain of the 1932 Clemson Tigers and their star punter and fullback.

Gene Willimon, ace tailback for the Tigers in '32 and '33. It was his bobble that gave USC their first TD of the day.
Willimon would become Director of IPTAY, and is a member of the Clemson Athletic Hall of Fame.

Meanwhile, back at the dorm. . .

In 1932, for the first time ever, the Gamecocks decided to go with co-captains. Here are those first two, Bill Gilmore and Harry Freeman.

Henry Willard who recovered a fumble for a USC TD on Big Thursday 1932.

Grayson Wolfe, the starting forward on Carolina's record-setting basketball teams of '32 and '33 (they went 35-3 over that two-year period), was also a star fullback and punter for USC.

Carolina's All-State selections for 1932: Earl Clary and Dave Meers.

Anxious players await the ref's call as Willard and Willimon are unscrambled in the end zone. Willard came up with the ball and a TD for USC.

1933

HAMBRIGHT PASSES USC TO VICTORY

It was October 19, 1933, and despite the Great Depression that had reduced much of the state to poverty, over 14,000 wildly exuberant fans showed up at the Fair Grounds for this year's shootout betwseen Carolina and Clemson on Big Thursday. Both men and women back in those days dressed in their Sunday finest for this event, leading some to joke that Big Thursday was South Carolina's biggest fashion show of the year.

This would mark Jess Neely's third year at Clemson, but to date his Tigers were not doing particularly well. Indeed, they had only a 9-0 win over NC State to show for their efforts, while losing to Georgia Tech 39-2 and tying both PC and George Washington.

As for the Gamecocks, they had fared little better to this point, with a single win over Wofford and losses to both Temple and Villanova. Even worse, their great running back, Earl Clary, had been injured in practice during the week and was not expected to play today against Clemson. Interestingly enough, Earl's little cousin from Gaffney, Wilton Clary, would replace him at halfback for this game, and his sterling performance would almost make fans forget about his more illustrious cousin.

Once the game got under way it became apparent to most that Carolina had the superior eleven on this occasion. And midway the first quarter the Gamecocks got the break they'd been waiting for. Harold Mauney took the snap and began what appeared to be an end sweep with Fred Hambright and Wilton Clary leading the way. But then, at the last moment, without breaking stride, Mauney tossed a short pass to a wide open Hambright who brought fans to their feet as he wove his way through the entire Tiger team 20 yards for a touchdown. Hambright then kicked the point, and Carolina took a 7-0 lead.

Carolina threatened Clemson's goal on several more occasions as the game progressed, but could not push across for another score. Clemson, on the other hand, could mount almost no threat to the Gamecocks offensively. On one occasion they did penetrate as far as the Carolina 32-yard line, but they could get no further. Nor did Clemson complete a single forward pass in this game. So, for the third consecutive year, the Gamecocks had shutout the Tigers.

Carolina would finish the season with a good 6-3-1 record, their last win a 16-14 decision over Auburn, one of their greatest victories in history, and were crowned co-champions of the Southern Conference.

Clemson would finish with a disappointing 3-6-2 record, including losses to Wofford, Mercer and Furman.

Earl Clary scores his second TD of the day as USC upset a great Auburn team 16-14, one of USC's greatest wins in history.

Earl Clary was named All-Southern and Honorable Mention All-American in 1933. He is a member of the USC Athletic Hall of Fame and the All-Time USC Football Team.

Jess Neely's 1933 Clemson Tigers would suffer through another 3-6-2 losing season, scoring a total of only 50 points against 11 opponents. But the Tigers would not have another losing season until 1941.

It was the final game of the '33 season, and Clemson lost 6-0 to Furman, a fitting finale to a dismal season.

But their loss to Furman was not nearly as demoralizing as their 14-13 loss to good old Wofford earlier in the season.

John Heinemann, captain of the '33 Clemson Tigers and a three-year starter at guard.

Bll Dillard, a devastating runner for the Tigers and a star in both basketball and track. He is a member of the Clemson Athletic Hall of Fame.

Carolina's All-State picks for 1933 : Arthur Moorhead, Freeman Huskey, Tom Craig.

Fred Hambright, who received the Jacobs Blocking Trophy in 1933, would later sign a contract with the New York Yankees of the American Football Conference, the first Gamecock ever to play pro football. He is a member of the USC Athletic Hall of Fame and the All-Time USC Football Team.

Fred Hambright snags a Harold Mauney pass as the Gamecocks bombed NC State 14-0 at Melton Field. (Note the USC dorms in the background. Melton Field previously known as Davis Field, was located at the corner of Sumter and Green Streets.)

An amazing shot from '33 captures Earl Clary as he vaults the line for a touchdown in Carolina's 30-7 loss to LSU.

1934

HENRY WOODWARD SPARKS CLEMSON WIN

It was 1934 and the big news in Columbia was the completion of Municipal Stadium at the State Fair Grounds. It was built with WPA money and WPA labor. The name would later be changed to Carolina Stadium, but for the moment it seated 18,000 fans and solved the problem of where to put everybody on Big Thursday.

The Gamecocks dedicated Municipal Stadium on October 6 by walloping a good VMI team 22-6. But a torrential rain had been falling since early morning, and thus only 10,000 fans showed up for this momentous occasion.

In fact, Carolina had enjoyed three wins against only one defeat going into Big Thursday, and even though their three wins came over fairly weak opponents, Gamecock fans were still optimistic as they awaited the arrival of the Clemson Tigers.

As for Jess Neely's Tigers, they were 1-3 coming into Big Thursday. Their losses were to such powers as Georgia Tech, Duke and Kentucky, while their only win was at the expense of PC by a score of 6-0.

Thus the experts went out on a limb and picked USC as a slight favorite to take their fourth consecutive win over the Tigers. After all, they reasoned, 3-1 is better than 1-3 regardless of who's on the schedule.

They made a terrible guess.

Some 17,000 fans turned out on a beautiful day for football, most expressing awe at Carolina's giant new stadium.

Clemson's Bill Dillard immediately served notice that Clemson would not be denied for the fourth straight year as he returned the opening kickoff 27 yards, to the Tiger 43 yard line. Then came quarterback Randy Hinson around end. He broke into the USC secondary, then raced 43 yards, down to the 17 before being brought down by Paul Gaffney. Clemson then gave up the ball on downs, but on the first play for Carolina Harold Mauney tried a short pass. It was intercepted by Henry Shore and returned to the Carolina four.

But again the Gamecocks held, making a sensational goal line stand. Then following a Carolina punt, Clemson moved to the USC 12. Four plays later Stanley Fellers kicked a field goal and the Tigers went up, finally, 3-0.

Several punts later, Wilton Clary fumbled while trying an end sweep, and Henry Shore recovered for Clemson at the Tiger 43. Again Shore threw to Bill Dillard, good for 25 yards. Then came a 15-yard penalty against Carolina, and the Tigers had a first down at the 14. Henry Woodward burst through on the next play, down to the USC one-yard line, and Tiger fans could already taste victory. Still, thanks to a rugged Carolina defense, it took Clemson four plays to move it in for a TD. But they did, Henry McCown carrying the ball. Fellers' kick was good, and the score became 10-0.

The third quarter was little more than a punting contest between Harold Mauney and Clemson's Alex Stevens.

In the fourth period Henry Woodward scored again for the Tigers from eight yards out. The kick failed, and the score became 16-0. Then, five minutes later, after Clemson stalled at the Carolina 15, Fellers again booted a field goal and the score became 19-0, which is how the game ended. By season's end, both Carolina and Clemson would show 5-4 records for their efforts.

In 1934 Carolina defeated Erskine 25-0 in the last game played at Melton Field. (It is interesting to note that some players still refused to wear helmets as late as 1934.)

Harold Mauney was an outstanding quarterback for the Gamecocks for three seasons and is a member of the USC Athletic Hall of Fame.

Carolina's Municipal Stadium was built in 1934 with WPA money and WPA labor, and would hold 17,000 fans.

The Carolina Gamecocks of 1934 would have another 5-4 winning season, though they'd lose to Clemson on Big Thursday.

Captain Tom Craig, an All-State tackle for the Gamecocks.

Henry Woodward, captain and quarterback of the '34 Tigers.

First Row: STEVENS, CROXTON, LEE, YARBROUGH, INABINET, WOODWARD, FELLERS, TROUTMAN, CUMMINGS, McCOWN, HINSON, BROWN, HENLEY, DILLARD, *Manager*.
Second Row: LEWIS, KISSAM, BLACK, DILLARD, WATSON, McCONNELL, S. W., BERRY, SHUFORD, BUSCHER, HORTON, SHORE, FOLGER, CATHCART.
Third Row: LAWTON, LANFORD, ROBINSON, MANESS, McCONNELL, T. S., ROBINSON, E. D., JETER, SNIDER, BRYANT, SEGARS, PRICE, OTEY, FORD.

The Clemson Tigers of 1934 would have a 5-4 record, their first winning season since 1930.

Alabama's celebrated Dixie Howell breaks away for a TD in the Tide's 40-0 win over Clemson in '35. (Note the Clemson player here wearing a face mask. Note too that for many years Clemson players were in the odd habit of wearing shin guards, such as those worn by baseball catchers.)

Streak Lawton scores on a 75-yard punt return as the Tigers drubbed Mercer 32-0. This remains one of the longest punt returns in the Clemson record book.

Stanley Fellers, who kicked two field goals for the Tigers on Big Thursday, kicks an extra point in Clemson's 7-0 win over Furman.

1935

TIGERS SWAMP GAMECOCKS, 41-0

1935 marked the departure of Billy Laval from the University, and in his place came Don McCallister who had played football under Bob Zuppke at Illinois, and who came to Carolina with an amazing 81-9 won-loss record as a high school coach in Toledo, Ohio.

Unfortunately for Gamecock fans, he would not do as well at Carolina. Indeed, over the next three years Jess Neely's Clemson teams would defeat USC by scores of 44-0, 19-0, and 34-6. As though that were not bad enough, McCallister would also lose three straight to Furman by scores of 20-7, 23-6, and 12-0. USC was 2-3 as Big Thursday arrived.

At Clemson, meanwhile, Neely's teams were beginning to kick into high gear. In '35 they would go 6-3 on the season, with losses only to Duke, Alabama, and Furman. They were 3-1 going into Big Thursday.

The Great Depression had also kicked into high gear, and colleges across America were taking extreme measures in hopes of raising money to support their athletic programs. USC's athletic department, for example, offered two five-year season tickets for $100 dollars (and got few takers).

Still, some 16,000 fans turned out on October 24 for Big Thursday 1935 to see if the heavily favored Tigers would live up their billing.

Sure enough, only two minutes into the game, Carolina's Paul Gaffney attempted to punt from the USC end zone, but the Tigers nailed Gaffney for a safety and a 2-0 lead.

Minutes later, following some superb offense by Joe Net Berry, Mac Folger, and Streak Lawton for Clemson and Wilton Clary and Bud Alexander for Carolina, Clary attempted an end run from the USC two, but was stopped behind the USC goal and the Tigers got another safety and a 4-0 lead.

Two minutes later Clemson blocked another Gaffney punt, Cliff Henley recovered at the USC 44, and three plays later Joe Net Berry scored from thirty yards out. C. J. Inabinet kicked the point, and Clemson led 11-0.

And so ended the first half, not a bad showing for the underdog Gamecocks so far. But the second half would become a whirlwind of Tiger scores.

Suffice it to say that Clemson scored 33 points over the next 30 minutes, with H. R. "General" Lee, Roddy Kissam, Net Berry, and Streak Lawton all getting in on the touchdown parade. And the final score was Clemson 41, Carolina 0. It was Carolina's worst loss to Clemson since the 51-0 shutout of 1900.

W. A. "Streak" Lawton who had a 75-yard punt return for a TD against Mercer in '34. Lawton averaged 17.5 yards per punt return during his career, still an all-time CU record.

Clarence Inabinet was named All-Southern for the Tigers in '35.

Henry Shore, captain of the Tigers in 1935, and alternate captain, Tom Brown.

The Tigers of '35 would go 6-3 on the season, with losses to only Duke, Alabama and Furman.

By 1935 Jess Neely had assembled one of the finest coaching staffs in the nation.

Tom Brown was named to the All-Southern team at tackle for the Tigers. He was a starter in four major sports, and is a member of the Clemson Athletic Hall of Fame.

Streak Lawton scored from 10 yards out on his first carry of the day as Clemson (in white jerseys) defeated The Citadel 6-0 on a crisp autumn day in Charleston in '35.

As frequently happened during the Early Era, Clemson took it on the chin from the Purple Hurricanes of Furman University, this time by a score of 8-6. This game was played at Sirrine Stadium in Greenville.

Wilburn Clary, a cousin of Earl Clary and a fine running back for the Gamecocks, finds running room againt NC State.

Don McCallister, coach of the Carolina Gamecocks, 1935-37.

Clay Alexander, captain of the '35 Gamecocks.

Paul Gaffney and Wilburn Clary were both named All-State for Carolina in '35. Clary received the team MVP Award.

Clay Alexander ignores the onrushing Tigers to get off a pass to Larry Craig.

Clemson fullback Tate Horton finds a big hole in the Gamecock line as the Tigers beat USC 41-0.

1936

JOE "NET" BERRY LEADS TIGER WIN

It was October 22, 1936 and an overflow crowd of 18,500 fans jammed into Municipal Stadium for the annual Big Thursday matchup between a disappointing Clemson team and a so-so Carolina squad.

The unpredictable Gamecocks had lost to VMI and Duke while beating VPI and a strong Florida team. Clemson, on the other hand, had handily beaten PC in their opener, then easily nailed VPI, but for the past three weeks had failed to even score in losses to Alabama, Duke and Wake Forest.

Kickoff had been moved up from noon until 2 p.m. for the first time today, and fans were edgy as they waited to see what their team would do.

But it wasn't until the second quarter rolled around that Clemson began to assert their superiority. They punted to the USC two, where the ball was downed by Sam McConnell. Ed Clary then punted to Net Berry who ran the ball back 11 yards to the USC 37. Then came a pass-lateral, Berry to Sam McConnell to Ben Pearson, a play that netted 40 yards, and the Tigers had

a first down at the USC 27. Then Net Berry fired a pass to Mac Folger who took it in for a Clemson TD. McConnell's kick missed, and thus Clemson led 6-0.

On Carolina's next possession, Ed Clary (also from Gaffney and a cousin of Earl and Wilburn) punted to Berry who raced it back to the USC 27, a run of some 38 yards. On third down Berry threw long to McConnell who went down at the USC seven. Runs by Folger and Berry took the ball to the one-foot line. Then Folger took it in for the score, Ben Pearson kicked the point, and Clemson led 13-0.

From that point on, until late in the fourth quarter, the game consisted of the teams exchanging punts.

But with only minutes remaining, Berry picked off a Ralph Dearth pass at the Clemson 38. Folger ran for nine yards, then Berry hit McConnell with an 18-yard pass to the Carolina 34. On the next play Folger faked a reverse and swept right end. He didn't pause until he'd crossed Carolina's goal for another Tiger TD and a final score of 19-0.

Captain Bob Johnson, winner of the Gamecocks' MVP Award in '36.

The 1936 Gamecocks went 5-7 on the year. It was hoped that the additional revenue gained from playing a 12-game schedule would help them stay afloat during the tough Depression years.

Ed Clary set an all-time USC record when he punted 15 times in Carolina's 7-0 win over Florida in '36. (Ed was from Gaffney and another cousin of Earl and Wilburn Clary.)

Paul Gaffney, a mainstay at guard for USC and named to the All-State team in '36.

Joe Net Berry gets ready to throw as Clemson beat VPI 20-0.

The Carolina cheerleaders of 1936 take an early Cocky for a walk.

The 1936 Clemson Tigers would go 5-5 on the season, including a big 14-13 win over Georgia Tech. For the third consecutive year they blanked the Gamecocks.

J. B. "Pinhead" Henson runs into big trouble after catching a short Lit Durham pass in Carolina's 24-7 loss to VMI.

Captain Joe Net Berry completed .583% of his passes in '35, still third best in the CU record book. He was named All-American in '36 and is a member of the Clemson Athletic Hall of Fame.

H D. Lewis collars Carolina's Ben Joe Williams for no gain on Big Thursday 1936.

T. M. "Mac" Folger, an All-Southern fullback and a member of the Clemson Athletic Hall of Fame.

Joe Net Berry hits Dusty McConnell with a pass for a Tiger first down.

1937

FIVE FUMBLES FOIL GAMECOCKS

The Tigers of '37 showed few signs of the greatness that would characterize them over the next two years. As expected, they had opened the season with a big win over PC but then had lost to all the biggies on their schedule--Tulane, Army and Georgia. Still, Jess Neely had recruited some fine football talent for Clemson, and among those young sophomores there were two in particular, Banks McFadden and Shad Bryant, who would become Tiger immortals before their playing days were over.

As for the Gamecocks, they were again playing a 12-game schedule, one that included such powers as UNC, Georgia, Alabama, Kentucky, Catholic and Miami. Of these, they tied UNC and actually beat Miami. And their losses were by respectable scores, so USC fans were somewhat hopeful as Big Thursday approached that the Gamecocks could break their three-game losing streak to the Tigers.

H. D. Lewis and Al Sanders, co-captains of the 1937 Tigers.

Some 19,000 fans turned out on a cloudy day to watch as these two old adversaries squared off.

Carolina began the game like gangbusters as they took the ball on the Clemson 41. Ed Clary ran for seven, then Rock Stroud for three, and the USC boys had a first down at the Clemson 31. At that point Ed Clary threw a long pass into the waiting hands of Bill Simpson in the Tiger end zone, and the Gamecocks went up 6-0. Ralph Dearth missed the point, but still, USC had their first score against Clemson since 1933.

During the next two series Clemson threats were stopped by Ed Clary who made pass interceptions on both occasions. Unfortunately for USC, the Gamecocks immediately fumbled the ball away following both interceptions, and now the Tigers found themselves with a first down at the USC four-yard line. Don Willis scored from there, Banks McFadden kicked the point, and Clemson went up 7-6.

Carolina again fumbled a moment later and Clemson recovered at the USC 32. Runs by Willis, Bob Bailey, and Banks McFadden gave Clemson a first down at the seven. Willis scored from there, his second TD of the game, and the Tigers led 13-6.

And so ended the first half. On the second play of the third quarter Carolina again fumbled and Clemson recovered at the USC 28. On first down, Ben Pearson broke off tackle and raced 28 yards for another Tiger score. Pearson then kicked the point, and Clemson led 20-6.

There then ensued a defensive struggle by both teams that would last until midway the fourth quarter. At that point USC's Jack Lyons got off a tremendous 66-yard punt, down to the Clemson 27.

Clemson's next series was all Shad Bryant. He carried the ball three times for a total of 73 yards on that drive, his final carry taking him into the USC end zone. His run, unfortunately, was called back and Clemson was penalized 15 yards for holding. But the Tigers came back, Dan Coleman going in for the score. Pearson's kick was good, and Clemson led 27-6.

On the next series Jack Lyons attempted to punt, but fumbled the ball and Clemson recovered at the Carolina 28. Following a hard fought drive Watson Magee scored again for Clemson and the Tigers were up 34-6. And thus ended the 1937 Big Thursday.

USC rushed for 474 yards in their 64-0 win over PC in '37, still an all-time Gamecock record.

The Clemson Tigers of 1937 would go 4-4-1 on the season, with wins over PC, Carolina, Wake Forest and Florida. As for their tie with Furman, Jess Neely now stood 1-4-2 with the Hurricanes. (Carolina stood 2-4-1 with Furman during that same time period.)

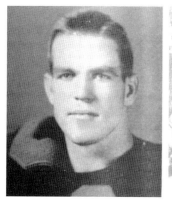

Ben Pearson, a great runner and kicker for the Tigers and hero of Big Thursday 1937.

Ben Pearson, so familiar to USC fans, kicks an extra point as Clemson beat Wake Forest 20-7 in '37.

A Clemson cadet of 1937.

Clemson routed the PC Blue Hose by a score of 46-0 in their opening game of the '37 season.

Bru Trexler carries for a first down as Clemson lost a close one to a great Army team at West Point by a score of 21-6. Banks McFadden returned a punt 75 yards for a TD in this game, one of the longest such runs in the CU record book.

The AP Sports Photo of the year in South Carolina in 1937: Jack Lyons breaks out for an apparent touchdown only to be tackled by an inebriated fan from The Citadel (right) who dashed out onto the field from the sideline. USC was granted the TD and went on to win 21-6. (The inebriated Bulldog fan was hauled off to the hoosegow.)

Ben Pearson cracks in for another Clemson score and a 20-6 Tiger lead over USC.

Ben Joe Williams being closely pursued by the Catholic University defense as USC fell 27-14. Ed Clary completed an 82-yard TD pass to Williams in this game, the 5th longest pass completion in the USC record book.

Jack Lyons, captain of the '37 Carolina Gamecocks.

Bob Snyder is up to his neck in purple alligators as he throws to the peerless Alex Urban on Big Thursday 1937.

1938

ERRORS AGAIN THWART GAMECOCKS

Gone now was Don McCallister from the Carolina scene and in his place came the personable Rex Enright, who had played ball under Knute Rockne at Notre Dame and later served as an assistant coach at the University of Georgia. His major objective, he was told upon his arrival at USC, was to beat Clemson--and hopefully everyone else.

And his '38 Gamecocks might have done just that, had they only had an extra point kicker on the team. Coming into big Thursday they had beaten Erskine 54-0, Xavier 6-0 and Davidson 25-0, but lost to both Wake Forest 20-19 and Georgia 7-6. By season's end they would have a winning 6-4-1 record against some truly tough competition.

As for Clemson, Jess Neely was finally putting it all together. The '38 Tiger team, though still a year away from the excellence they'd achieve in '39, was truly a team of all-stars. They'd go 7-1-1 on the season, a 20-7 loss to powerful Tennessee and a 7-7 tie with VMI the only blots on their record.

Some 19,000 fans crowded into the stadium to watch as the favored Tigers began to assert themselves early in the contest.

To begin the rout, Carolina's great Al Grygo fumbled at his own 27 and Gus Goins recovered for Clemson. Two plays later Clemson had a first down at the 16. Then came a reverse, Don Willis to Red Pearson, down to the three. Willis scored from there, Ben Pearson kicked the point, and Clemson was up early in the game 7-0.

On the next series Grygo passed the Gamecocks from their own 36 down to the Clemson 13. But then his next pass was picked off by Shad Bryant.

Following an exchange of punts, USC again lost a fumble, this time on their own 28. On first down Phil Chovan threw a long pass to Gus Goins in the USC end zone for the TD, and Clemson went up 13-0.

Five plays later, with the ball at their own 30, Shad Bryant turned left end and dashed 70 yards for another Tiger TD. Pearson's kick was good, and Clemson led 20-0.

Two minutes later Clemson was again on the march. From the USC 48, Dan Coleman ran for 21 yards, then had another run for 10 yards, down to the USC 17. Bob Bailey then threw a short pass to Lancaster who ran it into the end zone for a score. Aubry Rion kicked the point and Clemson led 27-0.

Clemson picked up in the third quarter where they'd left off in the second. Carolina attempted to punt from their own 40, but the kick was blocked. H. E. Miller picked the ball up and dashed 40 yards for a TD.

Pearson's kick was good, and Clemson increased their lead to 34-0. (And there were still 28 minutes left to play!)

But late in the third period the Gamecocks moved from their own 12 all the way for a touchdown. With the exception of a four-yard run from Jerry Huges, those 88 yards were gained by Al Grygo, the workhorse of the '38 Gamecocks. And the score became 34-6.

Late in the game, Jerry Hughes picked up a Tiger fumble and rambled 64 yards for another USC score. But that was it. The Gamecocks went down 34-12, their fifth consecutive loss to the Tigers.

Rex Enright, coach at Carolina 1938-42 and 1946-55. His length of service with the Gamecocks has never been approached by any other coach.

The great Shad Bryant had 779 yards in punt returns during his career, still an all-time CU record. (He returned ten punts vs. Furman in '39, another all-time CU record.)

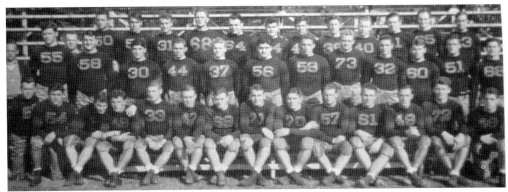

The Carolina Gamecocks of 1938 would go 6-4-1 on the season, losing three games because of missed extra points.

W. R. Howell and Larry Craig, co-captains of the '38 Gamecocks. Both were named to the All-State team. Craig later played for the Green Bay Packers, and is a member of the USC Athletic Hall of Fame and the All-Time USC Football Team.

Big cogs in USC's offensive machine of '38 were DeWitte Arrowsmith and Rock Stroud. Versus Davidson in '38 Arrowsmith returned a pass interception 90 yards for a TD, the 4th longest such run in the USC record book.

Ed Clary won USC's MVP award in both '37 and '38 and was the first Gamecock to play in a post-season game when he was chosen to play in the Blue-Gray game. (Yep, Ed was another Gaffney Clary!)

Ed Clary plunges in for a score to cut Georgia's lead to 7-6, but that's as close as USC could get.

Joe Hatkevich was named to the All-State team in '38.

104

Don Willis and Captain Charlie Woods. Both were named All-Southern in '38 and both are members of the CU Athletic Hall of Fame.

C. A. "Gus" Goins, an All-Southern end for the Tigers in '38, and Bob Bailey, an All-Southern back for the Tigers in '38.

Don Willis delivers the mail as Clemson and VMI tied 7-7 in a game played at Memorial Stadium in Charlotte.

Watson "Maggie" Magee, an ace punter for the Tigers.

USC sophomore sensation Al Grygo dashes in for a TD to cut Clemson's lead to 34-6. But it was too little too late and the Tigers won 34-12.

The great Banks McFadden, who would make Everybody's All-Everything teams in '39, rambles for yardage on Big Thursday 1938.

1939

TIGERS WIN FOR SIXTH STRAIGHT YEAR

Rex Enright had gotten his feet wet in '38 and now it was time to get down to business. Or so thought optimistic USC fans. But to the contrary, the Gamecocks of '39 would get off to one of their worst starts in years, losing to Wake Forest, Catholic University, and Villanova before eeking out a close 7-0 win over Davidson. More depressing, they knew that Clemson, who had already beaten USC for five straight years, had perhaps its strongest team in history.

As for Clemson, Jess Neely was back for his final year with the Tigers, and already his powerful eleven was drawing attention from across the nation. They had won their last five games of the '38 season and had now defeated both PC and NC State by wide margins to kickoff 1939. Indeed, the only blemish on their '39 record would be a 7-6 loss to Tulane, a team that would go on to become co-champions of the SEC.

That they would take their sixth straight from Carolina was a foregone conclusion. The question was by how much.

But hope blooms eternal in the hearts of football fans, and thus on October 19 fully 19,000 hopefuls turned out to watch this Big Thursday contest.

The Gamecocks refused to roll over and play dead, and thus it was midway the first quarter before Clemson began to assert themselves. Then, with a first down on their own 44, Shad Bryant turned left end for 36 yards down to the USC 20. On the next play Banks McFadden streaked down the sideline and into the end zone. Shad Bryant kicked the point, and Clemson led 7-0.

Midway the second period Ed Maness took a punt at his own 45 and ran it back to the USC 42. Then Maness, Trex Trexler and George Floyd took turns running it down to the Carolina 18. Then Trexler lateralled to Maness who took it in for another Clemson score. Norwood McElveen's kick was good, and Clemson led 14-0.

Clemson's next score came in the fourth period after a march of over 99 yards. Much of this came as a result of passing yardage from McFadden to Shad Bryant, Charlie Timmons and Joe Blalock. On the final play of this drive, from the USC 14, Trexler again lateralled the ball, this time to Aubry Rion, and Rion scored standing up, and Clemson led 20-0.

Five minutes later, now desperate to get on the scoreboard, the Gamecocks went to the air. But Hugh Jameson intercepted a Dutch Elston pass and returned it nine yards to the USC 36. Trexler broke through the line on the next play, but when he was hit at the 25, he lateralled the ball to George Floyd, who didn't pause until he'd crossed the goal line, giving Clemson a 27-0 win, their sixth straight over the Gamecocks.

Carolina would go on to finish the year with a grim 3-6-1 record.

As for Clemson, this was the year they'd been waiting for. They finished the season with a great 9-1 record, including their biggest win in history, a 6-3 upset of big-time Boston College in the 1940 Cotton Bowl.

The Tigers' starting eleven for 1939, the team that defeated nine opponents, including a 6-3 upset win over Boston College in the Cotton Bowl, a game which truly put Clemson College on the football map.
Linemen (L-R): Carl Black, George Fritts, Bill Hall, Walter Cox, Red Sharpe, Tom Moorer, Joe Blalock.
Backs (L-R): Shad Bryant, Charlie Timmons, Joe Payne, Banks McFadden, Aubry Rion.

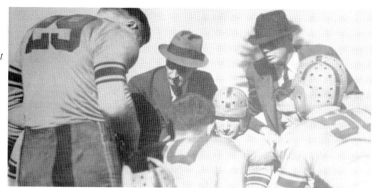

Jess Neely has a few words of advice for the team just before they kicked off to Presbyterian College in '39.

Banks McFadden around end as Clemson lost 7-6 to mighty Tulane, the Tigers' only loss of the '39 season. McFadden ran 90 yards from scrimmage for a TD vs. PC in '39, still the longest run from scrimmage in the CU record book.

Center Bob Sharpe, named to the All-Southern Team in '39 and '40.

Captain Joe Payne.

Joe Blalock, George Fritts, and Shad Bryant were named All-Southern in 1939 and to the Clemson Athletic Hall of Fame. Blalock and Fritts are members of the All-Time CU Football Team.

Banks McFadden was named All-American in both football and basketball in 1939, and was named America's Most Versatile Athlete by the Associated Press. He is also a member of the College Football Hall of Fame. Clemson has retired just three jersey's over the years. McFadden's was retired in both football and basketball. He is a member of Clemson's All-Time Football Team. (He also led the CU basketball team to the Southern Conference championship in '39, still the only conference basketball championship in Clemson history.)

Harvey Blouin, a speedy halfback for USC, won the team MVP award in '39.

Heber "Rock" Stroud and J. B. "Pinhead" Henson, co-captains of the 1939 Carolina Gamecocks.

Rock Stroud gives George Fritts a free ride as another Tiger rushes in to break up the fun.

Somewhere at the bottom of that stack of Gamecocks Shad Bryant is kicking for yardage.

Charlie Timmons, named All-Southern in '39, would score Clemson's only TD of the day as the Tigers upset Boston College 6-3 in the 1940 Cotton Bowl.

Chippy Maness dashes 18 yards for a touchdown and a 14-0 lead for Clemson on Big Thursday.

1940

FRANK HOWARD MAKES HIS DEBUT

Following his great triumphs of 1939 Jess Neely moved on to Rice Institute and in his place came the irrepressible Frank Howard, an assistant coach under Neely for the past ten years. Howard had spent his formative years in Mobile, Alabama and, despite being named to the All-American football team at guard in 1930, had actually attended his state university on an academic scholarship.

His Clemson team of 1940 was one of the best in the South, and would finish the season with six wins, two losses, a tie, and be crowned champions of the Southern Conference.

As for Coach Rex Enright and his Carolina Gamecocks of 1940, they picked up where they left off in '39 and were headed for another dismal losing season, this time going 3-6-1. So, whereas Carolina was 0-2 going into Big Thursday, Clemson was 4-0.

Regardless, 1940 would mark the first year of what would become one of the longest running football battles in the country. Indeed, Howard and Enright (with time out for World War II) would go toe to toe with one another for the next fifteen years.

A record crowd of some 21,000 jammed Municipal Stadium on October 24 to watch one of the most exciting Big Thursdays in history.

On Clemson's first drive, following a run of 15 yards by George Floyd and a 13-yard pass from Chippy Maness to Hugh Webb, the Tigers found themselves on the USC 34. Maness completed another pass for seven, then Floyd and Charlie Timmons ran the ball to the USC 12. Three plays later Floyd turned left end for four yards and a Tiger TD. Timmons' kick was good, and Clemson led 7-0.

And many fans had not even taken their seats. Some Carolina fans prepared to leave at that point.

Following several punt exchanges, USC's DeWitte Arrowsmith faked a kick from his own end zone and threw a pass which Charlie Wright intercepted and returned to the USC 16. Four plays later Joe Blalock circled around from his end position, took the hand-off from Timmons and ran it on into the end zone. Again the kick was good, and Clemson led 14-0.

Early in the third quarter Clemson's Booty Payne punted to Arrowsmith at the USC 25. He headed at full speed to the left sideline, the Tigers in hot pursuit. But then came Al Grygo

circling from the other direction. He took the lateral from Arrowsmith and dashed down the right sideline 75 yards for a TD. And the score became 14-6.

Five minutes later, Wright intercepted a Grygo pass and ran it back to the USC 30, then lateralled to Payne who made his way to the USC 15. Three plays later Maness ran it in from the three. The kick was good, and Clemson led 21-6.

And that was it for all practical purposes. Alex Urban did intercept a Booty Payne pass later in the game and he did return it 64 yards for a Carolina TD. But that was as lose as the Gamecocks could get, and the game ended a 21-13 victory for Clemson. (Clemson intercepted five USC passes in this game.)

For seven straight years now the Tigers had beaten the Gamecocks, and USC fans were beginning to shake their troubled heads.

This Clemson Rat of 1940 shows 'em the right way to do the jitterbug, the way they did it back home in Monks Corner.

George Floyd and Aubrey Rion. On September 21, versus PC, Floyd scored Clemson's first TD ever under new coach Frank Howard. Rion, sadly enough, was killed in the Battle of the Bulge during World War II.

Clemson's Charlie Timmons and Captain Red Sharpe. Both would be named All-Southern and both are members of the CU Athletic Hall of Fame and the CU All-Time Football Team.

Led by big Marion Craig, George Floyd circles end in Clemson's 13-0 loss to Tulane.

Captain Red Sharpe, Coach Frank Howard and Alternate-Captain Bill Hall.

Jim Blessing makes tough yardage in Clemson's 26-0 win over Wofford.

Chippy Maness pushes over for a TD as Clemson crushed Wake Forest 39-0.

The great Al Grygo and Captain Kirk Norton. Grygo was named All-Southern in 1940 and would go on to play pro ball with the Chicago Bears.

Jeep Urban would be named All-State and later play for the Green Bay Packers. Urban is a member of the USC All-Time Football Team.

Center Lou Sossamon was named All-American in '42.

Al Grygo follows Stan Nowak (63) and Ken Roskie (61) around end for a nice gain as USC lost to Georgia 33-2. Grygo returned a kickoff 90 yards for a TD vs. Davidson, the third longest KO return in the USC record book.

Jeep Urban intercepted this Tiger pass, then returned it 64 yards for a TD, but USC fell 20-13 on Big Thursday 1940.

The Tigers nail Buford Clary after a short gain. (Yes, Buford was also from Gaffney and a cousin of Earl, Wilburn and Ed Clary!)

This Chippy Maness pass fell incomplete.

1941

USC RUNS AND PASSES WAY TO WIN

Not since 1933, a period of some seven years, had the Gamecocks beaten Clemson and their chances seemed slim of doing so in 1941. They had a 1-1-1 record going into Big Thursday, with a 34-6 loss to Frankie Sinkwich and his Georgia Bulldogs, a 6-6 tie with Wake Forest, and an amazing 13-7 upset win over North Carolina. Hardly a record to get real excited about, despite having some truly great football talent on hand.

Clemson, on the other hand, was 4-0 going into Big Thursday, with wins over PC, VMI, NC State, and Boston College. Plus Clemson again fielded what many considered an all-star team, one that had aspirations to duplicate their feat of '39 and go to a major bowl game and win national recognition.

Another record crowd of some 23,000 crammed into Municipal Stadium on October 24 to witness this encounter.

Early in the contest Carolina proved that they were not to be taken lightly. With the ball on their own 33, Ken Roskie

Joe Blalock was named All-American in both 1940 and '41. He averaged 20.3 yards per reception in '41, still an all-time CU record. He is a member of both the CU Athletic Hall of Fame and the All-Time CU Football Team.

gained eight up the middle. Then came Carolina's newest star halfback, Stan Stasica, who started on an end sweep, then threw a short one to Harvey Blouin who made it down to the Tiger 13, a gain of 46 yards.

On the next play Roskie threw to Dutch Elston who trotted all alone into the end zone, and USC led 6-0.

Midway through the second quarter the Gamecocks struck again. With the ball on the Clemson 44 Stasica passed to Blouin down to the 30. Then Stasica ran to the 16. Roskie lost eight on the next play, but Stasica came back with a pass to Blouin down to the Tiger six. Two plays later Stasica tossed to Roskie in the end zone, and Carolina was up 12-0.

Butch Butler fumbled the ensuing kickoff and USC's John Leitner recovered at the Tiger 40. Fine runs by DeWitte Arrowsmith, Al Grygo and Stasica gave USC a first down at the Clemson 18. Then Arrowsmith burst off tackle for 15 yards and the Gamecocks were again knocking on the door.

On the next play Grygo went in for the TD and Carolina led 18-0. (Joe Patrone, Carolina's ace kicker, missed three extra points this afternoon.)

It wasn't until late in the third period that Clemson finally got on the scoreboard. With a first down at their own 40, Booty Payne spotted Harry Franklin all alone behind the USC secondary. He threw long, a perfect pass, and Franklin caught it at the 25 and ran unmolested all the way for a Tiger touchdown. Charlie Timmons' kick cut USC's lead to 18-7.

Midway the fourth quarter Clemson again began to move. With the ball at their own 41, Payne passed to Joe Blalock who lateraled to Charlie Timmons and Timmons ran it down to the Carolina 15. On the next play Payne was thrown for a 15 yard loss, but he came right back then with a pass completion to Bill Chipley down to the Carolina 10. Three plays later Payne ran the distance for another Tiger score, the kick was good, and the Gamecocks' lead was cut to 18-14. But that was as close as the Tigers could get, and Carolina walked away with an upset win, 18-14. At last, they had broken Clemson's seven-game win streak. Clemson's seven-game win streak (1934-40) is an all-time record for this series.

(Booty Payne passed for 202 yards in this contest, the first time any Clemson tailback had ever passed for over 200 yards in a single game.)

It might also be noted that some six weeks following today's game, those ugly bombs would fall at Pearl Harbor, and the world would never be the same again.

USC's Stan Stasica and Al Grygo, both named All-Southern. Grygo played for the Chicago Bears.

Carolina's Bobo Carter and Steve Nowak would both be named All-State.

Who's got the durned ball? Clemson beat Furman 34-6 in a game played in Greenville in '41.

George Fritts, three-time All-Southern, a member of the CU Athletic Hall of Fame, and a member of the CU All-Time Football Team. He was the first Tiger lineman to play in the NFL (Philadelphia Eagles).

Charlie Timmons scored 77 points for the Tigers in 1941, an all-time record for the Early Era. He is a member of CU All-Time Football Team.

Carolina co-captains, Dutch Elston and Harvey Blouin. Elston was named All-State, won the Jacobs Blocking Trophy, and was signed by the Clevland Rams. Blouin was named Honorable Mention All-American.

The Clemson Tigers of 1941. Linemen (L-R): Harold Pierce, George Fritts, Tom Wright, Charles Wright, Wade Padgett, Bull Cagle, Joe Blalock. (Backs) (L-R): Hawk Craig, Harry Franklin, Charlie Timmons, Booty Payne. (This team held Furman to -21 yards rushing in 1941, an all-time Clemson defensive record).

Clemson captain Wade Padgett meets with his Deacon counterpart in 1941.

Buford Clary goes for good yardage before being pulled down short of Clemson's goal line on Big Thursday.

Ken Roskie took a 5-yard pass from Stasica and scampered into the Clemson end zone.

Al Grygo goes in for USC's final touchdown of the day as the Gamecocks won 18-14.

1942

BUTCH BUTLER LEADS TIGER WIN

By the fall of 1942, with World War II in high gear, almost all of those young men who had played football for Carolina and Clemson in '41 were now in service. Thus both teams were forced to depend largely on untried youngsters in order to field a team at all.

There were a few major exceptions. John Leitner, Lou Sossamon and Ken Roskie were back with the Gamecocks, while Chip Clark, Wade Padgett and the illustrious Butch Butler were back to claim their positions with the Tigers.

The Gamecocks had opened the season with a surprising 0-0 tie with mighty Tennessee (who would go on to play in the Sugar Bowl). But since then they had lost to both UNC and West Virginia, and thus arrived on Big Thursday with an unenviable 1-2 record.

As for Clemson, they had opened the season with their usual win over PC (the first game ever played in their Memorial Stadium), then lost to NC State, Boston College, and tied VMI. Thus Clemson didn't have a lot to brag about, either. (Boston College held Clemson to -15 yards rushing in '42, an all-time CU record.)

As for Big Thursday, the first quarter became a punting contest between USC's Glen Rice and Clemson's Butch Butler. But in the next period Carolina took the ball at their own 43 and began a scoring drive. Bill McMillan went for 14 yards on a quick opener, then Ken Roskie carried the ball to the Tiger 15. Earl Dunham threw to John Leitner for five. Then Roskie went in for the TD. Lou Sossamon's kick failed, but Carolina was up 6-0.

Clemson then took the ball at their own 35. Butch Butler threw to Red Stacey, who lateraled to Chip Clark, who made it to the USC 15, a run of some 40 yards. Then Butler threw to Chip Clark in the end zone for the tying score. Dom Fucci blocked Johnny Sweatte's kick, and the score remained 6-6.

Midway through the third quarter Roskie fumbled at the USC 30 and Clemson recovered. On the next play Butler threw a 30-yard strike to Red Stacey for another Clemson score. This time Bill Milner blocked Sweatte's kick and Clemson went up 12-6.

Just after the fourth quarter began Butch Butler took off on one of the most thrilling runs ever seen on Big Thursday. From his own 35 Butler swept right end and behind great blocking dashed 65 yards for the game's final score. Sweatte again missed the extra point, but it really didn't matter. Clemson won 18-6

The Tigers in pre-game warmups just prior to their 24-6 loss to the Jacksonville Naval Air Station. Linemen (L-R): Red Stacy, Bull Cagle, Bill Hunter, Harold Pierce, Charles Wright, David Osteen, Chip Clark. Backs (L-R): Hawk Craig, Harry Franklin, Fred, McCown, Butch Butler.

The Carolina Gamecocks of '42 would go 1-7-1 on the year, one of their worst campaigns in history.

Lou Sossamon, co-captain of the '42 Gamecocks, was named to the AP All-American squad and would later play pro football with the New York Yankees. He is a member of the USC Athletic Hall of Fame and the USC All-Time Football Team.

Captain Charlie Wright of the '42 Tigers and John Leitner, co-captain of the '42 Gamecocks.

Walter Clark and Marion Craig would both be named All-State for the Tigers in '42.

Marion "Butch" Butler, one of the finest tailbacks ever to lead the Clemson Tigers, and John "Bull" Cagle, whose nickname well describes his play.

Butler set an all-time Clemson record in '42 when he punted 13 times in Clemson's 19-6 loss to Wake Forest. He also returned 88 punts during his career, another all-time Clemson record. (Butler was actually an army private stationed at Ft. Jackson during most of his playing career at Clemson!)

On September 19, 1942 Clemson dedicated Memorial Stadium with this 32-13 win over PC. Butch Butler (pictured here) had 192 yards rushing on the day.

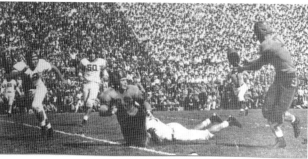

This lateral from Jack Stacey to Chip Clark gained 40 yards and led to Clemson's first TD on Big Thursday 1942.

It's Butch Butler again, this time breaking out for a TD against the Jacksonville Naval Air Station, a game lost by the Tigers 24-6.

Ken Roskie gave the Gamecocks the lead briefly, 6-0, when he plowed through the Tiger line for this TD

Katherine Edgerton (middle, top), a Carolina cheerleader in '42, is the daughter of USC coach Red Edgerton and the wife of USC All-American Lou Sossamon. As of this writing they have now been married for over 50 years.

Clemson zoot-suiters at the 1942 Christmas dance. They would trade these fancy duds for army fatigues in the near future.

117

1943

CLEMSON'S WORST GAME EVER

America's attention was elsewhere as summer turned into fall and the football wars of '43 began across the land. In both Europe and the Pacific the fighting was hot and furious, and hardly a family in the country did not have someone they cared for deeply slugging it out in those foreign lands. Football, suddenly, was not taken that seriously any more.

Gone from Carolina now was Rex Enright who had volunteered his services to the navy. In his place came Lt. Jim Moran, a naval officer, who would lead the Gamecocks to a 5-2 season, their best season, oddly enough, since 1928. Frank Howard, who was too old for military duty, was back for his fourth year with Clemson and lying awake nights wondering where he'd find eleven young men to play football on Saturday afternoons.

The problem for Howard was this: the government had initiated what was called a Naval V-12 Program which trained young men to become naval officers. Athletes from throughout the nation were enrolling in this program, and many were being sent to USC (a V-12 center), where some were expected to play football.

But Clemson had no such program. They did have an army OCS Program, but the young men enrolled in OCS were prohibited from playing football. Thus Howard was in a delimma as his team suffered through a 2-6 season, one of their worst in history. Still, somehow, Howard managed to keep the football program alive for the Tigers.

A good example of the bizarre things that were happening in '43 would be the case of Cary Cox. In '42 he had been the starting center for Clemson, but then he enrolled in the V-12 Program. Within a month he had been drafted by the navy and assigned to USC for training, which included playing football for the Gamecocks. For the Clemson game of '43 his teammates elected him game captain. Oddly enough, in '47 he would be elected captain of the Clemson Tigers, thus becoming the only man since the beginning of time to have served as captain of both the Gamecocks and the Tigers.

As for Big Thursday, in the second quarter Butch Butler punted for Clemson. (Butler by this time was an army private stationed at Ft. Jackson, but Coach Howard arranged for him to get weekend passes so that he could play football for Clemson on Saturdays!) The USC receiver fumbled the ball and Clemson recovered on the Gamecock nine-yard line. Two plays later Jim Taylor scored on an end-around, and the underdog Tigers took the lead 6-0.

Thanks largely to the super efforts of Butler, the Tigers went in at half time still nursing this 6-0 lead. Indeed, no less an authority than Tom Barton has called Butler's first half performance this day one of the greatest individual efforts in the history of Big Thursday.

But the second half belong to Carolina. Only minutes into this period R. M. Hodges, who had played for Tennessee in '42,

Military training for Clemson's cadets became deadly serious during the war years. Here they practice in downtown Anderson, S. C.

recovered a fumble at the Clemson 13. Two plays later Gene Wagnon went in and the score became tied, 6-6.

Only minutes later Phil Cantore missed the ball on a pitchout, chased it across field, then picked it up and dashed 70 yards for a touchdown. James Baughn's kick was good and USC led 13-6.

In the fourth quarter Brick Williams passed 30 yards to Cantore down to the Clemson three. Two plays later Williams took it into the end zone and USC went up 19-6.

As though that were not bad enough, only two minutes later Buck Williams swept right end 37 yards for another USC score. The kick was good and the Gamecocks stretched their lead to 26-6. And now the stampede was on.

Later in the peiod, following a Cantore run of 33 yards, USC had a first down at the Clemson three. Bill McMillan ran it in from there and Carolina led 33-6, the final score.

By game's end Clemson had one first down (which came about as the result of a penalty), eight yards rushing and zero yards passing. For Clemson this game remains their worst game in history offensively, while for Carolina it remains one of their finest game in history defensively.

Charlie Mims shows some fine defensive work as Clemson fell to Boston College 14-7 at a game played in Beantown in '42.

Coach Frank Howard, 1943.

It's Butch Butler going over for another score as Clemson beat Furman 12-7 in '42.

Cary Cox served as game captain for USC in '43, then as team captain for the Tigers in '47. (He remains the only man since the beginning of time to have served as captain of both the Gamecocks and the Tigers.)

Ralph "Pop" Jenkins remains the only Clemson player ever to serve as team captain on three occasions, 1944-46. He was named All-American in '46 and is a member of the CU Athletic Hall of Fame.

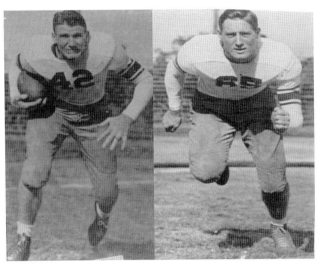

Bill McMillan and Neil Allen, co-captains of the '43 Gamecocks. McMillan would win the Jacobs Blocking Trophy in '43. Allen would again serve as captain in '47.

Dom Fusci and Ernie Bauer would both be named All-Southern in '43. Fusci is a member of the USC Athletic Hall of Fame.

Pat Thrash, an All-Southern end for USC in '43, and Phil Cantore, an All-State halfback for USC in '43.

Here, with only two minutes left in the first quarter, Phil Cantore is grabbed by one Tiger as two more rush in to help.

Pat Thrash takes a short Bill McMillan pass and is brought down immediately by the Tigers on Big Thursday 1943.

USC wartime coaches, Lt. Jim Blount and Lt. Jim Moran. In '43 they would guide USC to their best season since 1928.

1944

SID TINSLEY UPSETS THE GAMECOCKS

It was October 19, 1944, a cold rainy day in Columbia, as some 18,000 fans braved the weather to see if the Gamecocks would again humiliate the Tigers as they'd done in '43. Sports writers noted, by the way, that today was the first time it had rained on Big Thursday since 1896, a bad omen perhaps for the outmanned Clemson Tigers. As usual, the sports writers got it all wrong.

The Gamecocks were coached this year by Doc Newton, formerly of NC State, and he had quite a talented team on hand to meet the challenges of 1944. At this point they were 1-1-1 on the season, with a win over Newberry, a loss to Georgia Pre-Flight, and a tie with Miami.

Clemson, on the other hand, was not doing too badly, showing wins over PC and NC State, while losing 51-0 to Georgia Tech.

Carolina received the opening kickoff but couldn't move and Curly Kuldell punted to the Clemson 3. Sid Tinsley, from his tailback position, gained eight yards on first down, nine on second down. Then Came Billy "Tweetie" Poe on a reverse for 65 yards, down to the USC 15. Tinsley took it to the five on the next play, then Bill Rogers went in for the TD. Jack Miller's kick was good, and the underdog Tigers were up 7-0.

Two series later, by the way, Sid Tinsley punted from his own 14-yard line down to the Carolina 18, a kick of 68 yards, one of the longest in the Tiger record book.

Five minutes into the second quarter Jim Hunnicutt intercepted a Tinsley pass and ran it back to the Clemson 20. Kuldell hit George Harrison with an 11-yard pass, and Brick Bradford then ran down to the five. Mac Erwin, who was named All-State in '44, then went in for the TD and the score became 7-6.

Clemson took the second half kickoff and began a long touchdown march from their own 36. From the USC 41 Sid Tinsley, behind heavy blocking, turned left end and dashed all the way for another Clemson touchdown and the score became 13-6.

Three minutes into the final period Bill Rogers recovered a fumble at the USC 40, and the Tigers were again on the move. Rogers and Jack Miller (hero of Clemson's '48 win over Missouri in the Gator Bowl) alternated runs until they'd reached the USC five. Rogers then ran it in for the score, Miller kicked the point, and Clemson went up 20-6.

Carolina took the ensuing kickoff back to their own 20. From there, thanks to the fine running of Jim Hunnicutt, Brick Bradford, Mack Erwin, Charles Herdegan and Dan Harralson, they soon found themselves at the Tiger seven. A penalty took the ball to the two, and Hardegan then went in for the TD. John Tominack's kick was good, but that was as close as the Gamecocks could get. Clemson took another one, 20-13.

Mack Erwin, an All-State fullback for the Gamecocks in 1944.

Sid Tinsley, another in a long line of great tailbacks Coach Howard would recruit to run his single-wing machine. Tinsley rushed for 146 yards vs. USC in '44.

The Clemson Tigers of 1944 would go 4-5 on the season. They suprised all the experts by upsetting Carolina 20-13 on a soggy field in '44.

The Carolina Gamecocks of '44 would go 3-4-2 on the season. They upset UNC 6-0 that year, one of the few times USC had ever beaten UNC. (Many of these players are cadets in the Navy V-12 Program.)

Jim Hunnicutt and Jack Bradford, Carolina co-captains in '44.

In 1944 any young man seen on the USC campus dressed in civilian clothes was assumed to be either 4-F, a Nazi spy, or a 17-year-old freshman. The young fellow depicted here leaves little doubt as to his status.

The rain came down in sheets on Big Thursday '44. Here Jim Hunnicatt is brought down at the Clemson 20 after intercepting a Sid Tinsley pass. Mack Erwin would score for USC three plays later.

Clemson's Bill Rogers bulldozes an unidentified Gamecock to get the Tigers' second TD of the afternoon. (Note USC's V-12 marching band lined up on the sideline.)

Bill Farrow (top row, left), a native of Darlington, S. C., is pictured here with his Pi Kappa Alpha brothers at Rutledge College on the Horseshoe at USC in 1940. In December of '41, by now an Air Corps B-25 pilot, Farrow volunteered for Doolittle's famous raid on Tokyo. Forced to bail out over China, Farrow and his crew were interned by the Japanese as war criminals. On October 14, 1942, after months of starvation and terrible tortures, Farrow was cruelly executed by a Jap firing squad. Today his remains are interred at Arlington National Cemetary. The Air ROTC program at USC is named in his honor.

1945

GAME ENDS IN DEADLOCK, 0-0

The big news across America this fall concerned the surrender of the Japanese back in August of '45, thus ending the bloodiest war in America's history. And back came the veterans, many of them athletes, to colleges across the counry, including Clemson and Carolina.

For reasons that remain a mystery, Clemson seems to have made the transition from war to peace more quickly than Carolina, so that by the time football practice rolled around in September, Frank Howard had many of his old veterans back from the war and ready to resume their collegiate careers.

Rex Enright was still in the Navy, serving as athletic director at the Jacksonville Naval Air Station, and in his place came Johnny McMillan, a former USC star, and now football coach at Sumter High School. Under his direction Carolina would go 2-4-3 on the season and go to their first bowl game ever (!).

Frank Howard, back for his sixth season with the Tigers, would lead Clemson to a 6-3-1 record in '45, including big wins over both Tulane and Georgia Tech.

As for today's game, a record crowd of some 25,000 fans

Coach Johnny McMillan would lead USC to their first bowl game ever, a 26-14 loss to Wake Forest in the Gator Bowl.

overflowed Carolina Stadium (as it was called now) to enjoy the first peacetime Big Thursday since 1941.

Clemson fans noted that Butch Butler, one of their all-time favorite tailbacks, would again start for the Tigers as he'd done since 1942. What most didn't realize was that Butler had been drafted in late-'42 and had spent the past three years as an army private at Ft. Jackson. But Frank Howard, who was not one to let a little thing like World War II stand in his way when it came to fielding a football team, arranged with Butler's company commander (a Clemson graduate) for Butler to receive a pass every weekend to play tailback for the Tigers. In fact, he was still in service when Big Thursday '45 rolled around.

This odd situation would later prompt Butler to laugh, "Heck, I didn't know a soul on the team. The only time I ever saw 'em was on Saturday afternoon."

And Frank Howard joked, "Ol' Butler was the finest non-student tailback Clemson ever had."

As for the game itself, it was an offensive shutdown, with neither team able to score against the other, fumbles and pass interceptions being the main culprits.

Late in the third quarter Clemson did appear to score when, from their own 44, Butler threw a long pass to Eddie Freeman, who was racing down the sideline. Freeman caught the ball at the 15 and danced on into the end zone. But an official called Clemson offsides and the ball was brought back.

And so Big Thursday number-43 ended in an 0-0 tie, only the second time in history that neither team could score against the other (they also fought to a 0-0 tie in 1915).

Outstanding for Clemson that day were Butch Butler, Dewey Quinn, Carol Cox, Clint Dyer, Jim Hough, Chip Clark, Jim Sultis, Eddie Freeman, and Tweetie Poe.

Outstanding for Carolina were Bryant Meeks, Buck Isom, Ray Maginn, Dutch Brembs, Bill Carr, Bud Eades, Lyle Hanson, and Bobby Giles.

But the big news for USC in '45 concerned their invitation to play in the first Gator Bowl ever, featuring a re-match between the Gamecocks and Wake Forest. Many were puzzled as to how the 2-4-3 Gamecocks would get a bowl invitation, but some speculated that Rex Enright had used his influence with Jacksonville city fathers to finagle such an honor. At any rate, Carolina again fell to the Deacons in '45, this time by a score of 26-14.

1945 marked the final year of the Early Era of Carolina-Clemson football. At this point Clemson held the edge in this series by a whopping 28-13-2 margin.

Ralph "Pop" Jenkins, the only player ever to have served as captain of the Tigers for three consecutive years. He was named All-American and is a member of the Clemson Athletic Hall of Fame.

Sid Tinsley and Billy "Tweetie" Poe, two of the finest backfield aces ever to play for Clemson. Poe averaged 7.1 yards per carry in '45, still an all-time CU record.

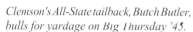

Clemson's All-State tailback, Butch Butler, bulls for yardage on Big Thursday '45.

Sid Tinsley is nailed by a host of Gamecocks after a nice gain for the Tigers.

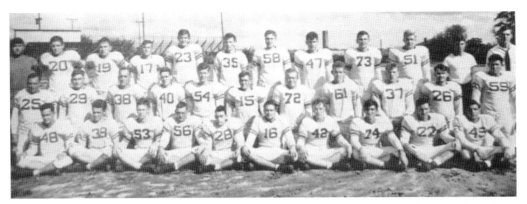

The Gamecocks of '45 would suffer through a 2-4-3 season, then receive an invitation to play Wake Forest in the first Gator Bowl ever.

Dutch Brembs and Bobby Giles would both be named All-State for the '45 Gamecocks.

Miss USC 1945 was honored at the Gator Bowl.

USC center and captain Bryant Meeks shakes hands with Wake Forest's captain just prior to kickoff in the first Gator Bowl ever. Meeks was named All-American and is a member of the USC Athletic Hall of Fame.

Dutch Brembs picked off this Deacon pass and dashed 90 yards for a USC touchdown. After 50 years, this remains an all-time Gator Bowl record.

THE MODERN ERA
1946 - 1996

1946

THE GAMECOCKS OUTLAST THE TIGERS

It was October 26, 1946. Frank Howard was still at Clemson, and Rex Enright had finally returned to assume his duties as head coach at Carolina, and a sense of normalcy that had not been felt for many years prevailed at both institutions.

Prior to Big Thursday USC had beaten both Newberry and Furman, while losing a close one (14-6) to mighty Alabama.

As for the Tigers, their only victory of the year had been over PC, while they'd lost to Georgia, NC State and Wake Forest.

And thus the Gamecocks were considered slight favorites as the teams prepared for Big Thursday.

But the most startling news this year had to do with the bogus football tickets that some enterprising counterfeiters from Pennsylvania had run off weeks prior to the game. Thousands of these were sold all over the country, and no one,

Chip Clark, captain of the '46 Tigers and an outstanding end. He was named All-Southern in '42, then All-American in '46, following his return from the war.

especially those taking up tickets at the gate, could tell the bogus tickets from the legitimate ones.

Thus, once the stadium was filled on game day, several thousand furious fans were left milling about outside the gates. Finally they decided to take action. They then stormed the gates, crowded into the stadium and filled every inch of space that was not already occupied by someone else. Indeed they stood six deep around the playing field. Frank Howard said that he spent the entire game standing behind some lady in a big hat.

"Every few minutes," said Howard, "I'd tap her on the shoulder and ask how Clemson was doing. She'd just turn around and glare at me, so I figured Clemson must not be doing too good."

As for the game itself, with two minutes remaining in the first quarter, USC finally struck for a score. With the ball at their own 38, USC's Bobby Giles took a pitchout, turned left end, then dashed 62-yards for a touchdown, and Carolina led 6-0.

Later in the quarter, after Clemson's star tailback, Bobby Gage, had moved the Tigers to within scoring range several times, the Gamecocks had the ball once again. With the ball on the Clemson 27, Carolina's great quarterback, Bo Hagan, threw to Doug Henson for ten yards, then to Pat Thrash for 13. Red Harrison then went in for the TD, and USC led 12-0.

But led by Bobby Gage, with only moments left in the half, the Tigers came back. Gage completed pass after pass, then hit Chip Clark with an 18-yarder in the USC end zone. Mavis Cagle's kick was good, and the Tigers trailed at half time 12-7.

Early in the second half Ralph Jenkins intercepted a Bo Hagan pass and Clemson again was on the move. Several plays later Gage hit Gerald Leverman in the end zone, Cagle's kick was good, and Clemson took the lead 14-12.

In the final period USC began a march from the Tiger 44. Earl Dunham completed a 22-yard pass to Bobby O'Hara, then Red Harrison ran to the 12. Then Harrison broke through all the way for another USC TD. Pete Lane's kick was good this time, and Carolina was back on top, 19-14.

On the next series Clemson was forced to punt, and USC took the ball at their own 44. Behind the fine runs of Bill Rutledge and Jim Hunnicutt, USC was suddenly at the Clemson seven. Then came Red Wilson in for another USC score. Again the kick was good, and USC went up 26-14. At that point the clock ran out, and USC had another victory on Big Thursday.

USC fullback Red Harrison won the team MVP award, the Jacobs Blocking Trophy, and was named All-Southern.

USC quarterback Bo Hagan would later become head coach at Rice University.

USC captain Earl Dunham.

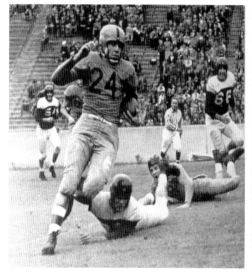

Fullback Dewey Quinn runs for yardage in Clemson's 19-7 loss to Wake Forest. Quinn is a member of the CU Athletic Hall of Fame.

Earl Dunham took this pass in for a TD in Carolina's 14-6 loss to Alabama.

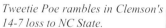

Tweetie Poe rambles in Clemson's 14-7 loss to NC State.

Denied admission to the game in '46, some 5,000 fans stormed the gates, then filled every inch of space in, on, and around the stadium, including the playing field. (This photo was taken as Bobby Giles streaked 62 yards for a USC touchdown).

Red Wilson went in for Carolina's final TD of the day on Big Thursday.

Hank Walker, being cheered on by Chip Clark, runs for good yardage on Big Thursday 1946.

Billy Poe is stopped on the USC 50-yard line. (It should be noted that Clemson players were still in the habit of wearing shin guards, a practice that went back to 1896.)

1947

PLUCKY GAMECOCKS WIN, 21-19

Neither Carolina nor Clemson were enjoying particularly good seasons as Big Thursday 1947 rolled around. The Gameocks had defeated Newberry and Furman while losing to both Maryland and Mississippi. Clemson had done even worse, beating only PC while losing to Boston College, Wake Forest and NC State. Such being the case, Big Thursday took on added significance this year, since it could be the game that would make or break the entire season for the participants.

Both schools had their secret weapons in '47. For Clemson it was tailback Bobby Gage, a young man out of Boys High in Anderson, S. C., who was now in his third season with the Tigers, and who would truly prove in '47 and '48 that he was the best tailback in America. In fact, he was now only a year away from claiming his All-American status.

At Carolina, meanwhile, they had a young freshman halfback, Bishop Strickland, from Mullins, S. C., whose name is still etched high up in the USC record book in almost every offensive catagory.

Fans were eager to see how these two stars would perform as they jammed Carolina Stadium on Big Thursday '47.

Eight minutes into the contest fans finally got a glimpse of Strickland's speed. With the ball at the Tiger 45, Strickland took a pitchout from Droopy Atwell, turned left end, then outraced everyone 55 yards for a USC touchdown. Pete Lane kicked the point, and USC led 7-0.

But the Tigers were not dismayed. Gage returned the kickoff to the Tiger 25, then Ray Mathews went for nine to the 34. On the next play Mathews took a handoff from Gage, cut up the middle, then dashed 66 yards for a Clemson touchdown, and the Tigers now trailed 7-6.

Then it was Carolina's turn. Gage attempted to punt from his two, but Neil Allen dove through, blocked the kick, and Jack Couch recovered for USC at the 19.

Atwell ran it down to the 15. Then, facing fourth and six, Strickland struggled his way down to the two. Then Atwell scored on the next play, the kick was made, and USC led 14-6.

But Clemson came right back. From their own 22, Mathews went for 16, Carol Cox for 22, then came a 15-yard penalty against USC, and the Tigers were again knocking at the door. Two plays later, from the USC nine, Cox passed to Oscar Thompson in the Carolina end zone, and the score became 14-12.

Oddly enough, neither team made a first down in the third quarter. But the fireworks resumed in the fourth when Carolina intercepted a Gage pass deep in Clemson territory and ran it back to the one. Bobby Giles scored on the next play, the kick was good, and USC led 21-12. Jim Reynolds would score Clemson's final touchdown, and Mavis Cagle would kick the point, but it was too little too late, and the Gamecocks walked away with a close win, 21-19.

Both teams did surprisingly well following this game. Carolina went on to a 6-2-1 season, including wins over Miami, The Citadel and Wake Forest, while tying Duke.

As for Clemson, they would finish 4-5-0, beating Furman, Duquesne, and Auburn in their final three games.

Clemson would defeat Furman University on November 8, 1947. They would not lose again until they fell to Rice on September 24, 1949, a win streak of 15 games, their longest win streak in history.

The Clemson Tigers of 1947 would go 4-5-0 on the season. They were still a year away from their great undefeated season of 1948.

USC's James "Droopy" Atwell, called the best second string quarterback in America.

Hank Walker caught 10 passes for 148 yards in the Tigers 34-18 win over Auburn in '47, still Number Two in the Clemson record book for receptions in a single game.

Cary Cox, captain of the '47 Clemson Tigers. In 1943 Cox served as captain of the Carolina Gamecocks.

Neil Allen, captain of the '47 Gamecocks. (He had also served as captain in 1943.)

The great Bobby Giles wound up a fine career with the Gamecocks in '47.

USC's Red Wilson, named to the All-State team at end.

In November of '47 USC's Harry DeLoach puts Carolina up 12-0 over The Citadel in a game played annually at the Orangeburg County Fair.

Bishop Srickland, named to the All-State team as a freshman in '47.

John Moorer goes in for a TD against Boston College, but the Eagles took it 33-22.

All-time Clemson great Ray Mathews runs for yardage as Clemson whacked Furman 35-7.

Red Wilson stops Bobby Gage after a short gain, one of the few times anybody would ever stop Bobby Gage.

Bishop Strickland, a 5-9 200 pound scatback, sets sail for a TD on Big Thursday 1947.

It's Strickland again, this time being pursued by Bobby Gage.

1948

CLEMSON BEATS USC—AND EVERYONE ELSE

Oscar Thompson and Tom Salisbury, heroes of the Tigers' undefeated '48 season.

Bobby Gage was an All-American tailback for Clemson in '48. In the opinion of many, Gage remains the finest football player ever to don the purple and orange of Clemson University. Gage averaged 8.8 yards per pass attempt during his career, still Number One in the CU record book. His 374 yards in total offense vs. Auburn in '47 remains another all-time Clemson record. His 24 career TD passes remains second in the record book.

By October 21, 1948, Big Thursday, Rex Enright's Gamecocks had defeated Newberry and Furman while losing to a strong Tulane team by a close score of 14-0. And there was a young freshman in Carolina's backfield in '48, a youngster named Steve Wadiak, recruited out of a semi-pro league in Chicago. Over the next four years he would become the finest football player in the history of Carolina football. Still, despite a great team of young men, fans were not optimistic about USC's chances on Big Thursday.

And little wonder. The Tigers appeared loaded for bear in 1948, and had already beaten PC, Boston College, Wake Forest and NC State, and their enthusiasm was at fever pitch to get their hands on Carolina, to avenge their losses to the Gamecocks over the past two years.

The first quarter was all Carolina. With about five minutes elapsed, freshman sensation Steve Wadiak took a pitchout at his own 32, then raced down to the Clemson 25, a run of some 43 yards the first time he ever touched the ball on Big Thursday. Then Bo Hagan threw to Red Wilson who took the ball at the 12 and danced on into the end zone. Bayard Pickett kicked the point, and USC took a surprising 7-0 lead.

The second quarter became a scoreless punting duel, and Carolina fans were beginning to hope.

Early in the third quarter Bishop Strickland fielded a Tiger punt, fumbled, and Oscar Thompson recovered for Clemson at the USC eight. Ray Mathews gained two, Carol Cox got four, then it was Cox again, this time going the distance for a Tiger score. Jack Miller's extra point try was wide, so the Gamecocks kept the lead, 7-6.

Steve Wadiak then returned the ensuing kickoff 46 yards, down to the Clemson 17, but a fumble a few plays later killed this promising USC drive.

Midway through the fourth quarter came the most essential play of the game, the one that would win it for Clemson.

Bo Hagan attempted to punt from the USC 28, but Phil Prince broke through and blocked the kick. Oscar Thompson picked up the bouncing ball and ran it in for a Clemson touchdown. Miller's kick was good, and Clemson won 13-7.

For Carolina this was a demoralizing loss. For Clemson it was just the impetus they needed to go on to a great undefeated season, one of their very best ever, and a victory over Missouri in the '48 Gator Bowl.

The '48 Gamecocks, despite an all-star lineup, would suffer through another 3-5 losing season. (Note: freshman Steve Wadiak is #33 in this photo.)

Carolina co-captains, Jack Couch and Al Faress.

Freshman sensation Steve Wadiak crosses the goal line all alone for his second TD of the day as USC upset Tulsa 27-7 in '48. Wadiak averaged 8.1 yards per carry in '48, a USC record that has never been approached by any other player.

Bob Martin and Phil Prince, co-captains of the '48 Tigers. It was Prince who blocked Hagan's punt on Big Thursday.

Frank Gillespie was named All-Southern in all three major sports, the only Tiger ever so honored, and Southern Conference Athlete of the Year in '48. He is a member of the Clemson Athletic Hall of Fame and the All-Time Clemson Football Team.

Ray Mathews, an All-Southern wingback, would go on to stardom with the Pittsburgh Steelers.

Clemson's '48 starting eleven, one of the finest in the history of Tiger football. They would go 11-0 on the season. Backs (L-R): Ray Mathews, Bob Martin, Fred Cone, Bobby Gage.
Line (L-R): Oscar Thompson, Phil Prince, Tom Salisbury, Frank Gillespie, Gene Moore, Ray Clanton, John Poulos.

Bobby Gage kept the Tigers going on Big Thursday '48.

Ray Mathews runs for daylight on Big Thursday 1948. In pursuit is USC's Ed Pasky.

Yep, it's Ray Mathews again!

Frank Howard called Fred Cone "The best football player I ever coached." A punishing fullback, he rushed for 31 TDs during his career, still Number-Two in the CU record book. He averaged scoring 10.2 points per game in 1950, still an all-time CU record. He was later named to two all-time NFL teams, the Green Bay Packers and the Dallas Cowboys. (Oddly enough, he led the NFL in field goal kicking in 1955.)

Gene Moore, Tom Salisbury and Dick Hendley in hot pursuit as Clemson downs Duquesne 42-0 in '48.

Bobby Williams gains yards vs. NC State (that's Bobby Gage wearing the face mask). Clemson took this one 6-0 (thanks to a Bobby Gage punt return of 90-yards for a TD) to keep their win streak alive.

Fred Cone scores his second TD of the day to give Clemson a 14-0 first half lead over Missouri.

Gage hit John Poulos with a pass for Clemson's only TD of the second half in the '49 Gator Bowl. Note: Poulos averaged 28.2 yards per reception in '47, number-two in the CU record book.

Jack Miller's field goal in the '49 Gator Bowl was the only field goal Clemson kicked all season. (Jim Miller is holding.)

Jack Miller won the game for Clemson over Missouri with this 33-yard fourth quarter field goal.

1949

BO HAGAN LEADS USC TO A BIG WIN

Unfortunately for Clemson, their undefeated season of '48 didn't carry over to '49. The Tigers had a great group of young men on hand that year, but they simply had not jelled as a team, and by the time the two teams met on Big Thursday, Clemson had beaten PC and NC State, tied Mississippi State, and lost to Rice. Indeed, they were still a year away from the greatness they were capable of, and would finish the '49 season with a mediocre 4-4-2 record.

As for the Gamecocks, Bo Hagan had been playing injured but that was truly no excuse for their poor showing prior to Big Thursday. They were, to put it kindly, 0-3 on the season, with losses to Baylor, Furman and UNC to show for their efforts. This, despite having a veteran line and one of the finest backfields in the South, including such all-stars as Bishop Strickland and Steve Wadiak. By season's end Carolina would struggle to a 4-6 season.

USC had recently filled in the south end of the field at Carolina Stadium, so that it now had a seating capacity of 35,000. And every seat was filled on October 20 as the fans came to cheer on their favorites.

Early in the first quarter Clemson would get a break when John Boyle (filling in for the injured Bo Hagan) threw a pass that was picked off by Jim Reynolds and returned to the USC 11-yard line. Several plays later Jackie Calvert, Clemson's latest All-American tailback, took a pitch from Fred Cone and raced in for a TD. Tommy Chandler's kick was good, and the Tigers led 7-0.

Just minutes later Boyle was again intercepted and the Tigers took over at their own 34. Several plays later Calvert threw a 15-yard TD pass to Glen Smith and Clemson led 13-0.

Steve Wadiak took the ensuing kickoff at the goal line and returned the ball 60 yards, to the Clemson 40. Fans were then startled to see the injured Bo Hagan limp onto the field to lead the USC offense. Then, behind the running of Wadiak and Strickland, and the passing of Hagan to Red Wilson, the Gamecocks found themselves at the Clemson one-yard line. Hagan sneaked it over from there, and now Clemson led 13-6.

On Clemson's next drive Harry DeLoach intercepted a Carol Cox pass and ran it back to the Tiger 22. After a five yard run by Strickland, Wadiak ran the ball on into the end zone. Bill Killoy's kick was good, and suddenly the underdog Gamecocks found themselves tied 13-13 with the Tigers.

The third quarter was scoreless, with both teams missing opportunities because of turnovers.

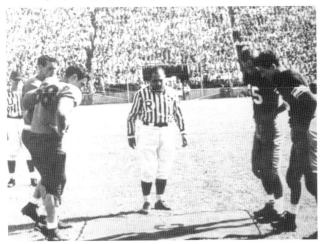

Captains from Carolina and Clemson meet for the coin toss just prior to kickoff on Big Thursday 1949.

Bob Hudson was an All-Southern end and is a member of the CU Athletic Hall of Fame.

But early in the fourth, following a brilliant 46-yard run by sophomore fullback Chuck Prezioso, Hagan again brought the USC faithful to their feet when he threw a 40-yard bomb to Jim Pinkerton for another TD. Again the kick was good, and amazingly the Gamecocks went up 20-13.

Then, with only two minutes left in the game, with Wadiak, Strickland, Prezioso and DeLoach carrying the load, the Gamecocks struck once again. Hagan took it in for the TD, his second of the day, the kick was good, and the Gamecocks led by 27-13. Only moments later the final seconds ticked off the clock and Big Thursday '49 was history. The appearance of Bo Hagan had made all the difference for Carolina.

Cecil Woolbright, captain of the '49 Gamecocks.

Steve Wadiak averaged 8.1 yards per carry as a freshman in '48, still an all-time USC record.

Bayard Pickett intercepted four passes vs. The Citadel in '49, still a USC record. (The Citadel completed seven passes in this game, four of those going to Pickett!)

Blackie Kincaid, an elusive USC halfback, and Red Wilson, an All-State end for four consecutive years.

Chuck Prezioso, a great halfback, and Bayard Pickett.

Ed Dew, USC's "Phantom Tackler," rushed in from the sideline to throw Jackie Calvert for a loss on this play. Oddly enough, the refs didn't see what happened and the play was allowed to stand.

Ed Pasky set an all-time USC record when he returned this pass interception 101 yards for a TD vs. Wake Forest in '49. (Pasky had 159 yards in interception returns in '49, still an all-time USC record.)

Jackie Calvert, another on Frank Howard's endless list of All-American tailbacks. He averaged 5.9 yards per carry during his career with the Tigers, still an all-time CU record.

Jackie Calvert's broken field running stumped defenders all year. Here he goes for yardage vs. USC on Big Thursday.

Dick Hendley, a devastating blocking back in Howard's single wing, won the Jacobs Blocking Trophy, and is a member of the CU Athletic Hall of Fame.

Tough Dick Hendley is finally brought down by two Gamecocks. Clemson was leading 13-6 at the time and seemed to have the game in the bag.

Bishop Strickland took a pitchout and raced around left end for yardage until stopped by Dick Hendley.

Ray Mathews, an All-Southern wingback, averaged 6.1 yards per carry in '49, still Number-Three in the CU record book. He also scored 28 touchdowns during his career, still Number-Three in the CU record book. (He once scored four TDs in a single game for the Pittsburgh Steelers, still an all-time Steeler record.)

Gene Moore, an All-Southern center and Captain of the '49 Tigers.

1950

WADIAK SPARKS USC TO AN UPSET TIE WITH TIGERS

Despite the presence of such all-time Gamecock stars as Hugh Merck, Larry Smith, Dave Sparks, Blackie Kincaid, Lip LaTorre, Bishop Strickland, Steve Wadiak, and Chuck Prezioso, the Gamecocks of 1950 had their usual problems trying to keep everybody healthy. Still, they had defeated both Furman and a strong Georgia Tech team coming into Big Thursday, while losing only to Duke.

At Clemson, meanwhile, they truly had one of their finest teams ever, a team of Tiger all-stars, and their record would prove it. They had run roughshod over their first three opponents, beating PC 55-0, Missouri 34-0, and NC State 27-0. Not a bad start. And of course they were heavily favored going into Big Thursday--which just shows how much the "experts" know.

A heavy rain the morning of October 19 had left the field a quagmire. Still, a record crowd of 35,000 showed up as the Gamecocks kicked off to the Tigers.

Three plays later Clemson punted and the ball went out on the USC 11. On first down, Ed Pasky handed off to Steve Wadiak who broke into the Tiger secondary, then made a dash down the right sideline and made it all the way to the Clemson 23 before being pulled down by Bob Hudson. Then came Strickland, bulling his way to the ten. On the next play Wadiak took it in for the score, Bill Killoy's kick was good, and USC was up 7-0.

And so it went, with both teams slugging it out in the mud. Then, with only a minute left in the half, Ray Mathews threw a bomb from his own 45 to a well-covered Billy Hair. But Hair wrestled the ball away from a Gamecock defender, then ran the remaining 20 yards for a Tiger score. Charlie Radcliff's kick was good, and the teams were tied 7-7 at half time.

In the third quarter Wadiak proved why he was considered one of the premier backs in America. With the ball at the USC 27, he took a handoff from Pasky and was apparently stopped at the line of scrimmage, but then he broke away and out raced everyone to the end zone, a run of 73 yards. The kick was good, and now the lowly Gamecocks were up 14-7.

In the fourth quarter, with Carolina seemingly in total control, Clemson began a drive from their own 43. Behind the running of Fred Cone and Mathews, and the passing of Billy Hair, plus some truly unfortunate penalties against Carolina, the Tigers made their way to USC's one-foot line. From there Cone simply waltzed through the Carolina line, Charlie Radcliff's kick was good, and again the two teams were tied, 14-14. And thus ended the game.

Steve Wadiak rushed for 256 yards in this game, a new Southern Conference single-game record. He averaged 13.5 yards per carry this day, and scored both USC touchdowns. He was later named Southern Conference Player of the Year.

Bishop Strickland was named All-State for four consecutive years, and to the All-Southern team in 1950. He later enjoyed an outstanding pro career, and is a member of the USC Athletic Hall of Fame.

Vince Gargano and Larry Smith. Gargano would win the Jacobs Blocking Trophy for Carolina in '50, while Larry Smith, an All-Southern center, would go on to play pro ball for the Hamilton Tiger-Cats. Smith is a member of the USC Athletic Hall of Fame.

As for Clemson, this tie would be the only blemish on their '50 record. They would go on then to enjoy a perfect season and upset a good Miami team 15-14 in the Orange Bowl. This was Clemson's second undefeated season in the past three years.

This 1950 Clemson team would average a phenomenal 6.1 yards per play, still an all-time Tiger record, and score 48 TDs, yet another all-time record. Their average of 34.4 points per game is still third in the CU record book.

Steve Wadiak, the Southern Conference Player of the Year in 1950, ran 96 yards from scrimmage for a TD vs. George Washington, still the longest run on record for USC.

Captain Dave Sparks, an All-Southern center for USC. He died a few years later while at the heigth of his career with the Washington Red Skins.

John "Lip" LaTorre, an excellent end for the Gamecocks whose tough play remains a legend at USC. He was named All-Southern in '52.

Clemson's varsity squad of 1950 would go 9-0-1, their second unbeaten season in the past three years, then upset Miami 15-14 in the Orange Bowl.

Clemson's 1950 all-star backfield. (L-R): Ray Mathews, Wyndie Wyndham, Fred Cone and Jackie Calvert. Mathews, Cone and Wyndham were named All-Southern, Jackie Calvert All-American. All four are members of the Clemson Athletic Hall of Fame.

Strom Thurmond and other dignitaries turned out en masse for Big Thursday 1950.

Steve Wadiak on his 73-yard TD jaunt to put the Gamecocks up 14-7 in the third period. He would rush for 256 yards on the day, a Southern Conference record.

Even Fred Cone found tough sledding through USC's defensive line. Cone averaged scoring 10.2 points per game in '50, still an all-time CU record. He also scored four TDs vs. Auburn in '50, tying another all-time CU record.

With only moments left in the '51 Orange Bowl game, Miami held a 14-13 lead over Clemson. But then Sterling Smith broke through and caught this Miami runner behind his goal line for a 2-point safety, and Clemson won, thanks to Smith, 15-14.

Did we win the Orange Bowl? Hell yes! The troops whoop it up in Miami following the game.

Fred Cone and Frank Howard congratulate a beaming Sterling Smith for his game-saving tackle.

1951

A GREAT TEAM WIN FOR USC

It was October 25, 1951, and most of the 35,000 fans who rushed through the gates to watch Big Thursday this year were aware that Clemson had been enjoying a record-setting unbeaten streak of 15 games before being upset by Pacific just the week before. And the Tigers were furious and just looking for a gamecock's neck to wring.

As for the Gamecocks, they were having their usual problems. Steve Wadiak was back for his senior year, along with such other notables as Don Early, Vince Gargano, Leon Cunningham, Billy Stephens, Lip LaTorre, and Chuck Prezioso. Still, despite such a great lineup, Carolina had managed to defeat The Citadel and Furman while losing badly to both Duke and UNC.

As for today's game, the first quarter became a punting duel that ended late in the period when Billy Hair punted a high spiraling kick to Billy Stephens waiting at his own 24. Stephens picked up a wall of blockers and dashed down the left sideline 76 yards for a TD. Chuck Prezioso's kick was good, and suddenly the Gamecocks were up 7-0.

Three minutes later, early in the second quarter, Leon Cunningham recovered Frank Kennedy's fumble at the Tiger 25. Behind the running of Wadiak and Gene Wilson, USC took it down to the Clemson one. Dick Balka took it over on the next play, and now USC led 13-0. And that was the half time score.

As for the third period, neither team could take advantage of several breaks that came their way and it ended with USC still leading 13-0.

Early in the fourth, with Clemson deep in their own territory, Billy Hair attempted to throw from his own 13. The ball was slightly deflected and Harry Jabbusch picked it off for Carolina and ran untouched into the Clemson end zone. Chuck Prezioso kicked the point, and Carolina led 20-0.

And that was the final score.

Following today's thrilling win, the Gamecocks would go on to beat West Virginia and Wake Forest while losing to George Washington and Virginia to give them a winning 5-4 record on the year.

As for Clemson, despite today's loss, they would go undefeated the rest of the season, with wins over Wake Forest, Boston College, Furman and Auburn, giving them a 7-3 record for the season.

They would also go to another bowl game (their third during the past four years), losing a re-match with Miami 14-0 in the '52 Gator Bowl.

(Clemson defeated Duquesne on November 5, 1949 and would not lose again until upset by Pacific on October 13, 1951, an unbeaten streak of 15 games, an all-time Clemson record.)

Billy Hair, an all-time great tailback who led Clemson to a 9-0-1 season in 1950, was twice named All-Southern and is a member of the CU Athletic Hall of Fame.

Rex Enright, Steve Wadiak (#37) and teammates celebrate their 34-14 spoiling of West Virginia's Homecoming in '51. (Note: Billy Stephens, #25, won the MVP Award in the '51 Carolina-Clemson game. Standing between Stephens and Wadiak is USC's all-time great end, John "Lip" LaTorre.)

In Memoriam

Stephan Wadiak

January 8, 1926
March 9, 1952

After a brilliant career, Steve Wadiak was killed in a car crash on March 9, 1952. A truly nice guy, it is said that grown men wept openly at his funeral.

Chuck Prezioso, a fine USC halfback, and Hootie Johnson, winner of the Jacobs Blocking Trophy.

Bobby Drawdy and Harry Jabbusch were both named to the All-State team for USC in 1951.

Captain Bob Patton and Dan DiMucci. Patton blocked a PAT attempt on the last play of the game against Wake Forest in '50, preserving Clemson's 13-12 win and keeping their win streak alive. He was named All-Southern for the Tigers in '51 and DiMucci All-State.

During his career with the Tigers Glenn Smith had 18 TD receptions, still an all-time CU record.

Don Wade and Frank Howard. Both are members of the CU Athletic Hall of Fame.

Team captains meet for the coin toss on Big Thursday 1951: Steve Wadiak, Glenn Smith, Bob Patton, and Don Wade, four of the finest young men ever to play on Big Thursday.

Buck George, moves for yardage in Clemson's 20-14 win over Rice. (George ran 90 yards from scrimmage for a TD vs. Furman in '51, tying an all-time Tiger record.)

Wadiak could mix it up with the best of them. Here he scrambles for a loose ball in USC's 21-6 loss to UNC.

Chuck Prezioso was beginning to feel mighty lonely out there.

Big Jim Shirley, an excellent single-wing fullback, breaks into the Carolina secondary on Big Thursday. (Shirley ran the ball 36 times vs. NC State in '51, an all-time CU record.)

Billy Hair returned the opening kickoff 73 yards in the '52 Gator Bowl. But Clemson finally fell to Miami 14-0.

Hootie Johnson is up to his neck in Tigers after taking this Dick Balka pass.

1952

GENE WILSON PULLS IT OUT FOR USC

A great many stars were gone now from the Clemson Tiger squad that had been to three bowl games over the past four years. And a glance at their '52 record indicates the results. They had beaten PC (no big surprise) in their opener, but then had lost to Villanova, Maryland, and Florida prior to Big Thursday.

Indeed, they almost didn't have to worry about Big Thursday in '52, for they had defied Southern Conference rules when they accepted a bowl bid in '51. And the same was true of Maryland. Thus the conference ruled that Clemson and Maryland were on probation and could not play any other conference schools for one year. This ruling did not sit well with the S. C. Legislature, and so they passed a state law that Clemson must play USC in football in 1952--whether the Southern Conference liked it or not. (The Southern Conference's stringent rules prohibiting post-season play led directly to the formation of the Atlantic Coast Conference in 1953.)

As for the Gamecocks, 1952 would see the appearance of Johnny Gramling, the granddaddy of a long line of great USC quarterbacks. And he had a fine supporting cast of players-- Gene Wilson, Bobby Drawdy, Hootie Johnson, Walt Shea, Frank Mincevich, Leon Cunningham, and Lip LaTorre. Still, they had, predictably, beaten Wofford and Furman while losing to both Army and Duke, the biggies on their schedule.

But they were favored to win this classic battle today, and they'd disappoint no one.

It would be totally accurate to describe today's fight as a classic defensive struggle. Indeed, Clemson completed not a single pass in this contest (except for two that landed in the hands of Carolina defensive backs), and they had only 103 yards rushing and five first downs.

The Gamecocks did little better. They had 95 yards passing and 125 yards rushing and 14 first downs.

As for the scoring, the only statistic that really counts, Carolina scored early, taking advantage of a Clemson fumble that Gene Wilson recovered at the Tiger 32. Johnny Gramling then went to the air, throwing to Clyde Bennett for 10 yards. Then he spotted Gene Wilson running between two Tiger defenders. Gramling threw a high pass that Wilson managed to take away from a Clemson defensive man at the two. From there he fell backwards into the end zone and the Gamecocks were on the board. The kick failed and USC led 6-0. And that is how the game finally ended.

Clemson would end the season with a poor 2-6-1 record, while Carolina would manage to go 5-5.

(The '52 Gamecocks held The Citadel to only one yard of total offense (-32 yards rushing, 33 yards passing), and all-time USC defensive record.)

In his first start as a Tiger tailback, freshman Don King rushed for a record 234 yards as Clemson tied Fordham University 12-12 in a major upset. This rushing effort would stand as an all-time Clemson record until 1983.

Tom "Black Cat" Barton and Earl Wrightenberry share a joke just before practice in 1952.

Charlie Radcliff, an early ace place kicker for the Tigers. His extra point kicks always seemed to make a difference on Big Thursday.

Tom "Black Cat" Barton, an All-American guard for the Tigers, and a member of the CU Athletic Hall of Fame.

Pete Cook, safety for the Tigers, whose eleven career interceptions is still Fourth Best in the CU record book.

Clemson's defensive team for 1952. Line (L-R): George Withers, Earl Wrightenberry, Barclay Crawford, Tom Barton, Nathan Gressette, Frank Gentry. Backs (L-R): Jimmy Wells, Bob Jolly, Pete Cook, Jimmy Quarles, Fred Knoebel. Note: in '51 Knoebel intercepted seven passes, number-two in the CU record book.

Clemson's offensive team for 1952. Line (L-R): Scott Jackson, Gary Byrd, Clyde White, J. C. Hudson, Joe Bryant, Charlie Wyatt, George Rodgers, Otis Kempson. Backs (L-R): Buck George, Red Whitten, Milton Pate, Billy Hair.

Jim Shirley, Ormand Wild, and George Rogers. All would be named to the All-State team in '52, Rodgers was named team captain.

Norris Mullis and Johnny Gramling. Mullis was named All-American in '52, while Gramling was the first USC QB to pass for over 1,000 yards in a single season. He was named All-Southern.

Don Early and Jess Berry would be named All-Southern for USC in 1952.

Team captains meet for the coin toss on Big Thursday 1952: George Rodgers and Billy Hair for the Tigers, Walt Shea and Lip LaTorre for USC.

Gene Wilson makes the catch that would give USC a 6-0 win over Clemson in '52.

Gene Wilson, one of the best running backs in the history of USC football.

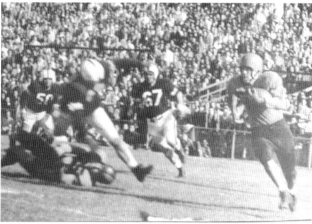

Billy Hair rambles for 25 yards on Big Thursday, but it was too little too late. Hair averaged 7.3 yards per carry in 1950, still an all-time Clemson record.

Ah, for the good old days! The night before the Clemson-Furman game these two Furman "spys" were caught on campus. They were taken to the Tom Clemson monument, their heads were shaved, and they were encouraged to salute Clemson College.

1953

HAROLD LEWIS GUIDES USC TO VICTORY

It was 1953 and Clemson and USC were now members of the Atlantic Coast Conference, a league composed of Maryland, Virginia, UNC, NC State, Duke, Wake Forest, USC and Clemson. These eight institutions had once been a part of the Southern Conference, but the lure of post-season play (plus less stringent entrance requirements) prompted these schools to begin a new conference.

Unfortunately, it would be a while before either USC or Clemson would have to worry about post-season play.

This was also the year that the NCAA abolished the two-platoon system, replacing it with a limited substitution rule.

It was also the year that Frank Howard finally threw in the towel and adapted the T-formation as his major offensive weapon. No more single-wing for the Tigers, and no one could have been happier than their opponents!

As for the Gamecocks, Johnny Gramling returned at quarterback. Plus there were such all-time great backs as Bill Wohrman, Gene Wilson, Carl Brazell and Mike Caskey, truly one of the finest backfields in the South.

Carolina would go 7-3 on the season in '53, Rex Enright's best record ever with the Gamecocks. Indeed, USC would beat both UNC and Virginia in '53, the first time they'd turned that trick since 1927.

As for Frank Howard, he was busy converting Don King,

one of the best single-wing tailbacks in America, to a T-formation quarterback. And King responded eagerly. Still, by the time Big Thursday rolled around, the Tigers had only a win over PC to show for their efforts while losing to Maryland and Miami and tying Boston College.

As for the Big Thursday game, both teams rocked along, showing plenty of offensive punch but stymied by turnovers, until late in the second quarter. At that point, from the Tiger 45, Johnny Gramling lofted a high spiraling pass to Clyde Bennett who had gotten the drop on a Clemson defender. Bennett took the pass and ran it in for USC's first score of the day. Jim Jarrett's kick was good, and the Gamecocks led 7-0.

But the most spectacular play of the day occurred just before half time when Mike Caskey took a Clemson punt in his own end zone, one that was well covered by the Tigers. But Caskey, a waterbug type runner, zigged and zagged until he saw a small opening. He then made his move, turned on the speed and appeared to be going all the way. But he was finally brought down by Buck George at the Clemson 37, a run of some 63 yards. The half ended at that point.

It was midway the third quarter that USC fans got their first look at a young quarterback from Lakeview, S. C. named Harold Lewis. He had just turned 17, and now he was subbing for the injured Johnny Gramling. From the Tiger 47 he threw to Bill

Nathan Gressette and Dreher Gaskin, co-captains of the '53 Tigers. Gressette was named All-State. Gaskin was named All-ACC and was chosen for the Senior Bowl. Gaskin caught three TD passes vs. Auburn in '53, an all-time Clemson record.

Don King, Clemson's all-purpose All-ACC quarterback, led the team in rushing, passing, punting and punt returns in '53. He also led Clemson in scoring during his career.

Wohrman down to the Clemson 21. Then he calmly tossed a long one to Joe Silas, running all alone in the Clemson end zone. Jarrett's kick was good, and now USC was up 14-0.

In the fourth period a poor USC punt went out of bounds on the Carolina 27-yard line. Behind the running of Larry Gressette and Jimmy Wells, Clemson made it to the USC 11.

From there Tommy Williams threw a perfect strike to Scott Jackson in the USC end zone. Pooley Hubert's kick was good, and now the Tigers were on the board. But Clemson could get no closer, and the game ended, a 14-7 win for USC.

This marked the first time since the 1931-33 seasons that USC had beaten Clemson for three straight years. In fact, Clemson had not won on Big Thurday now since 1948.

In the second quarter of Big Thursday, Bill McLellan intercepted a Gramling pass and returned it 30 yards before being wrestled to the turf.

Jimmy Wells (big brother of Joel Wells) blindsides a Boston College runner as big Buck Priester (son of Buck Priester, 1930-31) closes in for the kill. The game ended a 14-14 tie.

Bill McLellan, the Tigers' center in '53, would later become Athletic Director at Clemson.

Johnny Gramling and Clyde Bennett, USC's deadly passing duo, were also USC's first All-ACC players. Gramling's 2,007 career passing yards was an all-time USC record. Bennett's 64 career receptions was another all-time USC record. He was named All-American in '53.

Carl Brazell and Harold Lewis. In USC's first ACC game ever, a 20-7 loss to Duke, Brazell scored USC's only TD with a 70-yard punt return. Harold Lewis thrilled USC fans on Big Thursday when he came in and led the Gamecocks to their winning touchdown.

On the final play of the first half Mike Caskey brought fans to their feet when he returned this Don King punt from his own end zone all the way to the Clemson 37 before being nailed by Buck George.

Captain Gene Wilson averaged 6.5 yards per carry in '53, still fourth best in the USC record book.

Carl Brazell, at 5-8 and 155 pounds, is about to put the stop on big Scott Jackson--with a little help from his friends.

Gene Wilson electrified fans early in the game when he took a punt at his own 32 and returned it 68 yards for a Carolina touchdown. But a clipping penalty brought the ball back, and a fine run was nullified.

The Clemson coaching staff of 1953.

These Southern belles were selected as sponsors for the Clemson Tigers in 1953.

1954

PRICKETT BRILLIANT IN USC WIN

Frank Howard was headed into his fifteenth season as head coach of the Clemson Tigers as the '54 season began. Following their annual drubbing of Presbyterian College, they'd then lost close ones to both Georgia and VPI before defeating Florida.

As for the Gamecocks, the big story was the presence now of a young quarterback named Mackie Prickett who'd sparked USC to a magnificent upset win over a strong Army team in the season opener. They'd then lost to West Virginia but came back to beat Furman.

Clemson had an all-star backfield that year, with guys like Don King, Joel Wells, Joe Pagliei, and Billy O'Dell. And the same is true of Carolina. In addition to Prickett, there was Mike

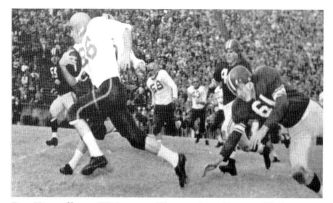

Don King off on a TD jaunt as Clemson beat Furman 27-6.

Tommy Williams goes in for a TD as Clemson defeated The Citadel 59-0 in '54. (Things were apparently getting pretty personal at this point!) Ken Moore ran the ball five times in this game, averaging 30.4 yards per attempt, an all-time CU record.

Caskey, Carl Brazell, and Bill Wohrman (famous as the finest blocker in the ACC).

The two teams were considered evenly matched as they lined up for the kickoff on Big Thursday, October 21, 1954.

The scoring began early and in an odd way. After holding Clemson at the USC eight, Carolina took over on downs but could not move the ball and attempted to punt from their own end zone. Bill Tarrer dropped the snap from center, fell on it in the end zone, and Clemson was awarded a 2-point safety.

Later in the period Carolina came back when Buck George fumbled at the Clemson 40. Prickett passed to Larry Gosnell for eight yards, then he himself ran for eight more. Then Tommy Woodlee went for another eight, and the Gamecocks were at the Clemson 16. Prickett picked up 11 yards on the option, then Crosby Lewis slugged it out down to the two. Carl Brazell made it to the one and Prickett sneaked it in on the next play. Joe Silas' kick was good, and Carolina took the lead 7-2.

Later, with one minute and 45 seconds remaining in the half, Carolina again was on the move from midfield. Brazell took a pitchout and moved to the Clemson 41. Then Prickett hit Brazell with a short pass, and the little speedster dashed down to the three. Prickett scored on the next play, and the score became Carolina 13, Clemson 2.

The final fireworks of the day came late in the fourth quarter. With the ball at their own 19-yard line, Joel Wells took a pitch from Don King, started to his right on an end sweep, then suddenly held up and fired a long pass downfield to an open Joe Pagliei at the USC 45. Pagliei caught the ball and ran the rest of the way for a Tiger TD, a play that covered some 81 yards. (This 81-yard TD pass remains the third longest pass play in the CU record book.) Final score USC 13, Clemson 8.

The Gamecocks had not lost to Clemson now since 1948, a period of six years.

Frank Mincevich was named to Look Magazine's All-American Team in '54, and is a member of the USC Athletic Hall of Fame.

Mackie Prickett was named All-ACC and Honorable Mention All-American. He was the total offensive leader in the ACC in '54.

Harry Lovell and Bill Wohrman, co-captains of the '54 Gamecocks. Lovell would be named All-State while Wohrman won the Jacobs Blocking Trophy and was named All-ACC. (Wohrman would later star in the popular TV series "Flipper.")

Carl Brazell in '54 was named All-ACC and was fourth in the nation in pass receptions

Center Leon Cunningham was named All-American and is a member of the USC Athletic Hall of Fame.

Mike Caskey in 1954 averaged 6.7 yards per carry, still second in USC's record book only to Steve Wadiak's 8.2 yards per carry in 1948.

Led by Leon Cunningham and Bill Wohrman, the Gamecocks parade Rex Enright across the field following their big 34-20 upset of a strong Army team in 1954. Carolina still recalls this win as one of their greatest ever.

Mike Caskey, the so-called Masked Marvel, dashes 62 yards for USC's final TD of the day to wrap up their 34-20 win over Army in '54. Bill Wohrman cheers him on.

Clemson captains for 1954: Clyde White, Scott Jackson, Mark Kane, and Buck George. White was All-ACC, won the Clemson Offensive MVP award, and played in the Blue-Gray Game. Jackson was All-ACC, and won Clemson's Defensive MVP award. Mark Kane was named All-State. Buck George was chosen for the North-South game.

Fullback Joe Pagliei led the ACC in punting in both '54 and '55.

Tackle Tommy Matto

Joe Pagliei ran through, around and over defenders. Here he makes a super run as Clemson beat PC 33-0.

Prickett faked a pitch right, then bootlegged the ball around left end for a TD and a 13-2 half time lead for USC.

Carl Brazell took this short Prickett pass, then ran for 47 yards, down to the Clemson three. USC scored three plays later to make the score 7-2, their favor.

1955

STRONG TIGERS TOO MUCH FOR USC

The Gamecocks would again field an all-star cast in '55, but predictably enough, as they prepared to meet the Clemson Tigers on October 20, they had beaten only Wofford and Furman, the little guys on their schedule, while losing to Wake Forest and Navy. Indeed, rumblings of discontent from disgruntled Gamecock fans (and the news media) could be heard from throughout the state.

As for Frank Howard and Clemson, they had won a total of only ten games (and lost a total of ten games) over the past three years, which was not a record to get real excited about. Still, Howard had proven that, given the proper circumstances, he could get the job done and that Clemson could hold their own with the best the nation had to offer. Thus Clemson fans were not nearly as vocal in their criticisms of Howard as USC fans were of Rex Enright.

And it's probably a good thing, for Clemson was on the threshold of their finest five-year performance in history. Indeed, over the next five years, with a record of 38-13-2, plus three bowl games, Coach Howard could boast of having one of the finest programs in America.

The Tigers were 3-1 going into Big Thursday, with wins over PC, Virginia and Georgia and a loss to Rice. And it didn't take long for the 35,000 fans on hand today to tell that Clemson was the stronger team.

Clemson scored the second time they touched the ball, with Charlie Bussey throwing to Willie Smith for the TD. Bussey's kick was good, and Clemson led 7-0.

Following a USC punt, the Tigers were again in business. From the Caroina 49, Joel Wells burst through the line for 46 yards. Then came Joe Pagliei in for the TD, the kick was good, and Clemson was up 14-0. And they still had another 50 minutes to play.

But things quieted down at that point and Carolina went in at half time down by a respectable 14-0 score.

Hugh Merck fumbled the second half kickoff and Clemson recovered at the USC 42. Three runs by Joel Wells, and the Tigers were again in the USC end zone. The kick was good, and their lead was 21-0.

But the Gamecocks were still not dead. From the Tiger 37, Bobby Bunch, subbing for Mackie Prickett, came in and led a

The late Mike Caskey and Carl Brazell take a break during the Furman game. Carl Brazell's 5.7 yards per carry during his career at USC remains an all-time Carolina record. Mike Caskey's 5.5 yards per carry during his career at USC remains number-five in the USC record book. His 6.7 yards per carry in '54 remains second only to Steve Wadiak's 8.2 yards per carry in '48.

Carolina drive that ended with Carol McClain dashing 15 yards for a touchdown. Joe Silas kicked the point, and Clemson led 21-7.

Then in the fourth period, with Bunch still at quarterback, Carolina moved from their own 25 down to the Clemson 24. Behind the running of Mike Caskey and Eddie Field, USC was suddenly on the Tiger eight. Field took it in on the next play, the kick was good, and now Clemson's lead was cut to 21-14.

With only seven minutes left on the clock, the Gamecocks tried an onsides kick. But Clemson recovered and quickly moved in for another score, Don King going over for the TD. The kick was good, and Clemson led 28-14, which was the final score.

Carolina would end the season with another poor 3-6 record, and an exhausted Rex Enright called it a day. With a record of 64-69-7 he remains both Carolina's winningest and losingest coach in history. Still, his record against Clemson was a very respectable 8-6-1. Enright would now devote his time to serving as Athletic Director at USC, a position he would hold until his death in 1960.

Hugh Bell and Carl Brazelll, co-captains of the '55 Gamecocks. Both were named to the All-ACC team.

Bobby Bunch, subbing for Mackie Prickett, led USC's comeback against Clemson on Big Thursday 1955.

Rex Enright resigned as head coach at USC following the 1955 season. He would remain as Athletic Director.

Joe Silas was named All-ACC and chosen for the Shrine Bowl game of '55.

Wingo Avery, an outstanding Tiger center.

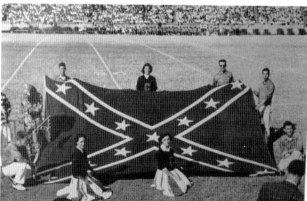

Waving the Confederate Battle Flag was once a large part of the football tradition in South Carolina. (Left) The Gamecock football team at West Point and (right) the Clemson cheerleaders.

Dick Marazza and Billy O'Dell were both named All-ACC. Marazza was named second team All-American.

Don King, captain of the Tigers in '55, won the MVP award and was named All-ACC.

If it wasn't Wells, it was big Joe Pagliei, seen here as he breaks into the USC secondary

Joel Wells moves out behind heavy blocking. It was this tough brand of football that made Frank Howard famous.

Carol McClain's 84-yard non-scoring punt return on Big Thursday '55 remains the longest such run in the USC record book.

Wells goes in for the score after taking a handoff from Don King, giving the Tigers a 21-0 lead.

1956

TIGERS CLAIM NARROW VICTORY

For the first time in eighteen years now (not counting the war years) Carolina had a new head coach, a young man who had served his apprenticeship under Jim Tatum and his great University of Maryland teams of the 1950s. His name was Warren Giese, and his gospel was a stout defense and a conservative offense. Three yards and a cloud of dust.

And it seemed to work. The Gamecocks had already played five games as they prepared for Big Thursday, beating Wofford, Duke (for the first time since 1931), UNC, and Virginia. Indeed the only blemish on their record at this point was a 14-6 loss to Miami, and the Gamecocks were feeling pretty good about themselves.

As for the Tigers, they had finished the 1955 season at 7-3 and were hoping for even better things in '56. Already they had beaten PC, NC State and Wake Forest while tying a good Florida team.

In fact, as those 35,000 fans stood for the National Anthem on Big Thursday 1956, they fully expected to see two very equal teams fight it out down to the wire. And they were right.

Clemson got a break fairly early in the opening period when Jim Coleman fielded a punt at his own 25 and dashed down the right sideline 39 yards to the Carolina 36.

Coleman then ran for five, and then came Joel Wells for 14 more. Two plays later Charlie Bussey ran it in from the one, and Clemson was on the board. Bussey then ran in for the extra point, and Clemson led 7-0.

Following that score neither team could move past their opponent's 20-yard line. But the Gamecocks did come close

to scoring in the fourth period. They moved all the way to the Clemson three when Don Johnson got the call. He shoved his way acrosss the goal line, apparently for a TD, but as he was hit the ball squirted out of his hands and into the waiting arms of Charlie Bussey. It was a touchback, and the Tigers walked away with a 7-0 win.

Oddly enough, it was Clemson that played the conservative-offense game today. The Tigers did not attempt a single pass all afternoon but relied on their great runners for all their yardage.

Clemson would go on then to have a great season, finishing with a 7-2-1 record, being crowned champions of the ACC, and playing Colorado in the Orange Bowl.

Carolina went on to win three of their last four games to finish with a 7-3 record, one of their best seasons in years.

USC gave up only 47.6 passing yards per game and allowed only 6.7 points per game in '56, all-time USC defensive records.

Coach Warren Giese, who believed that the best offense is a stout defense, is given a ride across field following USC's first win over Duke since 1931.

Carolina co-captains Mackie Prickett and Buddy Frick. Both would be named All-ACC. Prickett would win the team MVP award and play in the Blue-Gray game.

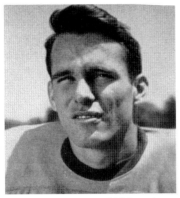

Jim Coleman averaged 19.3 yards per punt return in '55, number three in the CU record book.

Dick Marazza, named All-ACC and Honorable Mention All-American.

USC tackle Sam DeLuca, winner of the Jacobs Blocking Trophy, was named All-American in '56.

John Grdijan, named All-ACC, Honorable Mention All-American, and received the Most Outstanding Lineman in South Carolina Award.

Billy Hudson, an Honorable Mention All-American at tackle, is a member of the CU Athletic Hall of Fame.

Charlie Bussey, an All-ACC quarterback, an Academic All-American, and a member of the CU Athletic hall of Fame.

Charlie Horne runs for a touchdown in Clemson's 21-6 win over VPI in '56.

Joel Wells was an All-American in both '55 and '56 and would later start for the NFL champions New York Giants. He remains one of only three Clemson runners ever to average over five yards per carry during his career with the Tigers (so did Terry Allen and Cliff Austin). He is a member of the CU Athletic Hall of Fame.

Joel Wells scoots for yardage as Clemson downed VPI 21-6.

Frank Destino runs into heavy orange traffic as he plows into the Clemson line on Big Thursday 1956.

Alex Hawkins took this Mackie Prickett pass and appeared headed for pay dirt until a desperation tackle brought him down.

Jim Coleman set up Clemson's score when he took this Carolina punt at his own 25 and raced it back 39 yards to the USC 36. The Tigers scored several plays later.

Just a few minutes prior to kickoff as Clemson squared off against Colorado in the 1957 Orange Bowl.

After trailing 20-0 at half time, Bob Spooner put Clemson in the lead 21-20 with this fourth period TD. Colorado would come back to win it 27-21.

1957

TIGERS WIN ANOTHER THRILLER

The big news out of Columbia in '57 concerned Carolina Stadium. The remaining open end zone had now been filled in so that it could seat some 44,000 fans, an increase of almost 50% in seating capacity.

The other big news concerned USC's great running backs for 1957, King Dixon and Alex Hawkins. They were truly sensational, and, earlier in the season, had led USC to one of their greatest wins ever when they upset a strong Texas team 27-21. Indeed, the rejuvenated Gamecocks were coming off a good 7-3 season in '56 and were now 3-1 on the year, a 26-14 loss to Duke the only blemish on their record.

As for Clemson, they had enjoyed a fine season in '56 with a 7-2-2 record, which included a conference championship and a trip to the Orange Bowl. They had gotten off to a slow start in '57, with wins over PC and Virginia and losses to UNC and NC State. But by seasons' end they would look like the Clemson Tigers we'd all come to know, finishing with a good 7-3 record. Indeed, had it not been for a 7-6 loss to Duke, they could have had a super record.

As for Big Thursday, the Gamecocks found themselves in the unusual position of playing the favorite (mainly because of their win over Texas). But what the experts didn't know was that USC's starting quarterback, Bobby Bunch, was out with a shoulder injury, and both King Dixon and Alex Hawkins would see only limited action today because of injuries.

As for the game itself, the first quarter was scoreless, though USC behaved like the favorites they were, with Dixon, Hawkins and fullback Don Johnson repeatedly ripping off nice gains that came to naught.

There were only two minutes left in the half when Clemson began to move. From their own 18-yard line, Mike Dukes picked up a first down on two nice runs. Then Harvey White faked a pass and ran for another 20 yards and a first down at the USC 43. Then White hit Bill Mathis with a pass down to the 15-yard line. At that point, with only seconds on the clock, White found Sonny Quesenberry alone in the end zone, and suddenly the Tigers were up 6-0.

The third quarter also belonged to the Tigers. After an exchange of punts, Clemson began a drive from their own 23. Rudy Hayes ran twice and the Tigers were on the 39. White then fired a pass to Whitey Jordan who caught the ball on the dead run at the USC 25. Jordan was hit but kept his feet and staggered on, juggling the ball, then dropping it out of bounds at the Carolina one. Rudy Hayes took it over on the next play, White kicked the point, and Clemson was up 13-0. And that was the final score, the Tigers beating USC for the third straight year.

Nelson Weston and Julius Derrick, USC's bookend co-captains for '57. Both were All-State and Derrick would play in the North-South Shrine Game.

USC upset a great Texas team 27-21 in '57 after King Dixon ran the opening kickoff back 98 yards for a TD. Here Don Johnson breaks into the Texas secondary for a nice gain.

John Kompara and Tommy Addison would both be named All-ACC for Carolina. Addison would play with the Boston Patriots.

Tiger receiver Bill Few takes this Harvey White pass for a TD in Clemson's 26-7 win over Maryland.

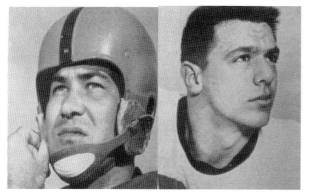

John Grdijan, co-captain of the '57 Tigers, and Ray Masneri. Both were named All-ACC, Grdijan at guard, Masneri at end. Grdijan is a member of the CU Athletic Hall of Fame.

Donnie Bunton and Dick DeSimone were named All-State for Clemson, Bunton at center, DeSimone at guard. DeSimone played in the North-South game.

Harvey White remains Clemson's only quarterback to be named All-ACC as a sophomore. He was also named Back of the Year in South Carolina. He is a member of the CU Athletic Hall of Fame.

Bob Spooner, a mainstay in Clemson's backfield for three years, 1955-57.

Whitey Jordan caught an essential pass from White on Big Thursday '57. He would later coach at Clemson for 14 years. (Jordan averaged an amazing 30.7 yards per reception in 1957, an all-time CU record.)

Bob Spooner plows into a gaggle of Terrapins as Clemson beat Maryland 26-7 while on thier way to a good 7-3 season.

USC captain Nelson Weston and Harold Olson take time out for a friendly chat on Big Thursday.

Eddie Beall stretches to haul in this Sam Spears pass to give USC good field position on Big Thursday.

Tiger fullback Rudy Hayes smashes over from the one to give Clemson their 13-0 margin of victory over Carolina.

1958

LOADED GAMECOCKS SURPRISE TIGERS

Carolina's two great Super Star running backs, King Dixon and Alex Hawkins, were back for their senior year in '58, and optimism was running high that the Gamecocks would improve on their 5-5 record of '57. And, so far, they were off to a fine start. Though they had lost to Army and UNC, they had beaten such powers as Duke and Georgia. By season's end they would be 7-3 and ranked 13th nationally.

As for Clemson, their backfield of '57 was back intact, including the peerless Harvey White, still the only Clemson quarterback to be named All-ACC for three consecutive years. They were undefeated coming into Big Thursday, with wins over Virginia, UNC, Maryland, and Vanderbilt. Indeed, by season's end Howard and his Tigers could boast an 8-2 season, have another conference championship under their belt, and be invited to play in the Sugar Bowl.

Still, despite Clemson's overall superior performance in '58, today would belong to the Gamecocks.

The first quarter ended in a scoreless tie. But in the second Clemson finally drew first blood when Harvey White kept the ball on an option and went into the end zone standing up for a touchdown. Clemson then wanted to try the new 2-point conversion play but White's pass fell incomplete and the score remained 6-0.

Minutes later, from the Clemson 38, Carolina was on the move. Bobby Bunch threw to Buddy Mayfield all alone in the left flat, and Mayfield dashed down to the Tiger 12 before being stopped. Then it was tough John Saunders getting the call. Seven times he ran the ball, finally pushing it across on his last shot, and USC was on the board. Bunch's pass for the two points was no good, and the score remained 6-6.

In the third quarter Carolina's Four Yards and a Cloud of Dust offense began to wear the Tigers down. Taking the ball at their own 43, they ran off 14 plays, with Bunch gaining 26 yards, Hawkins 19, and Saunders 12. Then Bunch sneaked into the end zone for another USC score. Hawkins ran the ball in for the two points, and Carolina led 14-6.

Early in the fourth quarter, behind the short runs of Saunders and Hawkins, the Gamecocks again scored, this time King Dixon taking the ball in. Bunch's pass for the two points failed, but with a 20-6 lead, the game seemed to be out of Clemson's reach anyway.

Late in the fourth, after a Clemson drive died at the USC 22, the Gamecocks again began a drive, with Saunders and Hawkins slamming through that big Tiger line for good yardage. Bunch completed only his second pass of the afternoon, again to Mayfield, good for eight yards. Finally, Hawkins drove in from the two, the try for two points failed, and USC had a 26-6 lead. Which is how the game finally ended.

Clemson, though defeated today, would go on to an 8-2 season, then meet LSU in the Sugar Bowl. It would be Frank Howard's fifth bowl trip.

All-American Alex Hawkins set an all-time USC record when he ran for six 2-point conversions in '59. He tied an all-time USC record by throwing three TD passes to King Dixon in USC's 24-7 win over Wake Forest in '58.

King Dixon, an All-ACC running back who later served as athletic director at USC. He is a member of the USC Athletic Hall of Fame.

Bill Thomas, captain of the '58 Tigers and an All-ACC selection.

Rudy Hayes, a tough fullback for the Tigers.

George Usry won the Jacobs Blocking Trophy in '59.

Charlie Horne points out the bad guys to Lou Cordileone as he goes for yardage in Clemson's 13-6 win over NC State.

Ray Masneri, an All-ACC selection and one of the finest ends ever to play for Clemson, takes this White pass for a first down in Clemson's 20-15 win over Virginia.

All-time Clemson great Bill Mathis takes a pass from Lowndes Shingler in Clemson's 26-21 win over UNC.

Frank James Howard, now in his nineteenth year as head coach at Clemson.

Alex Hawkins, ACC Player of the Year in '58 and an All-American, would go on to fame and fortune with the Baltimore Colts He is a member of the USC Athletic Hall of Fame.

Alex Hawkins charges into the Clemson secondary as USC marched 54 yards for a third period score, a typical USC drive that took 8 minutes and 26 seconds off the clock.

King Dixon appears undismayed as he attempts to elude these four angry Tigers.

John Saunders, winner of the ACC Jacobs Blocking Trophy, leads Alex Hawkins to the Promised Land on Big Thursday and a 26-6 Carolina win.

Bobby Bunch tries to pull down Doug Cline, but without much luck.

Harvey White seems to have these Chinese Bandits pretty well surrounded as Clemson finally went down 7-0 to LSU, the number-one team in the nation, in the 1959 Sugar Bowl.

Doug Cline remains the only Clemson running back ever to win the Jacobs Blocking Trophy.

1959

THE CURTAIN FALLS ON BIG THURSDAY

Sadly, after 64 years, 1959 would mark the last Big Thursday ever to be played. From now on the Carolina-Clemson game would be played on a home-and-home basis, usually the final game of the season for both teams, and thus one of the richest traditions in college football was coming to an end. It was an ending that many fans still deeply regret.

Carolina and Clemson had both enjoyed fairly good seasons prior to Big Thursday '59, with the Gamecocks having wins over Duke, Furman and Georgia while losing only to UNC. Clemson, on the other hand, had beaten UNC, Virginia, and NC State while losing only to Georgia Tech.

But the two teams were truly a study in contrasts. Whereas the Gamecocks relied on their big running backs, John Saunders, Kenny Norton and Phil Lavoie to grind out the yardage bit by bit, the Tigers were utilizing the arms of their two fine quarterbacks, Harvey White and Lowndes Shingler (both were from Greenwood, by the way) who could throw the ball as well as any quarterbacks in the country.

As for today's game, the first quarter was scoreless. But to begin the second, Harvey White capped a 62-yard march when he threw a 30-yard strike to Gary Barnes in the USC end zone, and Clemson took the lead, 6-0.

On the next series, Carolina took the ball at their own ten. Lavoie ran for five, but Steve Satterfield fumbled on the next play and Bob Morgan recovered for the Tigers at the 17.

With less than two minutes left in the half Clemson had to move fast. Bill Mathis gained two, but then George Usry lost one. White thus went to the air, hitting Usry with a pass down to the USC four. Mathis took it in on the next play, Len Armstrong kicked the point, and Clemson took the lead 13-0.

Early in the third period Clemson again recovered a fumble, big Harold Olson grabbing the ball at the USC 26. On first down, White zinged a pass to Bill Mathis standing all alone in the USC end zone, and the score became 19-0.

The Tigers' next score came early in the fourth quarter, the culmination of a 76-yard drive. White hit Sammy Anderson with a 15-yard pass, then came right back, completing another to Usry who ran it down to the USC five. Then Usry went in for the TD, and White threw to Barnes for the 2-point conversion, and Clemson led 27-0. And those were the final points ever scored on Big Thursday.

This was Carolina's worst loss to Clemson since 1939, by the way. But Clemson had 285 yards in total offense in this contest, while USC had only 118 (Carolina had only 38 yards in passing offense). And that, plus a couple of breaks, was the difference in the game.

Frank Howard's record against Carolina now, since becoming head coach of the Tigers in 1940, was eight wins, ten losses, and two ties.

Carolina went on to finish the season with a 6-4 record. Clemson, on the other hand, won a total of 8 games in '59 while losing only two. They would then go on to defeat a good TCU team in the 1960 Bluebonnet Bowl.

USC scored 13 2-point conversions in '59, four versus the University of Virginia, still all-time USC records.

Coach Warren Giese stands between USC co-captains Ed Pitts and John Saunders.

Pitts was named All-American, served as co-captain in the North-South All Star game, and is a member of the USC Athletic Hall of Fame. Saunders was named All-ACC and played in the North-South All Star game.

Phil Lavoie, an All-ACC halfback, ran for six 2-point conversions in '59, tying an all-time USC record.

Jake Bodkin, USC's All-ACC guard.

Jack Pitt, Carolina's All-ACC end.

Lowdnes Shingler and Harold Olson. Shingler was named MVP in the '60 Bluebonnet Bowl. Note: Olson was All-ACC and a member of Clemson's All-Time Football Team.

John Saunders, an All-ACC fullback, demonstrates here why he was considered one of the finest blockers in the South as he lowers the boom on a rash Terrapin. (A sharp elbow is worth a strong shoulder any day of the week!)

Bill Mathis and Doug Cline were both All-ACC and high draft picks. Note: Mathis returned a kickoff 99 yards for a TD against Georgia Tech in '59, the second longest such run in the CU record book.

Paul Snyder and Harvey White, co-captains of the '59 Tigers. Both were All-ACC.
White is a member of the CU Athletic Hall of Fame, and was a first round pick of the Boston Patriots.

Lou Cordileone was an All-American and a first round draft pick of the New York Giants. He is also a member of Clemson's All-Time Football Team.

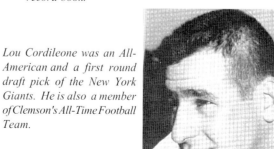

Kirk Phares draws a bead on Harvey White.

Clemson stops Jimmy Williams.

Gary Barnes took this White pass into the end zone for a 6-0 Tiger lead over Carolina.

Jack Morris gets a wheel around Clemson Corners as Dave Adams directs traffic.

The Clemson bench cheers the Tigers on just as they cross the goal line to take the lead from TCU, 10-7.

Sammy Anderson fights for extra yardage in Clemson's 23-7 win over TCU in the 1960 Bluebonnet Bowl.

Bob Morgan shows some fancy footwork as he breaks into the USC secondary.

1960

THE GAMECOCKS VISIT DEATH VALLEY

Coach Lonnie McMillan had dubbed Clemson's football stadium Death Valley after his Presbyterian College Blue Hose had fallen to the Tiger 76-0 on a brutally hot afternoon back in September of 1945, and the name had stuck. And now, on November 12, 1960, Death Valley is where Carolina and Clemson would meet for their annual shootout.

No more Big Thursday. And even the staunchest supporters of that august event had to admit that playing Carolina at home every year put Clemson at a distinct disadvantage, especially from the standpoint of proceeds.

So, after 65 years, here they were. The Tigers at this point were 4-3 on the season, while the Gamecocks were staggering along with a 1-5 record. Still, 4-3 is better than 1-5, so the experts had Clemson slightly favored as the game got underway.

The first period consisted of missed opportunities for both teams, with neither able to mount a drive of any substance.

But early in the second, after their drive stalled at the USC 22, Clemson's Lon Armstrong came in and kicked a field goal of 37 yards and the Tigers went up 3-0.

Later, as time ran out in the half, Lowndes Shingler attempted to scramble from his own 13, but John Jones tackled him behind the goal line to give USC a 2-point saftey.

The score stood at 3-2 until early in the fourth quarter. At that point Jack Morris fumbled at the USC seven, and Bob Coleman recovered for the Tigers. On first down Mack Matthews took a pitchout and went in for the TD. Armstrong kicked the point and Clemson's lead went to 10-2.

Two minutes later, from the USC 12, Tommy Pilcher pitched out to Jack Morris on an end sweep, but Gary Barnes nailed him behind the goal for a two-point safety, and Clemson took the lead by a score of 12-2. And that was the final score.

Clemson would go on to complete the season with a disappointing 6-4 record, while the Gamecocks would suffer through a dismal 3-6-1 season. As for Coach Giese, he would resign as head coach and assume the position of Athletic Director at USC.

Frank Howard, head coach and athletic director at Clemson College.

It was November 12, 1960, the first Carolina-Clemson game ever played at Death Valley, and here Tommy Pilcher scrambles out of the pocket in hopes of picking up a first down. (Pilcher, by the way, weighed in at 145 pounds.)

Dave Lynn, captain of the '60 Clemson Tigers.

Ron Scrudato, a fullback the Tigers called on in the clinch.

Gary Barnes, All-ACC and a member of Clemson's All-Time Football Team.

Calvin West, a tough guard for the Tigers.

Jake Bodkin and Jerry Frye, co-captains of the '60 Gamecocks. Bodkin was All-ACC and Lineman of the Year in South Carolina. Frye was All-ACC and played in the North-South Shrine game.

Wendell Black breaks out for a first down in Clemson's 21-6 loss to Duke.

Sammy Fewell, an All-ACC tackle for USC.

Quarterback Buddy Bennett averaged 5.1 yards per carry for USC in 1960, tops in the ACC.

Eddie Werntz was one of the top punters in the nation from 1960-62.

Carolina's ace running back, Billy Gambrell, shows the Tarheels that he has some pretty good heels of his own. He would be named All-American in 1962.

Lowndes Shingler options left as the Gamecocks begin to close in. That's Harry Pavilack waiting for the pitch.

Melvin Harris gets stopped for no gain as confused Gamecocks stumble about.

Buddy Bennett breaks up a Shingler pass to Gary Barnes. Barnes was named to the All-ACC team in '59.

1961

GAMBRELL SPARKS USC TO A BIG WIN

Warren Giese was now athletic diretor at Carolina, and in his place came his trusted assistant, Marvin "Moose" Bass, a man much admired for his warmth of personality and his self-effacing sense of humor. Indeed, one Clemson alumnus was quoted as joking, "They could have hired anyone but Marvin Bass. It's awful hard to hate a fellow like him." And he had a solid squad on hand to handle a tough schedule in '61, with backs like Billy Gambrell, Bob Anderson, Punky Holler, Carl Huggins, and Jim Costen, and such veteran linemen as John Caskey, Dave Lomas, John Jones, and Jim Moss.

Yet going into the Clemson game the Gamecocks were suffering through another of those dismal 2-5 seasons, and fans were not hopeful that they'd help themselves much when they went up against the Tigers.

Yet Clemson truly wasn't doing much better. The Tigers were 3-4 at this point, with impressive wins over Duke and Tulane. But many of their veterans were gone from the team of 1960 and it showed in several of their close defeats (their first three losses were by a total of 11 points).

It was an historical moment, November 11, 1961, the first time these two teams had ever squared off in Columbia when not surrounded by the State Fair.

The first quarter seemed to be a continuation of the 1960 sleeper with neither team able to do much against the other.

But early in the second quarter Clemson was on the move when little Tommy Pilcher intercepted a Jim Parker pass and returned it to the Tiger 42. Bill Gambrell, Carolina's peerless running back, was then called on to carry the mail, and after five attempts, he finally vaulted into the end zone. Dean Findley kicked the point and Carolina was up 7-0. (Note: Gambrell finished the day with 133 yards rushing.)

But Clemson came right back. Starting from their own 34, behind Parker's passing and the running of Elmo Lam and Bill McGuirt, they scored with only moments remaining on the clock when McGuirt went in from the two. Lon Armstrong kicked the point and the game was tied 7-7.

Early in the third quarter Clemson struck again. This time their drive started at their own 12. Behind the running of McGuirt, Lam and Harry Pavilack, the Tigers scored again, Lam taking it in from the three. Armstrong kicked the point and Clemson led 14-7.

But the Gamecocks still were not dead. Taking the ball at their own 48, Jim Costen threw to Billy Gambrell down to the Clemson 43. Then again Costen threw to Gambrell, this time to the Clemson 25. Then Dickie Day ran it down to the 15. And on the next play it was Day again, this time for 14 yards, down to the one. Jimmy Costen took in in from there on a sneak.

But on the kick attempt Calvin West broke through and blocked Armstrong's attempt, and the Tigers kept the lead at 14-13. At that point there were only ten minutes left in the game.

The Tigers began another march with the ensuing kickoff, and Carolina's hopes began to dim. But then Gambrell leaped high in the air to intercept a Parker pass and returned it to the Clemson 36. Dickie Day ran the ball on three consecutive plays. Then, on a quick opener, he was hit and the ball squirted from his hands. But luckily for the Gamecocks, Jimmy Costen plucked the loose ball out of the air at the 24 and set sail down the right sideline. No one touched him as he crossed the goal line. Then Gambrell ran it in for the 2-point conversion and USC led 21-14. And that was the final score.

Marvin Bass finished his first year at Carolina with a 4-6 record, but with a big win over Clemson. The Tigers, on the other hand, finished with a 5-5 record, the first time in seven years that Frank Howard had not had a winning season.

The personable Marvin Bass who became head coach of the Gamecocks in 1961. He beat Clemson his first year at the helm.

The Carolina Gamecocks of 1961.

Jim Costen, an All-State quarterback, signed with the Washington Red Skins.

Billy Gambrell, All-ACC.

John Caskey, All-ACC.

Note: Jim Moss, All-ACC, Lineman of the Year in South Carolina, and winner of the Jacobs Blocking Trophy.

Clemson co-captains, Calvin West and Ron Andreo.

Joe Anderson, Clemson's starting quarterback in both '61 and '62.

Harry Pavilack goes for yardage in Clemson's 27-0 romp over UNC.

Frank Howard and his main pals, Peahead Walker and Bill McLellan.

Ron Scrudato bulls over a Tulane lineman as Clemson went on to win 21-6.

Dave Sowell attempts to hurdle the LSU line as Carolina fell 42-0.

Jimmy Costen on a rollout. He threw two TD strikes against the Tigers today.

Tommy Pilcher intercepted this Parker pass, setting up USC's first TD of the afternoon.

Punky Holler just misses nabbing this Anderson pass to Mack Matthews.

1962

CLEMSON WINS A THRILLER, 20-17

In 1962 the Carolina-Clemson clash was moved to the final game of the season for both teams, and it has remained there ever since, restoring a sense of importance to the game it seemed to lack in both '60 and '61. And it was definitely important to both teams in '62, for neither came into this contest with a record to boast about. Clemson was 5-4 as November 24 rolled around, and Carolina 4-4-1.

Yet, despite their unenviable records, both teams were starting players who are still remembered as some of their finest in years.

In Carolina's backfield this year were two of their all-time greats, Dan Reeves and Billy Gambrell. Clemson answered with the presence of Jim Parker and Hal Davis.

Some 46,000 fans crammed into Death Valley this afternoon as the Gamecocks made an early mistake that cost them dearly. Jack McCathern punted for USC and the ball came down at the Carolina 41, then rolled around while USC players, assuming the ball was dead, just stood around watching. At that point, Clemson center Ted Bunton calmly picked up the loose ball and took off down the sideline. Only a last gasp tackle from McCathern saved a TD at that point, but still Clemson was in great field position. Three plays later Charlie Dumas went in for the score. Rodney Rogers kicked the point and Clemson went up 7-0.

But the Gamecocks came back. Only two minutes later, from the Tiger 45, Dan Reeves threw a perfect strike to Sammy Anderson who went into the end zone untouched. Dean Findley kicked the point and the score was tied 7-7.

Now, with only about eight minutes elapsed in the first quarter, Clemson was again on the march. Facing a fourth down at the Carolina eight, Rogers came in and booted a field goal, and the Tigers' lead became 10-7.

The second period was just as exciting as the first. Now it was Carolina's turn. Starting from their own 35, Reeves hit Sam Humphreys with a pass, then came Marty Rosen with a sparkling run to put the ball at the Tiger 34. Then it was Reeves and Pete DiVenere teaming up for yardage down to the Clemson 19. At that point Findley came in and kicked a field goal and again the teams were tied 10-10.

Following an exchange of punts, Carolina took the ball at their own 20 and began an 80 yard march that would result in another USC score when Reeves took it in from three yards out. The point was good, and now Carolina took the lead 17-10.

In the third quarter, following a TD pass from Reeves to Sammy Anderson which was nullified by a penalty (to the great

relief of the Tiger faithful), there then ensued an exchange of punts. Clemson took the ball at their own 22. Eleven plays later, from the USC 14, Parker ran it down to the six, then lateralled back to Elmo Lam who ran it in for the score. Rogers kicked the point, and again the score was tied, 17-17.

In the fourth quarter Clemson again began to use their terrific ground game to batter the Gamecocks. With the ball at the USC 15, Parker again optioned to Lam who went down to the four. But a great goal line stand by the Gamecocks stymied the Tigers and they had to settle for another Rogers' field goal. Score: Clemson 20, Carolina 17.

In the final moments of the game the excitement was still at fever pitch. Facing a fourth down at the Clemson 20, Reeves went back to try one more pass, but Tracy Childers sacked Reeves, and that was the ball game, one of the finest in recent memory.

Thus Clemson finished the season with a 6-4 record, Carolina with a 4-5-1 record.

(Mack Matthews averaged 24 yards per punt return for the Tigers in '62, an all-time CU record.)

Billy Gambrell, ACC Player of the Year in '62, AP All-American, winner of the MVP award in the Blue-Gray game, and a member of the USC Athletic Hall of Fame. He enjoyed a long pro career with the St. Louis Cardinals.

Coleman Glaze, end.

Joe Anderson, quarterback.

Oscar Thorsland, end.

Rodney Rogers, place kicker.

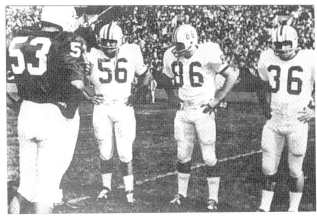

Tri-captains for the '62 Gamecocks, Dick Lomas (#56), John Caskey (#86) and Dick Day (#36), await the coin toss just before USC lost to Northwestern 37-20.

Don Chuy, All-ACC in '62, played six years with the Los Angeles Rams. He is a member of the Clemson All-Time Football Team.

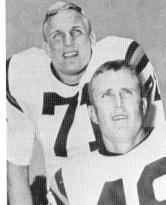

Clemson captain Dave Hynes and alternate captain Elmo Lam. Note: in '61 Elmo Lam averaged 22.4 yards per punt return, number-two in the CU record book.

The Clemson Tigers of 1962 would have a winning 6-4 season and finish second in the ACC.

John Caskey, captain of the '62 Gamecocks and an All-ACC end.

Jim Moss, All-ACC and winner of the Jacobs Blocking Trophy.

Ken Lester, All-ACC end.

Dan Reeves, All-ACC quarterback, and one of USC's finest football players ever.

Rodney Rogers kicked two field goals in Clemson's 20-17 win over Carolina in '62. His kicks beat both USC and Maryland that year.

Dan Reeves demonstrates the poise under fire that made him great as USC falls to Duke 21-8 in 1962.

Tracy Childers sacked Dan Reeves on the final play of the game to preserve Clemson's win.

Halfback Hal Davis sparked Clemson's final drive for a score as they edged out the Gamecocks 20-17 in '62.

1963

ASSASSINATION OF JFK POSTPONES GAME

The Carolina-Clemson game of 1963 had originally been scheduled to be played on November 23, and to be broadcast *live* on national TV. Well, somebody would choose just that weekend to assassinate the president of the United States. Officials from the two schools, not exactly hotbeds of political liberalism, initially announced that the game would go off as scheduled. But pressure from the federal government forced them to go into mourning, and thus the game was postponed until November 28 (Thanksgiving Day), and there would be no TV.

Perhaps it was just as well, since the Tigers and Gamecocks of '63 weren't enjoying the best of seasons. Clemson came into this game with a dismal 4-4-1 record, while poor Carolina was 1-7-1 at that point. (Following their win over Maryland on September 28, 1963 the Gamecocks would not win

Frank Howard with son Jimmy in the background. Jimmy's TD gave Clemson a 7-0 lead over Carolina in '63.

again until they upset The Citadel on November 7, 1964, a string of 15 non-wins, their longest in history.)

Only some 37,000 fans showed up for the game, possibly a result of its being played on Thanksgiving Day, or maybe a result of Carolina's poor showing to date. But those who came were in for a treat.

Midway the first quarter USC's Marty Rosen fumbled and Johnny Case recovered for Clemson at the Carolina 25. After three runs by Bob Swift, the Tigers were at the USC seven. At that point Jimmy Howard, Coach Howard's son, took a handoff and ran it in for the score. Frank Pearce kicked the point and the Tigers took the lead 7-0.

To open the second period the Gamecocks came storming back 52 yards for a score. Dan Reeves hit J. R. Wilburn with a pass down to the Clemson 38. Then a nine yard run from Rosen, plus a 15-yard penalty, put the ball at the 14. Reeves then passed to Billy Nies for the TD, Jack McCathern kicked the point, and the score was tied 7-7.

Minutes later Clemson quarterback Tommy Ray bobbled the ball and USC's Joe Prehodka recovered at the Tigers' 34. Carl Huggins ran it down to the ten. Then Jim Rogers found Charlie Williams in the end zone, and the Gamecocks were again on the board. The kick was good, and Carolina now led 14-7.

In the third period Wayne Bell intercepted a Dan Reeves' pass at the Clemson 30 and the Tigers began a 70-yard march from there, Mack Matthews accounting for 14 yards, Pat Crain 24, and Hugh Mauldin 17, including his run of seven yards for a TD. the kick was good, and now the score was tied 14-14.

Minutes later Clemson stopped Carolina at the USC 43. But three plays netted the Tigers nothing. Thus, facing a fourth down at the USC 18, Pearce came in and booted a field goal, and Clemson took the lead 17-14.

On the next drive the Gamecocks were again stopped on fourth down, this time at their own 48. Tommy Ray then passed to Meadowcroft for 13 yards. Matthews and Hal Davis ran it to the 22. Then came a 15-yard penalty against Carolina and the Tigers were again knocking at the door. Hal Davis took it in three plays later, the kick was good, and now Clemson led 24-14.

With time running out, Reeves led the Gamecocks on a desperate 42-yard drive. He passed to Wilburn for 17 yards, then to Ronnie Lamb for another 21, down to the Clemson four. Then he hit Marty Rosen in the end zone for the TD. Their two-point attempt failed, and now Clemson's lead was cut to 24-20, which was the final score.

Carl Huggins streaks 64 yards for a TD in USC's 20-19 loss to Wake Forest.

Marty Rosen breaks through for a TD in USC's 21-13 win over Maryland, their lone win of the '63 season.

Fleet Jim Parker looks awfully lonely out there as he carries the ball in the Tigers' 36-0 win over Wake Forest.

A trio of NC State tacklers struggle to bring down Hugh Mauldin.

Jim Parker and Tracy Childers, co-captains of the '63 Clemson Tigers.

Frank Pearce is true with this field goal in Clemson's win over UNC in '63.

M. D. Hathaway is greeted by an irate Tiger just before half time with USC holding a surprising 14-7 lead.

Doug Senter and Billy Nies go up for this Dan Reeves pass while a trio of Tigers ponder just who they should nail.

With Marty Rosen and Carl Huggins leading the way, Dan Reeves rolls out for a first down. He threw two TD passes in this game, but they weren't enough as Carolina fell to Clemson 24-20.

Hal Davis lunges into the USC end zone from six yards out to clinch Clemson's win over Carolina in '63.

1964

JIM ROGERS SAVES THE DAY FOR USC

Carolina had not won a game now since they beat Maryland back on September 28, 1963, a string of some 15 games without a win. But finally they beat The Citadel on November 7, 1964, and it was hoped that the jinx was broken. And apparently it was, for the very next week they played like world champions in beating Wake Forest 23-13. The bad news was that Carolina's All-American quarterback, Dan Reeves, had been injured against the Deacons and now he could hardly walk on his badly twisted ankle.

Still, they were ready for the Tigers!

And it was probably a good time, since this year's edition of the Tigers presented Frank Howard with the only losing season he'd had over the past eleven years. Indeed, they'd beaten Furman, Wake Forest and Virginia in '64 but that was it.

But now they were ready for the Gamecocks!

Of course the game was to be played at Death Valley and Tiger fans hoped that would give their team just the edge they needed.

Only minutes into the first quarter Clemson's Don Barfield punted down to the Carolina one. Ted Bunton downed the ball there and the Gamecocks took over. But four plays later Jack

McCathern, punting from his own end zone, kicked out at the USC 39. After nine plays, with Pat Crain and Hal Davis getting most of the yardage, Clemson was facing fourth down at the USC eight. Frank Pearce then came in and kicked a field goal to give Clemson the edge, 3-0.

Later, in the second quarter, Clemson again faced fourth down at the USC eight. But this time they went for it, were short by inches, and so Carolina dodged the bullet.

By midway the third period, with Reeves hobbling around on his injured ankle, the Gamecocks really had mounted no drives at all. But this time, with Carl Huggins and Marty Rosen getting the calls, they managed to move to the Clemson seven. On fourth down Reeves tried a sneak for the yardage but was stopped short.

It was in the fourth period that Clemson made their most threatening move of the entire game. They had a third and goal at the USC one-foot line. First USC stopped Jimmy Bell on a sneak, then on fourth down they popped Pat Crain who fumbled the ball. The Gamecocks took over at the seven.

Still, time was running short and Carolina was 93 yards away from a TD. It was no place for the faint of heart.

Tri-captains for the '64 Gamecocks, Pete DiVenere, Steve Cox, and Jim Johnson, huddle around Coach Marvin Bass.

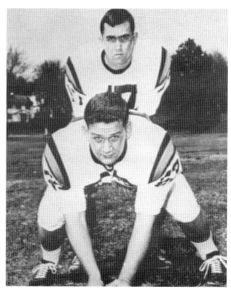

Clemson captain Ted Bunton and alternate captain Jimmy Bell.

Then a personal foul penalty moved the ball to the 24. Next a pass interference call moved it to the 36. The injured Dan Reeves left the game at this point and in his place came Jim Rogers. On first down Rogers threw long for J. R. Wilburn and this Gamecock speedster grabbed the ball and took it down to the Clemson 15, a play that covered 49 yards.

Two plays later Rogers again tried to pass, but he was chased out of the pocket by five furious Tiger linemen. He ran to the outside, looked downfield and realized that he was all alone, not an orange jersey between him and the goal line. He dashed in, and suddenly the Gamecocks were on the board. Jack McCathern kicked the point and Carolina led 7-3. And that was how this 62nd game between Carolina and Clemson ended.

Carolina finished the year with a 3-5-2 record, Clemson with a 3-7 record. It was the first time since 1954 that USC had finished with a better record than Clemson.

In addition to being a devastating running back, Kit Jackson set an all-time Clemson record with three interceptions vs. Wake Forest in '65.

Hugh Mauldin runs for yardage as Clemson falls to NC State 9-0 in '64.

Pat Crain, one of the toughest runners in the country, charges through an opening as Clemson lost to UNC 29-0 in '64.

Frank Liberatore breaks into the Deacon secondary as the Tigers beat Wake Forest 21-2 in '64.

Dan Reeves, an All-American for USC and later a great pro player and coach. He is a member of the USC Athletic Hall of Fame.

All-American Bobby Bryant returned this punt 49 yards as USC tied Georgia 7-7 in '64.

An alert Boy Scout helps Marty Rosen across the street following USC's 17-14 win over The Citadel.

Marty Rosen breaks into the Maryland seconday. He would play for the Winnipeg Blue Bombers.

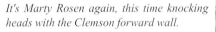

It's Marty Rosen again, this time knocking heads with the Clemson forward wall.

1965

CAROLINA AND CLEMSON PLAY FOR ACC CROWN

In 1965 the NCAA passed the Unlimited Substitution rule, the most significant rule change in the history of college football. Thanks to this rule players would no longer be expected to play for sixty minutes but could now specialize in either offense or defense, and they could rest when their team wasn't on the field. Thus, 1965 truly marks the beginning of the Modern Era in college football.

This year, for the first time ever, Carolina and Clemson found themselves playing for a conference championship. The Tigers at this point were 4-2 in the ACC, after recently being upset by both UNC and Maryland, so they had to beat Carolina today to become co-champions of the ACC.

As for USC, for several years the conference doormat, they were enjoying a 3-2 conference record, having lost only to Duke and Maryland. But for Carolina, there was a catch: in order to share in the ACC championship (along with Duke) they had to beat Clemson today, while UNC had to lose to Duke. It was a long shot at best. But after 73 years of being a bridesmaid, the Gamecocks were happy to have any shot at all.

It was a beautiful day for a game, with the temperature at 64-degrees, as 46,000 fans crammed into Carolina Stadium for this contest.

Early in the first quarter, following a USC fumble, the Tigers began a drive, with Phil Rogers, Bo Ruffner, Hugh Mauldin and Tommy Ray leading the way. Then on a fourth down at the USC four, Frank Pearce came in and booted a field goal and the Tigers went up 3-0.

Following several exciting runs by USC's Benny Galloway and Mike Fair that led nowhere, the first quarter ended.

In the second quarter USC was forced to punt from their own end zone and Clemson took over at the USC 45. After several runs by Mauldin and Ray, the Tigers faced a fourth and

two at the USC 25. Phil Rogers took a pitchout and ran the distance for the game's first TD. Pearce's kick gave Clemson a 10-0 lead, and Carolina's chances for a conference crown began to dim.

Following the ensuing kickoff, facing a third and 12 from their own 25-yard line, Mike Fair dodged the hard rushing Tiger linemen and heaved a long pass downfield to J. R. Wilburn who had gotten behind the Clemson defense. Wilburn snagged the ball and ran it down to the Tiger 25. From there, following runs by Phil Branson and Galloway, Jule Smith took it in from four yards out and the Gamecocks were on the board. Jimmy Poole kicked the point, cutting Clemson's lead to 10-7.

Later, Clemson was forced to punt and USC had the ball at the Tiger 41. A face mask penalty then moved the ball down to the Tiger 26. Four plays later Poole came in and booted a field goal and the score was tied 10-10.

Following another exchange of punts, Carolina began to move once again. Following pass completions from Fair to Wilburn and Smith, the Gamecocks were again knocking on the door at the Clemson eight. Branson ran to the seven, then Fair pitched out to Bob Harris who went in for the TD. Poole's kick made it 17-10 Carolina's favor.

Clemson then mounted two great drives but were turned away because of turnovers.

But finally, with time running out, Tommy Ray led the

Mike Fair looks downfield for J. R. Wilburn as USC lost a close one to Tennessee in '65.

Jim Rogers who scored Carolina's TD in their 7-3 win over Clemson in '64, runs for a first down here vs. Tennessee.

Tigers on one last attempt to win the game. Starting at their own 44, behind the passing of Ray to Ed McGee and Phil Rogers, Clemson was at the USC 24. Facing a fourth down at that point, Ray passed to Rogers down to the USC eight, and a first down. Then, facing a fourth down from the USC one, Ray tossed a pass to Rogers in the end zone and now Clemson trailed by one point, 17-16. They had to go for two.

The Tigers lined up as though to kick, but the ball was snapped to Jimmy Addison who threw to Ruffner in the end zone. But Bob Gunnels batted the ball away and Carolina walked away with a big 17-16 win.

Carolina thus shared the ACC championship with Duke in '65, at least for a few months. Then they were stripped of their crown because of recruiting violations and forced to forfeit their win over Clemson. Frank Howard, however, refused to accept the forfeit, saying, "As far as I'm concerned the score was 17-16. That's the way it'll stay."

John Boyette and Bill Hecht, co-captains of the '65 Tigers. Both were named All-ACC.

Hugh Mauldin, an All-ACC running back, is led by Mike Facciolo as he goes for a first down in Clemson's 3-0 win over TCU.

Ben Garnto took a pitchout at his own 6-yard line, then dashed 89 yards down to the Wake Forest five. This remains the longest non-scoring run from scrimmage in the USC record book. (It is also the second longest run from scrimmage in the USC record book.)

Jimmy Addison follows Tom Duley for an 18-yard pickup as Clemson defeated Virginia 20-14.

Frank Pearce, Clemson's ace place kicker for three years, 1963-65, boots a long one to give the Tigers a 3-0 win over TCU.

J. R. Wilburn took this pass down to the Clemson 25, a gain of 50 yards on the play before being rolled out of bounds. Wilburn was named Athlete of the Year in South Carolina in 1965.

Phil Branson breaks into the Clemson secondary only to be met by a big Tiger.

Tommy Ray can hardly see the forest for the trees.

Tom Duley stumbles through a hole in the Carolina line.

Tommy Ray completed 21 passes for 323 yards vs. UNC in '65, still an all-time Clemson passing records.

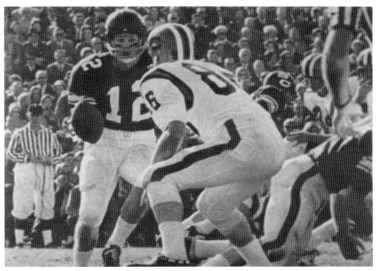

Mike Fair and Butch Sursavage have a brief confrontation in this game won by Carolina 17-16, giving them a share of the ACC crown in '65.

1966

CLEMSON UPENDS USC AND WINS ACC CROWN

Gone now after five years and a poor 17-29-4 record was Marvin Bass, the personable fellow loved by his players and fans alike. In his place came his opposite, Paul Dietzel, an aloof perfectionist who rarely rubbed elbows with the guys down on the field. But Dietzel had fashioned a national championship team at LSU back in '58, and had spent several years at West Point as successor to Army's Red Blaik, and USC thought he would be just the man to turn their dismal football fortunes around. Well, maybe he would be somewhere down the road, but he certainly didn't prove it in 1966 as the Gamecocks suffered through a disastrous 1-9 season, their worst in history.

As for the Tigers, Jimmy Addison was now playing quarterback and he had an experienced crew backing him up, on both offense and defense. Indeed, Clemson had lost to the biggies on their schedule, Georgia Tech, Alabama, and Southern Cal, but they had beaten all their ACC foes and appeared headed for another bowl game-- until they were upset by NC State in the ninth game of the season (NC State was the only team that Carolina beat all season!).

Still, a win over Carolina today would give them a 6-1 conference record and clear claim to their fourth ACC title.

Clemson took the opening kickoff and proved that they wanted that ACC title. From their own 28, behind the running of Buddy Gore and the passing of Jimmy Addison, they moved the ball all the way to the Carolina four, but a Tiger fumble then killed a terrific drive.

But two plays later the Gamecocks fumbled at their own 22 and Clemson recovered. Gore ran three times, putting the ball at the nine. Then Jacky Jackson scored from there, Don Barfield kicked the point, and Clemson led 7-0.

The Gamecocks then came back with an excellent 65-yard march of their own. After Bobby Bryant returned the kickoff 31 yards to the USC 45, Ben Garnto and Benny Galloway alternated runs down to the Clemson three. Mike Fair ran it in from there, Jimmy Poole's kick was good, and the score was tied 7-7.

Following an exchange of punts, Carolina moved 72 yards for another score. On one play Galloway dashed 36 yards on an end sweep, down to the Clemson 26, the most exciting play of the drive. Then Garnto went for 14 yards, down to the Tiger 12. But then, facing fourth down at the five, Jimmy Poole came in and booted a field goal to put USC up 10-7.

With only 2:19 left in the half Clemson moved once again. With Addison throwing to Phil Rogers, the Tigers suddenly found themselves at the USC 10. Two plays later Jackie Jackson ran it in from the three, Don Barfield's kick was good, and Clemson led 14-10 as the teams headed for the dressing rooms.

In the second half, following an exchange of punts, Clemson took over at the USC 49. On first down, Addison found Rogers

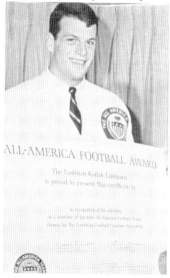

Wayne Mass was named to the All-American Team in '66. He is a member of the CU Athletic Hall of Fame.

Coach Frank Howard gained his 150th victory with a 27-3 win over UNC in '66.

Jimmy "The Needle" Addison averaged 149 passing yards per game in '66, an all-time clemson record.

all alone and fired a perfect strike to him, which Rogers took all the way for another TD. Again Barfield's kick was good, and Clemson led 21-10.

By now both Ben Garnto and Mike Fair were out of the game with injuries, and their absence was beginning to tell.

Late in the third quarter Ronnie Ducworth, a tough Tiger end, recovered a Carolina fumble at the USC 12. On first down Addison fumbled. But his alert teammate, Harry Olszewski, grabbed it and went all the way for another Tiger TD. Arthur Craig kicked the point and Clemson led 28-10. (No Clemson offensive lineman has scored a TD since Olszewski did it in 1966.)

As the clock wound down Clemson mounted one more march, this one of 81 yards. Jackson had a great run of 48 yards in this drive, and finally Addison passed to Edgar McGee for the score, Craig kicked the point, and Clemson won the game 35-10.

Buddy Gore had 130 yards rushing on the day, which gave him the ACC rushing title for '66.

Benny Galloway had 105 yards rushing for the Gamecocks.

This was Coach Howard's 151st win and it gave Clemson the ACC championship, Howard's fourth such title.

Clemson's All-Star cast for 1966. Standing: Wayne Page, Jimmy Catoe, Butch Sursavage, Wayne Mass, Buddy Gore. Front: Wayne Bell, Jimmy Addison, Harry Olszewski. (Olszewski is a member of both the Clemson Athletic Hall of Fame and the All-Time Football Team.)

Phil Rogers in action vs. Maryland. Rogers caught 11 passes vs. UNC in '65, an all-time CU record.

Billy Ammons blocks for Jacky Jackson.

Harry Olszewski clears the way for Buddy Gore in Clemson's 14-10 win over Maryland. (Clemson's Olszewsik and USC's Mike Fair became roommates while playing for the San Francisco '49ers. Fair would joke: "The toughest thing about making it with the '49ers was learning to spell Harry's last name.")

USC coach, Paul Dietzel, would compile a 42-43-1 record during his nine years at Carolina.

Bobby Bryant, captain of the '66 Gamecocks, returned a punt 98 yards for a TD vs. NC State in '66, an all-time USC record. He was named All-American, then went on to enjoy a remarkable 14-year pro career with the Minnesota Vikings, playing in four Super Bowls. He is a member of the USC Athletic Hall of Fame and the All-Time USC Football Team.

Ben Garnto scores from 35 yards out with this Mike Fair pass vs. Memphis State.

Harry Olszewski scores from 14 yards out with a fumble recovery to put Clemson up 28-10 over Carolina. He remains the last Clemson offensive lineman to score a TD.

Mac McElmurray forces Benny Gallowy to cough up the ball deep in Carolina territory.

Ben Garnto slices through the Tiger line for a first down. Garnto's 89-yard non-scoring run vs. Wake Forest is the longest such run in USC history.

1967

BUDDY GORE RIPS THE GAMECOCKS

It was a bright sunshiny day in Columbia, November 25, 1967, as over 43,000 fans streamed into Carolina Stadium to watch this 65th meeting between the Clemson Tigers and the Carolina Gamecocks.

The Gamecocks, led by Mike Fair and a sensational sophomore running back named Warren Muir, a transfer from West Point, were 5-4 at this point in the season, which was a marked improvement over their record of 1-8 this time last year. Indeed, for the first time in recent memory, they had already beaten both UNC and Duke during the same season.

As for Clemson, Jimmy Addison was back at quarterback, plus there was Buddy Gore, their record-setting junior running back who was just a few yards away from breaking every rushing record in the ACC record book. Indeed, the Tigers were 5-4 overall at this point, but 5-0 in the ACC and seeking another conference crown, one they were determined to get this very afternoon.

The first quarter was scoreless, but early in the second, with the Gamecocks threatening, Kit Jackson intercepted a Mike Fair pass and returned it to the Clemson 35. Three plays later they were facing fourth down at the USC 23. At that point Art Craig kicked a field goal and the Tigers were up 3-0.

Seven minutes later Clemson was again on a scoring march. Taking the ball at the USC 43, the Tigers ran 11 plays, with Gore carrrying on six of those, until they reached the two. Gore took a pitchout and went in for a TD, Craig kicked the point, and Clemson's lead went to 10-0.

The third quarter was pretty much a repeat of the second, with USC turnovers squelching any drives that amounted to anything. Midway the third, Clemson took the ball at their own 34. Gore was called on to run the ball on the next four plays, then on his fifth carry, he dashed 43 yards, down to the USC 13. Addison then threw to Ed McGee for the TD, Craig's kick was good, and Clemson led 17-0.

Pat Watson fumbled the kickoff. Ronnie Ducworth caught the ball in midair and returned it to the USC 26. Three plays later Addison bootlegged the ball around right end and went into the end zone for another Tiger score. Craig's kick was wide, so Clemson's lead became 23-0.

Two series later, Sammy Cain went back to punt for Clemson, but the ball sailed over his head. USC's Dave Lucas recovered at the Clemson 12. Five plays later, Mike Fair sneaked in for the TD from the one, but his attempted two-point conversion failed, and Clemson now led 23-6.

On the next series, the never-say-die Gamecocks were back in business when Pat Watson recovered an on-sides kick at the Clemson 48. Fair then threw a 33-yard pass to Freddy Zeigler, down to the Clemson 15. Three plays later Fair again sneaked in for a TD, and again his try for the two-point conversion failed, and Clemson's lead was cut to 23-12. And that is how the game ended.

Carolina concluded their season with a 5-5 record, while Clemson finished at 6-4 and another ACC championship, Coach Howard's fifth.

As for Buddy Gore, he rushed for 189 yards in today's game, a total of 1,045 for the season. Not only did this break an all-time Clemson single-season rushing record, it also broke the all-time ACC record set by Wake Forest's Brian Piccolo in 1964.

With time running out USC trailed Duke 17-14. Big Warren Muir then came in at fullback. Here he runs 14 yards for the TD that gave the Gamecocks a 21-17 upset win. In '69 he would be named All-American.

Buddy Gore, ACC Player of the Year in '67. He ran for 2,571 yards during his career with the Tigers, still Number-Three in the CU record book.

Pat Watson nails Kenny Stabler as USC fell to Alabama 17-0 in '67. Watson was named All-ACC in '69.

Ronnie Ducworth was named All-ACC in both '67 and '68, and served as Team Captain in '68. Here he lays the wood to a Duke runner foolish enough to try to run his end.

Frank Liberatore, All-ACC, drafted by the Washington Redskins.

Jacky Jackson, drafted by the Cleveland Browns.

Wayne Mass, All-American, drafted by the Chicago Bears.

Harry Olszewski, All-American and a member of the CU All-Time Football Team.

Phil Rogers is just one of three Tiger players ever to have over 100 career receptions.

Captains Don Somma and Jimmy Addison shake hands just before the big game.

Led by Buddy Gore who ran for 189 yards, the Tigers were too much for USC in '67. Here Gore runs for a big first down.

Mike Chavous took this Mike Fair pass for a 22 yard gain against Clemson.

Freddy Zeigler who would break all reception records at USC, takes this one for a first down versus the Tigers. Zeigler had twelve receptions for 199 yards and three TDs vs. Virginia in '68, all-time USC reception records.

It's Gore again, this time breaking into the USC secondary as he adds more yardage to his 189 total on the day.

After three years of leading the Gamecocks, Mike Fair climaxed his career with a great game against Clemson. He completed 12 passes, led his team in rushing yardage, and scored both USC touchdowns. Not a bad effort.

1968

TYLER HELLAMS TAMES THE TIGERS

It was November 23, 1968, a cool fall afternoon at Clemson's beautiful Memorial Stadium, as the Tigers prepared to go out and do what everyone expected them to do--smash the poor underdog Gamecocks. Indeed, a win today would give the Tigers, who were now 4-0-1 in the ACC, the conference championship and a chance at a nice bowl bid.

After all, Carolina was only 3-6 coming into today's game, with wins over UNC, Virginia and Wake Forest. They would be going nowhere come New Years Day.

And the Tigers had a veteran crew on hand to get the job done, guys like Joe Lhotski, Ivan Sutherland, Ronnie Ducworth, Richie Luzzi, Buddy Gore, and Sammy Cain.

At Carolina, in addition to their super fullback, Warren Muir, they now were starting Tommy Suggs at quarterback. Over the next three years, aided and abetted by such receivers as Freddy Zeigler and Rudy Holloman, Suggs would break every passing record at the University.

Some 53,000 fans crowded into Memorial Stadium for this contest, the largest turnout for any game ever played in the ACC.

Once the game got underway Jack Anderson quickly brought Clemson fans to their feet when he took the opening kickoff at his own goal line and then dashed 72 yards, down to the USC 28, where a last-gasp tackle by Tyler Hellams saved a sure touchdown. From there the Tigers drove to the USC five before they stalled. Jimmy Barnette then came in and kicked a field goal, and the Tigers were up 3-0. And there were still another 58 minutes left to play.

But from there on, it was all Gamecocks on offense. By the time the half ended, Clemson had stopped USC on their one, their two, their 11, their 13, their 18, and their 22. Pass interceptions, two by Bob Craig and two by John Fulmer, accounted for four of those stops.

(Later USC's Tommy Suggs would joke: "I was credited with making four solo tackles in the first half alone, which is pretty unusual for a quarterback.")

And thus things rocked along until midway the third quarter. At that point Clemson was forced to punt, and waiting to receive that kick was Tyler Hellams, standing at his own 27 yard line. Hellams made the catch, started up the middle of the field, then cut to the right sideline, dodged punter Sammy Cain, and didn't pause until he'd crossed the Clemson goal line, a TD run of 73 yards. The try for the extra point was good, and Carolina led 7-3. Which is how the game ended.

Nor was Carolina's win any fluke. They had 23 first downs to Clemson's six, they led in rushing yardage 185 yards to 100 yards (Buddy Gore ran for 92 of those); and in passing USC led 213 yards to 56 yards.

As a result of today's loss Clemson was denied their third straight conference title. The ACC crown now went to NC State.

Tommy Suggs fakes to Rudy Holloman, then bootlegs the ball as USC loses to Maryland 21-19.

Bob Mauro's face tells the story as he watches USC lose to the Terps. He would win the team MVP award in '68 and play in the Blue-Gray game.

Benny Galloway sprints down the sideline for USC's fourth TD of the day as the Gamecocks lost to Florida State 35-28.

Paul Dietzel confers with Tommy Suggs as USC fell to Duke 14-7. Suggs, a giant on the football field, stood 5-8 and weighed 155. He and receiver Fred Zeigler became the most effective passing duo in the history of USC.

Ronnie Ducworth and Jimmy Catoe would be named All-ACC in both '67 and '68.

Benny Padgett returns this interception for big yardage as USC upset Virginia 49-28. Tommy Suggs threw five TD passes in this game, a new USC record.

Joe Lhotski and Buddy Gore. Both were All-ACC, and Lhotski won the Jacobs Blocking Trophy. As for Gore, it is said that no other running back dominated the ACC during the 1960s the way Buddy Gore did.

Wayne Mulligan and John Cagle would both be named All-ACC in '68.

Rich Luzzi returned this missed field goal 108 yards for a TD vs. Georgia in '68. This remains the longest TD run in Clemson football history.

Rich Luzzi.

Linebacker Al Usher runs for good yardage with Buddy Gore's head in this shot. Usher's 59-yard non-scoring interception return vs. Georgia Tech in '70 remains an all-time USC record.

Howard's Rock, a gift from CU alumnus S. C. Jones.

Obviously a bird of humble origins, Cocky first appeared in '68.

It was midway through the third quarter and Clemson's 3-0 lead was looking bigger and bigger when Tyler Hellams took this Sammy Cain punt at his own 27. He started up the middle of the field, then cut to the right sideline. He didn't stop until he'd crossed Clemson's goal line some 73 yards away, giving USC a 7-3 win in '68. Hellams also stopped two big Clemson drives with pass interceptions in this contest.

1969

USC BEATS CLEMSON AND WINS ACC TITLE

For thirty years now Frank Howard had been the head coach of the Clemson Tigers. But 1969 would mark his final year in that position. He had become a legend not only in South Carolina but throughout the football world, and even Clemson's greatest enemies hoped that he would go out a winner. Such, unfortunately, was not to be as Clemson would finish the year with a disappointing 4-6 record, including a loss to Carolina in the final game of the season.

As for the Gamecocks, Paul Dietzel was now in his fourth year as head coach, and he had on hand one of the finest Carolina teams ever assembled, guys like Tommy Suggs, Freddy Zeigler, Warren Muir, Jim Mitchell, Tyler Hellams, Billy Ray Rice, Pat Watson, Don Buckner, Tony Fusaro, Rudy Holloman, Andy Chavous, Lynn Hodge, Dave Lucas, Billy DuPre and Dickie Harris.

In a word, the Gamecocks were loaded for bear in '69, and they would prove it as the season progressed. Indeed, they would lose only to such biggies as Georgia, Florida State, and Tennessee, while going 6-0 against all ACC opponents. Following their win over Clemson in the final game of the season, they would accept a bid to play West Virginia in the Peach Bowl, their first bowl trip since their visit to the Gator Bowl in 1945.

As for the game itself, Carolina racked up 17 points before Clemson even made a first down. The game was, in a word, a mis-match.

With six minutes gone in the first quarter, following a 73-yard drive, Rudy Holloman dashed seven yards for USC's first score. DuPre kicked the point and Carolina led 7-0.

Two minutes later, from a drive that started at their own 32, the Gamecocks scored again, this time with Warren Muir bulling in from three yards out. Again DuPre's kick was good, and USC led 14-0.

Only a minute into the second period, following a 43-yard drive, Billy DuPre kicked a 21-yard field goal and Carolina led 17-0.

Clemson still had not made a first down. But some five minutes later they got moving and drove 57 yards for their first score, Ray Yauger going in from the one. Jimmy Barnette's kick was good and USC now led 17-7.

Then, only moments later, Bill DePew blocked a Billy Parker punt. Charlie Mayer picked it up for the Tigers and ran it back to the USC 33. Tommy Kendrick then fired a 15-yard pass to Ray Yauger who weaved and dodged his way in for another Tiger TD. The kick was no good, and Carolina's lead was cut to 17-13. And thus ended the first half.

Early in the third quarter, after missing two scoring chances because of turnovers, the Gamecocks were again in business.

Starting from their own 43, USC then ran seven plays before Tommy Suggs hit Rudy Holloman with a 32-yard scoring pass. DuPre kicked the point, and USC led 24-13.

Carolina then recovered a fumble on their 31. From there they moved to the Clemson four. On fourth down DuPre kicked a field goal, and the score went to 27-13. Which was the final score.

Carolina's tremendous offense amassed 517 yards of total offense in this contest, 287 rushing and 230 passing. Warren Muir gained 127 yards rushing, while Freddy Zeigler caught nine passes for 122 yards. Rudy Holloman rushed for 65 yards, caught three passes for 71 yards, and scored twice.

Tommy Kendrick (1969-71) is still remembered as one of Clemson's greatest quarterbacks ever.

Georgia, infamous for their crude behavior, rudely push away Johnny Gregory (#88) who had rushed to the aid of his friend, Warren Muir.

George Ducworth (#88) and Charlie Mayer (#89) anchored the defensive line for the Tigers vs. Georgia Tech.

One of Clemson's most versatile athletes ever, Charlie Waters would go on to become an all-pro defensive back with the Dallas Cowboys. In '69, along with Ray Yauger and Ivan Southerland, Waters would be named All-ACC. He is a member of the CU Athletic Hall of Fame.

Frank Howard, a member of the Clemson coaching scene since 1931, head coach since 1940, decided to retire following the 1969 season. He has 165 wins to his credit along with eight conference championships. He is a member of the College Football Hall of Fame.

Ray Yauger woud be named All-ACC in both '68 and '69, and won the CU MVP Award for three consecutive years. He gained 2,439 yards during his career, still fifth best in the CU record book.

Clemson All-ACC linebacker Larry Hefner (1969-72).

USC's great All-American fullback Warren Muir takes it to the Deacons as Carolina beat Wake Forest 24-6 in '69.

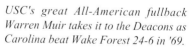

Tommy Suggs fires a pass to Freddy Zeigler in USC's 41-16 loss to Georgia. Suggs would break every passing record in the USC record book during his career with Carolina. He would win the MVP award in the '70 Blue-Gray game.

A walk-on for the Gamecocks in 1966, Fred Zeigler today remains second only to Sterling Sharpe as USC's all-time greatest receiver.

Clemson captains Charlie Tolley and Ivan Southerland meet with USC captains Pat Watson and Don Buckner just before kickoff in 1969. In '68 Pat Watson intercepted four passes vs. Wake Forest, tying an all-time USC record.

Rudy Holloman took a 32-yard Suggs' pass into the end zone, his second TD of the day, to up USC's lead to 24-13 over Clemson.

As for the Peach Bowl, USC's first appearance in a bowl game since 1945, a freezing rain had been falling for days and the entire town of Atlanta had become a quagmire by game night so that fans felt they were watching a mud wrestling contest instead of a football game. Carolina lost 14-3.

The elusive Tommy Suggs somehow breaks away from three Tiger defenders and picks his way for a first down during the big game of '69. Suggs would complete 15 passes today for 220 yards.

1970

TOMMY SUGGS LEADS USC TO VICTORY

For the first time since 1931 Clemson would see how it might feel to produce a football team without Frank Howard around to tell them how to do it. In his place had come Hootie Ingram, a former all-conference defensive back from the University of Alabama, and a Howard assistant. His first year as head coach would leave something to be desired, as the Tigers finished the season with a disappointing 3-8 record, their worst since they went 2-6-1 in 1952.

In Columbia, meanwhile, the big news concerned Coach Dietzel's plans to enlarge Carolina Stadium (over the objections of the USC faculty), and his plans to withdraw from the ACC. His logic (?) ran as follows: in order to pay for the stadium they must fill it on Saturday afternoons. In order to fill it, they must win games. In order to win games, they must have good players. In order to have good players, they must relax their entrance requirements. Which meant witdrawing from the ACC. His plans met with widespread objections from both the University and fans, but the Board of Trustees bought them and thus it was decided that 1970 would be USC's final year in the conference.

With Tommy Suggs back at quarterback, USC fans hoped the Gamecocks would pick up where they'd left off in '69, but such was not the case. Going into the final game of the season Carolina was 3-6-1, with wins over Wake Forest, VPI, UNC, and a tie with NC State.

Nor did the Tigers have much to brag about in the way of wins in '70. They were 3-7 going into the final game, with wins over The Citadel, Virginia and Maryland. But the game was being played at Death Valley, so anything might happen.

And it almost did.

Clemson entered the game as a two-touchdown underdog, but late in the first period they got on the scoreboard first when Larry Hefner intercepted a Suggs' pass and returned it 38 yards, down to the USC two-yard line. Ray Yauger took it in on the next play, Eddie Seigler kicked the point, and Clemson led 7-0.

Three minutes later Carolina came back. From the Clemson 49 USC ground out 31 yards, down to the Tiger 18. From there Suggs fired a pass to big Doug Hamrick who fought his way into the end zone. Billy DuPre kicked the point, and the game was tied.

Clemson's record-setting return man, Don Kelly, then ran back the ensuing kickoff 42 yards, down to the USC 48. A few moments later Eddie Seigler kicked a 30-yard field goal and Clemson led 10-7.

Ten minutes later, with time running out in the first half, Carolina took the ball at their own 42. Ten plays later they went back in front when Billy Ray Rice circled right end for a TD. Again DuPre's kick was good, and USC led 14-10. There was only 2:53 left on the clock at this point and fans thought they could relax.

Clemson ran three plays, then punted--which was a mistake. USC took the ball at their own 14. And Tommy Suggs

Don Kelly, an Academic All-American defensive back for Clemson, still holds most return yardage records in the ACC. Kelly ran back an interception 102 yards for a TD vs. Duke in 1970, an all-time Clemson record.

Dave Thompson, an All-American guard for Clemson and winner of the Jacobs Blocking Trophy in 1970. He played five years of pro ball with both Detroit and New Orleans.

Coach Hootie Ingram (1970-73) would complete his career with the Tigers with a 17-25-2 record.

started throwing. He completed a 27-yarder to Jim Mitchell, a 13-yarder to Haggard, then another to Haggard for 40 yards. And now USC was on the Clemson eight. DuPre came in then, as the final seconds ticked away, and kicked a field goal to put USC up 17-10.

But Clemson ran the second half kickoff back to their own 47. Tommy Kendrick fired a 21-yard pass to John McMakin, down to the USC 42. On the next play Ben Anderson broke off the right side of the line and went all the way for a touchdown. Seigler's kick tied it at 17-17.

Then it was Carolina's turn. From their own 47 they ran off six plays, including a 36-yard pass from Suggs to Billy Freeman, down to the one. Tommy Simmons smashed in from there, DuPre's kick was good, and Carolina again led 24-17.

In the fourth quarter, hoping to pad their lead, USC moved

80 yards for their next score, Suggs firing a 16 yard pass to Haggard in the end zone. DuPre's kick was good, and USC led 31-17. But still the game was not over.

On their next possession Clemson moved 55 yards in ten plays, concluding with Kendrick's eight-yard pass to Bobby Johnson for the TD. He then fired a completion to Oscar Carter for the two-pointer, and Carolina's lead was cut to 31-25.

Following the kickoff, Suggs moved the Gamecocks 60 yards in six plays, finally throwing a 35-yard TD strike to Jim Mitchell. DuPre was again true with his kick, and Carolina now led 38-25. There was 6:25 remaining on the clock.

Sure enough, Clemson bounced right back. Ray Yauger climaxed a 47-yard drive when he plunged over from one yard out for a touchdown. Seigler's kick was good, and Carolina led 38-32. And that, finally, was how the game ended, one of the most exciting in this long series.

Jim Sursavage and George Ducworth. Sursavage was captain of the '70 Tigers and an All-ACC linebacker. Ducworth was an outstanding defensive end for three years (1968-70) and the younger brother of Ronnie Ducworth.

B. B. Elvington and Jim Sursavage nail this Bulldog ball carrier in Clemson's 38-0 loss to Georgia in 1970.

It was a cold rainy day in late November when Clemson was beaten by UNC 42-7.

FUMBLE! In 1970 Clemson lost to Wake Forest by a score of 36-20.

Tommy Suggs established passing records that would stand at USC until broken by Todd Ellis. He received the team MVP award in 1970, then received the same award in the Blue-Gray game. He is a member of the South Carolina Athletic Hall of Fame.

Dickie Harris was named All-American after setting an all-time NCAA record by gaining 880 yards on 30 returns in 1970. (He also led USC in tackles in 1970.)

Billy DuPre, Carolina's ace place kicker, set field goal records that would stand for another ten years at USC. He is still remembered for his last second field goal that beat VPI in '69.

Doug Hamrick, a starter in the Blue-Gray game, takes a Suggs pass for a first down against Tennessee.

Dickie Harris off on another long jaunt in Carolina's 7-7 tie with NC State.

Tough Tommy Simmons is finally brought down by two Tigers. He would later go in for a TD to stretch Carolina's lead to 24-17.

1971

KENDRICK FIRES CLEMSON TO UPSET WIN

Over 57,000 jubilant fans turned out for the big game of 1971, the 69th annual shootout between the Carolina Gamecocks and the Clemson Tigers. Hootie Ingram's Tigers were a young team that had not lived up to expectations. They entered today's game with a mediocre 4-6 record, having lost badly to Georgia, Georgia Tech and Auburn (among others).

The Gamecocks were also a young team and especially missed their record-setting quarterback Tommy Suggs. In his place came Glenn Morris, previously untried at quarterback. Carolina's record of 6-4 (including a big win over Georgia Tech) was somewhat better than Clemson's, though they had lost to Duke, Georgia, Florida State and Tennesee--lost badly, in fact.

Still, the Gamecocks were not discouraged. This was their first year playing as an independent, and they knew that soon, just as Coach Dietzel had promised, they would become "the Notre Dame of the South."

Sports writers from throughout the state, those experts who always know about such things, said that Carolina was clearly the better team and that fans would be smart to put their money on the Gamecocks.

Well. . .

Those experts reckoned without the determined play of such Tiger defenders as Frank Wirth, Don Ethredge, Larrry Hefner and John Bolubasz. By day's end, in fact, the Tigers' defense would pick off six Carolina passes, an all-time record for this series.

The first quarter was scoreless, but only two minutes into the second Clemson drew first blood when their fine place kicker, Eddie Seigler, came in and to the amazement of everyone, calmly booted a 52-yard field goal to put the Tigers up 3-0.

Only a minute later Clemson safety Ben Anderson intercepted a Glenn Morris pass and returned it 12 yards to the USC 34. Aided by a pass interference call, Clemson found themselves on the USC 19. They scored seven plays later, Smiley Sanders taking it in from the two. Seigler's kick was good, and Clemson led 10-0 with 8:35 left in the half.

Three minutes later Bobby Johnson intercepted another Morris pass and returned it 14 yards to the Tiger 36. Clemson then moved 54 yards, including runs of 13 and 14 yards by Wade Hughes, down to the USC 10. From there Tommy Kendrick fired a pass to John McMakin in the end zone for another Tiger TD. Again Seigler's kick was good, and Clemson's lead went to 17-0.

Clemson kicked off to begin the second half, and for the next five minutes the Gamecocks played like men possessed.

Dickie Harris and Tommy Simmons were at the running back positions for USC today, and they carried the mail as Carolina moved in for a score. Simmons went over from the one, Tommy Bell kicked the point, and Clemson's lead was cut to 17-7. But that was as close as the Gamecocks could get, and thus this 69th meeting between these two teams went to the Clemson Tigers in a mild upset.

(USC's Bo Davies finished his career in '71 with 14 career interceptions, an all-time USC record.)

Cool Tommy Kendrick fires long in Clemson's 13-10 loss to Kentucky. Kendrick started 32 consecutive games for Clemson, still an all-time CU quarterback record. He completed 133 passes in 1970, yet another all-time CU record.

John McMakin nails a Duke runner as Clemson wins 3-0.

Clemson's rugged defense seems in control, but Auburn wins it in 1971 35-13.

And the Intercollegiate Good Will Award goes to. . .

USC's Dennis Ford (Offensive Lineman of the Year) and John LeHeup (Defensive Lineman of the Year). LeHeup, an All-American, is a memeber of the USC All-Time Football Team.

With the rain coming down like bullets, Chuck Mims runs for a first down in USC's 24-7 win over Georgia Tech.

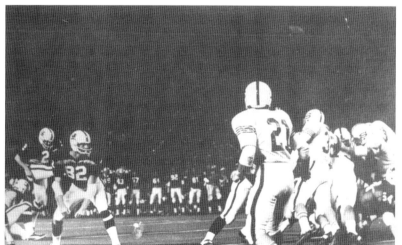

Tommy Bell boots a record 52-yard field goal in USC's 24-6 win over NC State. (This record was broken by Mark Fleetwood in 1982.)

For his career Dickie Harris returned 73 kickoffs for 1,946 yards and 77 punts for 825 yards, still all-time USC records. He is a member of USC's All-Time Football Team.

Smiley Sanders bulls his way into the end zone to boost Clemson's lead to 10-0 over the favored Gamecocks.

Tommy Simmons, the workhorse of the Gamecocks in '71, smashes in for a touchdown.

Jubilant Gamecocks celebrate the ref's signal for a TD, but it was too little too late, and the Tigers won it 17-7.

1972

WILLIAMSON SAVES THE DAY FOR CLEMSON

A freezing rain had been falling since dawn, and conditions had just gotten worse as the day wore on. In a word, it was a miserable day in the Blue Ridge, which is probably why only 45,000 fans showed up for today's big game between Carolina and Clemson. Plus there was the fact that neither team had a particularly good record in '72. Clemson was 3-7 going into today's contest, with wins over The Citadel, Virginia and Wake Forest. Nor did Carolina have much to cheer about. They were 4-6, with wins over Memphis State, Appalachian State, Wake Forest, and a big 24-21 upset win over Florida State.

Back on September 9, at halftime of the USC-Virginia game, old Carolina Stadium had its name officially changed to Williams-Brice Stadium. Which didn't seem to help the Gamecocks that much, since they still allowed themselves to be upset by Virginia 24-16.

Indeed, today was a day made more for huddling by a roaring fire than for going out of doors to watch a football game. But still some 45,000 hearty souls showed up.

The first quarter was scoreless, though USC did march from their own 33 down to the Clemson 14, but that threat ended when Jay Lynn Hodgin fumbled and the ball was nabbed by Clemson's John Price.

On their next possession USC threatened once again, but that drive ended when Jeff Siepe intercepted a Doby Grossman pass at the Clemson 21.

The second period was also scoreless, though Clemson did mount a drive into Gamecock territory. But that drive ended when Eddie Seigler's 51-yard field goal attempt fell short.

Indeed, Clemson made only three first downs in the first half, and two of those came as the result of penalties.

In the third period Wade Hughes, Clemson's leading runner in the game, was injured and was replaced by Heide Davis, who would be instrumental in their big scoring drive.

That came late in the third quarter when Clemson took the ball at their own 43-yard line. Then following Ken Pengitore's pass completions of 18 and 12 yards, the Tigers were at the USC 27. Several plays later Smiley Sanders went into the end zone from the one, and Clemson was on the board. Seigler's kick was good, and Clemson led 7-0 with only 20 seconds left in the period.

As the forth period advanced, Seigler missed on two more scoring opportunities, when his kicks sailed wide from both the 25 and 29.

There were only five minutes left on the clock when USC's backup quarterback, Bill Troup, came off the bench and led the Gamecocks on a big scoring drive. From their own 18 yard line Troup threw for 12 yards to Mike Haggard. Then on the next play he threw a screen pass to Tony Muldrow who caught the ball and streaked down the sideline all the way to the Clemson three. Hodgin took it in from there, and Clemson's lead was cut

Team captain Rick Brown moves for yardage in Carolina's 24-21 upset of Florida State.

USC quarterback Bill Troup demonstrates his ability as a hurdler as USC loses to Georgia Tech 34-6.

to 7-6. (Carolina had moved 82 yards in 36 seconds and four plays for this score.)

Then Doby Grossman came back in at quarterback and the Gamecocks were going for the two-pointer.

Grossman took the snap and rolled to his right. He spotted a receiver and threw a bullet. But Clemson's Jimmy Williamson dove for the ball, got a hand out, and batted it away.

The Gamecocks threatened twice more as the minutes ticked away, but one drive was ended with another Seipe interception of a Troop pass, and another with a failed field goal attempt. And the Tigers walked away with a tough 7-6 win on a rotten day for football.

Doby Grossman looks upfield while being pursued by a host of Yellow Jackets as USC went down 34-6.

Freshman Bobby Marino came in with 1:28 on the clock to boot this 38-yard field goal to give USC their upset win over Florida State.

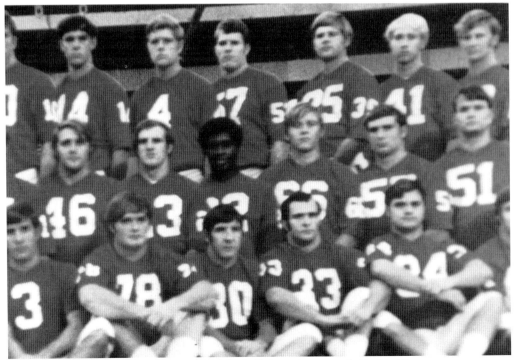

Jackie Brown, Carolina's first black football player, is surrounded by his '72 teammates.

Ken Pengitore spots a receiver as Clemson was upset 31-6 by Maryland. Eddie Seigler kicked two field goals in this game, one a 52-yarder.

Eddie Seigler adds three to Clemson's total, but it wasn't enough as the Tigers fell 29-10 to Rice.

Clemson took it on the chin from Oklahoma in '72 by a score of 52-3.

Jeff Grantz looks downfield on a cold, rainy day at Death Valley. Clemson scored seven points to Carolina's six to take this game, but everyone, winners and losers alike, seemed to be relieved that the game (and the season) was finally over.

1973

JEFF GRANTZ SPARKS USC TO BIG WIN

Gone now from the Clemson scene was Hootie Ingram, and in his place came Red Parker, a graduate of Arkansas A&M, and former head coach at The Citadel. Already the Tigers, a veteran club, were showing improvement over the past several years and were sporting a 5-5 record going into their final game of the season against Carolina.

As for the Gamecocks, the big news out of Columbia concerned USC's sensational sophomore quarterback, Jeff Grantz. Not only was he an excellent passer, he was also one of the finest runners ever to wear the garnet and black. Indeed, he had just broken USC's all-time rushing record when he ran for 260 yards in Carolina's 38-22 win over Ohio. Opponents found him truly hard to contain.

But November 24, 1973 was a beautiful day in Columbia, the opposite of the situation in '72, and over 53,000 fans turned out at Williams-Brice Stadium to watch today's contest.

The first quarter belonged to Clemson. They were some seven minutes into that period when Randy Spinks fumbled the ball and Bob Jones recovered for the Tigers at the USC 49. Several plays later Smiley Sanders went in from two yards out, but Bob Burgess' kick was wide left, and Clemson led 6-0.

Then, in the first minute of the second period, the Gamecocks drove 66 yards for a TD, Randy Chastain scoring from two yards out. Bobby Marino kicked the point and Carolina led 7-6.

Coach Red Parker (1973-76) would complete his 4-year stay at Clemson with a losing 17-25-2 record. In '73, his first year at the helm, the Tigers would go 5-6.

Jeff Grantz would rush for 260 yards against Ohio in '73, breaking an all-time record at USC. The NCAA named him America's Back of the Week for his play in USC's 41-28 win over Georgia Tech.

Mel Baxley returned an interception 102-yards for a touchdown vs. Georgia Tech, still an all-time USC record.

Four minutes later it was Carolina again getting on the board. Following a drive of 47 yards, down to the Clemson 20, Marino came in and drilled a 37-yard field goal to put USC up 10-6.

The first half ended with Clemson on the Carolina five, but they were unable to cash in before time expired.

Five minutes into the third period Clemson again scored after an 85-yard drive. Again it was Sanders going in, and this time Burgess' kick was good, and now Clemson led 13-10.

Following the ensuing kickoff, Carolina began a long drive of their own, one of 76 yards in 12 plays, with Jeff Grantz going over from the four. Marino's kick was good, and Carolina again took the lead, 17-13.

As though fans had not already been given enough excitement to last an entire season, Clemson then came back early in the fourth period with the go-ahead score when Smiley Sanders went in for his third TD of the afernoon. Burgess's kick was good, and the Tigers took the lead, 20-17.

Three minutes later, with the Tigers again driving, an injured Carolina player, Grahl Phillips, entered the game for his only play of the day--a big one.

For it was then that Ken Callicutt took a pitchout, turned end and was hit hard. The ball squirted from his hand, Phillips snagged it in midair and returned it 12 yards, down to the Clemson 20. Now USC was on the move, and Clemson's 20-17 lead didn't look so big anymore.

Four plays later Grantz scrambled all the way for another USC score, Marino's kick was good, and Carolina took the lead 24-20.

Late in the contest, Carolina would drive 87 yards for their final score, including a run of 43 yards by Jeff Grantz. Casper Carter took it in from the five, Jay Lynn Hodgin ran for the two-point conversion, and the Gamecocks led 32-20. And that was the final score.

Bobby Marino boots a 37-yard field goal to put USC up 10-6 over Clemson.

Clemson's defense took it on the chin from the Terrapins of Maryland, 28-13.

Jay Lynn Hodgin takes a handoff from Grantz. Hodgin would return a kickoff 93 yards for a TD against Houston in '73, the sixth longest KO return in USC history.

Ken Pengitore looks for Benny Cunningham in Clemson's 24-8 win over Duke.

1974

CALLICUTT, FELLERS LEAD CLEMSON ROMP

The 4-6 Gamecocks were concluding another dismal season as they prepared to meet a strong Tiger eleven on November 23 at Death Valley. Both fans and the Columbia press had grown disenchanted with Paul Dietzel at this point, and he had already announced his retirement as head coach, indicating that he would stay on at USC as athletic director. (Such was not to be, however, as University officials soon informed Dietzel that he would not remain at USC in any capacity.) The '74 Gamecocks began the season with a poor 0-5 record, their worst start in history.

Red Parker was now in his second season at Clemson, and the Tigers were doing reasonably well, sporting a 6-4 record coming into today's game. Indeed, they were 6-0 at Death Valley, with big wins over both Georgia and Georgia Tech. In fact, Clemson's 7-4 record of '74 was the best they'd had since 1959, the year they went to the Bluebonnet Bowl.

The Tigers were favored to take today's contest, and for obvious reasons. They had a tough offense, led by Mark Fellers and Ken Callicutt, that was truly loaded for bear.

Yet it was Carolina that drew first blood in today's game. Taking the ball at their own 11, the Gamecocks drove 89 yards in 16 plays, with Kevin Long going in from the two. Bobby Marino kicked the point and Carolina led 7-0.

But Clemson came right back. They drove 22 yards in three plays before big Ken Callicutt took a pitch and dashed 58 yards for the touchdown. The kick was blocked, and USC kept the lead, 7-6.

Two minutes later Dennis Smith intercepted a Jeff Grantz pass at the USC 44. Six plays later Mark Fellers ran it in from three yards out. The conversion failed, and Clemson now led 12-7.

Five minutes later it was Clemson again getting on the board. This time they drove 80 yards for the TD, Tony Mathews going over from the one. Callicutt ran for the two-point conversion, and Clemson led 20-7.

As though all this were not enough, on USC's next possession Grantz was again intercepted, this time by Ronnie Smith who returned the ball to the USC 31. Mark Fellers ran an option right from the five, and took the ball in for the TD. The conversion failed, and Clemson took the lead, 26-7.

As the clock wound down, Carolina then drove 59 yards for their second TD of the afternoon, Clarence Williams taking it in from the five. Marino kicked the point, and Clemson's lead was cut to 26-14.

As the third period got underway, Clemson picked up where they'd left off. Starting from their own 37 they drove 63 yards for their next score. Included in this drive was a run of 45 yards by Tony Mathews. Fellers again went in for the score, Bob Burgess kicked the point and Clemson led 33-14.

But Carolina was not dead. They drove 84 yards for their

A picture's worth a thousand words. Paul Dietzel concluded his disappointing career at USC with a devastating 39-21 loss to Clemson.

"Row, row, row your boat. . .Row, row, row. . ." Ron Bass (#10), Don Stewart (#74) and Captain Jerry Witherspoon (#65) discuss strategy as USC romped on UNC in '74 by a score of 31-23.

next score, Jay Lynn Hodgin going in from nine yards out for the TD. Marino kicked the point, and Clemson now led 33-21.

As for the fourth period, Clemson gave up fumbles deep in USC territory on three occasions. But then with just 12 seconds remaining, the Gamecocks tried a desperaton pass from their own 17. Dennis Smith picked it off and ran it back 31 yards for Clemson's final score of the day. The kick failed and Clemson walked away with a big 39-21 win.

Nor was today's win any fluke. Clemson had 433 yards rushing in this contest. Ken Callicutt had a remarkable 197 yards rushing, Tony Mathews 94 yards. Mark Fellers accounted for 229 yards in total offense and scored three touchdowns.

For Carolina the bright spot was Jay Lynn Hodgin, who had 127 yards rushing.

Tony Mathews takes off in Clemson's 29-28 loss to Tennessee.

Ken Callicutt carries the ball on a keeper for good yardage as Clemson fell to Texas A&M 24-0 to open the '74 season. Mitch Tyner had an 81-yard punt vs. Texas A&M in '73, an all-time CU Record.

Backup quarterback Ron Bass carried the ball 39 times vs. UNC in '74, an all-time USC record. (USC gained 468 yards rushing in this game, a Modern Era USC record. Bass rushed for 211 of those.)

Clemson walked all over Georgia in '74 to the tune of 28-24. They also beat Georgia Tech, the first time in sixty years they'd beaten both Georgia and Tech during the same season.

"Hey, we were only kidding!" Mike Farrell is hit after taking a Jeff Grantz pass good for 23 yards in USC's 24-14 loss to Houston.

Team captains meet for the coin toss before the 72nd meeting between Carolina and Clemson, this one at Death Valley. (Coach Dietzel very cleverly dressed his senior players in black helmets during the '74 campaign. By season's end they had four wins to show for their efforts.)

Ken Callicutt, Clemson's super soph running back, runs 58 yards for Clemson's first TD of the afternoon.

Co-captain Mark Fellers crashes in for the score that put Clemson up 12-7 over USC. Fellers completed a 97-yard TD pass to Craig Brantley vs. Virginia in '74, the longest pass play from scrimmage in the CU record book.

Jay Lynn Hodgin, who closed out a brilliant career with USC today, goes in to narrow the score 33-21, but USC could get no closer. Hodgin averaged 75.1 rushing yards per game during his three-year career at USC. Only Steve Wadiak, George Rogers and Duce Staley have better career rushing averages.

USC's All-American quarterback, Jeff Grantz, had a tough day against Clemson. Here we see why.

1975

GRANTZ AND COMPANY ROLL, 56-20

Gone now from USC was Paul Dietzel, and in his place came Jim Carlen, formerly head coach at Texas Tech. He was an abrasive, tell-it-like-it-is sort of fellow, who was as popular with his players as he was unpopular with the USC administration. Today he is remembered for having recruited some of the finest talent ever for the Gamecocks.

Even better, Jeff Grantz was back for his final year as quarterback for the Gamecocks, and he was backed up by two of the finest running backs in the South, Kevin Long and Clarence Williams. Plus they had an all-star line to do the heavy work. They were 6-5 going into the Clemson game, with big wins over Georgia Tech, Duke, Baylor, and Ole Miss. By season's end, they would accept a bid to play Miami of Ohio in the Tangerine Bowl.

At Clemson, meanwhile, Red Parker was now in his third year as head coach, and the Tigers were coming off a good 7-4 season in '74 and hopes were high that they would do even better in '75. But such was not to be. Ken Callicutt was one of their few stars returning from the previous year, and they were 2-8 going into the Carolina contest, with wins over Wake Forest and UNC.

Still, despite Carolina's superior performance to date, this was the Carolina-Clemson game, and no one expected what was about to happen.

Jeff and Joe Bostic anchored Clemson's offensive line from 1975-79. Jeff was named to the All-ACC team. Joe was named All-American and to the CU Athletic Hall of Fame. Both are members of the Clemson All-Time Football Team.

USC's first score came just three minutes into the contest. After a 33-yard USC march, fast Clarence Williams took a pitch and raced 36 yards for a TD. Marino's kick was good and USC lead 7-0. (Marino would not miss throughout the game.)

Moments later, after a 48-yard march, Grantz passed 34 yards to Randy Chastain for another TD, and Carolina went up 14-0.

Clemson then staged a comeback, moving 80 yards on their next possession. Mike O'Cain sneaked over from the one, but the kick missed and the score became 14-6.

Following the ensuing kickoff, the Gamecocks moved 70 yards for their next score, Williams going in from the nine. Now the score became 21-6.

On their next possession, Carolina moved 44 yards for another score, Grantz passing 13 yards to Phil Logan for the TD. Now USC led 28-6. Unfortunately for Clemson 2:33 still remained in the half. As the final seconds ticked away, Grantz threw 41 yards to Phil Logan for USC's fifth TD of the afternoon, and Carolina went in at halftime with a 35-6 lead.

But Clemson was not dead. They took the second half kickoff and moved 80 yards for a TD, O'Cain throwing six yards to Joey Walters for the score. Their two-point conversion try failed, and now USC led 35-12.

Carolina took the kickoff and drove 78 yards for their next score, Grantz hitting Logan with a three-yard pass, and USC led 42-12. And there were still six minutes left in the third quarter.

Three minutes later Grantz again moved Carolina in for a score when he dashed 19 yards on a keeper, and the Gamecocks were now up 49-12.

Clemson moved 83 yards on their next possession, O'Cain sneaking over from the three. He then threw to Stan Rome for the two pointer, and USC's lead was cut to 49-20.

Finally, with just 54 seconds on the clock, Grantz threw 19 yards to Stevie Stephens, and the score, the final score, became USC 56, Clemson 20.

Everyone, friend and foe alike, agreed that Jeff Grantz's performance today was phenomenal. USC had the ball nine times and scored nine touchdowns (one was called back because of a penalty). Indeed, USC did not punt all afternoon. They had 616 yards in total offense, 458 of those on the ground.

Grantz passed for five touchdowns and ran for another. (He accounted for 29 touchdowns in '75, which was number-one in the nation.)

Clemson climaxed a dismal 2-9 season this afternoon, while Carolina would wind up losing 20-7 to Miami in the Tangerine Bowl.

Kevin Long and Clarence Williams remain the only two Gamecock running backs ever to rush for over 1,000 during the same season. Only George Rogers and Duce Staley have gained more yards in a single season than Long and Williams.

Jim Carlen played center for Bobby Dodd at Georgia Tech, and is still remembered as one of the finest Gamecock coaches ever.

Jeff Grantz is still considered USC's most versatile quarterback ever. He was also a mainstay on the baseball team. In 1992 he was voted Carolina's all-time greatest quarterback, and is a member of the USC All-Time Football Team.

Bennie Cunningham, Clemson's All-American end, is a member of the CU All-Time Football Team.

Mike O'Cain stretches in for the go-ahead TD as the Tigers beat Wake Forest 16-14 in '75.

Craig Brantley was an ace receiver for the Tigers and one of the fastest men on the team. Brantley was on the receiving end of Fellers' 97-yard TD pass vs. Virginia in '74, an all-time CU record.

Clarence Williams goes in for one of his two touchdowns. He rushed for 160 yards in this game.

Jeff Grantz shows the form and the grace that made him an All-American. Grantz threw for five TDs today (tying an all-time USC record) and ran for another.

The scoreboard says it all! USC's 56 points in 1975 remains an all-time record for points scored in this series. (Clemson scored 51 points in 1900.)

As a result of their 7-4 record, USC was invited to play Miami of Ohio in the Tangerine Bowl. The Indians won 20-7.

Bobby Marino kicked eight extra points on the day as USC beat Clemson 56-20.

1976

THE TIGERS SMASH USC's BOWL HOPES

Clemson fans were complaining. Red Parker simply wasn't getting the job done. The Tigers were 2-9 in '75, and now, in '76, going into their annual game with Carolina, they were suffering through an equally bad year with a dismal 2-6-2 record. They were a young team, it is true, but they had a veteran quarterback in Mike O'Cain, and there was also Steve Fuller. So what was the problem?

As for the Gamecocks, gone now was Jeff Grantz and in his place came Ron Bass who could run and pass with the best of them. Plus there were those two record-breaking running backs, Clarence Williams and Kevin Long, and a supporting cast that could play for anybody in America. Indeed, the Gamecocks were 6-4 coming into today's game, with close losses to such powers as Georgia (20-12), Baylor (18-17) and Notre Dame (13-6). Indeed, it was widely rumored that a win today would give the Gamecocks a 7-4 record and a bid to the Peach Bowl.

Somehow, the experts had overlooked the presence of Tiger freshman Warren Ratchford, one of the finest running backs ever to play for Clemson. He gained 92 yards on only five carries, and all in the first quarter! And Mike O'Cain and Steve Fuller were brilliant in directing the team throughout the game.

Some 54,000 fans turned out for this contest, a record crowd at Frank Howard Field, despite the cold, dreary weather.

USC kicked off to Clemson, and the underdog Tigers immediately drove 81 yards for a score, Tracy Perry going in from the three. James Russell kicked the point, and Clemson was up 7-0.

Then the Gamecocks began a drive of their own, but Brian Kier intercepted a Ron Bass pass in the end zone and that was it. From their own 20 then, Clemson moved 80 yards for another score, and did it in just four plays, a run of 54-yards by Warren Ratchford highlighting the drive. Perry scored from 12 yards out, Russell kicked the point, and Clemson was up 14-0.

Several minutes later the situation was reversed. Steve Fuller fumbled the ball at the Clemson six, and Kerry DePasquale recovered for Carolina. But three Bass passes fell incomplete, and Britt Parrish came in and kicked a field goal. The Tigers went in at half time leading 14-3.

Early in the third quarter USC's Max Runager went back to punt, but the ball sailed over his head and Clemson recovered at the Carolina 16. Four plays later Steve Fuller kept the ball and scored from the five. Russell's kick was good, and Clemson increased their lead to 21-3.

As the third period came to a close, O. J. Tyler intercepted another Bass pass and Clemson took over on their own 29. They then moved 71 yards for their next score, Steve Fuller electrifying the crowd with a 27-yard scamper for the TD. Again Russell's kick was good and the Tigers led 28-3.

But the Gamecocks came back with a drive of their own. From their own 31 they moved the length of the field and scored when Ron Bass hit Phil Logan with a 17-yard pass in the Tiger end zone. Their 2-point conversion try failed, and Clemson led 28-9. And that was the final score.

This win increased Clemson's record to 3-6-2 for the season, and left Carolina with a 6-4 record. Plus it knocked Carolina out of any chance for a bowl bid.

Ron Bass accounted for 305 yards in total offense in this contest, while Phil Logan caught eight passes for 135 yards.

Warren Ratchford had 127 yards rushing for Clemson (he sat out the last three quarters with an injury), and Tracy Perry 104.

Clemson's Rex Varn, who intercepted two USC passes this afternoon, is the grandson of famed USC coach Rex Enright.

Ron Bass, one of the coolest Gamecock quarterbacks ever, rolls out in USC's 27-17 win over Georgia Tech.

Casper Carter and Zion McKinney put their heads together in USC's 10-7 upset loss to Wake Forest.

Mike O'Cain, captain of the '76 Tigers and a great quarterback.

Ken Callicutt, still remembered as one of Clemson's finest running backs ever.

It's Williams again, moving for yardage as Carolina lost to Clemson 28-9 in an upset in '76.

Clarence Williams is stood straight up by this tough Clemson defense as he tried for a first down.

Defensive end Russ Manzari collars a Tiger running back.

1977

BUTLER'S CATCH SINKS GAMECOCKS

Gone now, after two dismal seasons, was Red Parker, and in his place came Charlie Pell, an assistant under Parker. He would coach Clemson to an 8-2-1 season in '77 and a 10-1 season in '78, the first occasions since 1959 that the Tigers had been ranked in the top twenty. He was also named ACC Coach of the Year in both '77 and '78, an honor he truly deserved. He would leave Clemson to become head coach at Florida.

Pell had on hand in '77 Steve Fuller and Ken Callicutt, two of the finest backfield aces in the country, plus receivers like Jerry Butler who could have been playing pro ball.

At Carolina the big news was the return of such stalwarts as Ron Bass, Casper Carter, Spencer Clark, Zion McKinney, Phil Logan, Dave Prezioso, Jerome Provence, Steve Dorsey, punter Max Runager, and place kicker Britt Parrish.

Still, the Gamecocks were 5-5 coming into the Clemson game, though a few of their losses could easily have been wins, as they went down before Georgia 15-13, Duke 25-21, and NC State 7-3.

Tonight's game was viewed by some 56,000 fans at Williams-Brice Stadium plus a regional TV audience.

It is a game that is still talked about because of the heart stopping comebacks staged by both teams.

Clemson drew first blood midway the first quarter. Following a 90-yard drive, Warren Ratchford went over from the four for the score. Obed Ariri's kick was good and Clemson led 7-0.

Three minutes later Roy Eppes intercepted a Ron Bass pass and returned it 30 yards to the USC ten. From there Ariri came in and booted a field goal, and now the Tigers were up 10-0.

Just as the first period came to an end, Steve Ryan recovered a fumble at the Clemson 33, and the Tigers were again on the trail. This time it was Lester Brown going off tackle from the one, and the Tigers were up 17-0. And thus ended the first half. And Clemson fans were sitting on top of the world.

A win here tonight and their next stop would be Jacksonville, Florida, and the Gator Bowl where they would face Eastern power Pittsburgh.

Clemson then increased their lead to 24-0 midway the third period when Ken Callicutt raced 52 yards for a touchdown.

But three minutes later the Gamecocks finally showed signs of life when Spencer Clark made his sensational dash of 77 yards for a touchdown. Britt Parrish's kick was good and Clemson's lead was cut to 24-7.

Then, early in the fourth period, Clemson's lead was cut still further when Steve Dorsey capped a 67-yard drive with an 11-yard touchdown run. Parrish's kick was good and Clemson led 24-14.

Minutes later Clemson punter David Sims shanked a kick for only ten yards, the ball going out of bounds at the Tiger 38. Eleven plays later Steve Dorsey went over from the one. The 2-point conversion try was no good, but Clemson's big lead was now cut to 24-20.

Two minutes later Sims kicked for only 18 yards, this punt going out at the USC 48. Seven plays later the Gamecocks were again on the board following a 40-yard bomb from Bass to Phil Logan in the Clemson end zone. Parrish's kick made the score USC 27, Clemson 24.

(Phil Logan caught 105 passes for 2,063 yards during his career at USC. Only Sterling Sharpe and Robert Brooks have surpassed this mark.)

It was truly a miracle comeback, and the cheering the Carolina fans did could be heard all the way to Due West.

BUT--the Tigers did not fold at that point. Clemson then took the ensuing kickoff back to their own 33. From there, with the clock winding down, Fuller hit Rick Weddington with a 26-yard pass, and Dwight Clark with an 18-yarder. Then, from the 20, facing fourth and long, Steve Fuller rolled out with the ball, three Carolina linemen in hot pursuit. Then Fuller released his pass. The ball spiraled towards the goal, clearly over the head of his intended receiver, Jerry Butler. Gamecock fans heaved a sigh of relief. But then, at the last moment, Butler leaped high in the air, his fingertips seeming to barely brush the ball, and then, somehow, he came down with the ball clutched in his hands. He fell backwards into the end zone, the referee signaled a touchdown, and the Tigers had staged an amazing comeback of their own, winning 31-27 in the final seconds on a desperation pass that should never have been caught.

Obed Ariri remains one of Clemson's all-time greatest place kickers and one of their all-time leading scorers. He was named All-American in 1979. Arisi's 57 yard field goal vs. Wake Forest in '77 remains an all-time CU record.

The remarkable Bob Bradley, a Frank Howard confidante, was voted America's Most Outstanding Sports Information Director in '77. He is now Clemson's Sports Information Director Emeritus.

Lester Brown goes over for a TD against Maryland, but it wasn't enough as Clemson fell 21-14. Their only other loss in '77 would be a 21-17 decision to Notre Dame.

Team captain Steve Fuller runs for a first down as Clemson eased by NC State 7-3. Fuller threw for 1,655 yards in '77, an all-time CU record. He would be named All-American and is a member of the CU Athletic Hall of Fame. His jersey has been retired.

Britt Parrish set an all-time USC record when he booted four field goals to beat East Carolina 19-16 in 1977.

Team Captain Steve Fuller demonstrates the coolness under fire that made him great as he fires for yardage in Clemson's 31-13 win over VPI.

Lester Brown slams in from the one to give Clemson a big 17-0 lead over USC early in the second quarter.

Speedy Spencer Clark ignited USC's comeback when he dashed 77 yards for a TD to narrow Clemson's lead to 24-7. (He's seen here vs. Appalachian State.)

Here Ron Bass throws a 40-yard TD bomb to Phil Logan to put the Gamecocks up 27-24 over Clemson in a great comeback.

Spencer Clark runs for Carolina's only TD of the evening as the Gamecocks fell to Hawaii 24-7 in their 12th game of the '77 season.

THE BIG CATCH! Jerry Butler makes an amazing catch of this Steve Fuller pass to give Clemson a 31-27 comeback win over Carolina in '77.

Steve Fuller and the Tigers went down in defeat at the hands of national champion Pittsburgh by a score of 34-3 in the '77 Gator Bowl.

1978

BROWN AND FULLER BRILLIANT IN CLEMSON WIN

The brilliant Steve Fuller was now in his senior year as leader of the Tigers, a team sporting an excellent 9-1 record as they prepared for today's game againt the 5-4-1 Gamecocks.

Oddly enough, the '78 Gamecocks had lost to most of their ACC opponents while beating such SEC powers as Georgia and Ole Miss. Which suggested to fans that Carolina had the talent to win, if they could ever put it all together. USC fans were also talking about a young sophomore sensation named George Rogers who was breaking rushing records right and left for the Gamecocks that year.

Some 63,000 fans were on hand at Frank Howard Field on November 25 for this contest. For USC fans a win today would give them a 6-4-1 record and a modicum of respect following an othewise dismal season. For Tiger fans, on the other hand, they were bringing a great 9-1 record into this game and had already won the ACC championship and accepted a bid to play Ohio State in the Gator Bowl. Some fans worried that perhaps the Tigers, who had already proven themselves to be one of the finest teams in the land, might be prime candidates for an upset. They need not have worried.

Warren Ratchford returned the opening kickoff 42 yards to the Clemson 45. Six plays later Fuller went over from the one on a keeper. Obed Ariri's kick was good, and Clemson led 7-0. Zion McKinney fumbled the ensuing kickoff, Rick Wyatt recovered for Clemson, and the Tigers were back in business at the USC 35. Six plays later Lester Brown went in from the one, Ariri's kick was good, and Clemson led 14-0.

Five minutes later Rick Sanford fumbled a punt, and Jeff Bostic recovered for Clemson at the USC 26. Again it was Lester Brown going in for a Tiger score, and now Clemson's lead was 21-0, and there were still three minutes left in the first quarter.

But the Gamecocks came back in the second period. USC quarterback Garry Harper threw 41 yards to Horace Smith for one score, then scored the next one himself on a one-yard keeper following a drive of 80 yards. Britt Parrish's kicks were both good, and now Clemson's big lead was cut to 21-14.

There were still six minutes remaining in the first half, however, and the Tigers were not ready to shut down shop just yet.

They took the next kickoff at their own five, then drove 95 yards in just three minutes, Tracy Perry scoring from the seven. Ariri's kick was good, and Clemson led 28-14.

As though all that were not enough, on USC's next possession Harper was intercepted by Rex Varn who returned the ball to the USC 32. From there, with the seconds ticking down, Ariri kicked a field goal and the Tigers went in a halftime holding a 31-14 lead.

The third period was relatively quiet. Ariri hit on a 23-yarder for Clemson, and Parrish hit on a 20-yarder for USC. So Clemson now led 34-17.

Early in the fourth period Clemson again scored when Lester Brown went in from the two. The kick was good, and Clemson led 41-17.

Harold Goggins on the move in Clemson's 31-0 win over Villanova.

Lester Brown breaks out for the touchdown that would win this game for Clemson over UNC 13-9.

But then Carolina came right back with a score of their own when Johnnie Wright went in from the two. The kick was good, and Clemson led 41-24. Which was the final score.

Clemson had 397 yards rushing in this game. Lester Brown had 121 yards rushing and scored three touchdowns. Steve Fuller had 106 yards rushing and scored one touchdown. Marvin Sims had 104 yards rushing.

As for Carolina, they finished the game with 310 yards rushing, their celebrated sophomore, George Rogers, getting 123 of those--and all in the first half (he sat out the second with an injury).

Clemson would go on to upset Ohio State in the Gator Bowl 17-15 to complete a great 11-1 season, their best since 1950. (Charlie Pell resigned at the end of the season, and Danny Ford coached the team in the Gator Bowl.)

Charlie Bauman whose timely pass interception saved Clemson's 17-15 win over Ohio State in the '78 Gator Bowl.

Jerry Butler was named All-American in '78 and is a member of the CU Athletic Hall of Fame and the All-Time Football Team.

Max Runager, a member of the USC All-Time Football Team, enjoyed a long career in the NFL.

It was late in the game and USC held a 14-7 lead over Kentucky. But now the Wildcats had a first down at the Gamecock two and called time out. The grim expressions of these defensive warriors tells the story as they wait for play to resume. (Kentucky scored three plays later and the game ended, a 14-14 tie.)

Garry Harper sets 'em down as USC lost to Georgia Tech 6-3 in '78.

Lester Brown goes in for his second TD of the day to put Clemson up 21-0 over the Gamecocks. He scored 102 points in '78, fourth best in the nation.

Cliff Austin breaks through a gaping hole in the USC line.

Lester Brown moves in for his third touchdown of the afternoon as Clemson beat USC 41-23.

Steve Dorsey rips off big yardage against Clemson in '78.

The '78 Tigers won 11 games, including a 17-15 win over Ohio State in the Gator Bowl.

Steve Fuller had 161 yards of total offense in the Gator Bowl, and scored a touchdown. His 6,096 yards in total offense during his career remains an all-time Clemson record. He is a member of the CU Athletic Hall of Fame and the All-Time CU Football Team.

1979

TWO GREAT TEAMS FIGHT TO THE FINISH

1979 was certainly one of the most unusual years in the history of this long series with both Carolina and Clemson coming into the big game with excellent won-loss records and bowl bids on the line.

Clemson was 8-2 at this point with impressive wins over both Georgia and Notre Dame, and they would later play Baylor in the Peach Bowl. All in all, Coach Danny Ford was having a great year.

As for the Gamecocks, they were 7-3 going into today's game. Indeed, a win against Clemson would give them an 8-3 record, their best in history, and a bid to the Hall of Fame Bowl and a meeting with Missouri. Truly, this would be one of the most important games the Gamecocks had ever played.

Clemson took the opening kickoff back to their own 35, then marched to the USC 19 where they faced fourth and long. In came their old standby, Obed Ariri, who kicked a field goal, and the Tigers were up 3-0. There were now 9:35 remaining in the quarter.

Then back came the Gamecocks. Starting from their own 28, they then drove to the Clemson 17 before they stalled. Eddie Leopard came in and booted a field goal from there and the score was now tied 3-3 with only seconds remaining in the first quarter.

Then, midway the second period, an 80-yard Tiger drive finally ended at the USC 28. Ariri calmly kicked another field goal, and Clemson went up 6-3.

Carolina took the ensuing kickoff to their own 30. Facing third and 12, Garry Harper threw over the middle to Willie Scott and the big receiver then bulled his way for 61 yards, down to the Clemson nine. On the next play Harper again threw to Scott, and the Tigers were charged with interference, moving the ball to the one. George Rogers lost one yard on the next play, but then Harper came back with a pass to Ben Cornett who made a diving catch in the end zone for the touchdown. Eddie Leopard's kick was good, and Carolina took the lead 10-6. There were only four seconds showing on the scoreboard clock.

In the third period Leopard's 52-yard field goal try was short and Clemson took over at their own 35. They then drove to the USC seven but could go no further. Ariri's field goal closed USC's lead to 10-9.

Early in the fourth quarter, still protecting their one-point lead, the Gamecocks were facing third and long at their own 44. Harper then fired a 19-yard pass to Zion McKenney down to the Clemson 37. The drive finally died on the Clemson 21 and Leopard came in and kicked a field goal that gave Carolina a 13-9 lead. And that is how the game ended.

Despite the Gamecocks's win today, fans of both persuasions agreed that this had been a terrific game played between two terrific teams.

Billy Lott was outstanding for Clemson with 199 yards passing, while George Rogers had 103 yards rushing for USC.

A scene so dear to the Clemson faithful, the Tiger team running down the hill after rubbing Howard's Rock.

"Now hold on, Danny. This don't make sense worth a damn. In the first place, why would eight Polocks want to change a light bulb? In the second place, where'd they get a chair big enough. . ." Danny Ford and Jim Carlen, both good ol' Southern boys, enjoy a little jawing before the big game in '79.

Jim Stuckey, Clemson's All-American tackle, nails George Rogers after only a short gain on this play. Jim Stuckey is Clemson's career leader in tackles by a defensive lineman, and is a member of the CU Athletic Hall of Fame and the CU All-Time Football Team.

George Rogers rushed for 1,548 yards in '79, despite having sat out the second half in several games. He was a consensus All-American that year.

Obed Aariri would set three all-time NCAA records and be named All-American before he finished in 1980.

Captain Billy Lott pitches back to Chuck McSwain as the Tigers beat Virginia 17-7.

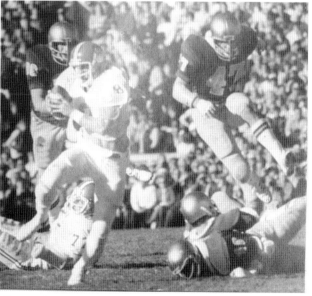

Clemson beat Notre Dame (at South Bend!) in '79 by a close 16-10 score. In the third period of that game Ariri kicked two field goals and Billy Lott broke loose for this 28-yard TD to give Clemson the win.

Robert Perlotte, an outstanding USC defensive back, returns this punt for good yardage against Clemson.

Ben Cornett stretches for this Garry Harper pass vs. Wake Forest. It was Cornett who scored the only TD of the day as USC beat Clemson in '79.

Garry Harper would win the game MVP award for his performance against Clemson.

Spencer Clark's last home game for the Gamecocks was a good one as his Gamecocks socked it to Clemson.

Lester Brown goes in for a TD as Clemson lost 24-18 to Baylor in the '79 Peach Bowl. Brown ran for 32 TDs during his career with the Tigers, still Number-One in the CU record book.

The Gamecocks would lose to Missouri 24-14 in the '79 Hall of Fame Bowl on a cold, rainy night in Birmingham.

1980

WILLIE UNDERWOOD IGNITES TIGER WIN

Clemson fans will always remember 1980 as a sort of a mediocre interval between the two great seasons of 1979 (8-3) and 1981 (11-0). Danny Ford was in his second full year as head coach and he led the Tigers to wins over all the little guys on their schedule--Rice, Western Carolina, VPI, and Virginia--while suffering losses to all the others, unless you consider USC to be one of the biggies.

As for Carolina, they were 8-2 going into the Clemson game, including a huge 17-14 win over gridiron giant Michigan, and a win today would give them their best season ever. Indeed, their two losses had been close ones, to Georgia and Southern Cal, and they had already accepted an invitation to meet Pittsburgh in the Gator Bowl, a win over Clemson being something of a foregone conclusion.

But the experts reckoned without the heroics of Willie Underwood, whose defensive exploits would save the day for the Tigers and spoil USC's ambitions for a 9-2 season.

Over 64,000 fans turned out at Death Valley to witness today's encounter on November 22, a cool, clear day in the Blue Ridge.

The first quarter rocked along, with neither team able to move too well against the other, until Clemson mounted a drive of some 60 yards that stalled at the USC 30. At that point Obed Ariri came in and kicked a 41-yard field goal, giving Clemson a 3-0 lead.

But the Gamecocks came right back. After their drive stalled at the Clemson 30, Eddie Leopard kicked a field goal to tie the score at 3-3. There were still two minutes remaining in the first quarter.

Ten minutes later, with 7:31 remaining in the second, Ariri was again called on by the Tigers. This time he was true with a 47-yarder and Clemson was ahead 6-3 at the half.

The third quarter was a re-play of the first with both teams running three plays and then punting.

But midway through the quarter Eddie Leopard did kick a 29-yard field goal to knot the score at 6-6.

But then, with only 32 seconds remaining in the period, with the Gamecocks again threatening at the Clemson 16, Willie Underwood suddenly stole a Garry Harper pass and returned it 64 yards, down to the USC 24. Six plays later Homer Jordan went in from the one. Ariri's kick was good, and Clemson now owned a 13-6 lead.

As though that news were not bad enough for the Gamecocks, on their very next possession Harper threw a short pass intended for Ben Cornett in the flat. But out of nowhere again came Willie Underwood. He picked off the toss and this time returned it 37 yards for another Clemson touchdown. The kick was good and the underdog Tigers now led 20-6.

The Gamecocks' hopes for their first 9-2 season ever were finally laid to rest.

Essentially this was the ball game, though Jeff McCall did add an insurance TD late in the game on a 15-yard run around right end. The kick was good and the final score became Clemson 27, USC 6.

The star for the Gamecocks in this contest was George Rogers who had 168 yards rushing on the day. He would soon be named the Heisman Trophy winner for 1980, the only player from any South Carolina college ever to be so honored.

The stars for Clemson were Willie Underwood, whose interceptions proved fatal to USC, and Obed Ariri.

Carolina would go on to lose to Pittsburgh in the Gator Bowl by a score of 37-9.

Obed Ariri would establishe three all-time NCAA records during his career with Clemson: most field goals in a season (23), most multiple field goals in a season (8), and most multiple field goals in a career (17).

(USC held Pacific to -39 yards rushing in 1980, an all-time USC defensive record.)

Johnnie Wright plows over the goal line to give USC a great 17-14 upset win over Michigan in 1980, one of USC's most impressive victories ever. (George Rogers had 242 yards rushing in this game.)

An All-Amercan in both 1979 and '80 and winner of the Heisman Trophy, George Rogers still holds most rushing records at USC. In 1980 he led the nation in rushing with 1,894 yards, an average of 157 yards per game. For his career, Rogers ran for 5,204 yards and scored 33 touchdowns.

Rogers was a guest on Bob Hope's All-American TV special. He is a member of the USC Athletic Hall of Fame and the All-Time USC Football Team. His jersey, number-38, has been retired.

Jack Cain (#12) and Willie Underwood (#20) come up fast to put the stop on George Rogers. Rogers would finish the day with 168 yards rushing.

Willie Underwood returns an interception for a TD vs. USC. He had 101 yards in interception returns in this game.

Eddie Leopard's second field goal of the day tied the score at 6-6, but thanks to Willie Underwood's two interceptions, Clemson would come back to win it 27-6. (Leopard kicked 10 extra points vs. Wichita State in '80, still an all-time USC record.)

Homer Jordan, Clemson's great sophomore quarterback, would lead the Tigers to a big win over USC in 1980, and to the national championship in 1981.

1981

CLEMSON BEATS USC AND GOES 11-0

1981 would prove to be Jim Carlen's last year at the helm for the Gamecocks. Unfortunately, it was a year of miscues and uncertainties, with no one knowing from week to week just who the starting quarterback would be or just what sort of offense the Gamecocks would be running. Carlen had announced at the beginning of the season (in an odd bit of reasoning) that he planned to de-emphasize the Gamecock passing game in order to create a more balanced, "wide open" offense. But since Carolina's rushing game averaged 150 yards per game less in '81 than in '80, the Gamecocks posed little threat to many of the teams on their schedule. Still, they were 6-4 going into the Clemson game, and indicated that they would not be intimidated by the Tigers.

As for Clemson, what can be said about their great '81 team that hasn't already been said. With Homer Jordan back at quarterback, and with such Tiger greats as Perry Tuttle, Jeff McCall, Jerry Gaillard, Donald Igwebuike, Jeff Bryant, Jeff Davis, Tim Childers, and the McSwain brothers, Chuck and Rod, back for another year, the Tigers were ready to play.

And they were 10-0 going into the Carolina game. They would go on to an 11-0 season, their first undefeated, untied team since the Bobby Gage days of 1948, then take the ACC crown, play Nebraska in the Orange Bowl for the national championship--and WIN! Not a bad year.

Some 53,000 fans showed up for this contest in Columbia on a beautiful fall afternoon. They had hardly taken their seasts when the underdog Gamecocks began a drive from their own 49 that ended with Johnnie Wright going off tackle from the one for a touchdown. Mark Fleetwood's kick was good and USC took a surprising 7-0 lead.

But it was a surprise that didn't last long. For on USC's next possession Chris Norman attempted to punt from the 28 and was swarmed by Clemson defenders. Rod McSwain blocked the punt and Johnnie Rembert chased it down and recovered in the end zone for a Clemson touchdown. But Bob Pauling's kick was no good, and USC kept the lead 7-6. And there were still six minutes remaining in the first quarter.

Some nine minutes later, now three minutes into the second quarter, Clemson took the lead for good when their 43-yard drive ended at the USC 33. Pauling kicked a field goal from there and Clemson went up 9-7.

Just before half time Hollis Hall intercepted a Gordon Beckham pass and returned it 27 yards, down to the USC 20. Six plays later Homer Jordan went in for the score on a keeper, the kick missed, and Clemson's lead was increased to 15-7.

But the Gamecocks were still game. Early in the third period Beckham threw ten yards to Horace Smith for another Carolina TD. The kick missed, but Clemson's lead was cut to 15-13.

But then the Tigers looked like national champions as they took the ensuing kickoff and marched 84 yards in 19 plays for the decisive score, Chuck McSwain blasting off tackle from the four. The kick was good, and Clemson led 22-13.

And for all practical purposes that was it, though Chuck McSwain did electrify the Tiger faithful with a great 23-yard run for another Clemson TD, and a 29-13 lead. There were still almost nine minutes remaining to play, but the exhausted Gamecocks could do no more.

(Clemson defeated Wake Forest 82-24 in '81, an all-time ACC record score. The Tigers rushed for 536 yards, an average of 8.7 yards per play, in this game, and scored 12 TDs, more all-time CU records.)

Chuck McSwain runs for a big first down as Clemson downed Nebraska 22-15 for the national championship in the 1981 Orange Bowl.

Gordon Beckham completed 16 of 17 passes vs. UNC in '81, still an all-time USC record, as the Gamecocks won 31-13.

Andrew Provence (#70) and company nail this Cavalier runner in USC's 21-3 win. Provence was named All-American in '82 and is a member of USC's All-Time Football Team.

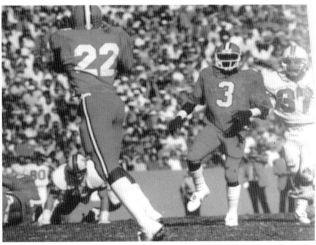

Jeff McCall ran for 28 yards with this Homer Jordan pass as the Tigers beat UNC 10-8 in '81.

Homer Jordan completes a short one to Perry Tuttle as Clemson defeated Virginia 27-0. Tuttle caught eight TD passes in '81, still an all-time Clemson record.

Gordon Beckham, trailed by Troy Thomas, options right as the Gamecocks fell to the Clemson Tigers, National Champions in 1981.

Johnnie Wright put the Gamecocks up 7-0 over the Tigers with this run for pay dirt. It was a lead that wouldn't last long. Wright remains USC's sixth all-time leading rusher.

1982

TOUGH TIGERS TRIP TIRED GAMECOCKS

It was 1982 and another Gamecock coach had just gone the way of the old gray goose. Yes, after annoying certain great powers in the USC administration, Jim Carlen had been sent packing, and in his place came his trusted assistant, Richard Bell. Under Coach Bell the Gamecocks had not done particularly well. By November 20, the day of the Clemson game, they had beaten Pacific, Richmond, Cincinnati, and Navy, the little guys on their schedule, while losing to all the biggies (which included a 28-23 loss to Furman).

But in all fairness to Bell, it is said that he inherited some big problems when he took over the program at USC, problems for which he should not be held responsible. Or, as one writer put it, Bell was a nice guy to whom none of it should ever have happened.

And Danny Ford and Clemson had a few problems of their own. After a 12-0 national championship season in '81, they were enjoying another phenomenal year in '82 with an 7-1-1 record coming into the USC game (their final game of the season would be played in Tokyo against Wake Forest). The problem was recruiting violations. The NCAA had accused them of such and said that the Tigers could not participate in any post season games in '82.

All to the delight of Gamecock fans, who began sporting bumper stickers which read: I Told On Danny.

November 20, 1982 was a bright, warm day at Frank Howard Field as a record crowd of 64,000 fans swarmed into the stadium to see what would happen when the powerful Tigers tangled with the lowly Gamecocks.

They didn't have long to wait.

The Gamecocks took the opening kickoff and moved for thirty yards before their record-setting place kicker, Mark Fleetwood, came in and booted a 30-yard field goal to put USC up 3-0.

(Fleetwood had earlier booted an incredible 58-yard field goal vs. Georgia, still an all-time USC record.)

Just three minutes later, however, Clemson stormed back 66 yards in just six plays for a touchdown, Cliff Austin going in from the nine. Bob Pauling kicked the point and Clemson took the lead 7-3.

Early in the second quarter Clemson padded their lead, driving 91 yards in 18 plays, when Chuck McSwain went over from the one for the score. Again the kick was good, and Clemson led 14-3. This drive consumed 7:25 off the clock.

In the third period Carolina made a comeback of sorts when they drove 77 yards only to have their march end at the Clemson

three. Fleetwood kicked his second field goal of the day and Clemson's lead was cut to 14-6.

Clemson immediatley began another drive of some 80 yards, Cliff Austin gaining 41 of those and Homer Jordan completing passes of 13 yards to Bubba Diggs and 18 yards to Frank Magwood. Austin scored from the two, the kick was good, and Clemson led 21-6.

Later, with only 7:37 remaining, Pauling kicked a 44-yard field goal to give Clemson their eighth win of the season, a 24-6 victory over Carolina. (And, yes, they went on to defeat Wake Forest in Tokyo's Mirage Bowl, giving them a 9-1-1 record in '82.)

Cliff Austin, with 1,064 rushing yards to his credit in '82, broke Buddy Gore's single-season rushing record in this game, and was voted Clemson's outstanding player of the afternoon. (Austin averaged 105.4 rushing yards per game in '82, still second in the CU record book.)

Carolina's freshman running back, Thomas Dendy, who gained 105 of USC's 145 rushing yards today, would be named most outstanding for the Gamecocks.

(Mark Fleetwood in 1982 kicked 39 of 53 field goal attempts during his career, a .736 average, still best in the USC record book.)

Harry Skipper returned a fumble 101 yards for a TD vs. Pacific, still an all-time USC record.

Coach Richard Bell would remain at USC for only the '82 season.

Carolina's Bill Bradshaw completed six passes against Clemson for 50 yards.

USC quarterback Gordon Beckham is interviewed by the press following Carolina's 24-6 loss to Clemson in '82.

Thomas Dendy (#35) set an all-time USC record when he rushed for 848 yards as a freshman. Here he clears the way for Todd Berry.

Team Captain Terry Kinard goes after a Doug Flutie fumble as Clemson tied Boston College 17-17 in '82. Kinard was named All-American in '82 and is a member of the CU Athletic Hall of Fame and All-Time Football Team.

Dale Hatcher still holds the CU punting record for seniors.

William Perry shuts down Bill Bennett as Clemson beat Duke 49-14 in '82. Perry was an All-American and is a member of the CU Athletic Hall of Fame and the CU All-Time Football Team.

Danny Ford sets the refs straight as his Tigers beat USC in '82.

1983

CLEMSON WINS AGAIN

Coach Richard Bell had departed USC and in his place came Joe Morrison, an all-time great pro player with the New York Giants, and a highly successful coach at both Chattanooga and New Mexico. Morrison was a friendly individual who knew when to be serious, and he was always serious when it came to football. Over the next six years, before his untimely death in 1989, he would lead Carolina to a place of prominence in the football world they had never known before, and furnish Gamecocks fans with a level of excitement and respectability they had never known before.

As for the '83 year, things were still somewhat unsettled at Carolina as a result of the abrupt departure of Coach Jim Carlen in '81, and that confusion was reflected in the 5-5 record they brought into the final game of the season. Indeed, the highlight of USC's season to date had been their incredible 38-14 romp over national power Southern California. (They played Georgia, Southern Cal, Notre Dame, and LSU in four successive weeks, which could further account for their 5-5 record.)

As for Clemson, as they walked into Williams-Brice Stadium that afternoon, they had won 29 games over the past three years and were anticipating another win today. Indeed, they were 8-1-1 at that point, their only loss being to Boston College, and their tie coming at the hands of Georgia. They were favored by nine points in today's clash.

Some 75,000 fans, a new record for this ancient series, paid to see today's contest. They were still streaming into the stadium when Clemson took the opening kickoff and drove 75 yards, down to the USC five, where they could go no further. But

Bob Pauling kicked a field goal and the Tigers went up 3-0.

Later, with only 46 seconds remaining in the first quarter, the Tigers struck again. This time it was Kevin Mack going in from the eight. Pauling's kick was no good, and Clemson led 9-0.

The Gamecocks took the ensuing kickoff and drove 80 yards for their first score of the afternoon. During this drive Quinton Lewis passed to Dominique Blasingame for 23 yards, and Allen Mitchell passed to Blasingame for another 29 yards. Finally, on fourth down at the Clemson 27, Mark Fleetwood kicked a field goal, and Clemson's lead was cut to 9-3.

Then, with five minutes remaining in the half, Clemson moved 53 yards before calling on Pauling for his second field goal of the day, a 47-yarder, and Clemson led 12-3.

Then came a long Carolina drive of 80 yards. Bill Bradshaw, now a wide receiver, hit Chris Wade on a 23-yard reverse-pass play, then Mitchell drilled one to Eric Poole for 16 yards, down to the Clemson seven. Quinton Lewis ran it in for the touchdown, Fleetwood kicked the point, and Clemson led 12-10.

Early in the third period the Tigers again drove for a score, this time going 80 yards with Kevin Mack and Stacey Driver taking turns carrying the ball. Mack went in from one yard out, Pauling kicked the point, and Clemson stretched their lead to 19-10.

Then, with six minutes remaining in the third, Chuckie Richardson intercepted Allen Mitchell and returned the ball to the USC 34. Four plays later Pauling kicked his third field goal of the day, this one a 42-yarder, and Clemson led 22-10.

Mike Eppley hands off to Kevin Mack as the Tigers tied Georgia 16-16 in '83. Eppley threw 28 TD passes during his career with the Tigers, still Number-One in the CU record book. His .593 completion percentage is another CU record. He would be named All-American in '84, and is a member of the CU Athletic Hall of Fame.

William Perry and William Devane, Clemson's "Bruise Brothers," anchored the Tiger defensive line, 1981-84.

With only 48 seconds remaining in the third, Mark Fleetwood kicked his second field goal of the afternoon and USC closed the gap to 22-13. And that is how the game ended, Clemson's fourth consecutive win over Carolina.

Clemson thus closed out another highly successful season, again going 9-1-1 on the year. But because of NCAA sanctions, they would not be going to any bowl games on New Years Day.

As for the Gamecocks, they closed out a 5-6 season under new coach Joe Morrison, and already could hardly wait til next year.

Clemson's defense was not famous for handling opponents gently in '83, as indicated in the above photo.

Kenny Flowers was quickly becoming a premier Tiger running back in '83.

Kent Hagood goes in for a TD as USC beat Navy 31-7 in '83. Hagood ran for 2,014 yards during his career at USC, an average of 5.5 yards per carry (second only to Carl Brazell's 5.7 average of 1952-55).

As a defensive back with the New York Giants, Joe Morrison won the NFL MVP award on three occasions. He compiled a 39-28-2 record during his six years at USC, including a 10-1 record in '84, USC's best season ever.

Carl Womble (#57) and Allen Mitchell (#11) look dejected as the final seconds tick down in USC's loss to Clemson.

Coach Joe Lee Dunn's famous Fire Ant defense dressed all in garnet and were tough to deal with.

Quinton Lewis scored from the seven to narrow Clemson's lead to 12-10.

Danny and Joe, both affable fellows, catch up on a little gridiron gossip just prior to the big game. In 1984 the NCAA would name Joe Morrison National Coach of the Year.

EVERYONE AGREES--IT'S A TOUCHDOWN!!! Kevin Mack scored both Clemson TDs as the Tigers beat Carolina 22-13 in '83.

1984

A GREAT GAMECOCK TEAM WINS IN MIRACLE FINISH

Mike Eppley was back for his senior season as quarterback of the Clemson Tigers, and he was supported by such great running backs as Kenny Flowers, Stacey Driver, and Richard Butler. On defense they had back their All-ACC linemen Terence Mack and the Perry brothers, William and Michael Dean. Indeed, following close losses to Georgia and Georgia Tech, the Tigers were enjoying a good 7-3 season as they prepared to host the Gamecocks on November 24 at Frank Howard Field.

At Carolina, meanwhile, the big news was their wading through a tough schedule, which included such powers as Georgia, Pittsburgh, Notre Dame, and Florida State, and winning them all. Indeed, this would be USC's best season in history, and they would have been undefeated going into the Clemson game had they not been the victims of an unbelievable upset at the hands of a Navy team that had beaten no one all year. Still, they were 9-1 as they jogged onto the field at Death Valley that fateful afternoon.

Much of Carolina's success in '84 was due to the arrival of a new quarterback, a young juco by the name of Mike Hold. He had shared the spotlight with Allen Mitchell all season, and had come into game after game, with USC trailing, and worked miracle after miracle, pulling it out for the Gamecocks with either his running or passing ability.

Carolina fans were eager to see what he could do against a tough Tiger team on this day.

Some 82,000 fans turned out on a glorious day in the Blue Ridge to witness this classic struggle, the 82nd between these two old adversaries. They noted that Clemson was dressed out in orange pants, to give them a psychological edge.

The first quarter rocked along with neither team making any headway. But then, following a turnover, Clemson took the ball on the USC 41. Six plays later Terrence Flagler went in from the nine, Donald Igwebuike kicked the point, and Clemson led 7-0.

Two minutes later Carolina mounted a drive of their own, marching from their own 13 down to the Clemson 23. They stalled at that point and brought in Scott Hagler who booted a field goal. Clemson now led 7-3.

Then the Tigers came back again, this time driving 85 yards for the game's next score, Stacey Driver going over from the one. Again the kick was good, and Clemson led 14-3. Mike Eppley had runs of 15 and 30 yards on this drive, by the way.

There were still eight minutes left in the half, and Clemson fans were beginning to feel much better about themselves.

Only moments later Thomas Dendy fumbled a Mike Hold pass and Keith Williams recovered for Clemson at the USC 37. Four plays later Steve Griffin went in from the 12 for Clemson's third TD of the first half. The kick was good, and Clemson padded their big lead to 21-3.

Now with three minutes remaining, the desperate Gamecocks mounted a drive of 83 yards, including a run of 51 yards by Thomas Dendy, and finally scored just moments before time expired when Quinton Lewis went over on fourth down from the four. Hagler's kick was good, and Clemson led 21-10 at the half.

Early in the third quarter Tony Guyton and Willie McIntee

Scott Hagler booted 45 of 45 extra points in '84, an all-time USC record.

James Seawright and Del Wilkes were both named to the All-American team in '84. Both are members of the USC All-Time Team.

broke through and tackled Mike Eppley behind the goal line, a 2-point safety for USC, which cut Clemson's lead to 21-12. This play would later be of extreme importance to the Gamecocks.

Later, midway the final quarter, following a drive of 56 yards, USC called on Hagler for yet another field goal, this one of 41 yards. It was good and Clemson now led 21-15. There was still 7:19 remaining in the game, and Clemson fans were beginning to wish that the big hand on that time clock would turn just a little faster.

Four minutes later, with just 3:07 remaining, USC took the ball at their own 16-yard line. Mike Hold completed a 36-yard pass to Chris Wade to the USC 48. Then came Quinton Lewis with a 16-yard run, and Thomas Dendy with an 18-yard run. Then Mike Hold picked up seven. Three plays later Hold kept again, this time going in for the TD that tied the score at 21-21. Hagler's kick gave the Gamecocks a 22-21 win in what is still remembered as one of the most exciting games ever in this long series.

Carolina finished their season at 10-1, losing finally to Oklahoma State in the Gator Bowl. Clemson, with a 7-4 record, was still prohibited from post-season play.

(The '84 Gamecocks finished the season with 5,095 yards in total offense and scored 381 points, all-time USC records.)

Fans got their first glimpse of Mike Hold when he came in to lead USC to a comeback upset of Georgia, 17-10.

Raynard Brown and Bryant Gilliard sparked USC's 38-26 upset of Florida State. Brown returned a kickoff 99 yards for a touchdown, while Gilliard had four pass interceptions, tying an all-time USC record. Gilliard was named All-American in '84 and is a member of the USC Athletic Hall of Fame.

Trailing Notre Dame 26-14 going into the 4th quarter, USC then scored 22 points to upset the irish 36-32. These jubilant Gamecocks ham it up after their big comeback win: (Top row, L-R): Harry South, Bill Barnhill, Carl Womble. (Middle row, L-R): Jim Walsh, Del Wilkes, Eric Poole, Jim Gatling. (Bottom row, L-R): Ray Carpenter, and Ken Robinson. Eric Poole averaged 21.3 yards per pass reception during his career at USC (46 catches for 982 yards), still an all-time USC record.

Carolina's Fire Ant defense set an all-time USC record when they blocked four punts in their 49-17 win over Kansas State.

Donald Igwebuike kicks his second of two field goals as Clemson beat UNC 20-12. He kicked 16 of 17 FGs in '81, an all-time CU record, and was named All-American in '84.

*Terrence Flagler goes over for another Clemson TD as the Tigers beat Appalachian State 40-7 in '84. They would win six more games by season's end. **Flagler was named All-American in 1986.***

Kevin Brown nails a Gamecock receiver after he takes a short pass from Mike Hold. At this point Clemson was holding a big 21-3 lead and seemed to have the game in the bag.

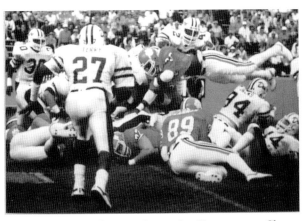

David Barnette crashes over for another Tiger score as Clemson romped on Duke 54-21.

A despondent Carolina squad looks on (or doesn't look on) during post-game ceremonies in the '84 Gator Bowl. They had just lost this one 21-14 on a crushing last minute Oklahoma State scoring drive.

With time running out in the fourth quarter Mike Hold went in from the one to tie the score at 21-21. Hagler kicked the point and Carolina walked away with a 22-21 miracle win over the Tigers, their first at Death Valley since 1970.

1985

TREADWELL, FLOWERS LEAD TIGER VICTORY

Fans who expected the Gamecocks to pick up just where they'd left off in '84 were disappointed as the '85 season progressed. Indeed, by the time November 23 and the Clemson game rolled around the Gamecocks had beaten the little guys on their schedule (The Citadel, Appalachian State, Duke, East Carolina, and Navy) but had lost to all the biggies, all five of them.

As for Clemson, Danny Ford's charges weren't doing much better. But they would win at Williams-Brice Stadium this afternoon, improve their record to 6-5, and accept an invitation to play Minnesota in the Independence Bowl. Not bad for a so-so team.

As usual, both teams felt the other out for the first ten minutes of the first quarter. But then, with 2:26 remaining, David Treadwell capped a 74-yard drive with a 27-yard field goal, and Clemson took the lead at 3-0.

But then, just three minutes later, Gleen Peacock covered a Kenny Flowers fumble at the Clemson 22, and suddenly the Gamecocks were back in business. Raynard Brown picked up 19 yards on a burst off tackle, then came Kent Hagood right up the middle and in for a touchdown. Scott Hagler's kick was good, and USC led 7-3.

Three minutes later, still in the second quarter, Mike Hold threw a 54-yard screen pass to Hagood for another USC score, but a penalty brought the ball back to the Clemson 27. But five plays later Hagood went over for his second touchdown of the day. The kick was good, and Carolina led 14-3. There was 10:12 showing on the clock at that point.

Four minutes later the Tigers began a comeback, culminating in a tremendous 49-yard Treadwell field goal. Carolina's lead was cut to 14-6.

Still later, with less than two minutes remaining, Clemson staged a brilliant 89-yard drive, in only nine plays, with Kenny Flowers going in from the two. Rodney Williams, the Tigers' fine freshman quarterback, then threw to Terrence Flagler for the two-point conversion, and the two teams went to the locker room all knotted at 14-14.

The third period had just gotten underway when Clemson's A. J. Johnson recovered a Hagood fumble at the USC 25. Five plays later Flowers went in for his second TD of the day, and Clemson suddenly took the lead at 21-14. It was a lead the Gamecocks could not overcome.

With only seconds left in the third period Hagler kicked an amazing 54-yard field goal to bring USC to within four points

of the Tigers, but that was as close as they could get.

With eight minutes left in the game, Clemson's 50-yard drive ended at the USC 30. From there Treadwell kicked his third field goal of the afternoon, and Clemson won by a score of 24-17.

For Carolina this was the end of the '85 road. Clemson would go on to lose by a score of 20-13 to Minnesota in the Independence Bowl.

(USC had 636 total yards vs. The Citadel, an all-time record.)

(Sterling Sharpe set an all-time USC record in '85 when he returned a kickoff 104 yards for a TD vs. Duke.)

And the USC Good Sportsmanship Award goes to. . .

Thomas Dendy rushed for 2,726 yards during his career at USC (still fifth best in the USC record book), an average of 5.5 yards per carry, still second only to Carl Brazell's 5.7 yards per carry (1952-55).

Derrick Little, USC's massive defensive tackle, surprises this Wolverine quarterback as Michigan won 34-3 in '85.

Tough Stacey Driver runs for daylight as the Tigers lost to Georgia 20-13.

Rodney Williams, hands off to Kenny Flowers as the Tigers beat Virginia 27-24 in '85.
(Rodney Williams completed 333 passes during his career for 4,647 yards. Both figures are still Number-Two in the CU record book.)
(Flowers ran for 2,914 yards during his career with the Tigers, still number-two in the CU record book.)

Keith Jennings took a short pass from Stacey Driver for Clemson's only TD of the evening as the Tigers lost to Minnesota 20-13 in the 1985 Independence Bowl.

Raynard Brown goes for a first down as USC fell to Clemson 24-17 in '85.

1986

THE BIG GAME ENDS IN TIE

Clemson was again enjoying an excellent year in '86. They had fought through a tough schedule and were showing a 7-1-2 record, including wins over both Georgia and Georgia Tech, as they made preperations to meet the Gamecocks on November 22 at Frank Howard Field.

As for the Gamecocks, the big news was the appearance of their new star quarterback, Todd Ellis, one of the top high school quarterbacks in America a couple of years before. Already he was rewriting the USC record book as far as passing was concerned, and was considered the most exciting USC quarterback ever. And catching the ball were such all-time great USC receivers as Sterling Sharpe and Ryan Bethea. The Gamecocks were showing a poor 3-6-1 record coming into today's game, but their losses were to such national powers as Nebraska (27-24), Georgia (31-26) and Miami (34-14). As for today's game, USC fans were predicting a win for the visiting team, despite Clemson's superior won-loss record.

The Gamecocks kicked off, which was a mistake, for Terrance Roulhac returned it 75 yards, down to the USC 25. Three plays later, following Ray Williams' run of 23 yards, Tracey Johnson took it in from the one, and Clemson was on the board. The center snap for the extra point was low, so Todd Schonhar picked it up and fired a perfect pass to Jim Riggs in the end zone for two points, and Clemson was up 8-0.

Seven minutes later Carolina drove 45 yards, down to the Clemson one. Harold Green went over from there, Scott Hagler kicked the point, and Clemson led 8-7.

Early in the second period there was another bad snap from center on an attempted field goal try, and again Todd Schonhar tried a pass. But this time Brad Edwards, USC's All-American safety, picked it off and returned it 61 yards for a touchdown. The point was good, and Carolina now led 14-8.

Then Clemson began another drive, this one of 70 yards. The score came on a Rodney Williams' pass of 35 yards to Roulhac in the end zone. David Treadwell's kick was good, and Clemson took the lead at 15-14.

There were still eleven minutes left in the second quarter.

A few minutes later Treadwell missed a field goal and USC took over at their own 28. Two plays later Todd Ellis fired a long pass of 72 yards to Sterling Sharpe who took it into the end zone. The kick was good, and Carolina re-gained the lead at 21-15.

Six minutes later Clemson drove to the Carolina 20. Treadwell kicked a field goal from there, and USC's lead was cut to 21-18.

And that would be the end of the scoring for the next 30 minutes. But then, with only 2:50 remaining on the clock, Treadwell kicked a field goal of 31 yards and the score was tied 21-21. And that is how the game finally ended, the first time since 1950 that these two teams had played to a tie.

Clemson, a hardnosed, grind-it-out team, had 237 yards on the ground, which accounted for most of their yardage and scoring.

For the Gamecocks, on the other hand, running a run-and-shoot offense, their yardage came through the air, 275 yards of it.

Again for Carolina this was the end of the road. But Clemson, now 7-2-2 on the season, would go on to win the ACC championship and defeat Stanford in the Gator Bowl.

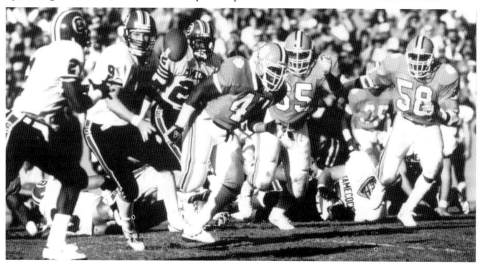

Todd Ellis pitches to Sterling Sharpe as USC and Clemson fought to a 21-21 tie in '86. Ellis threw for 3,020 yards and 20 touchdowns in '86, new records for USC. Sharpe caught 74 passes for 1,106 yards and 10 touchdowns in '86, more all-time USC records.

Terrence Flagler scored four TDs vs. Wake Forest and averaged 6.6 yards per carry in '86, still all-time CU records. He was name All-American in '86.

During his career at USC ('83-'86) Scott Hagler kicked 117 of 118 extra points, an all-time USC record.

David Treadwell's field goal beat Georgia 31-28 in the final moments. Treadwell would be named All-American in '88.

Freshman sensation Todd Ellis made his first appearance vs. Miami, the third-ranked team in the nation. He threw for 277 yards in that game, but USC lost 34-14.

Terrance Roulhac served as captain of the Tigers in '86. Roulhac won the NCAA kickoff return title with a 33-yards per return average in '86.

The Tigers defeated Stanford 27-21 in the '86 Gator Bowl.

1987

USC'S BEST TEAM EVER BEATS CLEMSON

Danny Ford came out with another of his great Clemson football teams in 87, and by the time they departed the Blue Ridge for Columbia the Tigers were 9-1 on the season, their only loss a shocking 30-28 upset at the hands of pesky NC State. Still, under the leadership of Rodney Williams, they had demolished everybody else on their schedule, including such outsiders as Georgia and Georgia Tech, and were again champions of the ACC and headed for a matchup against Penn State in the Citrus Bowl. They had also earned a number-eight national ranking. In a word, the Tigers were again loaded for bear, or Gamecock, as the case may be.

As for Carolina, Joe Morrison was now in his fifth year as head coach, and things, finally, were beginning to jell for his Gamecocks. He had recruited one of the best quarterbacks in America in Todd Ellis, plus some of the greatest receivers in the land. As for his Fire Ant defense, under Coach Joe Lee Dunn they had become one of the most feared gang of ruffians anywhere.

Indeed, they were 7-2 going into the Clemson game, with number-one Miami yet to be played, and were ranked number-12 nationally.

(Today, many Carolina fans still consider the '87 Gamecocks to be the best team ever produced by the University, better even than their 10-1 team of '84.)

These two teams met on November 21, a frigid evening in Columbia, with a record crowd of over 75,000 fans on hand, plus millions more watching at home on national TV.

The action in this contest was hot and furious from the very beginning, with Clemson taking the opening kickoff and moving 91 yards for their only score of the evening. Rodney Williams completed two passes to Keith Jennings for 44 yards in this drive and Tracy Johnson added another run of 14 yards. Then it was Wesley McFadden going in from the two for the TD. David Treadwell kicked the point and Clemson took the lead at 7-0.

Then, two minutes into the second quarter, Carolina drove to the Clemson 33 before they stalled. Collin Mackey came in at that point and booted a 49-yard field goal, narrowing Clemson's lead to 7-3.

Eight minutes later it was Carolina again getting on the board. Their drive this time began at their own 32. Following several running plays and a 38-yard pass from Todd Ellis to Kevin White, Mackie again booted a field goal, this one for 45 yards, and Clemson's lead was now 7-6.

There was no more scoring until late in the third quarter. At that point Rusty Seyles punted for 41 yards, and the ball was downed at the USC 17. On first down Todd Ellis found Ryan Bethea breaking across the middle. Bethea caught the ball on

Brad Edwards made a big interception as Carolina lost to Georgia 13-6. Edwards, named to the All-American Team in '87, returned three interceptions for touchdowns during his career, an all-time USC record, and later went on to become an all-pro with the Washington Red Skins.

Joe Morrison and Vice President George Bush have a friendly chat just prior to the Carolina-Clemson game of '87.

the dead run and appeared headed for a touchdown, but then a desperation tackle by Donnell Woolford brought him down at the six. The play covered 77 yards. Harold Green went in for the score on the next play, and USC took the lead 13-7.

(Todd Ellis' 77-yard non-scoring pass to Ryan Bethea remains an all-time USC record.)

In the fourth quarter, with 5:37 showing on the clock, Rodney Williams threw a short pass out in the flat, but USC's All-American safety, Brad Edwards, picked it off and ran 40

yards untouched for another Carolina score. Again Mackie's kick was good, and Carolina took the lead, and the game, by a final score of 20-7.

Clemson was now 9-2 on the season, and would go on to rout Penn State 35-10 in the Citrus Bowl.

As for Carolina, their Fire Ant defense held Clemson to just 166 yards in total offense, the lowest total ever for a Danny Ford-coached Tiger team. The Gamecocks finished the season with an 8-3 record, then went on to lose 30-13 to LSU in the Gator Bowl.

Joe Lee Dunn's defense finished in the top-ten of every NCAA defensive catagory in '87. The Fire Ants gave up only 1,158 yards rushing that season, an all-time USC record.

Sterling Sharpe became USC's all-time leading receiver in '87. During his career he hauled in 169 passes for 2,497 yards. He was named All-American in '87, and is one of only four USC players ever to have his jersey retired. He became an all-pro with the Green Bay Packers.

Harold Green, one of USC's finest running backs ever, punches over for a TD as Carolina smashed Virginia 58-10 in '87. Green scored 15 TDs in '87, still an all-time USC record.

Rodney Williams hands off to Terry Allen as the Tigers upended Virginia. Allen was named All-American in '87 and is a member of Clemson's All-Time Football Team.

The great Rodney Williams is brought down near the goal line as NC State upset Clemson 30-28. His 5,510 career total yards is still Number-Three in the CU record book.

Donnell Woolford returns a punt 67 yards for a TD as the Tigers beat Wake Forest 31-17. Woolford was named All-American in '87.

Collin Mackie scored 113 points for USC in 1987, an all-time Carolina scoring record.

Carolina's Fire Ant defense held Clemson's highly regarded offense to only 166 yards of total offense.

Tracey Johnson scored three TDs on the day as Clemson beat Penn State 35-10 in the Citrus Bowl, the Lion's worst bowl defeat in history.

Todd Ellis again finds himself under fire as USC fell to LSU 30-13 in the Gator Bowl. Ellis still managed to throw for 304 yards in that contest.

1988

GARDOCKI AND ERRORS BEAT GAMECOCKS

Danny Ford and his Tigers were enjoying another fabulous season as they prepared to host the Carolina Gamecocks in 1988. They were 8-2 at that point, with losses to only Florida State (24-21) and those pesky NC Staters (10-3) to mar their record. They had won their third consecutive ACC championship and would be headed for a meeting with tough Oklahoma in the Citrus Bowl come New Years Day. Indeed Coach Danny Ford was now recognized as one of the winningest coaches in America.

As for the Gamecocks, they themselves were enjoying a good season with an 8-2 record, their two losses coming at the hands of Georgia Tech (34-0) in a huge upset, and Florida State (59-0) in a real blowout.

Indeed, 1988 was a strange season for Carolina. In the first half of the season they looked like world beaters. They had romped over number-six Georgia by a score of 23-10, giving them a 4-0 record on the year and a number-seven national ranking. But then the coaches, who never quite knew what to do with Todd Ellis, changed offenses once again. From that point on, the Gamecocks seemed to struggle.

As for today's game, a record crowd of 85,000 jammed into Death Valley to watch this 86th meeting between the Gamecocks and the Tigers on a beautiful day in the Blue Ridge.

Clemson, with Rodney Williams at quarterback, took the opening kickoff and drove to the USC 35. At that point Chris Gardocki came in an kicked a 47-yard field goal to give the Tigers a 3-0 lead.

The Gamecocks then took the ensuing kickoff and drove for 61 yards, down to the Clemson nine. But Harold Green fumbled at that point, Dexter Davis recovered for Clemson, and the Tigers began a long drive of their own. After a 40-yard pass completion from Williams to Gary Cooper, plus four more running plays, Gardocki again came in and this time booted a 31-yarder to up Clemson's lead to 6-0.

Early in the second quarter Todd Ellis fumbled a snap from center, Levon Kirkland recovered for Clemson, and again they began a drive. And again Gardocki was called on for a field goal, this one of 38 yards, and the Tigers took the lead at 9-0.

On USC's next possession they were forced to punt. Clemson took the ball at their own 15 and then drove 85 yards for a touchdown, Terry Allen going in from the eight. Rusty Seyle's kick was good, and Clemson's lead went to 16-0.

The Gamecocks' George Rush took the kickoff and made a terrific return, down to the Clemson 33. Four plays later Ellis hit Robert Brooks with a zinger in the Tiger end zone. Collin Mackie's kick was good, and Clemson's lead was cut to 16-7.

With 4:56 left in the third Clemson truly took control of the game when Tracy Johnson went over from the one for a touchdown. The kick was no good, but the Tigers now led 22-7.

Some ten minutes later Rodney Williams added icing to the cake when he scored on a keeper from the seven. Seyle's kick was good, and Clemson led 29-7.

Carolina's Mackie added a 47-yard field goal with just four minutes remaining to cut Clemson's lead to 29-10, but it was too little too late, and the Tigers walked away with their ninth win of the season. They would go on to upset Oklahoma 13-6 in the Citrus Bowl.

Carolina would end the season with an 8-3 record, then lose to Indiana 34-10 in the Liberty Bowl.

Tragically, Coach Joe Morrison would die of a heart attack only a few weeks following the Liberty Bowl contest. Truly, he presented the most exciting brand of football to Carolina ever witnessed by Gamecock fans.

Robert Brooks makes his famous one-handed catch of an Ellis pass in the end zone to beat Georgia in '88. Brooks caught a 97-yard TD Todd Ellis pass against East Carolina in '88, the longest TD completion on record for the Gamecocks. He was named All-American in '91 and is a member of the USC All-Time Football Team. He went on to become an all-pro receiver with the Green Bay Packers.

Todd Ellis brought a level of excitement to USC football never seen before and totally rewrote the USC record book.

All-American Todd Ellis completed 747 passes for 9,953 yards during his career, still an all-time USC record.

Collin Mackie, with 330 points to his credit, remains USC's all-time leading scorer.

Ray Williams finished his career with the Tigers as one of their top men in receptions and return yardage.

Harold Green eludes a pack of NC State defenders for a TD as USC beat State 23-7.

Gary Cooper scored twice in Clemson's win over Maryland for the ACC title in '88. Cooper averaged 20.1 yards per reception during his career at Clemson. This remains second only to Joe Blalock's 20.3 average of 1939-41.

Tracy Johnson looks for that opening as Clemson thrashed UNC 37-14 in '88.

The captains meet on the field just moments before kickoff on November 19, 1988.

Todd Ellis, who would complete only 11 passes in the Clemson game, spots an open Harold Green.

Jesse Hatcher forced a fumble when he hit Todd Ellis. This mistake would prove costly for the Gamecocks.

Clemson rushed for 255 yards in this game, their massive offensive line dominating Carolina's defense.

Clemson held Oklahoma's vaunted offense to only 116 yards rushing and two field goals as the Tigers won the Citrus Bowl 13-6. Jesse Hatcher (#55) won the team MVP award for his fine defenive play in this contest.

1989

CLEMSON WINS IN LANDSLIDE, 45-0

The quarterback situation at Clemson was somewhat unsettled following the graduation of Rodney Williams, but the decision was soon made to go with Chris Morocco. It was a good decision, apparently, for the Tigers were enjoying another fabulous season under his direction with an 8-2 record as they prepared to meet the Gamecocks on November 18.

No one knew it at this date, but the bad news for Clemson fans was the departure of Danny Ford following the '89 season. During his eleven-year tenure at Clemson (1979-89) he had led the Tigers to an outstanding 96-29-4 record, which made him the third winningest coach in the nation. So it was not his ability to win that led to his troubles with the Great Powers at Tigerland.

The situation at Carolina was not quite as positive. Following the untimely death of Coach Joe Morrison, Sparky Woods had been hired to lead Carolina's fortunes. As head coach at Appalachian State, Coach Woods had been voted Southern Conference Coach of the Year on three occasions. Plus he was truly a nice guy and well known for running a clean program at ASU, which was important to USC's athletic department following Carolina's infamous steroid scandal in '88.

With Todd Ellis back for his senior season, Gamecock fans were hoping the team would pick up right where they'd left off in '88. And indeed they were rocking along with a good 5-1-1 record when tragedy struck. Todd Ellis went down with a severe injury vs. NC State and that was the end of his career. As for the team, they just weren't the same anymore and would go 1-3 on the rest of the season.

Today's game was played before 75,000 fans at Williams-Brice Stadium with millions more watching on national TV.

But it wasn't much of a game. The Tigers took the opening kickoff and drove 79 yards for a TD, Terry Allen going in from the 12. Rusty Seyle's kick was good, and Clemson led 7-0.

On USC's next possession Dick DeMasi's pass was picked off by Jerome Henderson and Clemson was back in business. They drove 54 yards this time, with Terry Allen again going in for the TD. The kick was good, and Clemson led 14-0. There were still five minutes left in the first quarter.

Ten minutes later Gardocki kicked a 28-yard field goal and Clemson led 17-0. Then, five minutes later, Clemson scored again, this time on a 12-yard pass from Chris Morocco to Rodney Fletcher. The kick was good and Clemson lead 24-0, which was the half time score.

If Gamecock fans were hoping that their team would re-group and make a big comeback in the second half, they were sadly disappointed.

With four minutes left in the third quarter Tony Kennedy scored on a 30-yard burst off tackle, the kick was good, and Clemson's lead went to 31-0. Then, two minutes into the fourth quarter, Junior Hall scored on a 22-yard run and the score went to 38-0.

Gamecock fans began streaming from the stadium at that point, and TV sets began to click off across the land. But the Tigers weren't finished. With nine minutes left, Tony Kennedy went in for his second TD of the day on a one-yard plunge, the kick was again good, and Clemson led 45-0. Which was the final score.

This was Clemson's greatest margin of victory since they'd beaten Carolina 51-0 in 1900.

Carolina was now 6-4-1 on the season, and their hopes for a bowl bid went down the drain with this loss. As for Clemson, they were now 9-2-0 and accepted a bid to play West Virginia in the Gator Bowl, a game they'd win by a score of 27-7.

(Robert O'Neal intercepted eight passes in '89, an all-time CU single-season record.)

Rob DeBoer ran for 165 yards as a freshman fullback vs. East Carolina.

Harold Green rushed for 3,005 yards during his career at USC. He also scored 33 TDs, tying George Rogers' all-time record. He was later an all-pro with the Cincinnati Bengals.

The peerless Robert Brooks takes a Dick DeMasi pass for yardage vs. Clemson.

Fullback Mike Dingle goes over for a TD as USC beat Western Carolina 24-3 in '89.

Coach Danny Ford and his family pose at Death Valley in '89. He was one America's winningest coaches at that time.

Carolina's defensive front five look troubled as Clemson seemed to score at will in '89. The Tigers won 45-0.

Coach Sparky Woods, formerly of Appalachian State, would lead USC to a 6-4-1 record in '89.

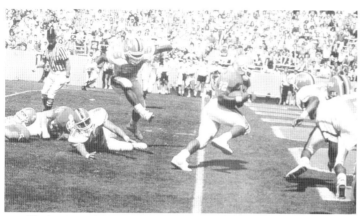

Wesley McFadden goes in for a TD as Clemson beat Virginia 34-20.

Stacy Long was named to the All-American Team in both 1989 and 1990 as one of the finest offensive linemen in America. He is a member of the CU All-Time Team.

Terry Allen led the ACC in rushing in both '87 and '88. He is still the Tigers' leader in career rushing yardage per game and Number-Two in total career rushing yardage.

Chris Morocco goes in for another score as Clemson whopped Maryland 31-7. Morocco completed .590 percent of his passes in '89, number two in the CU record book.

Here Clemson shows why they had one of the most feared offensive lines in the nation. The Tigers moved easily through the Mountaineers in the '89 Gator Bowl.

Chester McGlockton sacks West Virginia's Major Harris, then recovers in the end zone for a Tiger TD in the '89 Gator Bowl, a 27-7 win for Clemson.

253

1990

CLEMSON WINS ON LATE DRIVE

Gone now was Coach Danny Ford, and in his place came Ken Hatfield, a great coach with excellent credentials. As head coach at his old alma mater, the University of Arkansas, Hatfield had led the Razorbacks to two consecutive SWC championships (1988 and '89), proving pretty conclusively that he was a man with his head on straight. And his outstanding record at Clemson over the next four years would prove that the Tigers could not have chosen a better successor to Danny Ford. There was just one thing wrong--he wasn't Danny Ford. And many Clemson fans would never let him forget it.

Gone too was Chris Morocco, and thus DeChane Cameron got the nod to start at quarterback for the Tigers. And they were just as good in '90 as they had been in '89, with an 8-2 record coming into the USC game on November 18.

At Carolina, meanwhile, Sparky Woods was now in his second year as head coach and matters seemed to be well in hand. At quarterback was Bobby Fuller, a transfer from Appalachian State, who would prove to be one of USC's most successful field generals ever.

The Gamecocks were 5-4 coming into the Clemson game after having a real up-and-down season. They had beaten Duke, UNC, VPI and East Carolina, then allowed themselves to be upset by The Citadel 38-35.

But the big news at Carolina this year was their acceptance into the powerful Southeastern Conference. They would begin their SEC schedule in '92.

As for today's game, neither team scored until late in the first quarter. At that point Chris Gardocki went back to punt for the Tigers. But Ricky Ferguson blocked the kick and USC took over at the Clemson 12-yard line. Four plays later Collin Mackie came in and kicked a 22-yard field goal and USC took a surprising 3-0 lead over the favored Tigers.

The second quarter, however, belonged to Clemson. Fullback Rudy Harris scored twice for the Tigers in this period, once from the one and once from the seven, and Clemson was up 14-3.

But just before the half ended Mackie kicked another field goal for Carolina, this one of 42 yards, and so USC closed the gap to 14-6 at half time.

Scoring in the third quarter consisted only of a Chris Gardocki field goal which upped Clemson's lead to 17-6.

But the real fireworks started in the fourth quarter. With twelve minutes remaining, following another Mackie field goal, USC made a comeback when fullback Mike Dingle went in from four yards out for a touchdown. The 2-point conversion try failed, and Clemson's lead was cut to 17-15.

For a moment the outcome was in doubt, much to the consternation of Clemson fans, but eight minutes later the Tigers marched 84 yards for their final, and deciding score, when Tony Kennedy went in from the one. The kick was good, and the final score became 24-15.

USC would then go on to defeat West Virginia 29-10 on national TV and refuse a bid to play in the Independence Bowl.

Clemson would finish the season with a 10-2 record after defeating Illinois 30-0 in the Hall of Fame Bowl.

Clemson 's DeChane Cameron led the Tigers to a great 10-2 record in '90. His .547 completion percentage is still third in the CU record book.

Vance Hammond was an All-ACC defensive lineman in both '89 and '90.

Coach Ken Hatfield came to Clemson with excellent credentials. But he wasn't Danny Ford, and many Clemson fans would never let him forget it.

Chris Gardocki, Clemson's career punting leader, was chosen for the CU All-Time Football team as a placekicker. (Gardocki kicked a 57 yard field goal vs. ASU in '90, an all-time CU record.)

Ed McDaniel ranks third in career tackles with the Tigers. Here he puts the skids on a USC running back.

Fred Zeigler and Sterling Sharpe, USC's all-time greatest receivers, met at a reunion at Carolina. Zeigler is now a Columbia attorney; Sharpe a network sportscaster.

Ronald Williams breaks for a touchdown as Clemson smashed Georgia 34-3.

On September 25, 1990 Commissioner Roy Kramer invited USC to become a member of the Southeastern Conference. Looking on are Coach Sparky Woods and athletic director King Dixon.

Clemson's no. 1 defense held Illinois to just 59 rushing yards as they swamped the Illini 30-0 in the '91 Hall of Fame Bowl. Here Doug Thomas takes a DeChane Cameron pass into the end zone for another Tiger score.

A transfer from Appalachian State, Bobby Fuller threw for 4,896 yards (still fourth best in the record book) during his two years of eligibility at USC.

Mike Dingle, at 6-3 and 240 pounds, leaps over the East Carolina line for a TD as USC won 37-7.
(Dingle scored four TDs vs. VPI, tying an all-time USC record.)

Collin Mackie kicked 72 field goals and 92 consecutive extra points for a total of 330 points scored, all-time USC records. He also kicked five field goals vs. West Virginia, another all-time USC record.

Rob DeBoer led USC to a great 29-10 win over West Virginia in the final game of the '90 season.

Williams-Brice Stadium. In '90 skittish USC fans complained that they could see the upper East deck, the student section, dangerously swaying. USC officials thus moved the students to the lower East deck and prohibited the USC band from playing "Louie, Louie" at home football games. (We ain't kidding!)

1991

CAMERON, RUNNING GAME SINK USC

Ken Hatfield was in his second year as head coach of the Tigers, and as usual they were enjoying a great season, being 8-1-1 as they prepared to meet the Gamecocks on November 23. DeChane Cameron and Rodney Blunt were back in Clemson's backfield, and Hatfield said he wouldn't trade them for any other two backs in the country. As for Clemson's defense, they were their usual selves, which means that they were terrific.

As for Carolina, they appeared on paper to be a very sound football machine. With such super stars as Bobby Fuller, Brandon Bennett, and Robert Brooks back on offense, they could certany score points. But their weakness, in addition to an annoying inconsistency in general, was a defense that had trouble stopping any of the big boys. They were 3-5-2 going into the Clemson game, including a loss to East Carolina and a tie with Louisiana Tech, their first losing season since 1986.

Their chances today against number-12 Clemson were considered slim.

On Clemson's first possession of the game they marched 84 yards for a TD, Rudy Harris going in from the one. Nelson Welch's kick was good, and Clemson took an early 7-0 lead.

Just five plays later USC's Daren Parker took a bad snap from center, then got off a wobbly punt that went out of bounds at the Carolina 41. Eight plays later Nelson Welch booted a 21-yard field goal, and the Tigers were up 10-0.

But the Gamecocks came back with 6:04 remaining in the second quarter when Bobby Fuller hit Robert Brooks with a 16-yard TD pass. Marty Simpson's kick was good, and Clemson led 10-7.

But Clemson quieted the Carolina fans when DeChane Cameron hit Mike Samnick with a 31-yard pass on first down, then scampered around end for 31 yards and another Tiger touchdown. The kick was good, and Clemson's lead went to 17-7.

But with only seconds remaining on the clock Marty Simpson kicked a 27-yard field goal, and the Tigers' half time lead was cut to 17-10.

On their first drive of the second half, Cameron completed a 63-yard pass to Terry Smith and four plays later Welch kicked a 22-yard field goal, and Clemson increased their lead to 20-10.

(Nelson Welch kicked five field goals in three different games, an all-time CU record.)

Minutes later the Tigers were again on the move, this time driving 81 yards for their next score, Rodney Blunt bursting into the end zone from 16 yards out. Again the kick was good, and Clemson led 27-10.

But still the Tigers were not finished, not by a long sight. On their next possession they moved 69 yards for a score, Rudy Harris going in from the six for the TD. The kick was good, and Clemson padded their lead to 34-10.

Linebacker Joe Reaves, with a 3.8 GPR, was named Academic All-American in '91.

Jay Killen and Eddie Miller, co-captains of the '91 Gamecocks. Killen was chosen for the All-Independent team, while Miller was taken by the Indianapolis Colts.

During his career at Carolina the fleet Robert Brooks caught 120 passes for 2,211 yards, making him third in all-time receptions. He caught 19 career TD passes, an all-time USC record. He was named All-American in '91 and is a member of the USC All-Time Football Team.

With twelve minutes remaining, Bobby Fuller engineered a 53-yard drive in eight plays, Rob DeBoer going in from the two. Simpson's kick was good, and Clemson led 34-17.

On Clemson's next possession Cameron was injured and had to be helped from the field. In came Richard Moncrief. On his first snap from center he lofted a 25-yard pass to Terry Smith in the USC end zone for another touchdown. The kick was good, and Clemson increased their lead to 41-17.

To say that the USC stands now looked like Ghost Town, USA would be an understatement.

Still, the Gamecocks didn't quit. With just a minute left in the game, sub quarterback Wright Mitchell scrambled 15 yards for the final score of the afternoon. The kick was good, and the game ended, a 41-24 win for the Tigers, their fourth in a row over the Gamecocks.

DeChane Cameron accounted for 322 total yards in this contest, the third-best in Clemson history. The Tigers had a total of 503 yards in total offense, not a bad showing. They would then go on to defeat Duke in Tokyo, Japan, before losing to California in the Citrus Bowl.

Bobby Fuller was one of the few bright spots for Carolina. He passed for 303 yards, which were badly needed, since the Gamecocks rushed for only 16. They would finish the season with a 3-6-2 record.

(Mike Barber returned a fumble recovery 90 yards for a TD vs. UTC in '91, an all-time CU record.)

Bobby Fuller completed 373 of 634 passes for 4,896 yards during his career at USC. This .588 completion percentage remains second only to Steve Taneyhill's .605 completion percentage.

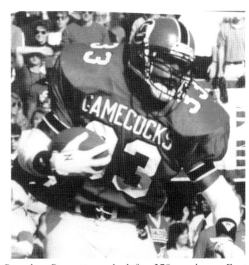

Brandon Bennette rushed for 278 yards vs. East Tennessee in '91, an all-time USC record.

Coach Sparky Woods poses with the mainstays of the '91 team: Gerald Dixon (#99), Robert Brooks (#49), Darren Parker (#1), and Bobby Fuller (#20).

Tailback Rodney Blunt was the Tigers' leading rusher in '91.

Jeb Flesch leads the way for DeChane Cameron as Clemson bombed USC 41-24 in '91.

All-American Rob Bodine and Chester McGlockton throw Bobby Fuller for a loss. The Gamecocks netted a total of 16 yards rushing in this game.

Jeb Flesch, a '91 All-American, was named the South's top lineman by the Atlanta Touchdown Club.

Levon Kirkland (#44) and Mike Barber (#12) again put the pressure on Bobby Fuller. Despite the pressure, Fuller completed 26 passes for 303 yards.

Clemson, all frocked out in their new purple jerseys, took it on the chin from California 37-13 in the Citrus Bowl.

Clemson led the nation in rushing defense in '91, and here All-American Levon Kirkland explains why to Bobby Fuller.

1992

TANEYHILL POWERS USC PAST CLEMSON

The Clemson faithful were not happy campers in 1992. The Tigers were 5-5 coming into today's game with Carolina, having lost four of their past five games. Indeed, this would be Clemson's first losing season since 1976, despite the fact that they were number-six nationally in rushing defense. With DeChane Cameron now departed, they simply weren't putting many points on the board.

The situation at Carolina was somewhat bizarre. They had begun playing their SEC schedule with a 28-6 loss to Georgia back in September, then proceeded to lose their next four games by rather convincing scores. But then, in the sixth game of the season, a young freshman quarterback named Steve Taneyhill finally was given a chance to show what he could do. What he could do was upset Mississippi State 21-6 with his terrific passing ability. Indeed, with Taneyhill at quarterback USC then went on to win five of their last six games, including a big

During the latter half of the '92 season USC went 5-1 under the leadership of their fine freshman quarterback, Steve Taneyhill. At season's end Sports Illustrated *named him Freshman of the Year and* Football News *named him to their Freshman All-American team.*

In 1992, after 31 years of service, Tom Price, USC's illustrious Sports Information Director, retired. He received numerous honors during his tenure and was recently named Historian of the USC Athletic Dept.

24-23 win over Tennessee. After four years without a win, the Gamecocks were ready for Clemson.

Some 85,000 fans turned out on November 21 at Death Valley to witness this contest. And they didn't have long to wait. Clemson took the opening kickoff and, behind quarterback Patrick Sapp, they moved to the USC ten on a drive that lasted for seven minutes. At that point Nelson Welch came in and kicked a 23-yard field goal, and Clemson led 3-0.

But following the ensuing kickoff Toby Cates beat Clemson's secondary and took a 46-yard toss from Steve Taneyhill. Six plays later Taneyhill hit Asim Penny with a 21-yarder for USC's first TD of the day. Marty Simpson's kick was good, and USC took the lead 7-3.

With two minutes remaining in the half, Tim Jones intercepted Taneyhill and returned it 26 yards for a Tiger touchdown. Welch's kick was good, and Clemson re-captured the lead at 10-7.

But the Gamecocks came right back. With only five seconds remaining on the clock, Simpson hit a 43-yard field goal, and thus the two teams went in at half time tied 10-10.

Clemson kicked off to open the second half, and Taneyhill quickly moved the Gamecocks deep into Tiger territory. Taneyhill then hit Cates with a 30-yard pass in the end zone for USC's second TD of the day. The kick was good, and Carolina now led 17-10.

Late in the third quarter Clemson drove to the USC 11, but a holding penalty moved them back to the 26. From there Welsch kicked a 40-yard field goal, and Carolina's lead was cut to 17-13.

Late in the game, after passing the Tigers dizzy, USC ran 10 consecutive rushing plays before Brandon Bennett dashed in for a TD from the four. The kick was good, and Carolina's lead became 24-13. And that was the final score, USC's first win over Clemson since 1988.

Both Clemson and Carolina finished the season with 5-6 records, which meant that neither team would have to worry about making preparations to participate in a big bowl game this year.

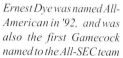

Ernest Dye was named All-American in '92, and was also the first Gamecock named to the All-SEC team

Ernest Dixon and Antoine Rivens, co-captains of the '92 Gamecocks.

Patrick Sapp ran the Tarheels dizzy with the option play as Clemson beat UNC 40-7 in '92.

Rodney Blunt finds daylight briefly as he's pursued by Cedric Bambury and Eric Sullivan. Clemson lost to Carolina 24-13 in '92.

For his outstanding play in USC's upset of Tennessee, Hank Campbell was named SEC Defensive Player of the Week.

Freshman sensation Steve Taneyhill led the Gamecocks to victory on the strength of his passing arm in '92.

1993

CLEMSON WINS IN COMEBACK

The Clemson Tigers were 7-3 coming into today's game with the Carolina Gamecocks, and would finish the season with a 9-3 record and a win over Kentucky in the Peach Bowl. You would assume that the above scenerio would gain the head coach a contract extension and a big fat raise. But no! Regardless of what Ken Hatfield might have accomplished, he still wasn't Danny Ford, and at the end of the '93 season he was told to find himself another job. (He would become head coach at Rice University in '94.)

As for Sparky Woods, his Gamecocks would post a 4-7 record in '93, their third consecutive losing season, and Sparky had also been told to move on. (He would become an offensive coach with the New York Jets.)

But to the 75,000 fans sitting through a cold drizzle at Williams-Brice today coaching problems were of little consequence. They only wanted to see which team could beat hell out of the other.

The Gamecocks took an early 3-0 lead thanks to a 37-yard Reed Morton field goal.

But Clemson answered on their next possession when Nelson Welch kicked a 37-yarder of his own to tie the score at 3-3.

But with four minutes left in the half, USC mounted an 84-yard drive that ended with Mike Reddick going in from the two. Reed Morton's kick was good, and Carolina led 10-3.

Then with only 13 seconds remaining in the half, Morton kicked a 27-yard field goal and USC padded their lead to 13-3.

But the Gamecocks had taken double-digit leads into five games earlier in the season only to see those leads dissolve and their sure wins become losses. The same thing happened today as the Tigers took over in the third quarter.

On their second possession, Nelson Welch kicked a 28-yard field goal to narrow the gap to 13-6. Then five minutes later Derrick Witherspoon went over from the five to knot the score at 13-13.

But the big score came with 1:02 remaining in the third when Andre Humphrey returned a punt 53 yards, down to the USC 43. Eight plays later Welch kicked a 31-yard field goal, and the Tigers went up 16-13. Which was the final score.

Following the 1993 season, Brandon Bennett had 2,201 yards rushing, and he still had another year to go.

David Turnipseed was named SEC Defensive Player of the week for his play against Georgia in '93.

Toby Cates, an excellent receiver and one of Steve Taneyhill's favorites.

Rob DeBoer turned down a six-figure baseball contract to play for USC in '93.

Stanley Prichett, called the best fullback in the SEC.

Reed Morton, with 57 points to his credit, led USC in scoring in '93.

Rodney Blunt, a great receiver as well as a devastating runner.

Nelson Welch tied an all-time Clemson record when he kicked five field goals vs. NC State in '93. His 301 total points is still Number-One in the CU record book. He was named All-American in '94.

Terry Smith caught a 21-yard TD pass with 20 seconds left to beat Kentucky 14-13 in the '93 Peach Bowl. During his career with the Tigers Smith caught 162 passes for 2,681 yards, still Number-One in the CU record book.

Stacy Evans brings down Patrick Sapp after a two yard gain.

Brandon Bennett runs for yardage as USC fell to Clemson 16-13 in '93.

1994

TANEYHILL, USC ROUT CLEMSON

There were new faces in the head coaching positions at both Clemson and Carolina as the '94 football season got underway. Tommy West, who had formerly served as head coach at UT-Chattanooga, was now at the helm at Clemson and Tiger fans were hoping the team would pick up right where they'd left off in '93. But such, unfortunately, was not to be. The Tigers were 5-5 coming into their season finale against USC, and would eventually end the season with a losing 5-6 record.

At Carolina, meanwhile, Brad Scott had replaced Sparky Woods as head coach, and Gamecock fans were hoping he'd brought with him a few of the tricks he'd learned as offensive coordinator under Bobby Bowden at Florida State. And sure enough, USC was doing unusually well under Coach Scott. Steve Taneyhill was back at quarterback, and the Gamecocks were 5-5 coming into the Clemson game, having lost a few close ones to some tough SEC opponents.

As had happened so often in the past, the first quarter was scoreless, with both teams feeling out the other. But the Gamecocks finally got rolling in the second when Steve Taneyhill hit Toby Cates with an 18-yard pass in the Clemson end zone for a TD. Reed Morton's kick was good, and USC led 7-0.

But the Tigers came right back. On their next drive Raymond Priester took a pitch and raced 15 yards for a Clemson touchdown. Nelson Welch's kick was good, and the score was tied 7-7.

But then, with only two minutes remaining before half time, Stanly Prichett took a little shovel pass from Taneyhill and burst through the Clemson line 14 yards for a touchdown. The kick was good, and USC went in at half time holding a 14-7 lead.

But it was the kickoff to open the second half that seemed to break the Tigers' back. Brandon Bennett took the kick at the goal line, then ran 11 yards upfield before suddenly stopping and tossing a lateral across field to Reggie Richardson. With a wall of blockers before him, Richardson dashed down the left sideline 85 yards before tripping over teammate Darrell Nicklow at the Clemson six.

(This remains the longest non-scoring kickoff return in USC history.)

Bennett went in on the next play, the kick was good, and USC now led 21-7.

Nor were the Gamecocks finished. Reed Morton kicked two field goals in the third quarter, one of 24 yards, the other of 33, and Carolina entered the fourth quarter with a 27-7 lead.

The biggest fireworks of the final quarter occurred with five minutes remaining when Benji Young intercepted a Nealon Green pass and returned it 27 yards for another Carolina touchdown. The kick was blocked, and USC took the lead 33-7. Which was the final score.

Coach Brad Scott, wife Daryle, and their two sons, John and Jeff. Coach Scott previously served as offensive coordinator under Bobby Bowden at Florida State.

Coach Tommy West, wife Lindsay, and their son, Turner. Coach West was head coach at UT-Chattanooga before coming to Clemson.

The illustrious Bob Fulton, the Voice of the Gamecocks on Gamecock Radio since 1952, retired following the '94 season. He's pictured here with his radio assistants. (L-R): Tommy Suggs, Bob Fulton, Todd Ellis, and Jim Powell.

Brandon Bennett completed his career in '94 with 3,055 yards rushing, the second leading rusher in the history of USC football. In 1991 (above) he rushed for 278 yards vs. East Tennessee, an all-time USC record.

Gamecock tri-captains go out for the coin toss just prior to their big win over Clemson in '94. (L-R): Tony Watkins, Brandon Bennett, and Toby Cates.

Steve Taneyhill was awarded the Carquest Bowl MVP award following USC's 24-21 win over a great West Virginia team. (Versus East Carolina Taneyhill completed 39 passes for 451 yards, an all-time USC record. He also completed 257 of 403 passes in '94, a .637 completion percentage. Both figures are more all-time USC records.)

Benji Young's 27-yard interception return for a TD sealed Clemson's fate in USC's 33-7 win in '94.

Brian Dawkins, one of Clemson's all-time great defensive backs, ranked eighth in the nation in interceptions in '94 and was named All-American.

The Tigers' great defense held Mayland scoreless as Clemson pulled a 13-0 upset in '94.

With 300 points to his credit, Nelson Welch became Clemson's all-time leading scorer in 1994, and was named All-American.

Lamarick Simpson was an All-ACC defensive tackle for Clemson in both '94 and '95.

Freshman Raymond Priester would become Clemson's most outstanding running backs in history. He scored the Tigers' only TD as they lost to USC in '94.

Quarterback Nealon Green would become one of Clemson's finest passer in history.

1995

PRIESTER KEYS CLEMSON WIN

It was November 18, and another of those seasons that sports fans throughout the state have come to expect. Clemson, led by Nealon Green and their all-time great running back, Raymond Priester, was 7-3 coming into their final game of the season, while USC was struggling along with a 4-5-1 record. Still, the Tiger team was not quite up to par, despite their good winning record, having lost to Florida State, Virginia, and Georgia. Indeed, as they arrived in Jacksonville for the Gator Bowl, one local sports writer joked that they were the worst 8-3 team in America.

The Gamecocks, despite their poor won-loss record, led by Steve Taneyhill, their record-breaking quarterback, had shown moments of brilliance. They had played LSU to a 20-20 tie, and beaten Mississippi State 65-39 and Vanderbilt 52-14, which suggests that they were not weak sisters by any means.

The game was played on a sunny afternoon in Columbia before 75,000 fans. A win for Carolina would be only for bragging rights, while a win for the Tigers would mean a trip to the Gator Bowl.

Carolina returned the opening kickoff to their ten-yard line. Eleven plays later they had marched the length of the entire field, finally scoring on a seven-yard toss from Steve Taneyhill to fast Monty Means. Reed Morton's kick was good, and USC went up 7-0. There were still ten minutes remaining in the first.

Five minutes later Antwuan Wyatt returned a USC punt 22 yards, all the way down to the Carolina 26-yard line. Six plays later Emory Smith bulled his way in from the one for the TD. Jeff Sauve's kick was good, and the score was tied 7-7.

Later, with only a minute remaining in the half, Reed Morton kicked a 27-yard field goal, and USC went in at halftime holding a surprising 10-7 lead. As though that were not bad enough for the Tigers, Raymond Priester had to be helped to the sideline with a severe hamstring injury.

In the third quarter Sauve tied the score on a 35-yard field goal. But then the Gamecocks roared back, driving 70 yards for a TD when Stanley Prichett took a three-yard pass from Taneyhill in the end zone. The kick was good, and USC again led, 17-10. There was 7:46 remaining in the third at that point.

Then Raymond Priester re-entered the game, which seemed to be just the spark the Tigers needed.

Four minutes later Wyatt took a short Green pass then dashed another 56 yards for a Clemson TD. The kick was good, and again the score was tied, 17-17.

And that was it. The fourth quarter belonged to the Tigers.

On Clemson's first possession of the fourth they moved 80 yards in ten plays, Priester going in from the six. The kick was good and Clemson took the lead for the first time today, 24-17.

Just three minutes later Clemson again scored, driving 46 yards with Green going over from the two. The kick was good, and Clemson increased their lead to 31-17. And that wasn't the end. There were still seven minutes left.

Following the ensuing kickoff, Leomont Evans intercepted a Taneyhill pass right on the Clemson goal line and returned the ball to the 24. The Tigers then drove 76 yards, with Emory Smith going in from the one. Again the kick was good, and the Tigers took the lead, and the game, by a score of 38-17.

With this loss the Gamecocks concluded a disappointing season with a 4-6-1 record.

Clemson, now 8-3, would go on to lose 41-0 to Syracuse in the Gator Bowl.

Raymond Priester set an all-time Clemson single-game rushing record when he ran for 263 yards in the Tigers' 34-17 win over Duke. He rushed for 110 yards per game in '95, another all-time record.

1995 marked the 100th year of Clemson football. In celebration, they broke out these old style uniforms popular in the 1930s. Here Nealon Green moves in Clemson's win over Furman.

The well dressed Clemson man of '95 observed the Centennial of Clemson Football.

Nealon Green, one of Clemson's all-time greatest quarterbacks, led Clemson to an 8-3 season and a trip to the Gator Bowl.

UPI named Anthony Simmons National Freshman of the Year.

The Clemson Sports Network features Jim Phillips, a veteran of 28 years as the Voice of the Tigers, supported by two of Clemson's finest quarterbacks ever, Mike Eppley and Rodney Williams.

Duce Staley, an All-SEC tailback, and USC's leading rusher in '95.

Reed Morton was twice named Academic All-American, and set an all-time USC record when he booted 11 PATs vs. Kent State in '95.

Defensive tackle Lamarick Simpson was an All-ACC performer in '95.

Cory Bridges caught five Taneyhill passes for 65 yards against the Tigers in '95.

Over the final 22 minutes of the game Clemson's defense held USC scoreless while the Tigers put 28 points on the board.

As the evening progressed, Clemson's big defense began to wear down the Gamecocks.

Big Emory Smith scored two touchdowns against the Gamecocks in '95. He tied an all-time CU record in '95 when he scored four TDs in the Wake Forest game.

Stanley Prichett's TD gave USC a 17-10 half time lead. (Prichett tied all-time USC records when he scored four TDs vs. Mississippi State in '95 and later had 12 receptions vs. Georgia.)

Steve Taneyhill completed 25 passes for 353 yards as USC fell to Clemson 38-17 in '95. He set a new NCAA record when he completed 40 of 46 passes (for 473 yards) vs. Mississippi State in '95. He completed 753 passes (a .605 completion percentage), including 64 TD passes, during his career at USC, more all-time records. Twice he completed five TD passes in a single game.

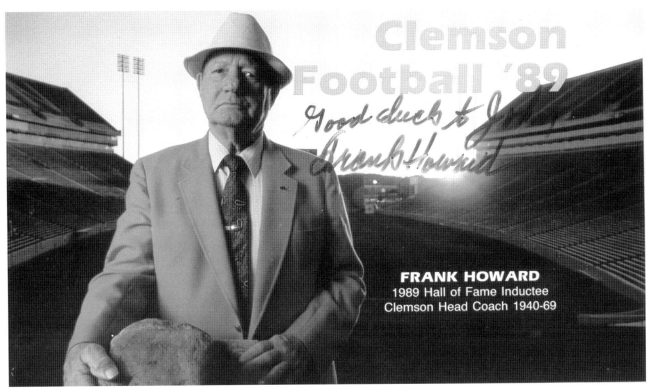

FRANK HOWARD
1989 Hall of Fame Inductee
Clemson Head Coach 1940-69

The End of an Era.

On January 28, 1996, only weeks after his beloved Clemson Tigers had celebrated their 100th year of football, Coach Frank James Howard departed this life. He originally arrived at Clemson to serve as assistant coach under Jess Neely in 1931. Then he became head coach in 1940, a position he would hold until 1969. He would then serve as athletic director for another five years. Truly, his death marked the end of an era, but the legend of Frank Howard will live on as long as there are Clemson Tigers and Blue Ridge mountains.

Frank Howard's first football team, the 1940 Clemson Tigers, went 6-2-1 on the season and were crowned Champions of the Southern Conference.

1996

USC DODGES BULLET, BEATS CLEMSON

The 1996 shootout between the Clemson Tigers and the Carolina Gamecocks will long be remembered as one of the most exciting on record. It all took place on a frigid November evening at Death Valley, with the 7-3 Tigers hoping for a bid to the Carquest Bowl, while the 5-5 Gamecocks were hoping a win would send them on their way to the Independence Bowl.

Clemson was led in '96 by their great record-setting quarterback Nealon Green and their equally great tailback, Raymond Priester, who had sparked the Tigers' to their big win over Carolina in '95.

As for Carolina, gone now was Steve Taneyhill, one of the finest passers in the nation, and in his place came Anthony Wright. And gone too was Stanley Prichett. But there was one old face in the USC backfield, a young juco transfer named Duce Staley who kept Gamecock fans on their feet through many a game.

Though the Tigers had a better record coming into tonight's game, USC had played a more rugged SEC schedule and had done fairly well. The experts thus considered this contest a tossup.

And they were pretty well correct.

The first half passed quickly, with the two teams seemingly well matched. Raymond Priester rushed for 113 yards, scored twice, and the Tigers went in at half time holding a 14-13 lead.

The fireworks started in the second half. Indeed, midway the third quarter Antwan Edwards picked off an Anthony Wright pass and returned it 58 yards, down to the USC two-yard line. A penalty moved them back to the seven. Three plays later USC's defense had allowed them only three yards. Matt Padgett came in at that point and kicked a field goal which put Clemson up 17-13.

But the tough Gamecocks then answered with 21 unanswered points. Indeed, there were just seven minutes remaining when freshman tailback Troy Hambrick made the most sensational run of the night, dashing 75 yards for a touchdown to put USC up 34-17. Still, despite the score, few fans left the stadium. And it's a good thing.

With 5:19 left Nealon Green hit Brian Wofford with a 12-yard pass for a touchdown. The kick was good, and USC's lead was cut to 34-24.

Still, with only five minutes remaining, USC held a 10-point lead, and Gamecocks fans were not too worried. But then, suddenly, the Tigers again had the ball. This time their drive ended with Green hitting Priester with a 10-yard TD pass, and now the Tigers had pulled to within three points of Carolina, 34-31. And there were still 2:47 remaining to be played.

Again Clemson took possession of the ball. Now there were only five seconds remaining on the clock and the Tigers had the ball at the USC 20. Time for one play. Matt Padgett, who had made seven of nine field goals during the past season, came in at that point to try a 37-yarder, a chip shot. Already the USC coaching staff was planning strategy for the over-time that was sure to follow.

But somehow Padgett's kick sailed wide to the left, and Carolina had dodged the bullet and walked away with a tough 34-31 win in this ninety-fourth meeting between these two schools.

Clemson, now with a 7-4 record, would go on to lose to LSU 10-7 in the Peach Bowl. Carolina, with a 6-5 record, had hoped this win would send them on to a bowl date, but SEC alignments caused the bid to go to Auburn instead.

Carolina's great sophomore quarterback, Anthony Wright, meets with the press following USC's thrilling 34-31 win over Clemson in '96. He laughed when asked how it felt to dodge Clemson's bullet that night.

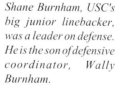

Shane Burnham, USC's big junior linebacker, was a leader on defense. He is the son of defensive coordinator, Wally Burnham.

The great Raymond Priester has now rushed for 3,010 yards, an all-time CU record. (And he still has another season to play!)

As for passing proficiency, Nealon Green is one of the top quarterbacks in Clemson history.

Big Tony Plantin, Clemson's defensive end, set an all-time record with seven quarterback pressures vs. Duke in '96.

Tony Horne led the Tigers in yards per catch in '96.

Matt Butler made Clemson's offensive line as a freshman.

Antwan Edward's 58-yard return of an interception, down to the USC two, set up Padgett's fourth quarter field goal.

Duce Staley's first TD of the evening put Carolina up 7-0. Here he is congratulated by a teammate while Dexter McCleon (#9) just shakes his head.

Reggie Richardson, one of USC's finest defensive backs ever. He returned a kickoff 85 yards vs. Clemson in '95.

Travis Whitfield trots off the field following the TD that gave USC a 34-17 lead. He was named USC's Most Improved Offensive Lineman in '96.

USC junior center, Paul Beckwith, became a leader on offense.

Freshman Zola Davis, promises to become an all-time great receiver for the Gamecocks. He was named to the All-SEC Freshman Team in '96.

USC safety Ben Washington gave Nealon Green something to think about.

Raymond Priester's 65-yard run set up Clemson's first TD of the evening.

Here, leading 17-14 early in the third quarter, Nealon Green looks for a receiver.

Troy Hambrick rushed for 135 yards vs. Clemson in '96, including a 75 yard TD run.

Staley goes in for his second TD of the evening, and Carolina was up 24-17.

Anthony Wright scores with only minutes remaining, and USC thought the game was over.

And were his coaches happy?

1997

TIGERS' 44 UNANSWERED POINTS ZAP GAMECOCKS

It was Saturday evening, November 22, 1997, a clear, pleasant evening in Columbia, though there was a distinct autumn chill in the air as some 83,700 fans (a new stadium record) filed into Williams-Brice Stadium for this 95th meeting between the Carolina Gamecocks and the Clemson Tigers.

This game always generated a great deal of excitement in the Palmetto State, of course. But the excitement generated by tonight's contest was extremely intense, for neither the Gamecocks nor the Tigers had lived up to expectations in '97 and it was hoped, by both persuasions, that the winner of tonight's game would be awarded a big bowl bid and thus salvage a modicum of respect from othewise disappointing seasons.

This was Coach Tommy West's fourth year with the Tigers, and in Raymond Priester and Nealon Green he had two of the finest backfield aces ever to play for the orange and purple. And of course Clemson had their usual terrific defensive team. Still, they came into tonight's contest sporting a mediocre 6-4 record. Which didn't sit particularly well with the Clemson faithful who don't tolerate too much Tom Foolery when it comes to football. But it should be pointed out that two of those losses had come at the hands of Florida State and UNC, two of the toughest teams in America. Yet Clemson had hung tough in both those contests and could have won them had the breaks gone a little more Clemson's way. In othe words, with just a little luck, Clemson could easily have been 8-2 coming in to tonight's game instead of 6-4. But, then, if bullfrogs had wings. . .

Back in Columbia, meanwhile, feelings of disappointment were even more intense. 1997 marked Coach Brad Scott's fourth year at the helm with the Gamecocks, and it had been trumpeted throughout the state that this was Brad Scott's team, a team of seniors, the team they had all been awaiting since the glory

years of Coach Joe Morrison back in the 1980s. Things, unfortunately, had not worked out as anticipated. The Gamecocks had easily whacked Central Florida in the opening game of the season, but then came Georgia, an also-ran in '96 who couldn't buy a game, and it was assumed that the Gamecocks would just add to their woes in '97. But such was not the case. Indeed, from the opening moment of that contest USC fans sat in stunned silence as the Bulldogs totally demolished the Gamecocks. But the Georgia game was just a harbinger of the bad things to come for USC as the season progressed, and now the Gamecocks were 5-5 as they prepared to dismantle Clemson and win that big bowl bid. (It should be pointed out, however, that USC's five losses came at the hands of Georgia, Auburn, Mississippi State, Florida and Tennessee, a gridiron Murder's Row by anyone's standards.)

And for the first 28 minutes of the first half it appeared that USC would indeed dismantle Clemson, despite the fact that the Tigers drew first blood on their opening drive. Starting from their own 23, Nealon Green guided the Tigers 67 yards in 12 plays before USC finally held at the ten. David Richardson came in at that point and booted a 20-yard field goal, and Clemson was up 3-0.

The Gamecocks, led by backup quarterback, Vic Penn, came right back, moving 86 yard in just under two minutes. The big play came on an option left with Troy Hambrick taking the pitch and racing 54 yards for a touchdown. Steve Florio's kick was good, and now the Gamecocks were up 7-3.

On their next possession Clemson was forced to punt, and Kevin Brooks returned it to the Tiger 47. Four plays later, Penn handed off to Hambrick on a draw play, and the big tailback raced 35 yards for another Gamecock touchdown. Again the kick was good, and now USC was up 14-3.

Troy Hambrick gained 109 yards on his first five carries of the evening and scored two TDs vs. Clemson in '97. On his third carry he dashed 54 yards for his first TD, then on his fifth carry (above) he dashed 35 yards for another. He was presented USC's MVP Award for his performance tonight.

Photo Courtesy of Ernie Rowell

The second quarter was truly a great one, with the Tigers again getting on the board early when their 62-yard drive stalled at the USC 17-yard line. From there Richardson kicked his second FG of the evening, cutting USC's lead to 14-6.

But then came a crucial series, with the Gamecocks starting a drive from their own 30. Penn guided them masterfully down the field, converting two big third-down plays by hitting Zola Davis with passes of 10 and 23 yards.

But then disaster struck.

With a first down at the Clemson 19, the Gamecocks got fancy and tried a trick play, a reverse, with Hambrick pitching back to Kerry Hood. The ball, unfortunately, never got to Hood. Instead, it was pitched ten feet over his head, bounced acrosss the field, and was finally recovered by Clemson freshman Chad Speck.

A collective gasp could be heard from the Gamecock faithful throughout the stadium.

In less than two minutes, then, Green moved the Tigers 75 yards in just six plays, Brian Wofford taking a seven-yard Green pass in for the touchdown, and suddenly the Tigers had pulled to within one point of the Gamecocks, 14-13. And thus ended the first half.

Gamecock fans could only shake their heads. Only two minutes earlier they had been sitting on top of the world, leading 14-6 with the ball on the Clemson 19 and about to score again. USC should have gone in at half time leading 21-6, and that might have done the Tigers in. But because of that one errant pitch, Carolina's lead had been cut to only one point. And now the Tigers looked like a team on fire.

And such indeed was the case.

Clemson wasted little time taking the lead once the second half got under way. With the ball at his own 45, Penn tossed a pass out to Shaw Mays. But an alert Antwan Edwards picked it off and returned it four yards, to the USC 44. Three plays later Green hit Tony Horne with a 17-yarder in the end zone, and Clemson took the lead 19-14.

And the rout was on.

Kerry Hood bobbled the ensuing kickoff out of bounds at the USC eight. Four plays later (from their three), Courtney Leavitt punted from his own end zone. Tony Horne took the kick at the USC 39, then wiggled all the way, almost untouched, into the USC end zone. Richardson's kick was good, and now Clemson led 26-14.

Carolina's next possessin was almost an exact replay of their last series. Again Penn tossed a pass out into the flat, and again Edwards was in the right place at the right time and again made the interception. Only this time he dashed 42 yards for another Tiger touchdown. Richardson's kick was good, and now Clemson's lead went to 33-14.

As though that were not bad enough, now, with just 41 seconds remaining in the third quarter, Mal Lawyer took a 15-yard Green pass into the end zone for another Tiger score. The kick was good, Clemson's lead went to 40-14, and Carolina fans began streaming from the stadium by the thousands.

And they still had 15 minutes left to play.

In the fourth quarter Clemson began to employ their running game more, with All-American Raymond Priester showing what he can do. On one play he dashed 24 yards, down to the USC 44. Then a few plays later Javis Austin took a pitchout and raced 19 yards for the Tigers' final TD of the evening. The kick was good, and Clemson's lead went to 47-14. The Tigers, after trailing 14-3, had now scored 41 unanswered points!

Then with just six minutes remaining, Carolina mounted a last drive of the evening, this one of 80 yards. Scott Moritz then scored from nine yards out, Florio's kick was good, and the game ended, a 47-21 blowout.

Not since Clemson defeated USC 51-0 in 1900 had they scored so many points against the Gamecocks.

For Carolina, it was the end of the road, though Clemson would receive that big bowl bid, and go on to lose to Auburn in the Peach Bowl.

Nealon Greene threw three TD passes vs. USC in '97, giving him 16 for the season, an all-time CU record.

Arturo Freeman, named to the All-SEC Freshman Team in '96.

Zola Davis, named to the All-SEC Freshman Team in '96, holds most freshman reception records at USC.

Darren Hambreck, one of the finest linebackers in the SEC, and the big brother of Troy Hambrick.

Jamar Nesbit, named to the All-SEC Freshman Team in '96.

Shane Burnham, leader of USC's defensive unit from his linebacker position.

Jason Lawson, originally a walkon fullback, has become a mainstay at end for USC.

Joey Unitas, son of NFL Hall of Famer Johnny Unitas, adds depth at QB for the Gamecocks.

Victor Penn, freshman backup QB to Anthony Wright, masterfully led USC in the Clemson game.

Ben Washington, a fine defensive back, named All-SEC in '97.

Scott Moritz scored USC's final TD of the evening in '97.

Cory Atkins, another of USC's outstanding linebackers. He won USC's Defensive Player of the Game vs. Clemson in '97.

Paul Beckwith, a mainstay at center for USC and an All-SEC selection.

Boo Williams, a crowd favorite, Williams shows promise of becoming an all-time great tailback for USC.

Travis Whitfield, a three-year starter at defensive tackle for USC.

Nealon Greene set 30 new records for CU quarterbacks during his career. He threw for 2,126 yards in '97 alone, and for 5,633 during his career. His .630 completion percentage in '97 was also a new CU record.

Antwan Edwards made two essential interceptions vs. USC in '97, one of which he returned 42 yards for a Tiger touchdown. He was name CU's Defensive Player of the Game.

Kenya Crooks, Clemson's leading receiver over the past two years.

Tony Horne caught a 17-yard TD pass to put Clemson up 19-14, then he later ran a punt back 39 yards for a TD to stretch Clemson' lead to 26-14.

Mal Lawyer took a 15-yard Greene pass into the end zone to run the score to 40-14. That was the end of the Gamecocks.

Anthony Simmons, Clemson's All-American linebacker.

Jim Bundren, Clemson's massive offensive tackle.

Brian Wofford caught Greene's TD pass with only moments left in the first half.

Ernie Rowell

Clemson drew first blood when David Richardson booted this 20-yard FG to put Clemson up 3-0.

Ernie Rowell

Raymond Priester over the past four years has become Clemson's all-time greatest running back, and now holds almost all rushing records for the Tigers, including rushing for a phenomenal 3,904 yards during his career.

Brian Wofford takes in this Nealon Greene pass just before half time to pull Clemson to within one point of USC, 14-13. The Gamecocks never recovered from this Tiger comeback.

Ernie Rowell

Ernie Rowell

Nealon Greene scrambles for good yardage as Clemson ran the clock down in the final quarter.

Ernie Rowell

Buck Priester runs for a crucial first down to keep a Clemson drive alive in their big third quarter.

The venerable Bob Bradley, Sports Information Director Emeritus, strolls the sideline at Clemson's Memorial Stadium where he's been a part of the action for over a half century now. He has seen it all and can truly tell some tales.

Art Baker, Special Consultant to Coach Brad Scott. If it pertains to football, Art has been there, done that. He has served as head coach at Furman, The Citadel, East Carolina, and was with Bobby Bowden at Florida State. He then served a successful stint as Executive Director of USC's Gamecock Club before being named Special Consultant to Coach Brad Scott. (He once served as Freshman Coach at Clemson University.)

POST SCRIPT

- 1997 marked the 95th meeting between USC and Clemson University.
- During the Early Era (1896-1945) these two teams played a total of 43 times. Clemson holds a big edge in those meetings by a margin of 28-13-2.
- During the Modern Era (1946-1997) Carolina and Clemson have played a total of 52 times. Again Clemson holds the edge by a margin of 28-22-2.
- Overall, Clemson leads in this series by a margin of 56-35-4, a .610 winning percentage.

Regardless, win or lose, this series is one of the oldest in America, and has furnished more excitement and entertainment to the citizens of this great land than anyone could possibly estimate. It has truly became a part of the great cultural heritage in the great state of South Carolina. It is this series, and others like it, that has made college football the worlds' greatest sporting event.

LONG MAY IT LIVE!

CLEMSON ALL-STARS AND SCORES SINCE 1896

CLEMSON ALL-STARS

THE FOLLOWING CLEMSON PLAYERS WERE NAMED ALL-AMERICAN AND/OR TO THE CLEMSON ATHLETIC HALL OF FAME (AHF).

Obed Ariri (1977-80), All-American
Boo Armstrong (1918-20), AHF
Stumpy Banks (1915-19), All-Southern, AHF
Tom Barton (1950-52), All-American, AHF
Joe Net Berry (1934-36), All-American, AHF
Joe Blalock (1939-41), All-American, AHF
Rob Bodine (1989-91), All-American
Joe Bostic (1976-78), All-American, AHF
Thomas Brown (1933-37), All-Southern, AHF
Jeff Bryant (1978-81), All-American, AHF
Shad Bryant (1937-39), All-Southern, AHF
Charlie Bussey (1954-56), All-ACC, AHF
Jerry Butler (1976-78), All-American, AHF
Jackie Calvert (1948-50), All-American, AHF
Dwight Clark (1975-78), All-ACC, AHF
Doug Cline (1957-59), All-ACC, AHF
Fred Cone (1948-50), All-Southern, AHF
Lou Cordileone (1957-59), All-American
Ben Cunningham (1973-75), All-American, AHF
Jeff Davis (1978-81), All-American, AHF
Brian Dawkins (1992-95), All-American
Bill Dillard (1932-34), All-State, AHF
Mike Eppley (1982-84), All-ACC, AHF
James Farr (1981-83), All-American
Terrence Flagler (1982-86), All-American
Jeb Flesch (1988-91), All-American
Mac Folger (1934-36), All-Southern, AHF
George Fritts (1939-41), All-Southern, AHF
Steve Fuller (1975-78), All-American, AHF
Bobby Gage (1945-48), All-American, AHF
Chris Gardocki (1988-90), All-American
Mutt Gee (1914-17), All-Southern, AHF
Frank Gillespie (1946-48), All-Southern, AHF
Buddy Gore (1966-68), All-ACC, AHF
John Grdijan (1955-57), All-ACC, AHF
Billy Hair (1950-52), All-Southern, AHF
R. G. Hamilton (1896), Team Captain, AHF
Dale Hatcher (1981-84), All-American
John Heisman (1900-03), Coach, AHF
Dick Hendley (1946-50), All-Southern, AHF
Frank Howard (1931-74), Coach, AHF
Bob Hudson (1947-50), All-Southern, AHF
Billy Hudson (1954-56), All-American, AHF
Donald Igwebuike (1981-84), All-American
Ralph Jenkins (1943-46), All-American, AHF

Bob Jones (1928-30), All-South, AHF
Terry Kinard (1979-82), All-American, AHF
Levon Kirkland (1988-91), All-American
Bull Lightsey (1922-25), All-Southern, AHF
Stacy Long (1986-90), All-American
Wayne Mass (1965-67), All-American
Ray Mathews (1947-50), All-Southern, AHF
Bill Mathis (1957-59), All-ACC, AHF
John Maxwell (1902-03), Team Captain, AHF
Ed McDaniel (1988-91), All-American
Banks McFadden (1937-39), All-American, AHF
Goat McMillan (1928-29), All-Southern, AHF
Lee Nanney (1978-81), All-American
Jess Neely (1931-39), Coach, AHF
Harry Olszewski (1965-67), All-American, AHF
Suzie Owens (1919-20), AHF
Michael Dean Perry (1984-87), All-American
William Perry (1981-84), All-American
John Phillips (1984-87), All-American
O. K. Pressley (1926-28), All-Southern, AHF
Steve Reese (1982-85), All-American
Johnny Rembert (1981-82), All-American
James Robinson (1979-83), All-American
Phil Rogers (1965-67), All-ACC, AHF
Wallace Roy (1923-25), All-South, AHF
Bill Schilletter (1911-14), Team Captain, AHF
Stacy Seegars (1990-93), All-American
Bob Sharpe (1938-40), Team Captain, AHF
Bob Smith (1950-69), Coach, AHF
Glenn Smith (1949-51), All-Southern, AHF
Jim Stuckey (1976-79), All-American, AHF
Dave Thompson (1968-70), All-American
Charlie Timmons (1939-41), All-Southern, AHF
David Treadwel (1985-87), All-American
Perry Tuttle (1978-81), All-American, AHF
Charlie Waters (1967-69), All-ACC, AHF
Nelson Welch (1991-94), All-American
Joel Wells (1954-56), All-American, AHF
Harvey White (1957-59), All-ACC, AHF
Gene Willimon (1933-77), IPTAY Director, AHF
Don Willis (1936-38), All-Southern, AHF
Windy Wyndham (1948-50), All-South, AHF
Charles Woods (1936-38), All-South, AHF
Donnell Woolford (1985-88), All-American

CLEMSON ALL-TIME TEAMS

(1896-1964)

Position	Name	Years			
QB/TB	Banks McFadden	1937-39	LB	Levon Kirkland	1988-91
Back	Fred Cone	1948-50	LB	Bubba Brown	1976-79
Back	Charlie Timmons	1939-41	Line	Michael Dean Perry	1984-87
End	Joe Blalock	1939-41	Line	William Perry	1981-84
End	Gary Barnes	1959-61	Line	Jim Stuckey	1976-79
C	Bob Sharpe	1938-40	Line	Jeff Bryant	1978-81
Line	Lou Cordileone	1957-59	P	Dale Hatcher	1981-84
Line	Harold Olson	1957-59			
Line	Don Chuy	1961-62		**(Offense)**	
Line	Frank Gillespie	1946-48			
Line	George Fritts	1939-41	QB	Steve Fuller	1975-78
P	Banks McFadden	1937-39	RB	Terry Allen	1987-89
			RB	Buddy Gore	1966-68
	(1965–1996)		TE	Bennie Cunningham	1973-75
	(Defense)		WR	Jerry Butler	1976-78
			WR	Perry Tuttle	1978-81
Back	Terry Kinard	1979-82	C	Jeff Bostic	1977-80
Back	Donnell Woolford	1985-88	OG	Joe Bostic	1975-79
Back	Dexter Davis	1988-90	OG	Harry Olszewski	1965-67
Back	Brian Dawkins	1992-95	OT	Wayne Mass	1965-67
LB	Jeff Davis	1978-81	OT	Stacy Long	1986-90
			PK	Chris Gardocki	1988-90

Date	Score	W L T	Site	Opponent	CU/Opp. AP Rank	Opp. Final Rec.	Opp. Final #Rank

 # - Denotes Bowl Game

1896 (2-1)

Date	Score	W/L/T	Site	Opponent		Opp. Final Rec.	
O. 28	14-6	W	A	Furman		2-3	
N. 12	6-12	L	A	S. Carolina		1-3	
N. 21	16-0	W	A	Wofford		2-2	

1897 (2-2)

O. 9	0-24	L	A	Georgia		2-1	
O. 23	10-0	W	A	Charlotte "Y"			
O. 25	0-28	L	A	N. Carolina		7-3	
N. 10	20-6	W	A	S. Carolina		0-3	

1898 (3-1)

O. 8	8-20	L	A	Georgia		4-2	
O. 20	55-0	W	H	Bingham			
N. 17	24-0	W	A	S. Carolina		1-2	
N. 24	23-0	W	N1	Georgia Tech		0-3	

N1 - Augusta, GA

1899 (4-2)

O. 7	0-11	L	A	Georgia		2-3-1	
O. 14	10-0	W	N1	Davidson		1-3-1	
O. 28	0-34	L	A	Auburn		3-1-1	
N. 9	34-0	W	A	S. Carolina		2-3	
N. 18	24-0	W	N1	N.C. State		1-2-2	
N. 30	41-5	W	N2	Georgia Tech		0-5	

N1 - Rock Hill, SC; N2 - Greenville, SC

1900 (6-0)

O. 19	64-0	W	H	Davidson		4-2	
O. 22	21-0	W	A	Wofford		1-2-1	
N. 1	51-0	W	A	S. Carolina		4-3	
N. 10	39-5	W	A	Georgia		2-4	
N. 24	12-5	W	N1	Virginia Tech		3-3-1	
N. 29	35-0	W	N2	Alabama		2-3	

N1 - Charlotte, NC; N2 - Birmingham, AL

1901 (3-1-1)

O. 5	122-0	W	H	Guilford			
O. 19	6-6	T	A	Tennessee		3-3-2	
O. 26	29-5	W	A	Georgia		1-5-2	
O. 31	11-17	L	N1	Virginia Tech		6-1	
N. 28	22-10	W	N2	N. Carolina		7-2	

N1 - Columbia, SC; N2 - Charlotte, NC

1902 (6-1)

O. 4	11-5	W	H	N.C. State		3-4-2	
O. 18	44-5	W	A	Georgia Tech		0-6-2	
O. 24	28-0	W	A	Furman		4-3-3	
O. 30	6-12	L	A	S. Carolina		6-1	
N. 8	36-0	W	H	Georgia		4-2-1	
N. 15	16-0	W	A	Auburn		2-4-1	
N. 27	11-0	W	A	Tennessee		6-2	

1903 (4-1-1)

O. 10	29-0	W	A	Georgia		3-4	
O. 17	73-0	W	A	Georgia Tech		2-5	
O. 28	24-0	W	N1	N.C. State		4-4	
N. 14	6-11	L	A	N. Carolina		6-3	
N. 21	24-0	W	A	Davidson		1-4	
N.26#	11-11	T	N2	Cumberland (TN)			

N1 - Columbia, SC; N2 - Montgomery, AL
SIAA Championship Game

1904 (3-3-1)

O. 8	18-0	W	N1	Alabama		7-3	
O. 15	0-5	L	H	Auburn		5-0	
O. 22	10-0	W	H	Georgia		1-5	
O. 27	5-11	L	N2	Sewanee		8-1-1	
N. 5	11-11	T	A	Georgia Tech		8-1-1	
N. 12	6-0	W	A	Tennessee		3-5-1	
N. 24	0-18	L	A	N.C. State		3-1-2	

N1 - Birmingham, AL; N2 - Columbia, SC

1905 (3-2-1)

O. 14	5-5	T	H	Tennessee		3-5-1	
O. 21	35-0	W	A	Georgia		1-5	
O. 25	25-0	W	N1	Alabama		6-4	
N. 11	26-0	W	A	Auburn		2-4	
N. 18	0-41	L	A	Vanderbilt		7-1	
N. 30	10-17	L	A	Georgia Tech		6-0-1	

N1 - Columbia, SC

1906 (4-0-3)

O. 13	0-0	T	H	Virginia Tech		5-2-2	
O. 20	6-0	W	H	Georgia		2-4-1	
O. 25	0-0	T	N1	N.C. State		3-1-4	
N. 3	0-0	T	A	Davidson		3-2-1	
N. 10	6-4	W	H	Auburn		1-5-1	
N. 19	16-0	W	H	Tennessee		1-6-2	
N. 29	10-0	W	A	Georgia Tech		5-3-1	

N1 - Columbia, SC

1907 (4-4)

S. 28	5-0	W	H	Gordon			
O. 9	35-0	W	H	Maryville			
O. 21	0-4	L	H	Tennessee		7-2-1	
O. 31	15-6	W	N1	N. Carolina		4-4-1	
N. 4	0-12	L	A	Auburn		6-2-1	
N. 7	0-8	L	N2	Georgia		4-3-1	
N. 9	6-10	L	H	Davidson		4-1-1	
N. 28	6-5	W	A	Georgia Tech		4-4	

N1 - Columbia, SC; N2 - Augusta, GA

1908 (1-6)

S. 26	15-0	W	H	Gordon			
O. 10	0-6	L	H	Virginia Tech		5-4	
O. 17	0-41	L	A	Vanderbilt		7-2-1	
O. 28	0-13	L	N1	Davidson		6-2-2	
N. 5	0-8	L	N2	Georgia		5-2-1	
N. 14	5-6	L	A	Tennessee		7-2	
N. 26	6-30	L	A	Georgia Tech		6-3	

N1 - Columbia, SC; N2 - Augusta, GA

1909 (6-3)

S. 27	26-0	W	H	Gordon			
O. 2	0-6	L	A	Virginia Tech		6-1	
O. 9	17-5	W	N1	Davidson		3-4-2	
O. 16	0-3	L	N2	Alabama		5-1-2	
O. 23	19-0	W	H	Port Royal			
N. 4	6-0	W	A	S. Carolina		2-6	
N. 10	5-0	W	N3	Georgia		1-4-2	
N. 13	17-0	W	A	The Citadel			
N. 25	3-29	L	A	Georgia Tech		7-2	

N1 - Charlotte, NC; N2 - Birmingham, AL; N3 - Augusta, GA

1910 (4-3-1)

S. 24	26-0	W	H	Gordon			
O. 1	0-3	L	H	Mercer			
O. 8	24-0	W	A	Samford			
O. 15	32-0	W	A	The Citadel		3-4	
O. 22	0-17	L	A	Auburn		6-1	
N. 3	24-0	W	A	S. Carolina		4-4	
N. 10	0-0	T	N1	Georgia		6-2-1	
N. 24	0-34	L	A	Georgia Tech		5-3	

N1 - Augusta, GA

1911 (3-5)

O. 14	0-29	L	H	Auburn		4-2-1	
O. 21	15-0	W	H	Samford			
O. 25	5-6	L	H	Florida		5-1	
N. 2	27-0	W	A	S. Carolina		1-4-2	
N. 4	18-0	W	A	The Citadel		5-2-2	
N. 9	0-22	L	N1	Georgia		7-1-1	
N. 18	6-30	L	N2	Mercer			
N. 30	0-31	L	A	Georgia Tech		6-2-1	

N1 - Augusta, GA; N2 - Columbia, SC

1912 (4-4)

O. 5	59-0	W	A	Samford			
O. 12	26-0	W	H	Riverside			
O. 19	6-27	L	A	Auburn		6-1-1	
O. 26	52-14	W	H	The Citadel		3-4	
O. 31	7-22	L	A	S. Carolina		5-2-1	
N. 7	6-27	L	N1	Georgia		6-1-1	
N. 16	21-13	W	A	Mercer			
N. 28	0-20	L	A	Georgia Tech		5-3-1	

N1 - Augusta, GA

1913 (4-4)

O. 4	6-3	W	H	Davidson		2-5	
O. 11	0-20	L	A	Alabama		6-3	
O. 18	0-20	L	H	Auburn		8-0	
O. 30	32-0	W	A	S. Carolina		4-3	
N. 6	15-18	L	N1	Georgia		6-2	
N. 8	7-3	W	A	The Citadel		3-4-2	
N. 17	52-0	W	A	Mercer			
N. 27	0-34	L	A	Georgia Tech		7-2	

N1 - Augusta, GA

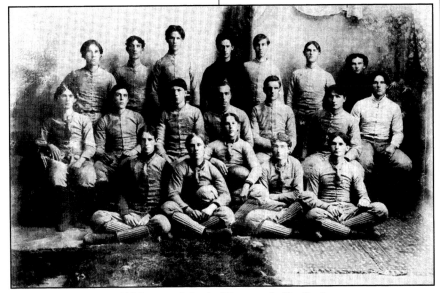

Clemson's 1896 team defeated Furman in the first game ever.

1914 (5-3-1)

O. 3	0-0	T	A	Davidson	5-1-1
O. 10	0-27	L	A	Tennessee	9-0
O. 17	0-28	L	A	Auburn	8-0-1
O. 22	57-0	W	A	Furman	2-5
O. 29	29-6	W	A	S. Carolina	5-5-1
O. 31	14-0	W	A	The Citadel	2-5
N. 7	35-13	W	A	Georgia	3-5-1
N. 14	27-23	W	N1	VMI	4-4
N. 26	6-26	L	A	Georgia Tech	6-2

N1 - Richmond, VA

1915 (2-4-2)

S. 25	94-0	W	A	Furman	5-3
O. 2	6-6	T	H	*Davidson	5-3-1
O. 9	3-0	W	A	Tennessee	4-4
O. 16	0-14	L	N1	Auburn	6-2
O. 28	0-0	T	A	S. Carolina	5-3-1
N. 6	7-9	L	N2	N. Carolina	4-3-1
N. 13	3-6	L	N3	VMI	6-2-1
N. 25	0-13	L	A	Georgia	5-2-2

* Dedication of Riggs Field
N1 - Anderson, SC; N2 - Greenville, SC; N3 - Richmond, VA

1916 (3-6)

S. 30	7-6	W	H	Furman	4-5
O. 7	0-26	L	N1	Georgia	6-3
O. 14	0-14	L	H	Tennessee	8-0-1
O. 20	0-28	L	A	Auburn	6-2
O. 26	27-0	W	A	S. Carolina	2-7
N. 11	7-37	L	N2	VMI	4-5
N. 16	0-3	L	N3	The Citadel	6-1-1
N. 22	40-0	W	H	Presbyterian	4-3
N. 30	0-33	L	N4	Davidson	5-3-1

N1 - Anderson, SC; N2 - Richmond, VA; N3 - Orangeburg, SC; N4 - Charlotte, NC

1917 (6-2)

S. 28	13-0	W	H	Presbyterian	8-1
O. 13	38-0	W	A	Furman	3-5
O. 19	0-7	L	H	Auburn	6-2-1
O. 25	21-13	W	A	S. Carolina	3-5
N. 1	27-16	W	A	Wofford	5-4
N. 8	20-0	W	N1	The Citadel	3-3
N. 17	55-7	W	N2	Florida	2-4
N. 29	9-21	L	N3	Davidson	6-4

N1 - Orangeburg, SC; N2 - Jacksonville, FL; N3 - Charlotte, NC

1918 (5-2)

S. 27	65-0	W	H	Camp Sevier	
O. 5	0-28	L	A	Georgia Tech	6-1
N. 2	39-0	W	A	S. Carolina	2-1-1
N. 9	13-66	L	H	Camp Hancock	
N. 16	7-0	W	N1	The Citadel	0-2-1
N. 23	67-7	W	H	Furman	3-5-1
N. 29	7-0	W	H	Davidson	2-1-1

N1 - Columbia, SC

1919 (6-2-2)

S. 27	53-0	W	H	Erskine	
O. 3	7-0	W	H	Davidson	4-4-2
O. 11	0-28	L	A	Georgia Tech	7-3
O. 17	0-7	L	A	Auburn	8-1
O. 25	14-0	W	H	Tennessee	3-3-3
O. 30	19-6	W	A	S. Carolina	1-7-1
N. 7	19-7	W	H	Presbyterian	4-3-2
N. 13	33-0	W	N1	The Citadel	4-4-1
N. 21	7-7	T	A	Furman	6-2-1
N. 27	0-0	T	A	Georgia	4-2-3

N1 - Orangeburg, SC

1920 (4-6-1)

S. 24	26-0	W	H	Erskine	
O. 1	7-7	T	H	Presbyterian	5-1-1
O. 2	26-6	W	H	Newberry	1-7
O. 9	13-7	W	H	Wofford	0-8-1
O. 15	0-21	L	H	Auburn	7-2
O. 23	0-26	L	A	Tennessee	7-2
O. 28	0-3	L	A	S. Carolina	5-4
N. 6	0-7	L	A	Georgia Tech	8-1
N. 11	26-0	W	N1	The Citadel	2-6
N. 20	0-14	L	A	Furman	9-1
N. 25	0-55	L	A	Georgia	8-0-1

N1 - Orangeburg, SC

Clemson defeated Boston College 26-13 in Fenway Park in 1941 behind two touchdowns by All-American Joe Blalock

1921 (1-6-2)

O. 1	0-14	L	A	Centre	
O. 7	34-0	W	H	Presbyterian	1-7
O. 14	0-56	L	A	Auburn	5-3
O. 21	0-0	T	A	Furman	7-2-1
O. 27	0-21	L	A	S. Carolina	5-1-2
N. 5	7-48	L	A	Georgia Tech	8-1
N. 10	7-7	T	N1	The Citadel	3-3-2
N. 18	0-13	L	H	Erskine	
N. 24	0-28	L	A	Georgia	7-2-1

N1 - Orangeburg, SC

1922 (5-4)

S. 30	0-21	L	H	Centre	
O. 7	57-0	W	H	Newberry	2-5
O. 13	13-0	W	H	Presbyterian	6-2-1
O. 26	3-0	W	A	S. Carolina	5-4
N. 4	7-21	L	A	Georgia Tech	7-2
N. 11	18-0	W	A	The Citadel	3-5
N. 18	52-0	W	H	Erskine	
N. 25	6-20	L	A	Furman	8-3
Dec.2	14-47	L	N1	Florida	7-2

N1 - Jacksonville, FL

1923 (5-2-1)

S. 29	0-0	T	H	Auburn	3-3-3
O. 6	32-0	W	H	Newberry	
O. 13	7-28	L	A	Centre	
O. 25	7-6	W	A	S. Carolina	4-6
N. 3	6-25	L	A	Virginia Tech	6-3
N. 9	12-0	W	H	Davidson	3-7
N. 17	20-0	W	H	Presbyterian	4-3-1
N. 29	7-6	W	A	Furman	9-2

1924 (2-6)

S. 27	60-0	W	H	Elon	
O. 4	0-13	L	A	Auburn	4-4-1
O. 11	14-0	W	H	Presbyterian	1-6-1
O. 23	0-3	L	A	S. Carolina	7-3
N. 1	6-50	L	H	Virginia Tech	4-2-3
N. 8	0-7	L	N1	Davidson	7-2-1
N. 15	0-20	L	N2	The Citadel	6-4
N. 27	0-3	L	H	Furman	5-5

N1 - Charlotte, NC; N2 - Anderson, SC

1925 (1-7)

S. 26	9-14	L	H	Presbyterian	3-6
O. 3	6-13	L	H	Auburn	5-3-1
O. 10	6-19	L	A	Kentucky	6-3
O. 22	0-33	L	A	S. Carolina	7-3
O. 29	0-13	L	A	Wofford	3-7
N. 7	0-42	L	H	Florida	8-2
N. 14	6-0	W	A	The Citadel	6-4
N. 26	0-26	L	A	Furman	7-3

1926 (2-7)

S. 18	7-0	W	H	Erskine	
S. 25	0-14	L	H	Presbyterian	7-2
O. 2	0-47	L	A	Auburn	5-4
O. 9	7-3	W	H	N.C. State	4-6
O. 21	0-24	L	A	S. Carolina	6-4
O. 28	0-3	L	A	Wofford	2-8
N. 6	0-33	L	A	Florida	2-6-2
N. 13	6-15	L	H	The Citadel	7-3
N. 25	0-30	L	A	Furman	8-1

1927 (5-3-1)

S. 24	0-0	T	H	Presbyterian	3-3-3
O. 1	3-0	W	H	Auburn	0-7-2
O. 8	6-18	L	A	N.C. State	9-1
O. 14	25-6	W	H	Erskine	
O. 20	20-0	W	A	S. Carolina	4-5
O. 29	6-0	W	H	Wofford	2-4-3
N. 5	13-0	W	H	The Citadel	3-6-1
N. 12	0-32	L	A	Georgia	9-1
N. 24	0-28	L	A	Furman	10-1

1928 (8-3)

S. 22	30-0	W	H	Newberry	3-5
S. 29	6-0	W	H	Davidson	2-8
O. 6	6-0	W	A	Auburn	1-8
O. 12	7-0	W	N1	N.C. State	4-3-1
O. 19	52-0	W	H	Erskine	
O. 25	32-0	W	A	S. Carolina	6-2-2
N. 3	7-26	L	A	Mississippi	5-4
N. 10	12-0	W	N2	VMI	5-3-2
N. 17	6-27	L	N3	Florida	8-1
N. 29	27-12	W	A	Furman	5-4
D. 8	7-12	L	A	The Citadel	6-3-1

N1 - Florence, SC; N2 - Lynchburg, VA; N3 - Jacksonville, FL

1929 (8-3)

S. 21	68-0	W	H	Newberry	0-5
S. 28	32-14	W	N1	Davidson	5-5
O. 5	26-7	W	H	Auburn	2-7
O. 11	26-0	W	N2	N.C. State	1-8
O. 18	30-0	W	A	Wofford	3-6
O. 24	21-14	W	A	S. Carolina	6-5
N. 2	6-44	L	A	Kentucky	6-1
N. 9	0-12	L	N3	VMI	8-2
N. 16	7-13	L	A	Florida	8-2
N. 23	13-0	W	H	The Citadel	5-4-1
N. 28	7-6	W	H	Furman	5-4-1

N1 - Charlotte, NC; N2 - Florence, SC; N3 - Norfolk, VA

1930 (8-2)

S. 20	28-7	W	H	Presbyterian	9-1	
S. 27	32-0	W	H	Wofford	2-9	
O. 3	13-7	W	N1	The Citadel	4-5-2	
O. 11	27-0	W	N2	N.C. State	2-8	
O. 17	75-0	W	H	Newberry	0-5-3	
O. 23	20-7	W	A	S. Carolina	6-4	
N. 1	0-27	L	A	Tennessee	9-1	
N. 8	32-0	W	N3	VMI	3-6	
N. 15	0-27	L	N4	Florida	6-3-1	
N. 27	12-7	W	A	Furman	6-3-1	

N1 - Florence, SC; N2 - Charlotte, NC; N3 - Norfolk, VA; N4 - Jacksonville, FL

1931 (1-6-2)

S. 25	0-0	T	H	Presbyterian	2-5-2
O. 3	0-44	L	A	Tennessee	9-0-1
O. 10	6-0	W	N1	N.C. State	3-6
O. 16	0-6	L	N2	The Citadel	5-4-1
O. 22	0-21	L	A	S. Carolina	5-4-1
O. 31	0-12	L	H	Oglethorpe	
N. 7	6-7	L	N3	VMI	3-6-1
N. 14	7-74	L	N4	Alabama	9-1
N. 26	0-0	T	A	Furman	5-2-2

N1 - Charlotte, NC; N2 - Florence, SC; N3 - Norfolk, VA; N4 - Montgomery, AL

1932 (3-5-1)

S. 23	13-0	W	H	Presbyterian	5-2-1
O. 1	14-32	L	A	Georgia Tech	4-5-1
O. 8	0-13	L	A	N.C. State	6-1-2
O. 14	19-0	W	H	Erskine	
O. 20	0-14	L	A	S. Carolina	5-4-2
O. 29	7-7	T	A	Davidson	4-4-1
N. 5	18-6	W	A	The Citadel	4-5
N. 11	18-32	L	H	Georgia	2-5-2
N. 24	0-7	L	A	Furman	8-1

1933 (3-6-2)

S. 23	6-6	T	H	Presbyterian	4-2-2
S. 30	2-39	L	A	Georgia Tech	5-5
O. 7	9-0	W	H	N.C. State	1-5-3
O. 13	0-0	T	A	%Geo. Wash.	
O. 19	0-7	L	A	S. Carolina	6-3-1
O. 28	0-13	L	N1	Mississippi	6-3-2
N. 4	13-0	W	N2	Wake Forest	0-5-1
N. 11	13-14	L	A	Wofford	3-6
N. 18	0-13	L	N3	Mercer	
N. 25	7-0	W	H	The Citadel	3-5-1
N. 30	0-6	L	A	Furman	6-1-2

% First night game
N1 - Meridian, MS; N2 - Charlotte, NC; N3 - Savannah, GA

1934 (5-4)

S. 22	6-0	W	H	Presbyterian	3-4-2
S. 29	7-12	L	A	Georgia Tech	1-9
O. 6	6-20	L	A	Duke	7-2
O. 13	0-7	L	A	Kentucky	5-5
O. 25	19-0	W	A	S. Carolina	5-4
N. 3	12-6	W	A	N.C. State	2-6-1
N. 10	0-40	L	A	Alabama	10-0
N. 17	32-0	W	N1	Mercer	
N. 29	7-0	W	H	Furman	5-4

N1 - Savannah, GA

1935 (6-3)

S. 21	25-6	W	H	Presbyterian	2-7
S. 28	28-7	W	A	Virginia Tech	4-3-2
O. 5	13-7	W	H	Wake Forest	2-7
O. 12	12-38	L	A	Duke	8-2
O. 24	44-0	W	A	S. Carolina	3-7
N. 2	13-0	W	N1	Mercer	
N. 9	0-33	L	A	Alabama	6-2-1
N. 16	6-0	W	A	The Citadel	4-3-1
N. 28	6-8	L	A	Furman	8-1

N1 - Augusta, GA

1936 (5-5)

S. 19	19-0	W	H	Presbyterian	3-6
S. 26	20-0	W	H	Virginia Tech	5-5
O. 3	0-32	L	A	Alabama	48-0-1
O. 10	0-25	L	A	Duke	119-1
O. 16	0-6	L	A	%Wake Forest	5-4
O. 22	19-0	W	A	S. Carolina	5-7
O. 31	14-13	W	A	Georgia Tech	5-5-1
N. 7	20-0	W	A	The Citadel	4-6
N. 14	6-7	L	A	Kentucky	6-4
N. 26	0-12	L	H	Furman	7-2

1937 (4-4-1)

S. 18	46-0	W	H	Presbyterian	0-10
S. 25	0-7	L	A	Tulane	5-4-1
O. 2	6-21	L	A	Army	7-2
O. 9	0-14	L	A	Georgia	6-3-2
O. 21	34-6	W	A	S. Carolina	5-6-1
O. 30	32-0	W	H	Wake Forest	3-6
N. 6	0-7	L	A	Georgia Tech	6-3-1
N. 13	10-9	W	A	Florida	4-7
N. 25	0-0	T	A	Furman	4-3-2

1938 (7-1-1, 3-0-1, 2nd in Southern Conf.)

S. 17	26-0	W	H	Presbyterian	6-4	
S. 24	13-10	W	A	Tulane	7-2-1	19
O. 1	7-20	L	A	Tennessee	11-0	#2
O. 8	7-7	T	N1	VMI	6-1-4	
O. 20	34-12	W	A	S. Carolina	6-4-1	
O. 28	7-0	W	A	%Wake Forest	4-5-1	
N. 5	27-0	W	N2	Geo. Wash.		
N. 12	14-0	W	A	Kentucky	2-7	
N. 24	10-7	W	H	Furman	2-7-1	

N1 - Charlotte, NC; N2 - Greenville, NC

1939 (9-1, 4-0. 2nd in Southern Conf.)

S. 23	18-0	W	H	Presbyterian		4-3-2	
S. 30	6-7	L	A	Tulane		8-1-1	5
O. 7	25-6	W	N1	N.C. State		2-8	
O. 19	27-0	W	A	S. Carolina		3-6-1	
O. 28	15-7	W	A	Navy		3-5-1	
N. 3	13-6	W	A	%Geo. Wash.			
N. 11	20-7	W	H	Wake Forest		7-3	
N. 18	21-6	W	A	Southwest.	16/-		
N. 25	14-3	W	A	Furman	15/-	5-4	
J. 1	6-3	W	N2	Boston Coll.	12/11	9-2	#

N1 - Charlotte, NC; N2 - Cotton Bowl, Dallas, TX

1940 (6-2-1, 4-0, Southern Conf. Champs)

S. 21	38-0	W	A	Presbyterian		6-4
S. 28	26-0	W	H	Wofford		3-4-2
O. 5	26-7	W	N1	N.C. State		3-6
O. 12	39-0	W	H	Wake Forest		7-3
O. 24	21-13	W	A	S. Carolina	13/-	3-6
N. 2	0-13	L	A	Tulane	10/-	5-5
N. 9	7-21	L	A	Auburn		6-4-1
N. 16	12-12	T	A	Southwestern		
N. 23	13-7	W	A	Furman		5-4

N1 - Charlotte, NC

1941 (7-2, 5-1, 3rd in Southern Conf.)

S. 20	41-12	W	H	Presbyterian		6-3
S. 27	36-7	W	A1	VMI		4-6
O. 4	27-6	W	N2	N.C. State		4-5-2
O. 11	26-13	W	A	Boston College		7-3
O. 23	14-18	L	A	S. Carolina	14/-	4-4-1
O. 31	19-0	W	A	%Geo. Wash.		
N. 15	29-0	W	H	Wake Forest		5-5-1
N. 22	34-6	W	A	Furman	18/-	3-4-2
N. 29	7-28	L	A	Auburn	16/-	4-5-1

A1 - Lynchburg, VA; N2 - Charlotte, NC

1942 (3-6-1, 2-3-1, 9th in Southern Conf.)

S. 19	32-13	W	H	#Presbyterian		6-4
S. 26	0-0	T	A1	VMI		3-5-1
O. 3	6-7	L	N2	N.C. State		4-4-2
O. 10	7-14	L	A	Boston College		*8-2
O. 22	18-6	W	A	†S. Carolina		1-7-1
O. 31	6-19	L	A	Wake Forest		6-2-1
N. 7	0-7	L	H	Geo. Wash.		
N. 14	6-24	L	A	Jax. N.A.S.		
N. 21	12-7	W	H	Furman		3-6
N. 28	13-41	L	A	Auburn	-/16	6-4-1

First game in Memorial Stadium
† Clemson's 200th win
A1 - Lynchburg, VA; N2 - Charlotte, NC

1943 (2-6, 2-3, T7th in Southern Conf.)

S. 25	12-13	L	H	Presbyterian	6-6
O. 2	19-7	W	N1	%N.C. State	3-6
O. 9	7-12	L	N2	VMI	2-6
O. 21	6-33	L	A	S. Carolina	5-2
O. 30	12-41	L	H	Wake Forest	4-5
N. 6	26-6	W	A	Davidson	0-5
N. 13	6-32	L	N3	Ga. Preflight	
N. 20	6-41	L	A	Ga. Tech	-/15	8-3	#13

N1 - Charlotte, NC; N2 - Roanoke, VA; N3 - Greenville, SC

1944 (4-5, 3-1, T3rd in Southern Conf.)

S. 23	34-0	W	H	Presbyterian		3-6	
S. 30	0-51	L	A	Georgia Tech		8-3	#13
O. 7	13-7	W	N1	N.C. State		7-2	
O. 19	20-7	W	A	Wake Forest		3-4-2	
O. 28	7-26	L	A	Tenn.	-/19	7-1-1	#12
N. 4	7-13	L	A	W. Forest	-/17	8-1	
N. 11	57-12	W	H	VMI		1-8	
N. 18	20-36	L	A	Tulane			
N. 24	7-21	L	A	Georgia		7-3	

N1 - Charlotte, NC

1945 (6-3-1, 2-1-1, 4th in Southern Conf.)

S. 22	76-0	W	H	Presbyterian		1-6	
S. 29	0-20	L	A	Georgia		9-2	#18
O. 6	13-0	W	A	%N.C. State		3-6	
O. 13	7-6	W	H	Pensacola NAS			
O. 25	0-0	T	A	S. Carolina		2-4-3	
N. 2	6-7	L	A	%Miami (FL)		9-1-1	#
N. 10	35-0	W	H	Virginia Tech		2-6	
N. 17	47-20	W	A	Tulane			
N. 24	21-7	W	A	Georgia Tech		4-6	
D. 1	6-13	L	H	W. Forest	16/-	5-3-1	

1946 (4-5, 2-3, 11th in Southern Conf.)

S. 21	39-0	W	H	Presbyterian	7-2	
S. 27	12-35	L	A	%Georgia	11-0	#3
O. 5	7-14	L	H	N.C. State	8-3	#18
O. 12	7-19	L	A	Wake Forest	6-3	
O. 24	14-26	L	A	S. Carolina	5-3	
N. 2	14-7	W	A	Virginia Tech	3-4-3	#
N. 9	13-54	L	A	Tulane		
N. 16	20-6	W	H	Furman	2-8	
N. 23	21-13	W	N1	Auburn	4-6	

N1 - Montgomery, AL

1947 (4-5, 1-3, 12th in Southern Conf.)

S. 20	53-0	W	H	Presbyterian	4-5-1	
S. 26	22-32	L	A	%Boston College	5-4	
O. 4	14-16	L	H	Wake Forest	6-4	
O. 11	0-18	L	A	%N.C. State	5-3-1	17
O. 23	19-21	L	A	S. Carolina	6-2-1	
O. 31	6-21	L	A	%Georgia	7-4-1	#
N. 8	35-7	W	A	Furman	2-7	
N. 15	34-13	W	A	%Duquesne	2-8	
N. 22	34-18	W	H	Auburn	2-7	

1948 (11-0, 5-0, Southern Conf. Champions)
Ranked 11th in AP

S. 25	53-0	W	H	%*Presbyterian		5-4	
O. 2	6-0	W	H	%N.C. State		3-6-1	
O. 9	21-7	W	A1	Miss. State		4-4-1	
O. 21	13-7	W	A	S. Carolina	14/-	3-5	
O. 29	26-19	W	A	%Boston Coll.	13/-	5-2-2	
N. 6	41-0	W	H	Furman		2-7	
N. 13	21-14	W	A	Wake Forest	10/19	6-4	#20/-
N. 20	42-0	W	H	Duquesne	9/-	2-7	
N. 27	7-6	W	A	Auburn	11/-	1-8-1	
D. 4	20-0	W	A	Citadel	10/-	2-7	
J. 1	24-23	W	N1	Missouri	10/-	8-3	#

* - First home night game
A1 - Mobile, AL; N2 - Gator Bowl, Jacksonville, FL

1949 (4-4-2, 2-2, 8th in Southern Conf.)

S. 17	69-7	W	H	%Presbyterian		5-4	
S. 24	7-33	L	A	%Rice		10-1	#5/-
O. 1	7-6	W	A	%N.C. State		3-7	
O. 8	7-7	T	H	%Miss. State		0-8-1	
O. 20	13-27	L	A	S. Carolina		4-6	
O. 29	21-35	L	H	%Wake Forest		4-6	
N. 5	27-40	L	H	Boston College		4-4-1	
N. 12	33-20	W	H	%Duquense		3-6	
N. 19	28-21	W	A	Furman		2-6-1	
N. 26	20-20	T	A1	Auburn		2-4-3	

A1 - Mobile, AL

1950 (9-0-1, 3-0-1, 2nd in Southern Conf.)
Ranked 10th in AP, 12th in UPI

S. 23	54-0	W	H	%Presbyterian	5-5	
S. 30	34-0	W	A	Missouri	4-5-1	
O. 7	27-0	W	H	%N.C. State	18/-	5-4-1
O. 19	14-14	T	A	S. Carolina	12/-	3-4-2
O. 28	13-12	W	A	Wake Forest	16/17	6-1-2
N. 4	53-20	W	H	Duquesne	14/-	2-6-1
N. 11	35-14	W	A	Boston Coll.	13/-	0-9-1
N. 18	57-2	W	H	Furman	11/-	2-8-1
N. 25	41-0	W	A	Auburn	11/-	0-10
J. 1	15-14	W	A1	Miami	10/15	9-1-1	#15/13

A1 - Orange Bowl, Miami, FL

1951 (7-3, 3-1, 5th in Southern Conf.)
Ranked 19th in AP

S. 22	53-6	W	H	%Presbyterian	5-4	
S. 29	20-14	W	A	%Rice	5-5	
O. 6	6-0	W	A	%N.C. State	18/-	3-7
O. 13	7-21	L	A	%Pacific	16/-	6-5
O. 25	0-20	L	A	S. Carolina	5-4	
N. 3	21-6	W	H	Wake Forest	6-4	
N. 10	21-2	W	H	Boston Coll.	3-6	
N. 17	34-14	W	A	Furman	3-6-1	
N. 24	34-0	W	H	Auburn	5-5	
J. 1	0-14	L	N1	Miami	19/15	8-3	#

N1 - Gator Bowl, Jacksonville, FL

1952 (2-6-1)*

S. 20	53-13	W	H	%Presbyterian	3-6	
S. 27	7-14	L	H	Villanova	7-1-1	
O. 4	0-28	L	A	Maryland	-/3	7-2	13/13
O. 11	13-54	L	A	Florida	8-3	#15/
O. 23	0-6	L	A	S. Carolina	5-5	
O. 31	13-0	W	A	%Boston Coll.	4-4-1	
N. 8	12-12	T	A	Fordham		
N. 15	14-27	L	A	Kentucky	1-9	20/20
N. 22	0-3	L	A	Auburn	2-8	

*Clemson ineligible for Southern Conf. Championship

First Year of ACC
1953 (3-5-1, 1-2, 6th in ACC)

S. 19	33-7	W	H	%Presbyterian	5-3-1	
S. 26	14-14	T	A	Boston College	5-3-1	
O. 3	0-20	L	H	#Maryland	-/3	10-1	#1/1
O. 9	7-39	L	A	%Miami	4-5	
O. 22	7-14	L	A	S. Carolina	7-3	
O. 31	18-0	W	H	Wake Forest	3-6-1	
N. 7	7-20	L	A	Georgia Tech	-/14	9-2-1	#8/9
N. 14	34-13	W	A	The Citadel		
N. 21	19-45	L	H	Auburn	-/14	7-3-1	#17/-

- Clemson's first ACC game

1954 (5-5, 1-2, 5th in ACC)

S. 18	33-0	W	H	%Presbyterian	6-3	
S. 25	7-14	L	A	Georgia	6-3-1	
O. 2	7-18	L	H	Virginia Tech	8-0-1	
O. 9	14-7	W	A1	%Florida	-/14	5-5
O. 21	8-13	L	A	S. Carolina	6-4	
O. 30	32-20	W	N2	Wake Forest	2-7-1	
N. 6	27-6	W	H	Furman	5-5	
N. 13	0-16	L	A	Maryland	-/17	7-2-1	#8/12
N. 20	6-27	L	A	Auburn	-/18	8-3	#13/-
N. 27	59-0	W	H	Citadel	2-8	

A1 - Jacksonville, FL; N2 - Charlotte, NC

1955 (7-3, 3-1, 3rd in ACC)

S. 17	33-0	W	H	%Presbyterian	3-5-1	
S. 24	20-7	W	A	Virginia	1-9	
O. 1	26-7	W	H	Georgia	4-6	
O. 8	7-21	L	A	%Rice	16/-	2-7-1
O. 20	28-14	W	A	S. Carolina	3-6	
O. 29	19-13	W	H	Wake Forest	5-4-1	
N. 5	21-16	W	N1	Virginia Tech	4-6	
N. 12	12-25	L	H	Maryland	-/2	10-1	#3/3
N. 19	0-21	L	N2	Auburn	-/12	8-2-1	#8/8
N. 26	40-20	W	A	Furman	1-9	

N1 - Roanoke, VA; N2 - Mobile, AL

1956 (7-2-2, 4-0-1, ACC Champions)
Ranked 19th in AP

S. 22	27-7	W	H	%Presbyterian	4-6	
S. 29	20-20	T	A	Florida	-/19	6-3-1
O. 6	13-7	W	A	%N.C. State	3-7	

O. 13	17-0	W	A	Wake Forest	2-5-3	
O. 25	7-0	W	A	S. Carolina	20/-	7-3
N. 3	21-6	W	H	Virginia Tech	13/-	7-2-1
N. 10	6-6	T	A	Maryland	11/-	2-7-1
N. 16	0-21	L	A	%Miami	13/8	8-1-1	6/6
N. 24	7-0	W	H	Virginia	4-6	
D. 1	28-7	W	H	Furman	2-8	
J. 1	21-27	L	N1	Colorado	19/20	8-2-1	#20/18

N1 - Orange Bowl, Miami, FL

1957 (7-3, 4-3, T3rd in ACC)
Ranked tied for 18th in UPI

S. 21	66-0	W	H	Presbyterian	0-8-1	
S. 28	0-26	L	H	N. Carolina	6-4	
O. 5	7-13	L	H	N.C. State	-/13	7-1-2	15/-
O. 12	20-6	W	A	Virginia	3-6-1	
O. 24	13-0	W	A	S. Carolina	5-5	
N. 2	20-7	W	H	%Rice	7-4	#8/7
N. 9	26-7	W	H	Maryland	5-5	
N. 16	6-7	L	A	Duke	14/11	6-3-2	#16/14
N. 23	13-6	W	H	Wake Forest	0-10	
N. 30	45-6	W	A	Furman	3-7	

1958 (8-3, 5-0, ACC Champions)
Ranked 12th in AP, 13th in UPI

S. 20	20-15	W	H	Virginia	18/-	1-9
S. 27	26-21	W	H	*N. Carolina	6-4	
O. 4	8-0	W	A	Maryland	10/-	4-6
O. 11	12-7	W	A	%Vanderbilt	8/-	5-2-3
O. 23	6-26	L	A	S. Carolina	10/-	7-3	15/-
N. 1	14-12	W	H	Wake Forest	19/-	3-7
N. 8	0-13	L	A	Georgia Tech	17/-	5-4-1
N. 15	13-6	W	A	N.C. State	2-7-1	
N. 22	34-12	W	H	Boston Coll.	16/-	7-3
N. 29	36-19	W	H	Furman	12/-	2-7
J. 1	0-7	L	N1	LSU	12/1	12-0	#1/1

* - Frank Howard's 100th win at Clemson
N1 - Sugar Bowl, New Orleans, LA

1959 (9-2, 6-1, ACC Champions)
Ranked 11th in AP

S. 19	20-18	W	A	N. Carolina	18/12	5-5
S. 26	47-0	W	A	Virginia	5/-	0-10
O. 3	6-16	L	A	Georgia Tech	7/8	6-5	#
O. 10	23-0	W	H	N.C. State	1-9	
O. 22	27-0	W	A	&S. Carolina	17/-	6-4
O. 31	19-0	W	A	%Rice	12/-	1-7-2
N. 7	6-0	W	A	Duke	10/-	4-6
N. 14	25-28	L	H	Maryland	11/-	5-5
N. 21	33-31	W	H	Wake Forest	19/-	6-4
N. 28	56-3	W	A	Furman	14/-	3-7
D. 19	23-7	W	N1	†TCU	11/7	8-3	#7/8

N1 - Bluebonnet Bowl, Houston, TX
& - Last Big Thursday Game
† - Clemson's 300th win

1960 (6-4, 4-2, 4th in ACC)

S. 24	28-7	W	A	Wake Forest	9/-	2-8
O. 1	13-7	W	H	Virginia Tech	7/-	6-4
O. 8	21-7	W	H	Virginia	8/-	0-10
O. 15	17-19	L	A	Maryland	8/-	6-4
O. 22	6-21	L	A	Duke	8-3	#10/11
O. 29	20-22	L	A	Vanderbilt	3-7	
N. 5	24-0	W	H	N. Carolina	3-7	
N. 12	12-2	W	H	&S. Carolina	3-6-1	
N. 19	14-25	L	A	Boston College	3-6-1	
N. 26	42-14	W	H	Furman	5-4	

& - First South Carolina game at Clemson

1961 (5-5, 3-3, T3rd in ACC)

S. 23	17-21	L	A	Florida	4-5-1	
S. 30	21-24	L	H	Maryland	7-3	
O. 7	27-0	W	A	N. Carolina	5-5	
O. 14	13-17	L	H	Wake Forest	4-6	
O. 21	17-7	W	A	Duke	7-3	#20/14
O. 28	14-24	L	A	Auburn	6-4	
N. 4	21-6	W	H	Tulane		
N. 11	14-21	L	A	S. Carolina	4-6	
N. 18	35-6	W	H	Furman	7-3	
N. 25	20-0	W	H	N.C. State	4-6	

1962 (6-4, 5-1, 2nd in ACC)

| S. 22 | 9-26 | L | A | Georgia Tech | 7-3-1 | # |
| S. 29 | 7-0 | W | A | N.C. State | 3-6-1 | |

O. 6	24-7	W	A	Wake Forest	0-10	
O. 13	16-24	L	H	Georgia	3-4-3	
O. 20	0-16	L	H	Duke	8-2	-/14
O. 27	14-17	L	H	Auburn	6-3-1	
N. 3	17-6	W	H	N. Carolina	3-7	
N. 10	44-3	W	A	Furman	4-6	
N. 17	17-14	W	A	Maryland	6-4	
N. 24	20-17	W	H	S. Carolina	4-5-1	

1963 (5-4-1, 5-2, T3rd in ACC)

S. 21	14-31	L	A	Oklahoma	-/4	8-2	10/8
S. 28	0-27	L	A	Georgia Tech	-/9	7-3
O. 5	3-7	L	H	N.C. State	8-3	#
O. 12	7-7	T	H	Georgia	4-5-1	
O. 19	30-35	L	A	Duke	5-4	
O. 26	35-0	W	A	Virginia	2-7	
N. 2	36-0	W	H	Wake Forest	1-9	
N. 9	11-7	W	A	N. Carolina	9-2	#-/19
N. 16	21-6	W	H	Maryland	3-7	
N. 28	24-20	W	A	&S. Carolina	1-8	

& - Only Clemson-S. Carolina game played on Thanksgiving Day

1964 (3-7, 2-4, 7th in ACC)

S. 19	21-7	W	H	Furman	3-7	
S. 26	0-9	L	A	N.C. State	5-5	
O. 3	7-14	L	A	Georgia Tech	7-3	
O. 10	7-19	L	A	Georgia	7-3-1	#
O. 17	21-2	W	H	Wake Forest	5-5	
O. 24	10-14	L	A	TCU	4-6	
O. 31	29-7	W	H	Virginia	5-5	
N. 7	0-29	L	H	N. Carolina	5-5	
N. 14	0-34	L	A	Maryland	5-5	
N. 20	3-7	L	H	S. Carolina	3-5	

1965 (5-5, 4-3, ACC Co-Champions)

S. 18	21-7	W	H	N.C. State	6-4	
S. 25	20-14	W	A	Virginia	4-6	
O. 2	6-28	L	A	Georgia Tech	7-3-1	
O. 9	9-23	L	A	Georgia	-/4	6-4
O. 16	3-2	W	A	Duke	6-4	
O. 23	3-0	W	H	TCU	6-5	#
O. 30	26-13	W	H	Wake Forest	3-7	
N. 6	13-17	L	A	N. Carolina	4-6	
N. 13	0-6	L	H	Maryland	4-6	
N. 20	16-17	L	A	S. Carolina	5-5	

1966 (6-4, 6-1, ACC Champions)

S. 24	40-35	W	H	Virginia	4-6	
O. 1	12-13	L	A	Georgia Tech	-/9	9-2	#8/8
O. 8	0-26	L	A	Alabama	-/4	11-0	#3/3
O. 15	9-6	W	H	Duke	4-6	
O. 22	0-30	L	A	Southern Cal.	-/5	7-4	#-/18
O. 29	23-21	W	H	Wake Forest	3-7	
N. 5	27-3	W	H	N. Carolina	2-8	
N. 12	14-10	W	A	Maryland	4-6	
N. 19	14-23	L	H	N.C. State	5-5	
N. 6	35-10	W	H	S. Carolina	1-9	

1967 (6-4, 6-0 ACC Champions)

S. 23	23-6	W	H	Wake Forest	4-6	
S. 30	17-24	L	H	Georgia	-/5	7-4	#-/18
O. 7	0-10	L	A	Georgia Tech	4-6	#
O. 14	21-43	L	A	Auburn	6-4	
O. 21	13-7	W	A	Duke	4-6	
O. 28	10-13	L	H	Alabama	8-2-1	#8/7
N. 4	17-0	W	H	N. Carolina	2-8	
N. 11	28-7	W	H	Maryland	4-6	
N. 18	14-6	W	H	N.C. State	-/10	9-2	#-/17
N. 25	23-12	W	A	S. Carolina	5-5	

1968 (4-5-1, 4-1-1, 2nd in ACC)

S. 21	20-20	T	A	Wake Forest	2-7-1	
S. 28	13-31	L	A	Georgia	8-1-2	#8/4
O. 5	21-24	L	A	Georgia Tech	4-6	
O. 12	10-21	L	H	Auburn	7-4	#16/-
O. 19	39-22	W	H	Duke	4-6	
O. 26	14-21	L	A	Alabama	8-3	#17/12
N. 2	24-19	W	A	N.C. State	6-4	
N. 9	16-0	W	H	Maryland	2-8	
N. 16	24-14	W	H	N. Carolina	3-7	
N. 23	3-7	L	A	S. Carolina	4-6	

Jim Riggs' fourth-down catch at Maryland in 1986 was the key play in Clemson's ACC Championship clinching tie.

1969 (4-6-0, 3-3-0, T3rd in ACC)

S. 20	21-14	W	A	Virginia		3-7	
S. 27	0-30	L	H	Georgia	-/7	5-5-1	#
O. 4	21-10	W	A	Georgia Tech		4-6	
O. 11	0-51	L	A	Auburn	-/20	8-3	#20/15
O. 18	28-14	W	H	Wake Forest		3-7	
O. 25	13-38	L	H	Alabama		6-5	#
N. 1	40-0	W	H	Maryland		3-7	
N. 8	27-34	L	A	Duke		3-6	
N. 15	15-32	L	A	N. Carolina		5-5	
N. 22	13-27	L	A	S. Carolina		7-4	#

1970 (3-8, 2-4, T6th in ACC)

S. 12	24-0	W	H	Citadel		5-6	
S. 19	27-17	W	H	Virginia		5-6	
S. 26	0-38	L	A	Georgia		5-5	
O. 3	7-28	L	A	Georgia Tech	-/15	9-3	#13/17
O. 10	0-44	L	A	Auburn	-/9	9-2	#10/9
O. 17	20-36	L	A	Wake Forest		6-5	
O. 24	10-21	L	H	Duke		6-5	
O. 31	24-11	W	A	Maryland		2-9	
N. 7	13-38	L	A	%Florida State		7-4	
N. 14	7-42	L	H	N. Carolina		8-4	#
N. 21	32-38	L	H	S. Carolina		4-6-1	

1971 (5-6, 4-2, 2nd in ACC)

S. 11	10-13	L	H	Kentucky		3-8	
S. 25	0-28	L	A	Georgia	-/14	11-1	#7/8
O. 2	14-24	L	A	Georgia Tech		6-6	#
O. 9	3-0	W	N1	Duke	-/14	6-5	
O. 16	32-15	W	N2	Virginia		3-8	
O. 23	13-35	L	A	Auburn	-/5	9-2	#12/5
O. 30	10-9	W	H	Wake Forest		6-5	
N. 6	13-26	L	A	N. Carolina		9-3	#-/18
N. 13	20-14	W	H	Maryland		2-9	
N. 20	23-31	L	H	N.C. State		3-8	
N. 27	17-7	W	A	S. Carolina		6-5	

N1 - Oyster Bowl, Norfolk, VA; N2 - Tobacco Bowl, Richmond, VA

1972 (4-7, 2-5, 5th in ACC)

S. 9	13-0	W	H	Citadel		5-6	
S. 23	10-29	L	A	%Rice		5-5-1	
S. 30	3-52	L	A	Oklahoma	-/2	11-1	#2/2
O. 7	9-31	L	A	Georgia Tech		7-4-1	#20/-
O. 14	0-7	L	H	Duke		5-6	
O. 21	37-21	W	H	Virginia		4-7	
O. 28	31-0	W	A	Wake Forest		2-9	
N. 4	10-26	L	H	N. Carolina		11-1	#12/14
N. 11	6-31	L	A	Maryland		5-5	
N. 18	17-42	L	A	N.C. State		8-3	#17/-
N. 25	7-6	W	H	S. Carolina		4-7	

1973 (5-6, 4-2, 3rd in ACC)

S. 8	14-12	W	H	Citadel		3-8	
S. 22	14-31	L	A	Georgia		7-4-1	#
S. 29	21-29	L	A	Georgia Tech		5-6	
O. 6	15-30	L	H	Texas A&M		5-6	
O. 13	32-27	W	H	Virginia		4-7	
O. 20	24-8	W	A	Duke		2-8	
O. 27	6-29	L	H	N.C. State		9-3	#16/-
N. 3	35-8	W	H	Wake Forest		1-9	
N. 10	37-29	W	A	N. Carolina		4-7	
N. 17	13-28	L	H	Maryland		8-4	#20/18
N. 24	20-32	L	A	S. Carolina		7-4	

1974 (7-4, 4-2, T2nd in ACC)

S. 14	0-24	L	A	Texas A&M	-/20	8-3	16/15
S. 21	10-31	L	A	%N.C. State	-/15	9-2-1	#11/9
S. 28	21-17	W	H	Georgia Tech		6-5	
O. 5	28-24	W	H	Georgia		6-6	#
O. 12	0-41	L	A	Maryland		8-4	#13/13
O. 19	17-13	W	H	Duke		6-5	
O. 26	28-29	L	A	Tennessee		7-3-2	#20/15
N. 2	21-9	W	A	Wake Forest		1-10	
N. 9	54-32	W	H	N. Carolina		7-5	#
N. 16	28-9	W	H	Virginia		4-7	
N. 23	39-21	W	H	S. Carolina		4-7	

1975 (2-9, 2-3, 5th in ACC)

S. 13	13-17	L	H	Tulane		5-6	
S. 20	0-56	L	A	%Alabama	-/14	11-1	#3/3
S. 27	28-33	L	A	Georgia Tech		7-4	
O. 4	7-35	L	A	Georgia		9-3	#19/19
O. 11	16-14	W	H	Wake Forest		3-8	
O. 18	21-25	L	H	Duke		4-5-2	
O. 25	7-45	L	H	N.C. State		7-4-1	
N. 1	7-43	L	H	Florida State		3-8	
N. 8	38-35	W	A	N. Carolina		3-7-1	
N. 15	20-22	L	H	Maryland		9-2-1	#13/11
N. 22	20-56	L	A	S. Carolina		7-5	#

1976 (3-6-2, 0-4-1, 7th in ACC)

S. 11	10-7	W	H	Citadel		6-5	
S. 18	0-41	L	H	Georgia	-/9	10-2	#10/10
S. 25	24-24	T	A	%Georgia Tech		4-6-1	
O. 2	19-21	L	A	Tennessee		6-5	
O. 9	14-20	L	H	Wake Forest		5-6	
O. 16	18-18	T	H	Duke		5-5	
O. 23	21-38	L	A	N.C. State		3-7	
O. 30	15-12	W	A	%Florida State		5-6	
N. 6	23-27	L	H	N. Carolina		9-3	#
N. 13	0-20	L	A	Maryland	-/6	11-1	#8/11
N. 20	28-9	W	H	S. Carolina		6-5	

1977 (8-3-1, 4-1-1, 2nd in ACC)
Ranked 19th in AP

S. 10	14-21	L	H	Maryland	-/10	8-4	#
S. 17	7-6	W	A	Georgia	-/17	5-6	
S. 24	31-14	W	A	Georgia Tech		6-5	
O. 1	31-13	W	A	Virginia Tech		3-7-1	
O. 8	31-0	W	H	Virginia		1-9-1	
O. 15	17-11	W	A	Duke		5-6	
O. 22	7-3	W	H	N.C. State	20/-	8-4	#-/19
O. 29	26-0	W	H	Wake Forest	16/-	1-10	
N. 5	13-13	T	A	N. Carolina	13/-	8-3-1	#17/14
N. 12	17-21	L	H	Notre Dame	15/5	11-1	#1/1
N. 19	31-27	W	A	S. Carolina	15/-	5-7	
D. 30	3-34	L	N1	%Pittsburgh	11/10	9-2-1	#8/7

N1 - Gator Bowl, Jacksonville, FL

1978 (11-1-0, 6-0-0, ACC Champions)
Ranked Tied for 6th in UPI, 6th in AP

S. 16	58-3	W	H	^Citadel		5-6	
S. 23	0-12	L	A	Georgia	8/-	9-2-1	#16/15
S. 30	31-0	W	H	Villanova		5-6	
O. 7	38-0	W	H	Virginia Tech		4-7	
O. 14	30-14	W	A	Virginia		2-9	
O. 21	28-8	W	H	Duke		4-7	
O. 28	33-10	W	A	N.C. State	20/-	9-3	#18/19
N. 4	51-6	W	H	Wake Forest	16/-	1-10	
N. 11	13-9	W	H	N. Carolina	15/-	5-6	
N. 18	28-24	W	A	Maryland	12/11	9-3	#20/-
N. 25	41-23	W	H	S. Carolina	10/-	5-5-1	
D. 30	17-15	W	N1	%Ohio State	7/20	7-4-1	#

N1 - Gator Bowl, Jacksonville, FL
^ - Clemson's 100th win in Death Valley

1979 (8-4, 4-2, T2nd in ACC)

S. 8	21-0	W	H	Furman		5-6	
S. 15	0-19	L	H	Maryland		7-4	
S. 22	12-7	W	H	*Georgia		6-5	
O. 6	17-7	W	H	Virginia		2-8	
O. 13	21-0	W	A	Virginia Tech		5-6	
O. 20	28-10	W	A	Duke		2-8	
O. 27	13-16	L	H	N.C. State		7-4	
N. 3	31-0	W	H	Wake Forest	-/14	8-4	#
N. 10	19-10	W	A	N. Carolina	18/-	8-3	#15/14
N. 17	16-10	W	A	Notre Dame	14/-	7-4	
N. 24	9-13	L	A	S. Carolina	13/19	8-4	#
D. 31	18-24	L	N1	Baylor	18/20	8-4	#14-15

N1 - Peach Bowl, Atlanta, GA
* - Clemson's 400th victory

1980 (6-5, 2-4, T4th in ACC)

S. 13	19-3	W	H	Rice		5-6	
S. 20	16-20	L	A	Georgia	-/10	12-0	#1/1
S. 27	17-10	W	H	W. Carolina		3-7-1	
O. 4	13-10	W	H	Virginia Tech		8-4	#
O. 11	27-24	W	A	Virginia		4-7	
O. 18	17-34	L	H	Duke		2-9	
O. 25	20-24	L	A	N.C. State		6-5	
N. 1	35-33	W	A	†Wake Forest		5-6	
N. 8	19-24	L	H	N. Carolina	-/14	11-1	#10/9
N. 15	7-34	L	A	Maryland		8-4	#
N. 22	27-6	W	H	S. Carolina	-/14	8-4	#

† - Clemson's 100th ACC win

1981 (12-0, National Champions, 6-0, ACC Champions)
Ranked 1st by AP and UPI

S. 5	45-10	W	H	Wofford		6-5	
S. 12	13-5	W	A	%Tulane		6-5	
S. 19	13-3	W	A	Georgia	-/4	10-2	#6/5
O. 3	21-3	W	A	Kentucky	14/-	3-8	
O. 10	27-0	W	H	Virginia	9/-	1-10	
O. 17	38-10	W	H	Duke	6/-	6-5	
O. 24	17-7	W	H	N.C. State	4/-	4-7	
O. 31	82-24	W	H	Wake Forest	3/-	4-7	
N. 7	10-8	W	A	N. Carolina	2/8	10-2	#9/8
N. 14	21-7	W	H	Maryland	2/-	4-7	
N. 21	29-13	W	A	S. Carolina	2/-	6-6	
J. 1	22-15	W	N1	%Nebraska	1/4	9-3	#11/9

N1 - Orange Bowl, Miami, FL

1982 (9-1-1, 6-0, ACC Champions)
Ranked 8th in AP

S. 6	7-13	L	A	%Georgia	11/7	11-1	#4/4
S. 11	17-17	T	H	Boston Coll.	16/-	8-3-1	#
S. 25	21-10	W	H	W. Carolina		6-5	
O. 2	24-6	W	H	Kentucky		0-10-1	
O. 9	48-0	W	A	%Virginia		2-9	
O. 6	49-14	W	H	Duke	20/-	6-5	
O. 23	38-29	W	A	N.C. State	18/-	6-5	
N. 6	16-13	W	H	N. Carolina	13/18	8-4	#18/13
N. 13	24-22	W	A	Maryland	11/18	8-4	#20/20
N. 20	24-6	W	H	S. Carolina	10/-	4-7	
N. 27	21-17	W	N1	Wake Forest	10/-	3-8	

N1 - Mirage Bowl, Tokyo, Japan
Note - Wake Forest game played N. 28 in Tokyo

1983 (9-1-1, 7-0 vs. ACC Teams)
Ranked 11th in AP, 10th in USA Today

S. 3	44-10	W	H	W. Carolina		11-3	
S. 10	16-31	L	A	%Boston Coll.		9-3	#19/20
S. 17	16-16	T	H	Georgia	-/11	10-1-1	#4/4
S. 24	41-14	W	H	Georgia Tech		3-8	
O. 8	42-21	W	H	Virginia		6-5	
O. 15	38-31	W	A	Duke		3-8	
O. 22	27-17	W	H	N.C. State		3-8	
O. 29	24-17	W	H	Wake Forest		4-7	
N. 5	16-3	W	A	N. Carolina	-/10	8-4	#
N. 12	52-27	W	H	Maryland	17/11	8-4	#
N. 19	22-13	W	A	S. Carolina	13/-	5-6	

Clemson ineligible for ACC title

1984 (7-4, 5-2 vs. ACC Teams)

S. 1	40-7	W	H	App. State	4/-	4-7	
S. 8	55-0	W	A	%Virginia	3/-	8-4	#20/17
S. 22	23-26	L	A	Georgia	2/20	7-4-1	#
S. 29	21-28	L	A	Georgia Tech	13/20	6-4	
O. 6	20-12	W	H	N. Carolina		5-5-1	
O. 20	54-21	W	H	Duke		2-9	
O. 27	35-34	W	A	N.C. State		3-8	
N. 3	37-14	W	H	Wake Forest		6-5	
N. 10	17-10	W	H	Virginia Tech		8-4	#
N. 17	23-41	L	A1	Maryland	20/-	9-3	#12/11
N. 23	21-22	L	H	S. Carolina	-/9	10-2	#11/13

A1 - Baltimore, MD, Memorial Stadium
Clemson ineligible for ACC title

1985 (6-6, 4-3, T3rd in ACC)

S. 14	20-17	W	A	Virginia Tech		6-5	
S. 21	13-20	L	H	Georgia		7-3-2	#
S. 28	3-14	L	H	Georgia Tech		9-2	#19/18
O. 5	7-26	L	A	%Kentucky		5-6	
O. 12	27-24	W	H	Virginia		6-5	
O. 19	21-9	W	A	Duke		4-7	
O. 26	39-10	W	H	N.C. State		3-8	
N. 2	26-10	W	H	Wake Forest		4-7	
N. 9	20-21	L	A	N. Carolina		5-6	
N. 16	31-34	L	H	Maryland		9-3	#18/19
N. 23	24-17	W	H	S. Carolina		5-6	
D. 21	13-20	L	N1	%Minnesota		7-5	#

N1 - Independence Bowl, Shreveport, LA

1986 (8-2-2, 5-1-1, ACC Champions)
Ranked 17th in AP, 19th in UPI, 18th in USA Today

S. 13	14-20	L	H	Virginia Tech		10-1-1	#
S. 20	31-28	W	A	Georgia	-/14	8-4	#20/-
S. 27	27-3	W	A	Georgia Tech		5-6	
O. 4	24-0	W	H	Citadel		3-8	
O. 11	31-17	W	A	%Virginia	20/-	3-8	
O. 18	35-3	W	H	Duke	17/-	4-7	
O. 25	3-27	L	A	N.C. State	16/20	8-3	#
N. 1	28-20	W	A	Wake Forest		5-6	
N. 8	38-10	W	H	N. Carolina		7-5	
N. 15	17-17	T	A1	Maryland	15/-	5-5-1	
N. 22	21-21	T	H	S. Carolina	19/-	3-6-2	
D. 27	27-21	W	N2	Stanford	-/20	8-4	#

A1 - Baltimore, MD, Memorial Stadium; N2 - Gator Bowl, Jacksonville, FL

1987 (10-2-0, 6-1-0, ACC Champions)
Ranked 12th in AP, 10th in UPI, 11th in USA Today

S. 5	43-0	W	H	W. Carolina	9/-	4-7	
S. 12	22-10	W	A	Virginia Tech	10/-	2-9	
S. 19	21-10	W	H	Georgia	8/18	9-3	#13/14
S. 26	33-12	W	H	Georgia Tech	9/-	2-9	
O. 10	38-21	W	H	Virginia	8/-	8-4	#
O. 17	17-10	W	H	Duke	7/-	5-6	
O. 24	28-30	L	H	N.C. State	7/-	4-7	
O. 31	31-17	W	H	Wake Forest	14/-	7-4	
N. 7	13-10	W	A	N. Carolina	10/-	5-6	
N. 14	45-16	W	H	Maryland	9/-	4-7	
N. 21	7-20	L	A	&S. Carolina	8/12	8-4	#15/15
J. 1	35-10	W	N1	Penn State	14/20	8-4	#

N1 - Florida Citrus Bowl, Orlando, FL

1988 (10-2-0, 6-1-0, ACC Champions)
Ranked 8th in UPI, 9th in AP, 10th in USA Today

S. 3	40-7	W	H	Virginia Tech	4/-	3-8	
S. 10	23-3	W	H	Furman	3/-	13-2	
S. 17	21-24	L	H	Florida State	3/10	11-1	#3/3
S. 24	30-13	W	A	Georgia Tech	12/-	3-8	
O. 8	10-7	W	A	Virginia	11/-	7-4	
O. 15	49-17	W	H	Duke	11/22	7-3-1	
O. 22	3-10	L	A	N.C. State	9/24	8-3	#17/-
O. 29	38-21	W	A	Wake Forest	15/-	6-4-1	
N. 5	37-14	W	H	N. Carolina	17/-	1-10	
N. 12	49-25	W	A	Maryland	16/-	5-6	
N. 19	29-10	W	H	S. Carolina	15/25	8-4	#
J. 1	13-6	W	N1	Oklahoma	9/10	9-3	#14/14

N1 - Citrus Bowl, Orlando, FL

1989 (10-2-0, 5-2-0, 3rd in ACC)
Ranked 12th in AP, 11th in UPI, 12th in USA Today

S. 2	30-0	W	H	Furman	12/-	12-2	
S. 9	34-23	W	A	%Florida St.	10/16	10-2	#3/2
S. 16	27-7	W	A	%Virginia Tech	7/-	6-4-1	
S. 23	31-7	W	H	Maryland	7/-	3-7	
S. 30	17-21	L	A	Duke	7/-	8-4	#
O. 7	34-20	W	H	Virginia	15/-	10-3	#18/15
O. 14	14-30	L	H	Ga. Tech	14/-	7-4	
O. 21	30-10	W	H	N.C. State	-/12	7-5	#
O. 28	44-10	W	H	Wake Forest	22/-	2-8	
N. 4	35-3	W	A	N. Carolina	21/-	1-10	
N. 18	45-0	W	A	%S. Carolina	15/-	6-4-1	
D. 30	27-7	W	N1	%W. Virginia	14/17	8-3-1	#21/-

N1 - Gator Bowl, Jacksonville, FL

1990 (10-2-0, 5-2-0, T2nd in ACC)
Ranked 9th by AP, UPI, and USA Today

S. 1	59-0	W	H	Lg. Beach St.	10/-	6-5	
S. 8	7-20	L	A	Virginia	9/14	8-4	#23/15
S. 15	18-17	W	A1	Maryland	16/-	6-5	
S. 22	48-0	W	H	App. State	17/-	6-5	
S. 29	26-7	W	H	Duke	19/-	4-7	
O. 6	34-3	W	H	Georgia	16/-	4-7	
O. 13	19-21	L	A	Ga. Tech	15/18	11-0-1	#2/1
O. 20	24-17	W	A	N.C. State	22/-	7-5	#
O. 27	24-6	W	A	$Wake Forest	19/-	3-8	
N. 3	20-3	W	H	N. Carolina	18/-	6-5	
N. 17	24-15	W	H	S. Carolina	17/-	6-5	
J. 1	30-0	W	N2	Illinois	14/18	8-4	#25/24

A1 - Baltimore, MD, Memorial Stadium; N2 - Hall of Fame Bowl, Tampa, FL
$ - Clemson's 500th victory

1991 (9-2-1, 6-0-1, ACC Champions)
Ranked 18th in AP, 17th in USA Today

S. 7	30-0	W	H	App. State	8/-	8-4	
S. 21	37-7	W	H	Temple	8/-	2-9	
S. 28	9-7	W	H	Georgia Tech	7/19	8-5	#
O. 5	12-27	L	A	%Georgia	6/-	9-3	#17/20
O. 12	20-20	T	H	Virginia	18/-	8-3	#
O. 26	29-19	W	H	N.C. State	19/12	9-3	#
N. 2	28-10	W	H	Wake Forest	16/-	3-8	
N. 9	21-6	W	A	%N. Carolina	15/-	7-4	
N. 16	40-7	W	H	Maryland	15/-	2-9	
N. 23	41-24	W	A	S. Carolina	14/-	3-6-2	
N. 30	33-21	W	N1	Duke	13/-	4-7	
J. 1	13-37	L	N2	California	13/14	10-2	#8/8

N1 - Tokyo, Japan; N2 - Citrus Bowl, Orlando, FL
Note - Duke game played Dec. 1 in Tokyo

1992 (5-6-0, 3-5-0, 7th in ACC)

S. 5	24-10	W	H	Ball State	13/-	5-6	
S. 12	20-24	L	H	%Florida St.	15/5	11-1	#2/2
S. 26	16-20	L	A	%Gia. Tech	16/-	5-6	
O. 3	54-3	W	H	UTC	25/-	2-9	
O. 10	29-28	W	A	Virginia	25/10	7-4	
O. 17	21-6	W	H	Duke	19/-	2-9	
O. 24	6-20	L	A	N.C. State	18/23	9-3	#17/17
O. 31	15-18	L	A	Wake Forest		8-4	#25/-
N. 7	40-7	W	H	N. Carolina	-/18	9-3	#19/18
N. 14	23-53	L	A	Maryland		3-8	
N. 21	13-24	L	H	S. Carolina		5-6	

1993 (9-3-0, 5-3-0, 3rd in ACC)
Ranked 23rd in AP, 22nd in USA Today

S. 4	24-14	W	H	UNLV	22/-	3-8	
S. 11	0-57	L	A	Florida State	21/1	12-1	#1/1
S. 25	16-13	W	H	Georgia Tech		5-6	
O. 2	20-14	W	H	N.C. State	-/24	7-5	#
O. 9	13-10	W	A	Duke		3-8	
O. 16	16-20	L	H	Wake Forest		2-9	
O. 23	27-0	W	H	ETSU		5-6	
O. 30	29-0	W	H	Maryland		2-9	
N. 6	0-24	L	A	%N. Carolina	-/16	10-3	#21/20
N. 13	23-14	W	H	Virginia	-/18	7-5	#
N. 20	16-13	W	A	S. Carolina	24/-	4-7	
D. 31	14-13	W	N1	%Kentucky	23/-	6-6	#

N1 - Peach Bowl, Atlanta, GA

1994 (5-6, 4-4, 5th in ACC

S. 3	27-6	W	H	Furman	24/-	3-8	
S. 10	12-29	L	H	N.C. State	22/-	9-3	#17/17
S. 17	6-9	L	A	Virginia		9-3	#15/13
O. 1	13-0	W	H	Maryland		4-7	
O. 8	14-40	L	A	Georgia		6-4-1	
O. 15	13-19	L	A	Duke	-/25	8-4	#
O. 22	0-17	L	A	Florida State	-/7	11-1	#4/5
O. 29	24-8	W	H	Wake Forest		3-8	
N. 5	28-17	W	A	N. Carolina	-/19	8-4	#-/21
N. 12	20-10	W	H	Georgia Tech		1-10	
N. 19	7-33	L	H	S. Carolina		7-5	#

Note- UNC ranked 12th in USA Today prior to game.

1995 (8-4-0, 6-2, 3rd in ACC)

S. 2	55-9	W	H	W. Carolina		3-7	
S. 9	26-45	L	H	Florida State	-/1	10-2	#4/5
S. 16	29-14	W	A	%Wake Forest		1-10	
S. 23	3-22	L	H	Virginia	-/11	9-4	#16/16
S. 30	43-22	W	H	N.C. State		3-8	
O. 7	17-19	L	H	%Georgia		6-6	#
O. 21	17-0	W	A	Maryland		6-5	
O. 28	24-3	W	A	Georgia Tech		6-5	
N. 4	17-10	W	H	N. Carolina		7-5	#
N. 11	34-17	W	H	Duke	24/-	24/-	3-8
N. 18	38-17	W	A	S. Carolina	24/-	4-6-1	
J. 1	0-41	L	N1	Syracuse	23/-	9-3	#19/17

N1 - Gator Bowl, Jacksonville, FL

1996 (7-5-0, 6-2-0, 2nd in ACC)

A. 31	0-45	L	A	N. Carolina		10-2	#10/10
S. 7	19-3	W	H	Furman		9-4	
S. 21	24-38	L	A	%Missouri		5-6	
S. 28	21-10	W	H	Wake Forest		3-8	
O. 5	3-34	L	A	Florida State	-/2	11-1	#3/3
O. 12	13-6	W	A	Duke		0-11	
O. 19	28-25	W	H	Georgia Tech	-/22	5-6	
N. 2	35-3	W	H	Maryland		5-6	
N. 9	24-16	W	A	Virginia	-/15	7-5	#
N. 16	4-17	W	H	N.C. State		3-8	
N. 23	31-34	L	H	%S. Carolina	22/-	5-6	
D. 28	7-10	L	N1	%LSU	-/17	10-2	#12/3

N1 - Peach Bowl, Atlanta, GA

1997 (7-5, 4-4, 5th in ACC)

S. 6	23-12	W	H	App. State	18/-	7-4	
S. 13	19-17	W	A	N.C. State	19/25	6-5	
S. 20	28-35	L	H	Florida State	16/5	11-1	#3/3
S. 27	20-23	L	A	%Georgia Tech	17/-	7-5	#
O. 4	39-7	W	H	Texas El-Paso		4-7	
O. 11	7-21	L	H	%Virginia		7-4	
O. 25	20-9	W	A	Maryland		2-9	
N. 1	33-16	W	A	Wake Forest		5-6	
N. 8	29-20	W	H	Duke		2-9	
N. 15	10-17	L	H	N. Carolina	-/8	11-1	#4/6
N. 22	47-21	W	A	%S. Carolina		5-6	
J. 1	17-21	L	N1	%Auburn	-/13	10-3	#13/12

N1 - Peach Bowl, Atlanta, GA

USC
ALL-STARS
AND
Scores
Since
1896

USC ALL-STARS

THE FOLLOWING USC PLAYERS WERE NAMED ALL-AMERICAN AND/OR TO THE USC ATHLETIC HALL OF FAME (AHF).

Clyde Bennett (1951-53), All-American
Ed "Bru" Boineau (1928-30), AHF
Robert Brooks (1988-91), All-American
Bobby Bryant (1964-66), All-American, AHF
Earl Clary (1931-33), All-Southern, AHF
Larry Craig (1935-38), All-Southern, AHF
Leon Cunningham (1951-54), All-American, AHF
Sam DeLuca (1954-56), All-American
King Dixon (1956-58), All-ACC, AHF
Brad Edwards (1985-87), All-American
Todd Ellis (1986-89), All-American
Dominic Fusci (1943-46), All-Southern, AHF
Billy Gambrell (1960-62), All-American, AHF
Bryant Gilliard (1982-84), All-American
Jeff Grantz (1973-76), All-American, AHF
Tatum Gressette (1920-21), AHF
Fred Hambright (1931-33), All-Southern, AHF
Dickie Harris (1969-71), All-American
Roy Hart (1985-87), All-American
Alex Hawkins (1956-58), All-American, AHF
Luther Hill (1911-15), Team Captain, AHF
John LeHeup (1970-72), All-American
Harold Mauney (1932-34), AHF

Bryant Meeks (1945-46), All-American, AHF
Frank Mincevich (1952-54), All-American, AHF
Warren Muir (1967-69), All-American
Norris Mullis (1950-52), All-American
Rut Osborne (1915-17), AHF
Ed Pitts (1957-59), All-American
Mackie Prickett (1954-56), All-ACC, AHF
Andrew Provence (1980-82), All-American
Dan Reeves (1962-64), All-ACC, AHF
Bill Rogers (1924-26), All-State, AHF
George Rogers (1977-80), Heisman Trophy, AHF
Rick Sanford (1976-78), All-American
James Seawright (1982-84), All-American
Sterling Sharpe (1985-87), All-American
Larry Smith (1949-51), All-Southern, AHF
Lou Sossamon (1940-42), All-American, AHF
Bishop Strickland (1947-50), All-Southern, AHF
Tommy Suggs (1968-70), All-ACC, AHF
Steve Taneyhill (1992-95), All-American
Alfred Von Kolnitz (1911-13), AHF
Steve Wadiak (1948-51), All-American, AHF
Del Wilkes (1982-84), All-America
Fred Zeigler (1967-69), All-ACC, AHF

An early shot of the Gamecocks (dark jerseys) in action versus the Tigers (orange jerseys) at the State Fair Grounds on Big Thursday. 1909. It is interesting to note the old wooden grandstands. One also notes that there appear to be as many female fans on hand as male fans.

USC ALL-TIME TEAMS

(1894-1945)

Position	Name	Years
Back	Bru Boineau	1928-30
Back	Earl Clary	1931-33
Back	Tatum Gressette	1920-21
Back	Fred Hambright	1931-33
Line	Lou Sossamon	1940-42
Line	Larry Craig	1935-37
Line	Luke Hill	1911-15
Line	Dom Fusci	1942-43
Line	Joe Wheeler	1920-23
Line	Skimp Harrison	1942-44
Line	Julian Beal	1927-29
Line	Alex Urban	1938-40

(1946–1996)
(Defense)

Back	Bobby Bryant	1964-66
Back	Brad Edwards	1984-87
Back	Dick Harris	1969-71
Back	Rick Sanford	1975-78
LB	Ed Baxley	1979-80
LB	Cory Miller	1988-90
LB	James Seawright	1981-84
Line	Roy Hart	1983-87

Line	Kevin Hendrix	1985-88
Line	John LeHeup	1970-72
Line	Andrew Provence	1980-82
Line	Emanuel Weaver	1980-81

(Offense)

QB	Jeff Grantz	1972-75
RB	George Rogers	1977-80
RB	Harold Green	1986-89
RB	Steve Wadiak	1947-50
TE	Jay Saldi	1968-70
TE	Willie Scott	1977-80
WR	Sterling Sharpe	1983-87
WR	Fred Zeigler	1967-69
C	Mike McCabe	1973-75
C	Bryant Meeks	1945-46
OG	Steve Courson	1973-76
OG	Del Wilkes	1980-84
OT	Chuck Slaughter	1978-81
OT	Dave DeCamilla	1968-70
P	Max Runager	1976-78
PK	Collin Mackie	1987-90
Returns	Robert Brooks	1988-91

1892   Won 0, Lost 1   No Coach
Furman   0-44   Dec. 24   at Charleston, S.C.

1893 No team

1894   Won 0, Lost 2   No Coach
Georgia   0-40   Nov.   3   at Columbia
Augusta Y   4-16   Nov.   11   at Columbia

1895   Won 2, Lost 1   No Coach
Columbia AA   20- 0   Nov.   2   at Columbia
Furman   14-10   Nov.   8   at Columbia
Wofford   0-10   Nov.   14   at Columbia

1896   Won 1, Lost 3   Coach W. H. Whaley
Charleston Y   4- 6   Oct.   31   at Charleston
Clemson   12- 6   Nov.   12   at Columbia
Wofford   4- 6   Nov.   19   at Columbia
Furman   0-12   Nov.   26   at Greenville, S.C.

1897   Won 0, Lost 3   Coach W. P. Murphy
Charleston Y   0-4   Oct.   23   at Charleston, S.C.
Clemson   6-18   Nov.   11   at Columbia
Charleston Y   0-6   Nov.   26   at Columbia

1898   Won 1, Lost 2   Coach W. Wertenbaker
Bingham   16- 5   Oct.   18   at Columbia
Clemson   0-24   Nov.   17   at Columbia
Davidson   0- 6   Nov.   24   at Charlotte, N.C.

1899   Won 2, Lost 3   Coach I. O. Hunt
Columbia Y   5- 0   Oct.   15   at Columbia
Clemson   0-34   Nov.   9   at Columbia
Bingham   11- 5   Nov.   15   at Columbia
Bingham   6-18   Nov.   22   at Asheville, N.C.
Davidson   0- 5   Nov.   30   at Charlotte, N.C.

1900   Won 4, Lost 3   Coach I. O. Hunt
Georgia   0- 5   Oct.   20   at Athens
Guilford   10-0   Oct.   25   at Columbia
Clemson   0-51   Nov.   1   at Columbia
N.C. A&M   12- 0   Nov.   10   at Columbia
Furman   27- 0   Nov.   17   at Greenville, S.C.
Davidson   0- 5   Nov.   22   at Charlotte, N.C.
N.C. A&M   17- 5   Nov.   29   at Raleigh, N.C.

1901   Won 3, Lost 4   Coach B. W. Dickson
Georgia   5-10   Oct.   12   at Augusta
Furman   12- 0   Oct.   22   at Columbia
Bingham   11- 6   Oct.   24   at Asheville, N.C.
Davidson   5-12   Oct.   30   at Columbia
Georgia Tech   0-13   Nov.   9   at Atlanta
N.C.M.A   47- 0   Nov.   12   at Columbia
Wofford   5-11   Nov.   18   at Spartanburg, S.C.

1902   Won 6, Lost 1   Coach C. R. Williams
Guilford   10- 0   Oct.   15   at Columbia
N.C.M.A   60- 0   Oct.   21   at Columbia
Bingham   28- 0   Oct.   25   at Columbia
Clemson   12- 6   Oct.   30   at Columbia
St. Albans   5- 0   Nov.   6   at Columbia
Furman   0-10   Nov.   14   at Greenville, S.C.
Charleston M.C   80- 0   Nov.   28   at Columbia

1903   Won 8, Lost 2   Coach C. R. Williams
Columbia Y   24- 0   Oct.   2   at Columbia
Welsh Neck   89- 0   Oct.   6   at Columbia
North Carolina   0-17   Oct.   10   at Columbia
Georgia   17- 0   Oct.   17   at Athens
Guilford   29- 0   Oct.   23   at Columbia
Tennessee   24- 0   Oct.   29   at Columbia
Davidson   29-12   Nov.   8   at Charlotte, N.C.
N.C. A&M   5- 6   Nov.   14   at Raleigh
Charleston   6- 0   Nov.   21   at Charleston, S.C.
Georgia Tech   16- 0   Nov.   26   at Atlanta

1904   Won 4, Lost 3, Tied 1   Coach Christie Benet
Welsh Neck   14- 0   Oct.   7   at Columbia
North Carolina   0-27   Oct.   15   at Chapel Hill
Guilford   21- 4   Oct.   20   at Columbia
Georgia   2- 0   Oct.   26   at Columbia
N.C. A&M   0- 0   Nov.   5   at Raleigh
Davidson   0- 6   Nov.   12   at Columbia
Charleston A.C.   0- 6   Nov.   19   at Charleston, S.C.
Wash. and Lee   25- 0   Nov.   24   at Sumter, SC

1905   Won 4, Lost 2, Tied 1   Coach Christie Benet
Welsh Neck   14- 0   Oct.   13   at Columbia
Bingham   19- 6   Oct.   20   at Columbia
N.C. A&M   0-29   Oct.   26   at Columbia
Davidson   6- 4   Nov.   4   at Charlotte, N.C.
Bingham   5- 5   Nov.   11   at Asheville, N.C.
Virginia Tech   0-34   Nov.   18   at Roanoke
The Citadel   47- 0   Nov.   30   at Charleston, S.C.

1906 No team — Trustees abolished football

1907   Won 3, Lost 0   Coach Douglas McKay
Charleston   14- 4   Nov.   16   at Columbia
Georgia College   4- 0   Nov.   21   at Columbia
The Citadel   12- 0   Nov.   28   at Charleston, S.C.

1908   Won 3, Lost 5, Tied 1   Coach Christie Benet
Ridgewood   0- 0   Oct.   3   at Columbia
Charleston   17- 0   Oct.   10   at Columbia
Georgia   6-29   Oct.   17   at Athens
Charleston AA   4-15   Oct.   22   at Columbia
Davidson   0-22   Oct.   29   at Columbia
Georgia M.S   19- 5   Nov.   4   at Augusta
Bingham   6-10   Nov.   7   at Columbia
North Carolina   0-22   Nov.   14   at Chapel Hill
The Citadel   12- 0   Nov.   26   at Charleston, S.C.

1909   Won 2, Lost 6   Coach Christie Benet
N.C.M.C   0- 5   Oct.   9   at Columbia
Georgia Tech   0-59   Oct.   16   at Atlanta
Wake Forest   0- 8   Oct.   23   at Columbia
Charleston   17-11   Oct.   28   at Columbia
Clemson   0- 6   Nov.   3   at Columbia
Davidson   5-29   Nov.   13   at Davidson, N.C.
Mercer   3- 5   Nov.   20   at Macon, Ga.
The Citadel   11- 5   Nov.   25   at Charleston, S.C.

1910   Won 4, Lost 4   Coach John H. Neff
Charleston   8- 0   Oct.   8   at Columbia
Georgia M.S   14- 0   Oct.   15   at Augusta
Lenoir   33- 0   Oct.   22   at Columbia
Wake Forest   6- 0   Oct.   27   at Columbia
Clemson   0-24   Nov.   3   at Columbia
Davidson   0-53   Nov.   12   at Davidson, N.C.
North Carolina   6-23   Nov.   19   at Durham, N.C.
The Citadel   0- 5   Nov.   24   at Charleston, S.C.

1911   Won 1, Lost 4, Tied 2   Coach John H. Neff
Georgia   0-38   Oct.   7   at Athens
Charleston   16- 0   Oct.   14   at Charleston, S.C.
Florida   6- 6   Oct.   21   at Columbia
Clemson   0-27   Nov.   2   at Columbia
North Carolina   0-21   Nov.   11   at Chapel Hill
Davidson   0-10   Nov.   18   at Columbia
The Citadel   0- 0   Nov.   30   at Charleston, S.C.

1912   Won 5, Lost 2, Tied 1   Coach N. B. Edgerton
Wake Forest   10- 3   Oct.   5   at Columbia
Virginia   0-19   Oct.   14   at Charlottesville
Florida   6-10   Oct.   19   at Gainesville
Charleston   68- 0   Oct.   26   at Charleston, S.C.
Clemson   22- 7   Oct.   31   at Columbia
North Carolina   6- 6   Nov.   9   at Chapel Hill
Porter   66- 0   Nov.   16   at Columbia
The Citadel   26- 2   Nov.   28   at Columbia

1913   Won 4, Lost 3

		Coach N. B. Edgerton		
Virginia	0-54	Oct.	4	at Charlottesville
Wake Forest	27-10	Oct.	11	at Columbia
North Carolina	3-13	Oct.	18	at Columbia
Clemson	0-32	Oct.	30	at Columbia
Florida	13- 0	Nov.	8	at Columbia
Davidson	10- 0	Nov.	15	at Davidson, N.C.
The Citadel	42-13	Nov.	26	at Columbia

1914   Won 5, Lost 5, Tied 1

		Coach N. B. Edgerton		
Mach. Mates	30- 7	Sept.	30	at Columbia
Georgia Tech	0-20	Oct.	3	at Atlanta
North Carolina	0-48	Oct.	12	at Chapel Hill
Virginia	7-49	Oct.	17	at Charlottesville
Newberry	13-13	Oct.	24	at Columbia
Clemson	6-29	Oct.	29	at Columbia
Wofford	25- 0	Nov.	4	at Spartanburg, S.C.
Wake Forest	26- 0	Nov.	7	at Columbia
Davidson	7-13	Nov.	14	at Columbia
Newberry	47- 6	Nov.	19	at Newberry, S.C.
The Citadel	7- 6	Nov.	26	at Columbia

1915   Won 5, Lost 3, Tied 1

		Coach N. B. Edgerton		
Newberry	29- 0	Oct.	2	at Columbia
Presbyterian	41- 0	Oct.	9	at Columbia
N.C. A&M	19-10	Oct.	21	at Raleigh
Clemson	0- 0	Oct.	28	at Columbia
Wofford	33- 6	Nov.	4	at Spartanburg, S.C.
Cumberland	68- 0	Nov.	6	at Columbia
Virginia	0-13	Nov.	13	at Columbia
Georgetown	0-61	Nov.	20	at Washington, D.C.
The Citadel	0- 3	Nov.	25	at Columbia

1916   Won 2, Lost 7

		Coach Rice Warren		
Newberry	0-10	Oct.	7	at Columbia
Wofford	23- 3	Oct.	14	at Columbia
Tennessee	0-26	Oct.	21	at Knoxville
Clemson	0-27	Oct.	26	at Columbia
Wake Forest	7-33	Nov.	4	at Columbia
Virginia	6-35	Nov.	11	at Charlottesville
Mercer	47- 0	Nov.	18	at Columbia
Furman	0-14	Nov.	23	at Greenville, S.C.
The Citadel	2-20	Nov.	30	at Columbia

1917   Won 3, Lost 5

		Coach Dixon Foster		
Newberry	38- 0	Oct.	6	at Columbia
Florida	13-21	Oct.	13	at Gainesville
Clemson	13-21	Oct.	25	at Columbia
Erskine	13-14	Nov.	3	at Columbia
Furman	26- 0	Nov.	8	at Florence, S.C.
Wofford	0-20	Nov.	17	at Spartanburg, S.C.
Presbyterian	14-20	Nov.	24	at Columbia
The Citadel	20- 0	Nov.	29	at Columbia

1918   Won 2, Lost 1, Tied 1

		Coach Frank Dobson		
Clemson	0-39	Nov.	2	at Columbia
Furman	20-12	Nov.	16	at Greenville, S.C.
Wofford	13- 0	Nov.	23	at Columbia
The Citadel	0- 0	Nov.	28	at Orangeburg, S.C.

1919   Won 1, Lost 7, Tied 1

		Coach Dixon Foster		
Presbyterian	0- 6	Sept.	27	at Columbia
Erskine	6- 0	Oct.	4	at Columbia
Georgia	0-14	Od.	11	at Athens
Davidson	0- 7	Oct.	18	at Columbia
Clemson	6-19	Oct.	30	at Columbia
Tennessee	6- 6	Nov.	8	at Columbia
Wash. and Lee	0-26	Nov	15	at Lexington, Va.
Florida	0-13	Nov.	22	at Columbia
The Citadel	7-14	Nov.	27	at Columbia

1920   Won 5, Lost 4

		Coach Sol Metzger		
Wofford	10- 0	Oct.	2	at Columbia
Georgia	0-37	Oct.	9	at Columbia
North Carolina	0- 7	Oct.	16	at Chapel Hill
Presbyterian	14- 0	Oct.	21	at Augusta, Ga.
Clemson	3- 0	Oct.	28	at Columbia
Davidson	0-27	Nov.	6	at Davidson, N.C.
Navy	0-63	Nov.	13	at Annapolis, Md.
Newberry	48- 0	Nov.	20	at Columbia
The Citadel	7- 6	Nov.	25	at Charleston, S.C.

1921   Won 5, Lost 1, Tied 2

		Coach Sol Metzger		
Erskine	13- 7	Oct.	1	at Columbia
Newberry	7- 0	Oct.	8	at Columbia
North Carolina	7- 7	Oct.	15	at Columbia
Presbyterian	48- 0	Oct.	22	at Columbia
Clemson	21- 0	Oct.	27	at Columbia
Florida	7- 7	Nov.	5	at Tampa
Furman	0- 7	Nov.	12	at Greenville, S.C.
The Citadel	13- 0	Nov.	24	at Columbia

1922   Won 5, Lost 4

		Coach Sol Metzger		
Erskine	13- 0	Sept.	29	at Columbia
Presbyterian	7- 0	Oct.	7	at Columbia
North Carolina	7-10	Oct.	14	at Chapel Hill
Wofford	20- 0	Oct.	20	at Columbia
Clemson	0- 3	Oct.	26	at Columbia
Sewanee	6- 7	Nov.	4	at Columbia
Furman	27- 7	Nov.	11	at Columbia
The Citadel	13- 0	Nov.	16	at Orangeburg, S.C.
Centre	0-42	Nov.	30	at Danville, Ky.

1923   Won 4, Lost 6

		Coach Sol Metzger		
Erskine	35- 0	Sept.	29	at Columbia
Presbyterian	3- 7	Oct.	6	at Columbia
N. C. State	0- 7	Oct.	13	at Raleigh
Newberry	24- 0	Oct.	19	at Columbia
Clemson	6- 7	Oct.	25	at Columbia
North Carolina	0-13	Nov.	3	at Columbia
Furman	3-23	Nov.	10	at Greenville, S.C.
The Citadel	12- 0	Nov.	15	at Orangeburg, S.C.
Wash. and Lee	7-13	Nov.	17	at Columbia
Wake Forest	14- 7	Nov.	29	at Columbia

1924   Won 7, Lost 3

		Coach Sol Metzger		
Erskine	47- 0	Sept.	27	at Columbia
Georgia	0-18	Oct.	4	at Athens
N. C. State	10- 0	Oct.	11	at Columbia
Presbyterian	29- 0	Oct.	17	at Columbia
Clemson	3- 0	Oct.	23	at Columbia
The Citadel	14- 3	Oct.	29	at Orangeburg, S.C.
North Carolina	10- 7	Nov.	1	at Chapel Hill
Furman	0-10	Nov.	8	at Columbia
Sewanee	0-10	Nov.	15	at Columbia
Wake Forest	7- 0	Nov.	27	at Columbia

1925   Won 7, Lost 3

		Coach Branch Bocock		
Erskine	33- 0	Sept.	26	at Columbia
North Carolina	0- 7	Oct.	3	at Columbia
N.C. State	7- 6	Oct.	11	at Raleigh
Wofford	6- 0	Oct.	16	at Columbia
Clemson	33- 0	Oct.	22	at Columbia
The Citadel	30- 6	Oct.	28	at Orangeburg, S.C.
Virginia Tech	0- 6	Oct.	31	at Richmond
Furman	0- 2	Nov.	14	at Greenville, S.C.
Presbyterian	21- 0	Nov.	20	at Columbia
Centre	20- 0	Nov.	28	at Columbia

1926	Won 6, Lost 4		Coach Branch Bocock		
Erskine	41- 0	Sept.	25	at Columbia
Maryland	12- 0	Oct.	2	at Columbia
North Carolina	0- 7	Oct.	9	at Chapel Hill
Wofford	27-13	Oct.	15	at Columbia
Clemson	24- 0	Oct.	21	at Columbia
The Citadel	9-12	Oct.	28	at Orangeburg, S.C.
Virginia	0- 6	Oct.	30	at Columbia
Virginia Tech	19- 0	Nov.	6	at Richmond
Furman	7-10	Nov.	13	at Greenville, S.C.
N.C. State	20-14	Nov.	20	at Columbia

1927	Won 4, Lost 5		Coach Harry Lightsey		
Erskine	13- 6	Sept.	24	at Columbia
Maryland	0-26	Oct.	1	at College Park
Virginia	13-12	Oct.	8	at Charlottesville
North Carolina	14- 6	Oct.	15	at Columbia
Clemson	0-20	Oct.	20	at Columbia
The Citadel	6- 0	Oct.	27	at Orangeburg, S.C.
Virginia Tech	0-35	Nov.	5	at Richmond
Furman	0-33	Nov.	12	at Greenville, S.C.
N.C. State	0-34	Nov.	24	at Columbia

1928	Won 6, Lost 2, Tied 2		Coach Billy Laval		
Erskine	19- 0	Sept.	22	at Columbia
Chicago	6- 0	Sept.	29	at Chicago, Ill.
Virginia	24-13	Oct.	6	at Charlottesville
Maryland	21- 7	Oct.	13	at Columbia
Presbyterian	13- 0	Oct.	19	at Columbia
Clemson	0-32	Oct.	25	at Columbia
The Citadel	0- 0	Nov.	1	at Orangeburg, S.C.
North Carolina	0- 0	Nov.	10	at Chapel Hill
Furman	6- 0	Nov.	17	at Columbia
N. C. State	7-18	Nov.	29	at Raleigh

1929	Won 6, Lost 5		Coach Billy Laval		
Erskine	26- 7	Sept.	28	at Columbia
Virginia	0- 6	Oct.	5	at Columbia
Maryland	26- 6	Oct.	12	at College Park
Presbyterian	41- 0	Oct.	18	at Columbia
Clemson	14-21	Oct.	24	at Columbia
The Citadel	27-14	Oct.	31	at Orangeburg, S.C.
North Carolina	0-40	Nov.	9	at Columbia
Furman	2- 0	Nov.	16	at Greenville, S.C.
Florida	7-20	Nov.	23	at Columbia
N. C. State	20- 6	Nov.	30	at Raleigh
Tennessee	0-54	Dec.	7	at Knoxville

1930	Won 6, Lost 4		Coach Billy Laval		
Erskine	19- 0	Sept.	20	at Columbia
Duke	22- 0	Sept.	27	at Durham, N.C.
Georgia Tech	0-45	Oct.	4	at Atlanta
Louisiana State	7- 6	Oct.	11	at Columbia
Clemson	7-20	Oct.	23	at Columbia
The Citadel	13- 0	Oct.	30	at Orangeburg, S.C.
Furman	0-14	Nov.	8	at Greenville, S.C.
Sewanee	14-13	Nov.	15	at Columbia
N. C. State	19- 0	Nov.	22	at Columbia
Auburn	7-25	Nov.	27	at Columbus, Ga.

1931	Won 5, Lost 4, Tied 1		Coach Billy Laval		
Duke	7- 0	Sept.	26	at Columbia
Georgia Tech	13-25	Oct.	3	at Atlanta
Louisiana State	12-19	Oct.	10	at Baton Rouge
Clemson	21- 0	Oct.	22	at Columbia
The Citadel	26- 7	Oct.	29	at Orangeburg, S.C.
Furman	27- 0	Nov.	7	at Columbia
Florida	6- 6	Nov.	14	at Tampa
N. C. State	21- 0	Nov.	21	at Columbia
Auburn	6-13	Nov.	26	at Montgomery, Ala.
Centre	7- 9	Dec.	5	at Columbia

1932	Won 5, Lost 4, Tied 2		Coach Billy Laval		
Sewanee	7- 3	Sept.	24	at Columbia
Villanova	7- 6	Oct.	1	at Philadelphia, Penn.
Wake Forest	0- 6	Oct.	8	at Charlotte, N.C.
Wofford	19- 0	Oct.	14	at Columbia
Clemson	14- 0	Oct.	20	at Columbia
Tulane	0- 6	Oct.	29	at New Orleans, La.
Louisiana State	0- 6	Nov.	5	at Columbia
Furman	0-14	Nov.	12	at Greenville, S.C.
The Citadel	19- 0	Nov.	19	at Columbia
N. C. State	7- 7	Nov.	24	at Raleigh
Auburn	20-20	Dec.	3	at Birmingham, Ala.

1933	Won 6, Lost 3, Tied 1		Coach Billy Laval		
Wofford	31- 0	Sept.	23	at Columbia
Temple	6-26	Sept.	29	at Philadelphia, Penn.
Villanova	6-15	Oct.	7	at Columbia
† Clemson	7- 0	Oct.	19	at Columbia
The Citadel	12- 6	Oct.	26	at Orangeburg, S.C.
† Virginia Tech	12- 0	Oct.	28	at Blacksburg
Louisiana State	7-30	Nov.	5	at Baton Rouge, La.
† N. C. State	14- 0	Nov.	11	at Columbia
Furman	0- 0	Nov.	19	at Columbia
Auburn	16-14	Dec.	2	at Birmingham, Ala.

1934	Won 5, Lost 4		Coach Billy Laval		
Erskine	25- 0	Sept.	29	at Columbia
† V.M.I	22- 6	Oct.	6	at Columbia
† N. C. State	0- 6	Oct.	13	at Raleigh
The Citadel	20- 6	Oct.	18	at Orangeburg, S.C.
† Clemson	0-19	Oct.	25	at Columbia
† Virginia Tech	20- 0	Nov.	3	at Columbia
Villanova	0-20	Nov.	10	at Philadelphia, Penn.
Furman	2- 0	Nov.	17	at Greenville, S.C.
† Wash. and Lee	7-14	Nov.	29	at Columbia

1935	Won 3, Lost 7		Coach Don McCallister		
Erskine	33- 0	Sept.	21	at Columbia
† Duke	0-47	Sept.	28	at Durham, N.C.
† N. C. State	0-14	Oct.	5	at Columbia
Davidson	6-13	Oct.	12	at Davidson, N.C.
The Citadel	25- 0	Oct.	17	at Orangeburg, S.C.
† Clemson	0-44	Oct.	24	at Columbia
† Virginia Tech	0-27	Nov.	2	at Blacksburg
Furman	7-20	Nov.	16	at Columbia
† Wash. and Lee	2- 0	Nov.	23	at Columbia
Florida	0-22	Dec.	7	at Tampa

1936	Won 5, Lost 7		Coach Don McCallister		
Erskine	38- 0	Sept.	19	at Columbia
† V.M.I.	7-24	Sept.	26	at Lexington, Va.
†Duke	0-21	Oct.	3	at Columbia
Florida	7- 0	Oct.	10	at Columbia
† Virginia Tech	14 -0	Oct.	17	at Columbia
† Clemson	0-19	Oct.	22	at Columbia
† The Citadel	9- 0	Oct.	30	at Orangeburg, S.C.
Villanova	0-14	Nov.	7	at Columbia
† Furman	6-23	Nov.	14	at Greenville, S.C.
† North Carolina	0-14	Nov.	21	at Columbia
Xavier (Ohio)	13-21	Nov.	26	at Cincinnati
Miami (Fla.)	6- 3	Dec.	11	at Miami

1937	Won 5, Lost 6, Tied 1		Coach Don McCallister		
Emory & Henry	45- 7	Sept.	18	at Columbia
† North Carolina	13-13	Sept.	25	at Chapel Hill
Georgia	7-13	Oct.	2	at Columbia
Alabama	0-20	Oct.	9	at Tuscaloosa
† Davidson	12- 7	Oct.	16	at Columbia
† Clemson	6-34	Oct.	21	at Columbia
† The Citadel	21- 6	Oct.	29	at Orangeburg, S.C.
Kentucky	7-27	Nov.	6	at Lexington
† Furman	0-12	Nov.	13	at Columbia
Presbyterian	64 - 0	Nov.	20	at Columbia
Catholic	14-27	Nov.	25	at Washington, D.C.
Miami (Fla.)	3- 0	Dec.	3	at Miami

† Southern Conference Game

1938   Won 6, Lost 4, Tied 1   Coach Rex Enright

Erskine	53- 0	Sept.	19	at Columbia
Xavier (Ohio)	6- 0	Sept.	24	at Cincinnati
Georgia	6- 7	Oct.	1	at Columbia
† Wake Forest	19-20	Oct.	8	at Columbia
† Davidson	25- 0	Oct.	14	at Sumter, S.C.
† Clemson	12-34	Oct.	20	at Columbia
Villanova	6- 6	Oct.	28	at Orangeburg, S.C.
Duquesne	7- 0	Nov.	5	at Columbia
† Furman	27- 6	Nov.	12	at Greenville, S.C.
Fordham	0-13	Nov.	19	at New York, N.Y.
Catholic	7- 0	Nov.	28	at Washington, D.C.

1939   Won 3, Lost 6, Tied 1   Coach Rex Enright

† Wake Forest	7-19	Sept.	23	at Wake Forest, N.C.
Catholic	0-12	Sept.	29	at Columbia
Villanova	0-40	Oct.	6	at Philadelphia, Penn.
† Davidson	7- 0	Oct.	13	at Sumter, S.C.
† Clemson	0-27	Oct.	19	at Columbia
West Virginia	6- 6	Oct.	27	at Orangeburg, S.C.
Florida	7- 0	Nov.	4	at Columbia
†Furman	0-20	Nov.	11	at Columbia
Georgia	7-33	Nov.	18	at Athens
Miami (Fla.)	7- 6	Nov.	25	at Columbia

1940   Won 3, Lost 6   Coach Rex Enright

Georgia	2-33	Oct.	5	at Columbia
Duquesne	21-27	Oct.	11	at Pittsburgh, Penn.
† Clemson	13-21	Oct.	24	at Columbia
Penn State	0-12	Nov.	2	at University Park
Kansas State	20-13	Nov.	9	at Columbia
† Furman	7-25	Nov.	16	at Greenville, S.C.
Miami (Fla.)	7- 2	Nov.	22	at Miami
† Wake Forest	6- 7	Nov.	28	at Charlotte, N.C.
† The Citadel	31- 6	Dec.	8	at Charleston, S.C.

1941   Won 4, Lost 4, Tied 1   Coach Rex Enright

† North Carolina	13- 7	Sept.	27	at Chapel Hill
Georgia	6-34	Oct.	4	at Athens
† Wake Forest	6- 6	Oct.	11	at Columbia
† Clemson	18-14	Oct.	23	at Columbia
† The Citadel	13- 6	Oct.	31	at Orangeburg, S.C.
Kansas State	0- 3	Nov.	8	at Manhattan
† Furman	26- 7	Nov.	15	at Columbia
Miami (Fla.)	6- 7	Nov.	21	at Miami
Penn State	12-19	Nov.	29	at Columbia

1942   Won 1, Lost 7, Tied 1   Coach Rex Enright

Tennessee	0- 0	Sept.	26	at Columbia
† North Carolina	6-18	Oct.	3	at Chapel Hill
West Virginia	0-13	Oct.	10	at Morgantown
† Clemson	6-18	Oct.	22	at Columbia
† The Citadel	14- 0	Oct.	30	at Orangeburg, S.C.
Alabama	0-29	Nov.	7	at Tuscaloosa
† Furman	0- 6	Nov.	14	at Columbia
Miami (Fla.)	6-13	Nov.	21	at Miami
† Wake Forest	14-33	Nov.	27	at Charlotte, N.C.

1943   Won 5, Lost 2   Coach J. P. Moran

Newberry	19- 7	Sept.	25	at Columbia
176th Infantry	7-13	Oct.	2	at Columbia
Presbyterian	20- 7	Oct.	9	at Columbia
† Clemson	33- 6	Oct.	21	at Columbia
Charleston C.G	20- 0	Oct.	29	at Orangeburg, S.C.
† North Carolina	6-21	Nov.	6	at Columbia
† Wake Forest	13- 2	Nov.	25	at Charlotte, N.C.

1944   Won 3, Lost 4, Tied 2   Coach William Newton

Newberry	48- 0	Sept.	23	at Columbia
Ga. Pre-Flight	14-20	Sept.	30	at Columbia
Miami (Fla.)	0- 0	Oct.	7	at Miami
† Clemson	13-20	Oct.	19	at Columbia
Charleston C.G	6- 6	Oct.	27	at Orangeburg, S.C.
† North Carolina	6- 0	Nov.	4	at Chapel Hill
Presbyterian	28- 7	Nov.	11	at Columbia
† Duke	7-34	Nov.	18	at Columbia
† Wake Forest	13-19	Nov.	23	at Charlotte, N.C.

1945   Won 2, Lost 4, Tied 3   Coach Johnnie McMillan

† Duke	0-60	Sept.	22	at Durham, N.C.
Presbyterian	40- 0	Sept.	29	at Columbia
Camp Blanding	20- 6	Oct.	6	at Columbia
Alabama	0-55	Oct.	13	at Montgomery
† Clemson	0- 0	Oct.	25	at Columbia
Miami (Fla.)	13-13	Nov.	9	at Miami
† Wake Forest	13-13	Nov.	22	at Charlotte, N C.
† Maryland	13-19	Dec.	1	at Columbia
Wake Forest	14-26	Jan.	1	at Jacksonville, Fla.
(1946 Gator Bowl)				

1946   Won 5, Lost 3   Coach Rex Enright

Newberry	21- 0	Sept.	29	at Columbia
Alabama	6-14	Oct.	5	at Columbia
† Furman	14- 7	Oct.	11	at Greenville, S.C.
† Clemson	26-14	Oct.	24	at Columbia
† The Citadel	19- 7	Nov.	1	at Orangeburg, S.C.
† Maryland	21-17	Nov.	9	at College Park
† Duke	0-39	Nov.	16	at Columbia
† Wake Forest	0-35	Nov.	28	at Charlotte, N.C.

1947   Won 6, Lost 2, Tied 1   Coach Rex Enright

Newberry	27- 6	Sept.	20	at Columbia
† Maryland	13-19	Sept.	27	at Columbia
Mississippi	0-33	Oct.	4	at Memphis, Tenn.
† Furman	26- 8	Oct.	11	at Columbia
† Clemson	21-19	Oct.	23	at Columbia
Miami (Fla.)	8- 0	Oct.	31	at Miami
† The Citadel	12- 0	Nov.	7	at Orangeburg, S.C.
† Duke	0- 0	Nov.	15	at Durham, N.C.
† Wake Forest	6- 0	Nov.	27	at Charlotte, N.C.

1948   Won 3, Lost 5   Coach Rex Enright

Newberry	46- 0	Sept.	24	at Columbia
† Furman	7- 0	Oct.	1	at Greenville, S.C.
Tulane	0-14	Oct.	9	at New Orleans, La.
† Clemson	7-13	Oct.	21	at Columbia
West Virginia	12-35	Oct.	30	at Morgantown
† Maryland	7-19	Nov.	6	at Columbia
Tulsa	27- 7	Nov.	13	at Tulsa, Okla.
† Wake Forest	0-38	Nov.	25	at Columbia

1949   Won 4, Lost 6   Coach Rex Enright

Baylor	6-20	Sept.	24	at Waco, Texas
† Furman	7-14	Sept.	30	at Columbia
† North Carolina	13-28	Oct.	8	at Columbia
† Clemson	27-13	Oct.	20	at Columbia
† Maryland	7-44	Oct.	29	at College Park
Marquette	6- 3	Nov.	5	at Milwaukee, Wis.
Miami (Fla.)	7-13	Nov.	11	at Miami
Georgia Tech	3-13	Nov.	19	at Atlanta
† Wake Forest	27-20	Nov.	23	at Columbia
† The Citadel	42- 0	Dec.	3	at Columbia

1950   Won 3, Lost 4, Tied 2   Coach Rex Enright

† Duke	0-14	Sept.	23	at Columbia
Georgia Tech	7- 0	Sept.	30	at Atlanta
† Furman	21- 6	Oct.	6	at Greenville, S.C.
† Clemson	14-14	Oct.	19	at Columbia
† George Washington	34-20	Oct.	27	at Washington, D.C.
Marquette	13-13	Nov.	3	at Columbia
† The Citadel	7-19	Nov.	11	at Charleston, S.C.
† North Carolina	7-14	Nov.	18	at Columbia
† Wake Forest	7-14	Nov.	25	at Columbia

1951   Won 5, Lost 4   Coach Rex Enright

† Duke	6-34	Sept.	22	at Columbia
† The Citadel	26- 7	Sept.	29	at Columbia
† Furman	21- 6	Oct.	6	at Columbia
† North Carolina	6-21	Oct.	13	at Chapel Hill, N.C.
† Clemson	20- 0	Oct.	25	at Columbia
† George Washington	14-20	Nov.	3	at Columbia
† West Virginia	34-13	Nov.	10	at Morgantown
Virginia	27-28	Nov.	17	at Charlottesville
† Wake Forest	21- 0	Nov.	24	at Columbia

† Southern Conference Game

1952 — Won 5, Lost 5 — Coach Rex Enright

Wofford	33- 0	Sept. 20	at Columbia
Army	7-28	Sept. 27	at West Point, N.Y.
† Furman	27- 7	Oct. 4	at Greenville, S.C.
† Duke	7-33	Oct. 11	at Columbia
Clemson	6- 0	Oct. 23	at Columbia
Virginia	21-14	Nov. 1	at Norfolk
† The Citadel	35- 0	Nov. 8	at Charleston, S.C.
† North Carolina	19-27	Nov. 15	at Columbia
† West Virginia	6-13	Nov. 22	at Columbia
† Wake Forest	14-39	Nov. 29	at Winston-Salem, N.C.

1953 — Won 7, Lost 3 — Coach Rex Enright

* Duke	7-20	Sept. 19	at Columbia
The Citadel	25- 0	Sept. 26	at Columbia
Virginia	19- 0	Oct. 3	at Charlottesville
Furman	27-13	Oct. 10	at Columbia
* Clemson	14 -7	Oct. 22	at Columbia
Maryland	6-24	Oct. 31	at College Park
* North Carolina	18- 0	Nov. 7	at Columbia
West Virginia	20-14	Nov. 14	at Morgantown
Wofford	49- 0	Nov. 21	at Columbia
* Wake Forest	13-19	Nov. 26	at Charlotte, N.C.

1954 — Won 6, Lost 4 — Coach Rex Enright

Army	34-20	Sept. 25	at West Point, N.Y.
West Virginia	6-26	Oct. 2	at Columbia
Furman	27- 7	Oct. 9	at Greenville, S.C.
* Clemson	13- 8	Oct. 21	at Columbia
* Maryland	0-20	Oct. 30	at Columbia
* North Carolina	19-21	Nov. 6	at Chapel Hill
* Virginia	27- 0	Nov. 13	at Columbia
* Duke	7-26	Nov. 20	at Durham, N.C.
* Wake Forest	20-19	Nov. 27	at Columbia
The Citadel	19- 6	Dec. 4	at Charleston, S.C.

1955 — Won 3, Lost 6 — Coach Rex Enright

Wofford	26-7	Sept. 17	at Columbia
* Wake Forest	19-34	Sept. 24	at Winston-Salem, N.C.
Navy	0-26	Oct. 1	at Columbia
Furman	19- 0	Oct. 8	at Columbia
* Clemson	14-28	Oct. 20	at Columbia
* Maryland	0-27	Oct. 29	at College Park
* North Carolina	14-32	Nov. 5	at Norfolk, Va.
* Duke	7-41	Nov. 12	at Durham, N.C.
* Virginia	21-14	Nov. 26	at Charlottesville

1956 — Won 7, Lost 3 — Coach Warren Giese

Wofford	26-13	Sept. 15	at Columbia
* Duke	7- 0	Sept. 22	at Columbia
Miami (Fla.)	6-14	Sept. 28	at Miami
* North Carolina	14-0	Oct. 6	at Columbia
*Virginia	27-13	Oct. 13	at Richmond
* Clemson	0-7	Oct. 25	at Columbia
Furman	13- 6	Nov. 3	at Greenville, S.C.
* N. C. State	7-14	Nov. 10	at Raleigh
* Maryland	13- 0	Nov. 17	at Columbia
Wake Forest	13- 0	Nov. 22	at Charlotte, N.C.

1957 — Won 5, Lost 5 — Coach Warren Giese

* Duke	14-26	Sept. 21	at Columbia
Wofford	26- 0	Sept. 28	at Columbia
Texas	27-21	Oct. 5	at Austin
Furman	58-13	Oct. 12	at Columbia
* Clemson	0-13	Oct. 24	at Columbia
* Maryland	6-10	Nov. 2	at Columbia
* North Carolina	6-28	Nov. 9	at Chapel Hill
* Virginia	13- 0	Nov. 16	at Charlottesville
* N. C. State	26-29	Nov. 23	at Columbia
* Wake Forest	26- 7	Nov. 30	at Winston-Salem, N.C.

1958 — Won 7, Lost 3 — Coach Warren Giese

* Duke	8- 0	Sept. 20	at Columbia
Army	8-45	Sept. 27	at West Point, N.Y.
Georgia	24-14	Oct. 4	at Athens
* North Carolina	0- 6	Oct. 11	at Chapel Hill
* Clemson	26- 6	Oct. 23	at Columbia
* Maryland	6-10	Nov. 1	at College Park
Furman	32- 7	Nov. 8	at Greenville, S.C.
* Virginia	28-14	Nov. 15	at Columbia
* N. C. State	12- 7	Nov. 22	at Columbia
* Wake Forest	24 -7	Nov. 27	at Columbia

1959 — Won 6, Lost 4 — Coach Warren Giese

* Duke	12- 7	Sept. 19	at Columbia
Furman	30- 0	Sept. 26	at Columbia
Georgia	30-14	Oct. 3	at Columbia
* North Carolina	6-19	Oct. 10	at Chapel Hill
* Clemson	0-27	Oct. 22	at Columbia
* Maryland	22- 6	Oct. 31	at Columbia
* Virginia	32-20	Nov. 7	at Charlottesville
Miami (Fla.)	6-26	Nov. 13	at Miami
* N. C. State	12- 7	Nov. 21	at Columbia
* Wake Forest	20-43	Nov. 28	at Charlotte, N.C.

1960 — Won 3, Lost 6, Tied 1 — Coach Warren Giese

* Duke	0-31	Sept. 24	at Columbia
Georgia	6-38	Oct. 1	at Athens
Miami (Fla.)	6-21	Oct. 14	at Miami
* North Carolina	22- 6	Oct. 22	at Columbia
* Maryland	0-15	Oct. 29	at College Park
Louisiana State	6-35	Nov. 5	at Baton Rouge
* Clemson	2-12	Nov. 12	at Clemson, S.C.
* N. C. State	8- 8	Nov. 19	at Columbia
* Wake Forest	41-20	Nov. 26	at Columbia
* Virginia	26- 0	Dec. 3	at Columbia

1961 — Won 4, Lost 6 — Coach Marvin Bass

* Duke	6- 7	Sept. 23	at Columbia
* Wake Forest	10- 7	Sept. 30	at Winston-Salem, N.C.
Georgia	14-17	Oct. 7	at Athens
Louisiana State	0-42	Oct. 14	at Columbia
* North Carolina	0-17	Oct. 21	at Columbia
* Maryland	20-10	Oct. 28	at Columbia
* Virginia	20-28	Nov. 4	at Charlottesville
* Clemson	21-14	Nov. 11	at Columbia
* N. C. State	14-38	Nov. 18	at Raleigh
Vanderbilt	23- 7	Nov. 25	at Nashville, Tenn.

1962 — Won 4, Lost 5, Tied 1 — Coach Marvin Bass

Northwestern	20-37	Sept. 22	at Evanston, Ill.
* Duke	8-21	Sept. 29	at Durham, N.C.
Georgia	7- 7	Oct. 6	at Columbia
* Wake Forest	27- 6	Oct. 13	at Columbia
* North Carolina	14-19	Oct. 20	at Chapel Hill
* Maryland	11-13	Oct. 27	at College Park
* Virginia	40- 6	Nov. 3	at Columbia
* N. C. State	17- 6	Nov. 10	at Columbia
Detroit	26-13	Nov. 17	at Detroit, Mich.
* Clemson	17-20	Nov. 24	at Clemson, S.C.

1963 — Won 1, Lost 8, Tied 1 — Coach Marvin Bass

* Duke	14-22	Sept. 21	at Durham, N.C.
* Maryland	21-13	Sept. 28	at Columbia
Georgia	7-27	Oct. 5	at Athens
* N. C. State	6-18	Oct. 12	at Columbia
* Virginia	10-10	Oct. 19	at Charlottesville
* North Carolina	0- 7	Oct. 26	at Columbia
Tulane	7-20	Nov. 2	at Columbia
Memphis State	0- 9	Nov. 9	at Memphis, Tenn.
* Wake Forest	19-20	Nov. 16	at Winston-Salem, N.C.
* Clemson	20-24	Nov. 28	at Columbia

† Southern Conference Game
* Atlantic Coast Conference Game

1964 — Won 3, Lost 5, Tied 2 — Coach Marvin Bass

* Duke	9- 9	Sept. 19	at Columbia
* Maryland	6-24	Sept. 26	at College Park
Georgia	7- 7	Oct. 3	at Columbia
Nebraska	6-28	Oct. 10	at Lincoln
Florida	0-37	Oct. 17	at Gainesville
* North Carolina	6-24	Oct. 24	at Chapel Hill
* N. C. State	14-17	Oct. 31	at Raleigh
The Citadel	17-14	Nov. 7	at Columbia
* Wake Forest	23-13	Nov. 14	at Columbia
* Clemson	7- 3	Nov. 21	at Clemson, S.C.

1965 — Won 5, Lost 5 — Coach Marvin Bass

The Citadel	13- 3	Sept. 18	at Charleston, S.C.
* Duke	15-20	Sept. 25	at Columbia
* N. C. State	13- 7	Oct. 2	at Columbia
Tennessee	3-24	Oct. 9	at Knoxville
* Wake Forest	38- 7	Oct. 16	at Columbia
Louisiana State	7-21	Oct. 23	at Baton Rouge
* Maryland	14-27	Oct. 30	at Columbia
* Virginia	17- 7	Nov. 6	at Charlottesville
Alabama	14-35	Nov. 1	at Tuscaloosa
* Clemson	17-16	Nov. 2	at Columbia

1966 — Won 1, Lost 9 — Coach Paul Dietzel

Louisiana State	12-28	Sept. 17	at Baton Rouge
Memphis State	7-16	Sept. 24	at Columbia
Georgia	0- 7	Oct. 1	at Columbia
* N. C. State	31-21	Oct. 8	at Raleigh
* Wake Forest	6-10	Oct. 15	at Columbia
Tennessee	17-29	Oct. 22	at Knoxville
* Maryland	2-14	Oct. 29	at College Park
Florida State	10-32	Nov. 5	at Columbia
Alabama	0-24	Nov. 12	at Tuscaloosa
* Clemson	10-35	Nov. 26	at Clemson, S.C.

1967 — Won 5, Lost 5 — Coach Paul Dietzel

Iowa State	34- 3	Sept. 16	at Columbia
* North Carolina	16-10	Sept. 23	at Columbia
* Duke	21-17	Sept. 30	at Durham, N.C.
Georgia	0-21	Oct. 7	at Athens
Florida State	0-17	Oct. 14	at Tallahassee
* Virginia	24-23	Oct. 21	at Columbia
* Maryland	31- 0	Oct. 28	at Columbia
* Wake Forest	21-35	Nov. 4	at Winston-Salem, N.C.
Alabama	0-17	Nov. 18	at Tuscaloosa
* Clemson	12-23	Nov. 25	at Columbia

1968 — Won 4, Lost 6 — Coach Paul Dietzel

* Duke	7-14	Sept. 21	at Columbia
* North Carolina	32-27	Sept. 28	at Chapel Hill
Georgia	20-21	Oct. 5	at Columbia
* N.C. State	12-36	Oct. 12	at Raleigh
* Maryland	19-21	Oct. 19	at College Park
Florida State	28-35	Oct. 26	at Columbia
* Virginia	49-28	Nov. 2	at Charlottesville
* Wake Forest	34-21	Nov. 9	at Winston-Salem, N.C.
Virginia Tech	6-17	Nov. 16	at Columbia
*Clemson	7- 3	Nov. 23	at Clemson, S.C

1969 — Won 7, Lost 4 — Coach Paul Dietzel

* Duke	27-20	Sept. 20	at Columbia
* North Carolina	14- 6	Sept. 27	at Columbia
Georgia	16-41	Oct. 4	at Athens
* N. C. State	21-16	Oct. 11	at Columbia
Virginia Tech	17-16	Oct. 18	at Blacksburg
* Maryland	17- 0	Oct. 25	at Columbia
* Florida State	9-34	Nov. 1	at Tallahassee
Tennessee	14-29	Nov. 8	at Knoxville
* Wake Forest	24- 6	Nov. 15	at Winston-Salem, N.C.
* Clemson	27-13	Nov. 22	at Columbia
West Virginia	3-14	Dec. 30	at Atlanta, Ga.
(Peach Bowl)			

1970 — Won 4, Lost 6, Tied 1 — Coach Paul Dietzel

Georgia Tech	20-23	Sept. 12	at Atlanta
* Wake Forest	43- 7	Sept. 19	at Columbia
* N. C. State	7- 7	Sept. 26	at Raleigh
Virginia Tech	24- 7	Oct. 3	at Columbia
* North Carolina	35-21	Oct. 10	at Chapel Hill
* Maryland	15-21	Oct. 17	at College Park
Florida State	13-21	Oct. 24	at Columbia
Georgia	34-52	Oct. 31	at Athens
Tennessee	18-20	Nov. 7	at Columbia
* Duke	38-42	Nov. 14	at Columbia
* Clemson	38-32	Nov. 21	at Clemson, S.C.

1971 — Won 6, Lost 5 — Coach Paul Dietzel

Georgia Tech	24- 7	Sept. 11	at Columbia
Duke	12-28	Sept. 18	at Durham, N.C.
N. C. State	24- 6	Sept. 25	at Columbia
Memphis State	7- 3	Oct. 2	at Memphis, Tenn.
Virginia	34-14	Oct. 9	at Columbia
Maryland	35- 6	Oct. 16	at Columbia
Florida State	18-49	Oct. 23	at Tallahassee
Georgia	0-24	Oct. 30	at Columbia
Tennessee	6-35	Nov. 6	at Knoxville
Wake Forest	24- 7	Nov. 20	at Columbia
Clemson	7-17	Nov. 27	at Columbia

1972 — Won 4, Lost 7 — Coach Paul Dietzel

Virginia	16-24	Sept. 9	at Columbia
Georgia Tech	6-34	Sept. 16	at Atlanta
Mississippi	0-21	Sept. 23	at Columbia
Memphis State	34- 7	Sept. 30	at Columbia
Appalachian St	41- 7	Oct. 14	at Columbia
Miami (Ohio)	8-21	Oct. 21	at Columbia
N. C. State	24-42	Oct. 28	at Raleigh
Wake Forest	35- 3	Nov. 4	at Columbia
Virginia Tech	20-45	Nov. 11	at Blacksburg
Florida State	24-21	Nov. 18	at Columbia
Clemson	6- 7	Nov. 25	at Clemson, S.C.

1973 — Won 7, Lost 4 — Coach Paul Dietzel

Georgia Tech	41-28	Sept. 15	at Columbia
Houston	19-27	Sept. 21	at Houston, Texas
Miami (Ohio)	11-13	Sept. 29	at Columbia
Virginia Tech	27-24	Oct. 6	at Blacksburg
Wake Forest	28-12	Oct. 13	at Winston-Salem, N.C.
Ohio Univ.	38-22	Oct. 20	at Columbia
Louisiana State	29-33	Oct. 27	at Columbia
N. C. State	35-56	Nov. 3	at Columbia
Appalachian St	35-14	Nov. 10	at Columbia
Florida State	52-12	Nov. 17	at Tallahassee
Clemson	32-20	Nov. 24	at Columbia

1974 — Won 4, Lost 7 — Coach Paul Dietzel

Georgia Tech	20-35	Sept. 14	at Atlanta
Duke	14-20	Sept. 21	at Columbia
Georgia	14-52	Sept. 28	at Athens
Houston	14-24	Oct. 5	at Columbia
Virginia Tech	17-31	Oct. 12	at Columbia
Mississippi	10- 7	Oct. 19	at Oxford
North Carolina	31-23	Oct. 26	at Columbia
N. C. State	27-42	Nov. 2	at Raleigh
Appalachian St	21-18	Nov. 9	at Columbia
Wake Forest	34-21	Nov. 16	at Columbia
Clemson	21-39	Nov. 23	at Clemson, S.C.

1975 — Won 7, Lost 5 — Coach Jim Carlen

Georgia Tech	23-17	Sept. 13	at Columbia
Duke	24-16	Sept. 20	at Durham, N.C.
Georgia	20-28	Sept. 27	at Columbia
Baylor	24-13	Oct. 4	at Columbia
Virginia	41-14	Oct. 11	at Columbia
Mississippi	35-29	Oct. 18	at Jackson
Louisiana State	6-24	Oct. 25	at Baton Rouge
N. C. State	21-28	Nov. 1	at Raleigh
Appalachian St	34-39	Nov. 8	at Columbia
Wake Forest	37-26	Nov. 15	at Columbia
Clemson	56-20	Nov. 22	at Columbia
Miami (Ohio)	7-20	Dec. 20	at Orlando, Fla.
(Tangerine Bowl)			

1976	Won 6, Lost 5		Coach Jim Carlen		
Appalachian St	21-10	Sept.	4	at Columbia
Georgia Tech	27-17	Sept.	11	at Atlanta
Duke	24- 6	Sept.	18	at Columbia
Georgia	12-20	Sept.	25	at Athens
Baylor	17-18	Oct.	2	at Waco, Texas
Virginia	35- 7	Oct.	9	at Columbia
Mississippi	10- 7	Oct.	16	at Columbia
Notre Dame	6-13	Oct.	23	at Columbia
N. C. State	27- 7	Oct.	30	at Columbia
Wake Forest	7-10	Nov.	13	at Columbia
Clemson	9-28	Nov.	20	at Clemson, S.C.

1977	Won 5, Lost 7		Coach Jim Carlen		
Appalachian St	32-17	Sept.	3	at Columbia
Georgia Tech	17- 0	Sept.	10	at Columbia
Miami (Ohio)	42-19	Sept.	17	at Columbia
Georgia	13-15	Sept.	24	at Columbia
East Carolina	19-16	Oct.	1	at Columbia
Duke	21-25	Oct.	8	at Columbia
Mississippi	10-17	Oct.	15	at Oxford
North Carolina	0-17	Oct.	22	at Chapel Hill
N. C. State	3- 7	Oct.	29	at Raleigh
Wake Forest	24-14	Nov.	12	at Winston-Salem, N.C.
Clemson	27-31	Nov.	19	at Columbia
Hawaii	7-24	Nov.	26	at Honolulu

1978	Won 5, Lost 5, Tied 1		Coach Jim Carlen		
Furman	45-10	Sept.	9	at Columbia
Kentucky	14-14	Sept.	16	at Columbia
Duke	12-16	Sept.	23	at Durham, N.C.
Georgia	27-10	Sept.	30	at Columbia
Georgia Tech	3- 6	Oct.	7	at Atlanta
Ohio Univ	24- 7	Oct.	14	at Columbia
Mississippi	18-17	Oct.	21	at Columbia
North Carolina	22-24	Oct.	28	at Columbia
N. C. State	13-22	Nov.	4	at Raleigh
Wake Forest	37-14	Nov.	18	at Columbia
Clemson	23-41	Nov.	25	at Clemson, S.C.

1979	Won 8, Lost 4		Coach Jim Carlen		
North Carolina	0-28	Sept.	8	at Chapel Hill
Westem Michigan	24- 7	Sept.	15	at Columbia
Duke	35- 0	Sept.	22	at Columbia
Georgia	27-20	Sept.	29	at Athens
Oklahoma State	23-16	Oct.	6	at Columbia
Mississippi	21-14	Oct.	20	at Columbia
Notre Dame	17-18	Oct.	27	at Notre Dame, Ind.
N. C. State	30-28	Nov.	3	at Columbia
Florida State	7-27	Nov.	10	at Tallahassee
Wake Forest	35-14	Nov.	17	at Columbia
Clemson	13- 9	Nov.	24	at Columbia
Missouri	14-24	Dec.	29	at Birmingham, Ala.
(Hall of Fame Bowl)				

1980	Won 8, Lost 4		Coach Jim Carlen		
Pacific	37- 0	Sept.	6	at Columbia
Wichita State	73- 0	Sept.	13	at Columbia
Southern Cal	13-23	Sept.	20	at Los Angeles
Michigan	17-14	Sept.	27	at Ann Arbor
N. C. State	30-10	Oct.	4	at Columbia
Duke	20- 7	Oct.	11	at Columbia
Cincinnati	49- 7	Oct.	18	at Columbia
Georgia	10-13	Nov.	1	at Athens
The Citadel	45-24	Nov.	8	at Columbia
Wake Forest	39-38	Nov.	15	at Columbia
Clemson	6-27	Nov.	22	at Clemson
Pittsburgh	9-37	Dec.	29	at Jacksonville, Fla.
(Gator Bowl)				

1981	Won 6, Lost 6		Coach Jim Carlen		
Wake Forest	23- 6	Sept.	5	at Winston-Salem, N.C.
Mississippi	13-20	Sept.	12	at Columbia
Duke	17- 3	Sept.	19	at Columbia
Georgia	0-24	Sept.	26	at Athens
Pittsburgh	28-42	Oct.	3	at Columbia
Kentucky	28-14	Oct.	10	at Lexington
Virginia	21- 3	Oct.	17	at Columbia
North Carolina	31-13	Oct.	24	at Chapel Hill
N. C. State	20-12	Oct.	31	at Columbia
Pacific	21-23	Nov.	7	at Columbia
Clemson	13-29	Nov.	21	at Columbia
Hawaii	10-33	Dec.	5	at Honolulu

1982	Won 4, Lost 7		Coach Richard Bell		
Pacific	41- 6	Sept.	4	at Columbia
Richmond	30-10	Sept.	11	at Columbia
Duke	17-30	Sept.	18	at Columbia
Georgia	18-34	Sept	25	at Columbia
Cincinnati	37-10	Oct.	2	at Columbia
Furman	23-28	Oct.	16	at Columbia
Louisiana State	6-14	Oct.	23	at Baton Rouge
N. C. State	3-33	Oct.	30	at Raleigh
Florida State	26-56	Nov.	6	at Columbia
Navy	17-14	Nov.	13	at Columbia
Clemson	6-24	Nov.	20	at Clemson, S.C.

1983	Won 5, Lost 6		Coach Joe Morrison		
North Carolina	8-24	Sept.	3	at Columbia
Miami (Ohio)	24- 3	Sept.	10	at Columbia
Duke	31-24	Sept.	17	at Durham, N.C.
Georgia	13-31	Sept.	24	at Athens
Southern Cal	38-14	Oct.	1	at Columbia
Notre Dame	6-30	Oct.	8	at Columbia
Louisiana State	6-20	Oct.	22	at Baton Rouge
N.C. State	31-17	Oct.	29	at Columbia
Florida State	30-45	Nov.	5	at Tallahassee
Navy	31- 7	Nov.	12	at Columbia
Clemson	13-22	Nov.	19	at Columbia

1984	Won 10, Lost 2		Coach Joe Morrison		
The Citadel	31-24	Sept.	8	at Columbia
Duke	21- 0	Sept.	22	at Columbia
Georgia	17-10	Sept.	29	at Columbia
Kansas State	49-17	Oct.	6	at Columbia
Pittsburgh	45-21	Oct.	13	at Columbia
Notre Dame	36-32	Oct.	20	at South Bend
East Carolina	42-20	Oct.	27	at Columbia
N.C. State	35-28	Nov.	3	at Raleigh, N.C.
Florida State	38-26	Nov.	10	at Columbia
Navy	21-38	Nov.	17	at Annapolis
Clemson	22-21	Nov.	24	at Clemson
Oklahoma State	14-21	Dec.	28	at Jacksonville, Fla.
(Gator Bowl)				

1985	Won 5, Lost 6		Coach Joe Morrison		
The Citadel	56-17	Aug.	31	at Columbia
Appalachian State	20-13	Sept.	7	at Columbia
Michigan	3-34	Sept.	21	at Columbia
Georgia	21-35	Sept.	28	at Athens
Pittsburgh	7-42	Oct.	5	at Pittsburgh
Duke	28- 7	Oct.	12	at Columbia
East Carolina	52-10	Oct.	26	at Greenville
N.C. State	17-21	Nov.	2	at Columbia
Florida State	14-56	Nov.	9	at Tallahassee
Navy	34-31	Nov.	16	at Columbia
Clemson	17-24	Nov.	23	at Columbia

1986	Won 3, Lost 6, Tied 2		Coach Joe Morrison		
Miami, (Fla)	14-34	Aug.	30	at Columbia
Virginia	20-30	Sept.	7	at Charlottesville
Westem Carolina	45-24	Sept.	13	at Columbia
Georgia	26-31	Sept.	27	at Columbia
Nebraska	24-27	Oct.	4	at Columbia
Virginia Tech	27-27	Oct.	11	at Blacksburg
East Carolina	38- 3	Oct.	25	at Columbia
North Carolina St.	22-23	Nov.	1	at Raleigh
Florida State	28-45	Nov.	8	at Columbia
Wake Forest	48-21	Nov.	15	at Columbia
Clemson	21-21	Nov.	22	at Clemson

1987	Won 8, Lost 4		Coach Joe Morrison		
Appalachian State	24 - 3	Sept.	5	at Columbia
Western Carolina	31- 6	Sept.	12	at Columbia
Georgia	6-13	Sept.	26	at Athens

CAROLINA VS. CLEMSON

Nebraska	21-30	Oct.	3	at Lincoln
Virginia Tech	40-10	Oct.	10	at Columbia
Virginia	58-10	Oct.	17	at Columbia
East Carolina	34-12	Oct.	24	at Columbia
North Carolina St.	48- 0	Oct.	31	at Columbia
Wake Forest	30- 0	Nov.	14	at Winston-Salem
Clemson	20- 7	Nov.	21	at Columbia
Miami, Fla	16-20	Dec.	5	at Miami
Louisiana State	13-30	Dec.	31	at Jacksonville
(Mazda Gator Bowl)				

1988   Won 8, Lost 4   Coach Joe Morrison

North Carolina	31-10	Sept.	3	at Columbia
Western Carolina	38- 0	Sept.	10	at Columbia
East Carolina	17- 0	Sept.	17	at Columbia
Georgia	23-10	Sept.	24	at Columbia
Appalachian State	35- 9	Oct.	1	at Columbia
Virginia Tech	26-24	Oct.	8	at Blacksburg
Georgia Tech	0-34	Oct.	15	at Atlanta
North Carolina St	23- 7	Oct.	29	at Raleigh
Florida State	0-59	Nov.	5	at Columbia
Navy	19- 7	Nov.	12	at Columbia
Clemson	10-29	Nov.	19	at Clemson
Indiana	10-34	Dec.	28	at Memphis
(Liberty Bowl)				

1989   Won 6, Lost 4, Tied 1   Coach Sparky Woods

Duke	27-21	Sept.	2	at Columbia
Virginia Tech	17-17	Sept.	9	at Columbia
West Virginia	21-45	Sept.	16	at Morgantown
Georgia Tech	21-10	Sept.	23	at Columbia
Georgia	24-20	Sept.	30	at Athens
East Carolina	47-14	Oct.	7	at Columbia
Western Carolina	24- 3	Oct.	21	at Columbia
North Carolina St.	10-20	Oct.	28	at Columbia
Florida State	10-35	Nov.	4	at Tallahassee
North Carolina	27-20	Nov.	11	at Chapel Hill
Clemson	0-45	Nov.	18	at Columbia

1990   Won 6, Lost 5   Coach Sparky Woods

Duke	21-10	Sept.	1	at Columbia
North Carolina	27- 5	Sept.	8	at Columbia
Virginia Tech	35-24	Sept.	22	at Blacksburg
Georgia Tech	6-27	Sept.	29	at Atlanta
East Carolina	37- 7	Oct.	13	at Columbia
The Citadel	35-38	Oct.	20	at Columbia
North Carolina St.	29-38	Oct.	27	at Raleigh
Florida State	10-41	Nov.	3	at Columbia
Southern Illinois	38-13	Nov.	10	at Columbia
Clemson	15-24	Nov.	17	at Clemson
West Virginia	29-10	Nov.	22	at Columbia

1991   Won 3, Lost 6, Tied 2   Coach Sparky Woods

Duke	24-24	Sept.	7	at Columbia
at West Virginia	16-21	Sept.	14	at Morgantown
Virginia Tech	28-21	Sept.	21	at Columbia
at East Carolina	20-31	Sept.	28	at Greenville
East Tennessee St.	55-7	Oct.	5	at Columbia
Louisiana Tech	12-12	Oct.	12	at Columbia
Georgia Tech	23-14	Oct.	19	at Columbia
N. C. State	21-38	Nov.	2	at Columbia
at Florida State	10-38	Nov.	9	at Tallahassee
at North Carolina	17-21	Nov.	16	at Chapel Hill
Clemson	24-41	Nov.	23	at Columbia

1992   Won 5, Lost 6   Coach Sparky Woods

Georgia*	6-28	Sept.	5	at Columbia
Arkansas*	7-45	Sept.	12	at Columbia
East Carolina	18-20	Sept.	19	at Columbia
at Kentucky*	9-13	Sept.	26	at Lexington
at Alabama*	7-48	Oct.	3	at Tuscaloosa
Mississippi State*	21-6	Oct.	17	at Columbia
at Vanderbilt*	21-17	Oct.	24	at Nashville
Tennessee*	24-23	Oct.	31	at Columbia
Louisiana Tech	14-13	Nov.	7	at Columbia
at Florida*	9-14	Nov.	14	at Gainesville
at Clemson	24-13	Nov.	21	at Clemson

1993   Won 4, Lost 7   Coach Sparky Woods

at Georgia*	23-21	Sept.	4	at Athens
at Arkansas*	17-18	Sept.	11	at Fayetteville
Louisiana Tech	34-3	Sept.	18	at Columbia
Kentucky*	17-21	Sept.	23	at Columbia
Alabama*	6-17	Oct	2	at Columbia
East Carolina	27-3	Oct.	9	at Columbia
at Mississippi State*	0-23	Oct.	16	at Starkville
Vanderbilt*	22-0	Oct.	23	at Columbia
at Tennessee	3-55	Oct.	30	at Knoxville
Florida	26-37	Nov.	13	at Columbia
Clemson	13-16	Nov.	20	at Columbia

1994   Won 7, Lost 5   Coach Brad Scott

Georgia*	21-24	Sept.	3	at Columbia
Arkansas*	14-0	Sept.	10	at Columbia
Louisiana Tech	31-6	Sept.	17	at Columbia
at Kentucky*	23-9	Sept.	24	at Lexington
at Louisiana State*	18-17	Oct	1	at Baton Rouge
East Carolina	42-56	Oct.	8	at Columbia
Mississippi State*	36-41	Oct.	16	at Columbia
Vanderbilt*	19-16	Oct.	22	at Nashville
Tennessee	22-31	Oct.	29	at Columbia
at Florida	17-48	Nov.	12	at Gainesville
Clemson	33-7	Nov.	19	at Clemson
West Virginia	24-21	Jan.	2	at Ft. Lauderdale,FL
(1995 Carquest Bowl)				

1995   Won 4, Lost 6, Tied 1   Coach Brad Scott

at Georgia*	23-42	Sept.	2	at Athens
at Arkansas*	21-51	Sept.	9	at Fayetteville
Louisiana Tech	68-21	Sept.	16	at Columbia
Kentucky*	30-35	Sept.	23	at Columbia
Louisiana State*	20-20	Sept.	30	at Columbia
Kent	77-14	Oct.	7	at Columbia
at Miss. State*	65-39	Oct.	14	at Starkville
Vanderbilt*	52-14	Oct.	21	at Columbia
at Tennessee*	21-56	Oct.	28	at Columbia
Florida*	7-63	Nov.	11	at Columbia
Clemson	17-38	Nov.	18	at Columbia

1996   Won 6, Lost 5   Coach Brad Scott

Central Florida	33-14	Sept.	7	at Columbia
Georgia*	23-14	Sept.	14	at Columbia
East Carolina	7-23	Sept.	21	at Columbia
Mississippi State*	10-14	Sept.	28	at Columbia
at Auburn*	24-28	Oct.	5	at Auburn
at Kentucky*	25-14	Oct.	12	at Lexington
Arkansas*	23-17	Oct.	19	at Columbia
at Vanderbilt*	27-0	Oct.	26	at Nashville
Tennessee*	14-31	Nov.	2	at Columbia
at Florida*	25-52	Nov.	16	at Gainesville
at Clemson	34-31	Nov.	23	at Clemson

1997   Won 5, Lost 6   Coach Brad Scott

Central Florida	33-31	Sept.	6	at Columbia
at Georgia*	15-31	Sept.	13	at Athens
at East Carolina	26-0	Sept.	20	at Greenville
at Mississippi State*	17-37	Sept.	27	at Starkville
Auburn*	6-23	Oct.	4	at Columbia
Kentucky*	38-24	Oct.	11	at Columbia
at Arkansas*	39-13	Oct.	18	at Little Rock
Vanderbilt*	35-3	Oct.	25	at Columbia
at Tennessee*	7-22	Nov.	1	at Knoxville
Florida*	21-48	Nov.	15	at Columbia
Clemson	21-47	Nov.	21	at Columbia
* SEC game				

300